Aspects of American English

Aspects
of
American English
Second Edition

Elizabeth M. Kerr
The University of Wisconsin–Milwaukee

Ralph M. Aderman
The University of Wisconsin–Milwaukee

Harcourt Brace Jovanovich, Inc.
New York   Chicago   San Francisco   Atlanta

Prepared in consultation with David Levin, Stanford University

ISBN: 0-15-503821-4

Library of Congress Catalog Card Number: 76-151068

Printed in the United States of America

Copyrights and Acknowledgments

BASIC BOOKS, INC., for "The Nature and History of Linguistics" by William G. Moulton, Chapter 1 of *Linguistics Today*, edited by Archibald A. Hill. Copyright © 1969 by Basic Books, Inc., Publishers, New York. Reprinted by permission.

COLUMBIA UNIVERSITY PRESS for "Big Daddy's Dramatic Word Strings" by Dan Isaac from *American Speech*, Vol. 40 (December 1965). Reprinted by permission of Columbia University Press.

BERGEN EVANS for "Editor's Choice—You Couldn't Do Woise." Copyright © 1963. For "Now Everyone Is Hip About Slang" from *The New York Times Magazine* (March 22, 1964). Both reprinted by permission of the author.

MRS. CHARLES C. FRIES for "Standard English" from *American English Grammar* by Charles C. Fries. Reprinted with the permission of Mrs. Charles C. Fries.

ROBERT A. HALL, JR., for "Language Has System" and "There's Nothing Wrong with Your Language" from *Linguistics and Your Language* by Robert A. Hall, Jr. (1960). Reprinted by permission of the author.

HARCOURT BRACE JOVANOVICH, INC., for "What Is Language?" from *Introduction to Linguistic Structure* by Archibald A. Hill. Copyright © 1958 by Harcourt Brace Jovanovich, Inc. For "Words and Meanings" from *The Origins and Development of the English Language* by Thomas Pyles. Copyright © 1954 by Harcourt Brace Jovanovich, Inc. For "How Many Clocks?" from *The Five Clocks* by Martin Joos. Copyright © 1961, 1962, 1967 by Martin Joos. All reprinted with the permission of Harcourt Brace Jovanovich, Inc.

HARPER & ROW, PUBLISHERS, INC., for "Slang and Its Relatives" and "Speech Communities" from ·*Understanding English* by Paul Roberts. Copyright ©

Introduction

Language has its own character, developed by the countless generations of people who have used it; thus, knowing a language well helps one to better understand the countries and the peoples who have made it what it is and who continue to participate in its evolution. Americans have adapted the English language to their purposes, and American English has taken on new vigor and distinctive color in the New World. One purpose of this book is to help students understand their linguistic heritage.

We believe that language is a primary concern of the college English course. In recent years teachers and students have increasingly come to realize that the way a person expresses himself—his choice of words, his pronunciation and distinctive dialectal characteristics, his grammar and style—can influence his social and economic status. Often an individual clearly reflects his linguistic background without realizing that this background may evoke a negative or unsympathetic response in those who are listening to him or reading his writing. Through the essays and exercises in this book we hope to focus the attention of the student on some of the basic principles of language and the significant elements of American English. Careful study and close analysis will help the student to understand and appreciate the forces that determine whether or not a particular linguistic pattern is accepted, tolerated, or rejected in a given cultural context.

We believe this book has certain distinct virtues. Its concentration on American English will meet the needs of all students, not just those of the English major. Those using it will come to understand that skill in language underlies distinguished achievement in any branch of learning. They will find that sentence structure, grammar, usage, and vocabulary are not just rules in a handbook or artificial exercises, but subjects about which they will read and write and make their own observations. They will learn why the use of standard English is important and why a variety of styles suitable to the different purposes and occasions of communication is necessary. Instructors will find that the selections can be coordinated easily with other readings that they may wish to use in a composition course, such as modern fiction and drama, and that the selections on basic principles of the development of the English language are pertinent to historical courses in English or American literature. In addition, the selections are all suitable for study as examples of modern expository writing. Some can serve as models for techniques of documentation, and all are useful sources for preparing documented papers of various lengths, or for research papers involving library work.

Each selection is followed by study questions, and suggested topics for written assignments will be found at the end of each part. Topics for long papers, which may be based on the text or extended into research papers, are listed at the back of the book. The study questions and topics for papers emphasize the student's observation of language in use and the application of general principles to the particular language of his own environment. They also stress basic problems in exposition: definition, analysis, comparison, classification, and exemplification are repeatedly called for.

These selections are not technical: the material is modern, much of it recent, and it is addressed to the general reader. Complete chapters, sections, or articles are given, with at most minor deletions. The scientific point of view is usually represented, and attention is given also to the contrasting prescriptive view of grammar and usage, and the historical explanation of that view. We have tried to avoid overemphasis on any particular linguistic theory or mode of analysis. Recent developments reveal a flexibility on the part of linguists as they readily embrace and then quickly discard new theories and methods. A number of the essays suggest some of the recent approaches; but in presenting an overview of current linguistic trends as they relate to American English, we have not committed ourselves to any school. No word lists or glossaries are included; such valuable raw material is available in *American Speech* or *Publications of the American Dialect Society*. Although articles dealing with specific phenomena of language had to be kept within the limits of this relatively small volume, a number of our suggestions for theme topics refer to other articles that are useful as models to show students how to use their own data.

As the table of contents indicates, the general principles of language are covered first. The order of selections within each part is from general to specific, although the selections can, of course, be used in any order desired. Parts II through V apply the four "approaches to language" identified and explained by Charles C. Fries in his *American English Grammar* (1940). Part II, "Historical Aspects," includes material on the history of the English language only as a basis for consideration of American English and of the chief differences between British and American English. Part III, "Geographical Aspects," provides material that enables the instructor to stress whatever regional variety of American English is used by the students. Part IV, "Literary and Colloquial Aspects," includes the indispensable essay by John S. Kenyon that distinguishes between cultural levels and functional varieties of language and recognizes colloquial standard English as a correct variety of style. This part is an excellent basis for the study of varieties of style in literary selections. Part V, "Social or Class Aspects," presents differing attitudes toward language, some of them reflecting the viewpoints of minority groups of language users. The social and economic advantage to the students of using acceptable English is further stressed, both in selections and in study questions.

As suggested above, this text may be used in a variety of ways: in a two-semester course in composition the first two parts might be used in the first semester, supplemented by other readings exemplifying problems in exposition; in the second semester, the remainder of the book might be supplemented by fiction, drama, and formal and informal essays to illustrate varieties of style and levels of usage. Research papers might be based on the application of material in the text to a work of modern American fiction. In a one-semester course in composition, the instructor might streamline the material by assigning only what seems essential. The book might also be used as a text in an introductory course in language or in a more advanced course if supplemented by some of the many excellent paperback books on linguistics. Whatever the course, teachers can devise their own assignments or adapt suggestions in the text to their own specific needs. Many of the topics can easily be varied, thus allowing for and stimulating student originality, and avoiding repetition of specific subjects. The sources quoted in entries in general dictionaries and the works listed in Wentworth and Flexner, *Dictionary of American Slang* (1960), will suggest modern authors whose works might be suitable for special study of modern written English or dialogue. For papers requiring extensive use of the library, the bibliography will serve as a basis for further research. The books listed in our bibliography include articles and books in their bibliographies and thus serve as a guide to the sources most valuable for the study of American English.

We wish to acknowledge the valuable expert advice given us by Miss Verna Newsome, Professor Emeritus of English at the University of Wisconsin–Milwaukee. We wish also to thank Dr. Albert H. Marckwardt of Princeton University, Dr. Thomas Pyles of Northwestern University, and Dr. John Algeo of the University of Florida, who read and criticized earlier versions of the manuscript.

E. M. K.
R. M. A.

Contents

part 4   Literary and Colloquial Aspects   227

part 5   Social or Class Aspects   311

Aspects of American English

part 1

Principles of Language

In recent years students of language have come more and more to recognize that language is a living, changing instrument, that the characteristics of each set of language patterns differ in some details from all others, and that it is impossible to superimpose the grammar of one language upon another. The descriptive or scientific linguist tries to set forth the characteristics of a language without forcing it into a preconceived pattern suitable for a different set of linguistic patterns. The use of Latin grammar to explain the operation of English is a classic misapplication and one which has stubbornly resisted the efforts of scientific linguists to change it. In this section the discussion of different aspects of language by several experts provides a foundation of principles of language upon which the student can build as he examines various aspects of American English. The student should consider these principles when he is working on the topics for short or long papers on specific aspects of American English.

That language is a complex instrument is becoming even more apparent as linguists methodically examine it and apply their discoveries in new theories and hypotheses. The ideas presented in this section are commonly accepted as some of the bases of the new approach to language, an approach marked by cautious impersonality and a vigorous insistence upon describing patterns of linguistic behavior. As the student begins to comprehend some of the principles of the scientific linguist, he can more easily understand some of the aspects of American English.

1

What Is Language?

Archibald A. Hill

In the opening chapter of Introduction to Linguistic Structures (1958) *Professor Hill discusses five of the characteristics of language that distinguish it as a human activity.*

1. SOME BASIC ASSUMPTIONS

The subject of linguistics presents an initial difficulty because the word which designates it is unfamiliar. The word can easily be defined as the scientific analysis of language, but it is doubtful if such a definition is meaningful to anyone who lacks familiarity with this kind of analytic activity. It is far better to begin by defining language, since language is closer to the reader's experience. Yet even the definition of language presents unsuspected difficulties and needs preliminary discussion before it is attempted directly.

If a group of educated speakers are asked to define the language they are using, the reply will probably be "All the words and sentences used to express our thoughts." The definition is satisfactory in everyday situations, since long practice has made plain what is meant, and consequently most hearers know how to respond accurately. But for all that, the definition is not sufficiently accurate to be the basis for analysis. Terms like "words and sentences," which seem transparent to a speaker of a Western language, would be more misleading than enlightening if applied to some languages. Moreover, there are phenomena similar to language which this definition does not identify. Most important, the definition identifies language activity by thought. Language activity can be observed, and is therefore subject to verification. Thought can be observed only by subjective introspection, and so is not subject to verification. Language activity is therefore more knowable, thought less knowable. Obviously a definition must define the less knowable by the more knowable if it is to cast light. In what follows, such a definition will be attempted. There must first be a warning, the need for which will be clearer as we advance. A definition is not a description. A definition gives only those characteristics which have diagnostic value for recognition. A description attempts to give all characteristics, preferably in the order of their importance. A definition necessarily leaves out much and may make use of relatively trivial characteristics, but it is not to be condemned for that reason.

Most professional students of language proceed from a few assumptions, one of which is that the fundamental forms of language activity are the sequences of sounds made by human lips, tongues, and vocal cords—the phenomena usually distinguished by the narrower name of "speech." Though this first assumption may seem like a truism, it is important, since many who accept it verbally still act as if they did not believe it. Some few even deny it. There are only two reasons for questioning the assumption. Writing has great permanence and great prestige. Further, the basis of our education is training in the manipulation of written symbols of ever-increasing complexity. Highly literate people, and those who would like to be literate, are therefore apt to think of writing as the real center of language and of speech as peripheral and derived—often badly—from the written forms.

There are a number of facts which should settle this question of priority. First, speech reaches back to the origins of human society; writing has a history of only about seven thousand years.[1] Also, no contemporary community of men is without language, even though it is probably still true that most of the world's several thousand language communities remain in the preliterate stage, without benefit of alphabet or even picture symbol. Individual members of literate communities, furthermore, learn their language some years before they learn to read or write it; and adults, even adults who are professional writers, carry on a good deal more speech activity in daily living than activity involving writing. The final fact is that all writing systems are essen-

---

[1] The great antiquity of language, as compared with writing, is a reasonable assumption, but it is often presented without evidence. To arrive at the conclusion that language is older than writing, linguists and anthropologists start from the observed fact that in modern communities, all organized cooperative activity rests firmly and necessarily on language as the means of controlling and directing interaction. This being so in all observed communities, it is assumed by archaeological anthropologists that when remains of past communities show material evidence of social organization, these remains are those of communities which possessed language. Communities which show such evidences of social organization also show artifacts or other evidences which are much older than the remains of any communities which show evidences of even primitive systems of writing. It is possible that early human communities possessed some other form of highly organized communication, such as the gesture language which has been occasionally proposed since the days of Locke (cf. Max Müller, *Lectures on the Science of Language*, London, 1862, p. 31). But though possible, such a nonvocal symbol system is unlikely. Language is now a universal activity; it is an extra and unnecessary hypothesis to suppose something else.

tially representations of the forms of speech, rather than representations of ideas or objects in the nonlinguistic world. There are exceptions to this statement, like the Arabic numbers which work independently of the words for numbers in the Western languages. The exceptions, however, are in a minority disproportionate to the majority of symbols which always indicate the forms of language. The point can be driven home by a pair of simple examples. The symbol for *one* in Japanese writing is a single stroke, that for *two* two strokes, and so on. It might be thought that such a symbol has no relation to the Japanese word for *one* (*ichi*) but represents instead the nonlinguistic ideas of "oneness." Actually the occurrence of the single stroke is correlated with the occurrence of the word. It occurs not only in the number but also in such forms as *ichiji, primary*. The Japanese symbol, therefore, has a quite different range from the letter sequence *one* of English, which is not used in the dissimilar word *primary*. The one-stroke symbol corresponds with the occurrence of the Japanese word *ichi*, proving that the one-stroke symbol is a representation of the word (though an understandably pictorial one), and not a direct representation of the idea of oneness.

Written symbols can be understood, furthermore, insofar as they fit into a linguistic structure, even when they refer to nothing in the nonlinguistic world. Thus, if an English text should have the sentence "He *sprashes* it," the second word could immediately be recognized as a verb in the third person singular and as a sequence of sounds quite in accord with English structural habits, though it represents nothing in the outside world at all. For the purposes of this book, therefore, the linguist's assumption that language is a set of sounds will be adopted. It is no contradiction of this assumption that the sounds can be secondarily translated into visual marks, grooves on a wax disk, electrical impulses, or finger movements.

Linguists assume that the description and analysis of language must begin with description of the sounds and their patterning and that description of meaning must be put off until the first task is done. Such an attitude is often misunderstood to be a denial of meaning, but this is not true. The linguist's desire to put off analysis of meaning is no more than an application of the principle of working from the more knowable to the less knowable, and though linguistics has not as yet had very striking results in semantic analysis, it can be hoped that the next few decades will see results of real value in semantics.

2. THE DEFINING CHARACTERISTICS OF LANGUAGE

Working with the assumptions given above, linguists can offer a set of five defining characteristics which serve to set off language from other forms of symbolic behavior and to establish language as a purely human activity. Often animal communication will have one or more of these five characteristics, but never all of them.

First, language, as has been said, is a set of sounds. This is perhaps the least important characteristic, since the communication of mammals and birds is also a set of sounds. On the other hand, the system of communication which is in some ways most strikingly like language, that of bees, is a set of body movements, not sounds. It would be easy, further, to imagine a language based on something else than sound, but no human language is so constructed. Even the manual language of the deaf is derived from the pre-existent spoken language of the community.

Second, the connection between the sounds, or sequences of sounds, and objects of the outside world is arbitrary and unpredictable. That is to say, a visitor from Mars would be unable to predict that in London a given animal is connected with the sound sequence written *dog*, in Paris with the sequence *chien*, in Madrid with *perro*. The arbitrary quality of language symbols is not infrequently denied, for a number of reasons. Sometimes the denial is based on nothing more than the notion that the forms of one's native language are so inevitably right that they must be instinctive for all proper men. Sometimes the denial is more subtle. It is often maintained that all language, even though now largely arbitrary, must once have been a systematic imitation of objects by means of sound. It is true that there are some imitative words in all languages, but they are at best a limited part of the vocabulary. It is easy to imitate the noise of a barking dog, for instance, but difficult if not impossible to imitate a noiseless object, such as a rainbow. Though imitative words show similarity in many languages, absolute identity is rare. A dog goes "bow-wow" in English, but in related languages he often goes "wow-wow" or "bow-bow." The imitative words do not, after all, entirely escape from the general arbitrariness of language. The imitative origin of language appears, therefore, at worst unlikely and at best unprovable. The same injunction holds for theories of language origin which speculate that it is an imitation of facial or other gestures.

If it is assumed that language is arbitrary, what is meant by the statement? Just that the sounds of speech and their connection with entities of experience are passed on to all members of any community by older members of that community. Therefore, a human being cut off from contact with a speech community can never learn to talk as that community does, and cut off from all speech communities never learns to talk at all. In essence, to say that language is arbitrary is merely to say that it is social. This is perhaps the most important statement that can be made about language.

In contrast, much of animal communication is instinctive rather than social. That is to say, all cats mew and purr, and would do so even if they were cut off from all communication with other cats. On the other hand, some animal communication seems to share the social nature of human speech and is therefore learned activity. A striking example is the barking of dogs, which is characteristic only of the domesticated animal, not of dogs in the wild state. Similarly, the honey dances of bees may not be altogether without an arbitrary element. It is also likely that when more is known of the cries and chatterings of the great apes in the wild state, a considerable social element in their communication may be found. Nor should it be thought that all human communication is social. A part of our communication consists of instinctive reactions which accompany language, like the trembling of fear or the suffusion of blood which accompanies anger. Yet even in the nonlinguistic accompaniments of speech, the tones of voice and the gestures, it is now clear that there is more of arbitrary and socially learned behavior than had at one time been supposed.

Third, language is systematic. I cannot hope to make this statement completely clear at this point, since the whole of this book is devoted to an exposition of the system of language. However, some observations may now be made about the system of language. As in any system, language entities are arranged in recurrent designs, so that if a part of the design is seen, predictions can be made about the whole of it, as a triangle can be drawn if one side and two angles are given. Suppose there is an incomplete sentence like "John —s Mary an —." A good deal about what must fill the two blanks is obvious. The first must be a verb, the second a noun. Furthermore, not all verbs will go in the first blank, since it requires a verb whose third person singular is spelled with –s and which can take two objects (that is, not such a verb as *look* or *see*). Nor will all nouns fit in the second place, since an initial vowel is required, and the noun must be one which takes an article. There is no difficulty in deciding that the sentence could be either "John gives Mary an apple" or "John hands Mary an aspirin," but not "John *gaves* Mary an *book*." [2]

Another observation that can be made about language systems is that every occurrence of language is a substitution frame. Any sentence is a series of entities, for each of which a whole group of other entities can be substituted without changing the frame. Thus the sentence "John gives Mary an apple" is such a substitution frame. For *John* there can be replacements like *he, Jack, William, the man, her husband,* or many

---

[2] . . . [A]n asterisk placed before a form means that it is believed to be impossible. In historical treatments of language, on the other hand, an asterisk before a form indicates that it has been reconstructed by comparison but is not actually recorded. These two uses of the asterisk should not be confused.

others. For the verb, entities like *buys*, *takes*, *offers*, as well as the alternatives *hands* or *gives*, may be used. This characteristic of extensive substitutability for all parts of any language utterance is of some importance in that it enables us to say that parrots, no matter how startlingly human their utterances may be, are not carrying on language activity. A parakeet may produce the sentence "Birds can't talk!" with human pitch, voice tones, and nearly perfect sounds. But the bird never says "Dogs can't talk!" or "Birds can't write!" His utterance is a unit, not a multiple substitution frame.

Still another characteristic of language systems is that the entities of language are grouped into classes, always simpler, more predictable, and more sharply separated than the infinite variety of objects in the world. For instance, a whole series of objects is grouped under the single word *chair*, and *chair* is put into the large class of nouns. In dealing with objects in the outside world it may be difficult to decide whether something is a chair, a stool, or merely a rock. In language, we think of nouns and verbs as quite separate and are apt to say that the one class represents things, the other events. But in the outside world, as the physicists tell us, it is often hard to decide whether an object is best described as thing or as event.

To return once more to the defining characteristics of language, the fourth characteristic is that it is a set of symbols. That is to say, language has meaning. In this form the statement is a platitude and does not distinguish language from other activities which are also symbolic. The nature of language symbols turns out to be rather different from the symbols of other types of communication. The simplest nonlinguistic symbol can be defined as a substitute stimulus. Pavlov's famous dogs, fed at the sound of a bell, eventually began to drool at the sound of the bell even when no food was present. The dogs were responding to a substitute stimulus. Nonlinguistic symbols can also be substitute responses, and these can also be taught to animals. A dog who learns to "speak" at the sight of food has learned such a substitute response. In human speech, however, one of the most striking facts is that we can talk about things which are not present, and we can talk about things which ordinarily produce a strong physical reaction without experiencing that reaction. For instance, I can talk about apples even though there are none in the room, and I can talk about them without always making my mouth water, even when I am hungry. This type of language, which occurs without an immediately present stimulus or response, is called "displaced speech," and it is obviously of great importance. It is what enables man to know something of the past and of the world beyond the limited range of his vision and hearing at a given moment.

The crucial fact in producing this almost miraculous and purely human effect seems to be that a given language entity can be both substitute stimulus and substitute response, and can also be a stimulus for further language responses or a response to other language stimuli. I can talk about apples when they are absent because "something reminds me of them." That is, I can make language responses to what is before me, and these language responses can stimulate the further response *apple* without any direct physical stimulus to my vision, touch, or smell. *Apple* can call forth still further language entities, like *pear* or *banana*, in an endless chain; these entities are also both stimuli and responses. When human speakers do this, they are setting up what philosophers call a "universe of discourse." The ability to make connected discourse within the symbol system is what enables men to talk at length, and profitably, about things they have never seen. By means of language men make elaborate models of distant experience and eventually test their accuracy by acting upon them. All that is known of animal communication leads to the supposition that precisely what is absent from it is the kind of symbolic activity here described, symbolic activity connected not merely with experience but with all parts of the symbol system itself. We believe, in short, that animals are incapable of displaced speech.

The paragraphs above are rather general, so that a concrete example may be helpful. Let us suppose that two speakers of English are together in a room. One of them is cold. A direct response for him would be to close the window.

Instead of this he can use the substitute response, which is also substitute stimulus: "John, please close the window for me." John can either close the window or reply with a further substitute: "Just a minute. Wait until I finish this page." Such a reply may produce acceptance or may lead to a discussion of John's procrastinating character, of the fact that his parents did not discipline him properly in youth and that modern young people are generally rebellious and unmannerly. To all of this John may reply that modern times are marked by progress and the disappearance of old taboos. In the meantime the window may have been quietly closed, or completely forgotten in the warmth of discussion. What is important is that each speaker has begun reacting, not to the immediate situation, but to the other speaker's language and to his own. And in so doing, each has been building a model of general social conditions, of wide scope and ultimately of some value, even in a random and unchecked conversation of the sort described.

We are now ready to turn to the last defining characteristic of language, the fact that it is complete. By this is meant that whenever a human language has been accurately observed, it has been found to be so elaborated that its speakers can make a linguistic response to any experience they may undergo. This complex elaboration is such a regular characteristic of all languages, even those of the simplest societies, that linguists have long ago accepted it as a universal characteristic. Nevertheless, in early books about language, and in the descriptions by linguistically untrained travelers today, there are statements that tribe X has a language with only two or three hundred words in it, forcing the tribe to eke out its vocabulary by gesture.[3] Linguists maintain that all such statements are the product of lack of knowledge, and are false. Skepticism about such statements is borne out by the fact that in all instances where it was possible to check on tribe X, its language proved to be complete as usual, whereupon the statement was transferred to tribe Y, whose language was as yet unknown. The statement that human language is complete once again serves to distinguish it from animal activity. In the communication of bees, for instance, the subjects of systematic discourse are severely limited. Bees cannot, apparently, make an utterance equivalent to "The beekeeper is coming."

The statement that human language is always complete should not be interpreted to mean that every language has a word for everything. Obviously the ancient Greeks had no words for automobiles or atom bombs, and probably the modern Yahgan of Tierra del Fuego lack them as well. The completeness of language lies rather in the fact that a speaker of ancient Greek would have been perfectly capable of describing an automobile had he seen one, and further that had automobiles become important in ancient Greece, the speakers of Greek would have been perfectly capable of coining a word for them. It is a characteristic of vocabulary that, except in languages which have gone out of use, it is always expansible, in spite of the fact that resistance to new forms may frequently appear. Since language enables the user to make appropriate responses to all things and since vocabulary is thus characteristically "open," differences in vocabulary between two languages are not an accurate measure of the differences in efficiency or excellence of the two tongues. The fact that Eskimo does not have as highly developed a vocabulary of philosophy as does German merely indicates that the Eskimos are less interested in philosophy; on the other hand, Eskimo has a highly developed vocabulary for various kinds of snow, indicating that snow is important in Eskimo society. The completeness of

---

[3] A typical recent statement of this sort was reported by Leonard Bloomfield in "Secondary and Tertiary Responses to Language," *Language*, XX, 1944, p. 49 *n*.

"A physician, of good general background and education, who had been hunting in the north woods, told me that the Chippewa language contains only a few hundred words. Upon question, he said that he got this information from his guide, a Chippewa Indian. When I tried to state the diagnostic setting, the physician, our host, briefly and with signs of displeasure repeated his statement and then turned his back to me. A third person, observing this discourtesy, explained that I had some experience of the language in question. This information had no effect."

For a good general account of the completeness of primitive languages and the use of gesture as a substitute among mutually unintelligible language groups, consult Ralph L. Beals and Harry Hoijer, *An Introduction to Anthropology*, Macmillan, New York, 1956, pp. 508–11.

human language and the openness of vocabulary make a groundless chimera of the occasionally expressed fear that a language might so degenerate as to become useless.

We can now attempt a definition of language, though the definition will be cumbersome. Language is the primary and most highly elaborated form of human symbolic activity. Its symbols are made up of sounds produced by the vocal apparatus, and they are arranged in classes and patterns which make up a complex and symmetrical structure. The entities of language are symbols, that is, they have meaning, but the connection between symbol and thing is arbitrary and socially controlled. The symbols of language are simultaneously substitute stimuli and substitute responses and can call forth further stimuli and responses, so that discourse becomes independent of an immediate physical stimulus. The entities and structure of language are always so elaborated as to give the speaker the possibility of making a linguistic response to any experience. Most of the above can be paraphrased by saying that every language is a model of a culture and its adjustment to the world. . . .

STUDY QUESTIONS AND EXERCISES

1. How does acquirement of language, as evidence of "normal" intelligence, compare with acquirement of such other skills as reading, writing, and arithmetic or with creativity in art and music? Is it conceivable that a physically and mentally normal human being, brought up in a human community, with or without schooling, would be unable to use spoken language? Is it conceivable for such a person, without schooling, to lack any or all of the other skills listed above? What do you conclude about speech as a human attribute?

2. Discover from people whose native language is not English, what sounds a child learns in imitation of animal sounds, as an American child learns "bow-wow" for dog, "meow" for cat, "quack" for duck, "baa" for sheep, and so forth. If various members of a class investigate a number of languages, do the results show identity of sounds, similarity, or dissimilarity among languages? What do the findings imply as to the imitative origin of language? * Nursery words, such as *mama* and *papa* show greater similarity, even among unrelated languages, than do onomatopoetic words. Can you think of any likely reason for this exception to the arbitrariness of language?

3. What special "family words" for objects or people do you use in your own home? How did these words originate?

* See Noel Perrin, "Old Macberlitz Had a Farm," *The New Yorker* (January 27, 1962), pp. 28–29, and Paul Koht's letter in reply, *The New Yorker* (February 24, 1962), p. 125.

4. In German, *Gift* means "poison" and *Brief* means "letter"; in French, *lice* means "lists" or "arena" and *mince* means "slender"; in Spanish, *cola* means "tail" and *sin* means "without." Give other examples to illustrate the arbitrary quality of language.

5. Children invent secret languages, such as pig Latin. What is the principle of transposition in: "Amscray, erehay omescay ethay opcay"? In James Joyce's *A Portrait of the Artist as a Young Man*, Chapter 4, the Dedalus children use a different kind of pig Latin: their parents have "Goneboro toboro lookboro atboro aboro houseboro" because "theboro landboro lordboro willboro putboro usboro outboro." What is the principle here? Are you familiar with any other secret languages? If so, what are the principles?

6. The four basic sentence patterns in English can be illustrated as follows:

    a. Birds chirp.
    b. The bird is small.
    c. Birds are travelers.
    d. The child saw the bird.†

Using these four patterns as "substitution frames" to which modifiers may be added, what do you discover about "extensive substitutability"?

7. From your own earliest memories of nursery rhymes and fairy tales, illustrate how a child talks about things he has never seen. By observing a small child and his speech and responses to words, can you determine what constitutes his "universe of discourse"?

8. Many words in modern English have as their roots ancient Greek and Latin words. Look up *stereophonic* in a recent dictionary; note the original meanings of *stereo* and *phonic* and all the words for modern inventions and concepts that have been derived from these roots. Look up *sinister* and *conduct* in the dictionary. Are their modern meanings similar to the Latin meanings? If not, can you suggest how their meanings might have changed through time?

9. This selection presents an inductive definition of language. What does *inductive* mean as a method of reasoning and a principle of organization? What is the *genus* of language, in Hill's definition? What are the *differentiae*?

---

† Verna L. Newsome, *Structural Grammar in the Classroom* (Oshkosh: Wisconsin Council of Teachers of English, 1961), p. 13.

2

Language Has System

Robert A. Hall, Jr.

This selection from Linguistics and Your Language (1960) *examines the approaches toward language systems that the scientific linguist may follow in his investigations.*

Up to now, in general, grammarians and teachers and those who have told others how to talk and what to do about their language, have done so on a purely *normative* basis—that is, setting up rules or norms and insisting that people follow them. Sometimes the normative grammarian has justified his dicta by appealing to "logic," sometimes to tradition, and sometimes to just the weight of his own say-so; but his attitude has always been authoritarian, i.e., depending on the force of authority and not on accurate observation and reasoning. The scientific attitude, on the other hand, rejects normative commands, and tries to base its conclusions on the greatest possible accuracy in observing facts, with the greatest possible objectivity, and on as careful reasoning and analysis as we can apply to the facts at our command. A true scientist also wants others to know as much of the truth as he can find out and make known, so that others also can follow his line of argument and, where possible, carry on up to and beyond whatever point he has reached. Now if we were to proceed immediately to the linguistic analyst's recommendations for changing our current ideas and behavior connected with language, we would be skipping an essential step in the process; and the linguist, by presenting his findings and his advice without first giving his reasons for so doing, would be converting himself from a scientist into simply another normative grammarian. In this process, there would be no gain; there is no use of substituting Language Authoritarian No. 2 for Language Authoritarian No. 1. What we need to do is rather to find out how we can escape entirely from the clutches of authoritarianism of any kind in language, and how we can ourselves acquire the essentials of a scientific attitude, and if we need to or want to, go ahead on our own in studying and thinking about language without being dependent on "authority."

When we want to imagine how things would seem to somebody who could look at us in a wholly objective, scientific way, we often put our reasoning in terms of a "man from Mars" coming to observe the earth and its inhabitants, living among men and studying their existence dispassionately and in its entirety. Such a "man from Mars," or some equally impartial observer, would notice, among the first things he saw in any human group, that its members cooperate by means of signals. They lend each other a hand, literally, in many undertakings, and they are able to exchange the use of all their faculties. We can build skyscrapers and bridges, manoeuver airplanes and battleships, warn each other of coming dangers and tell each other of past happenings, by means of signals. Theoretically, of course, any one of the five senses—touch, smell, taste, sight or hearing—could be used to make such signals. But our senses of touch, smell and taste do not distinguish very clearly or sharply between various feelings, smells or tastes, and our memories for these senses are not as exact as they are for sight or hearing. These last two senses are more nearly on a par with each other, so far as clearness and sharpness of distinction and memory go: we can distinguish a signal that we see, and can remember it, just about as clearly as one that we hear. But hearing has certain advantages over sight, for signalling purposes: we can hear sounds coming from any direction, whereas we can see only things that are more or less in front of us; and we have, built into our bodies from birth, a pretty complex group of organs that we can use for making sounds, and a wide range of sounds that we can make—whereas the range of visible signals we can make unaided is quite limited. Furthermore, we can make sounds with the organs of our respiratory tract (what cigarette advertisements call the "T-zone") without interfering with what we are doing with the rest of our body—working, resting, etc.—but any visible signals we might try to make (say, with arm signals) necessarily involve major disturbance to whatever else we might be trying to do at the same time.

So our "man from Mars" would observe that humans communicate by means of signals, and that these signals are primarily *oral* and *aural* —made with the mouth and other "organs of speech," and heard with the ear. He would observe this in any community he was in, from the Australian Bushmen to the tribes of the Congo, from the Navaho sheepherders to the aristocracy of Buckingham Palace. In fact, this is the major, basic characteristic that he would find differentiating humans from other living beings: humans talk, and talk extensively. They are not, by any means, the only living beings to communicate by means of auditory signals; but in the various animals that communicate with each other, the range and extent of communication is much less.

Furthermore, our "man from Mars" or our ideal linguistic analyst would see that when humans talk, their talk is not just a continual succession of babble, of sounds no two of which are alike or ever come in a given order. That is the way that monkeys gabble and jabber, or that babies prattle; but in grown people's speech, the world over, the same sounds and the same combinations of sounds keep recurring more or less frequently. In short, there are *partial resemblances* in the utterances that people make; and, because people's utterances have partial resemblances, we can say that all language has *system*—in its sounds and in the way these sounds are put together. If anything has system, we can describe it, by saying briefly and compactly what are the partial resemblances of the elements of the system; our "man from Mars" or our ideal analyst could make a series of statements about these systems of auditory signalling, about these *languages,* he observed among humans, and thus could make a description of their speech. If he were to do this, he would be engaging in the most fundamental type of scientific analysis as applied to language, in *descriptive linguistics.*

Another very important thing that our observer would see is that these signals always occur in connection with other things—in the last analysis, in connection (direct or indirect) with something in the world around us, with reality. (Let's leave aside all philosophical discussion as to the nature of reality, and simply assume reality as something we take as fact, in the way we all do in normal living.) That is to say, when the word *book* occurs in our speech, it normally occurs in connection, direct or indirect, with an object of the general type that might be described as "a series of sheets of paper in some way fastened together, or a composition or part of a composition that might be written on such a series of sheets of paper or other writing materials." The connections in which a word occurs, the situations with respect to which we use it, are the word's *meaning.* If a child has just learned some new word, say *grass,* and uses it to refer to some object that we normally call by some other name, such as a person's hair or the fur on a coat, we simply say that the child "doesn't know what *grass* means"—he hasn't yet learned in what situations it is and is not used. That is one of the basic features of a linguistic signal—it has to have meaning; if it has no meaning, it is not a signal, and does not come under the subject-matter of linguistics.

On the other hand, the meaning of a word is not by any means fixed, not so much as its sound; for instance, the sound of the word *book* is reasonably definite and always predictable throughout the English-speaking world, but it has many different meanings, as in *a big book* (referring to the actual tome), *a long book* (the composition contained in a book, even before it's printed and bound), or *Book I of the poem* (referring to a part of the composition). The word *book* also has many special uses in phrases such as "to throw the book at someone," "to speak by the book," in England "to book a ticket," and so forth. The meanings and uses of even such a simple word as *book* are much less easily definable and predictable, and change much more rapidly, than the sounds and grammatical form of the word. Hence the linguistic scientist considers it better to study language first from the point of view of its *form* (sounds and combinations of sounds), and tries to avoid, as much as possible, basing his analysis on the shifting sands of meaning.

In so doing, the linguistic analyst gets away at the outset from the approach to language that we find in a considerable part of the Latin and English grammar we learn in our schools—the approach based on meaning rather than form. Even our traditional definitions of the "parts of speech" like nouns, adjectives, verbs and so on, are based on meaning more than on anything else. Most of us probably were taught that a noun was supposed to be "the name of a person, place or thing"; an adjective, "the name of a quality or accidence"; and a verb, "the name of an action or state of being." Unfortunately, however, this approach is inefficient and keeps us from getting an accurate idea of the way the system of signalling, the language itself, as opposed to its meanings, is built. Meanings vary not only from one dialect to another, but from one person to another, or even in one person's usage: how many of us use the words *Communist* or *Fascist* in exactly the same meaning as the next man does, or are absolutely sure of the exact meaning of every word we use? For that matter, some meanings just will not fit into the definitions that grammarians give for linguistic classes such as the "parts of speech." Take the word *reflection*. In English, the word *reflection* is certainly a noun, just as much as *book, typewriter, ribbon, hat* or any of the other thousands of nouns of the language; but is *reflection* the name of a person, place or thing? It is hardly any of these; a reflection always involves motion, whether that of a light-wave or of a sound-wave or of anything else being reflected off something. It is more of an action, a happening, than a thing. Yet the word *reflection*, as any speaker of English who has learned a little grammatical terminology will tell us, is most certainly a noun.

The reason we say that *reflection* is a noun is, not that it refers to a person, place or thing (for *reflection, light, matter* and many other nouns do not), but that it fits into the system of the English language in the same way as do other words which we call nouns. The word *reflection* can take the suffix *–'s* (*reflection's*); it can, if necessary, be used in the plural (*reflections*); it can have the word *the* used before it (*the reflection*). Those things are true of all English nouns; and they are all features, not of the nouns' meaning, but of their form. At this stage of our work, the only use we make of a word's meaning is to determine whether the word is a true linguistic signal or not, and whether it belongs together in our analysis with other signals that have the same meaning (as when we classify *went* as the past of *go*); otherwise, it is much safer to keep to the form, which is constant, and can be identified and described with much less trouble than the meaning.

Our analysis has to be *formal* first of all; this implies that it will also be somewhat on an abstract plane, and that we will be analyzing language itself before we come to examine the situations in which it is used. Language naturally does not exist in a void, nor yet in a lifeless world of logic or abstraction. People talk, and use language in all their activities, from the most everyday, commonplace contacts to the most intellectual type of reasoning; that is, language is above all social in the way it works, and we shall have occasion to take up its social function later on. But we must first find out *what* language is, before we examine *how* it functions in the wider context of human affairs. Similarly the chemist, even though he may ultimately be interested in the function and use of some fertilizer or dyestuff, first analyzes it and studies its formal characteristics in terms of the frame of reference which has been worked out for chemical analysis.

Our study of language, in addition to being formal, needs to be *descriptive* at the outset, before we proceed to further more advanced analyses. What we need, first of all, is to get as clear and complete an idea as we can get of the structure of any language we're working on, as it exists or existed at a particular point of time, without letting our picture of the language be distorted by extraneous considerations. There are two types of undesirable approach which we are especially likely to introduce, and which can easily distract our attention from the work of pure description: the *prescriptive* approach, and the historical. On this first point, the analyst's task is not to prescribe what "should" or "should not" be said; his job is to describe what actually *is* said, with as completely scientific and objective an approach as a human is capable of. He is interested in noting down factors of meaning such as the social connotations of "incorrect" forms, but considerations of "correctness" should never induce him to omit from his study or analysis such forms as *ain't, he done.* From the scientific point of view, the truly sub-standard *it ain't,* the supposedly sub-standard *it's me,* the standard *I'm tired,* and all other types of speech (literary, dialectal, rustic, slang, criminal argot, etc.) are of absolutely equal merit. That is to say, questions of merit or value just do not enter into the picture of linguistic analysis, however important they may be in the study of literature. Matters of "correctness," of standard versus non-standard, are socially determined and are relevant only from the point of view of meaning, not of linguistic form. In the same way, the chemist or the biologist studies all chemical or biological phenomena with an impersonal, scientific attitude. Our culture has come to accept this situation with regard to the physical sciences, before it has extended the same recognition to the social sciences such as anthropology, of which linguistics is a branch. No one would now say to a biologist working on *spirochaeta pallida:* "That organism is the cause of syphilis, and venereal diseases must not even be discussed; therefore you must stop working in your laboratory and reporting your findings on spirochetes."

Likewise, the scientific linguist approaches all linguistic systems with what he hopes is an equally unprejudiced eye, no matter what is the level of culture or civilization of the people who use them. Whether we consider American, West European, Bush Negro African, aboriginal Australian, or American Indian civilization to be the highest and "best," we must use the same approach and the same methods for analyzing their languages. This is true even for such lowly and usually despised media of communication as Pidgin English; and, when we study Pidgin English with a serious intent and go at it without preconceived notions as to its merit or fitness for use, we find that even Pidgin has a structure and a value of its own.

The other distortion we mentioned, that which comes from a premature introduction of the historical viewpoint, is not basically anti-scientific, as is the prescriptive approach; but its bad effects are just as great, and lead to just as faulty a picture of the state of affairs. At present, in English, the Romance languages, and other languages of the Indo-European family, nouns are definitely distinct from adjectives: among other things, nouns in English have their plural in –s, adjectives do not have a plural formation; adjectives can have adverbs in –ly formed on them, nouns cannot. The present state of affairs, however, seems to have developed out of an earlier condition in which, some thousands of years ago, there was no distinction between the two parts of speech. So far, so good; if we state these two situations separately, and then tell the historical relation between the two, no harm is done. But definite harm is done if we do as one scholar did, and make the statement "Grammatically, nouns and adjectives are identical; their functional differentiation . . . was a later development." Identical at what point of time?—in Indo-European, yes; in modern English, Romance, etc., or even Latin and Greek, no; and the statement, as it stands, is inaccurate and confusing. It is as if we were to say "Maine is really a part of Massachusetts, and Vermont a section of New York; their functional differentiation was a later development," just because that was the situation in earlier times. Historical considerations should not be allowed to obscure our first aim, which is to find out the facts as they are or were at whatever given point of time we are studying; then, if we want to study historical development, we can do so by comparing two or more sets of descriptive data.

What the linguistic analyst does, therefore, when he begins to work on any particular language or on any feature of language in general, is to get rid of any preconceptions he may have concerning the social standing or "merit" of language. Then he has to get a clear idea of the language's structure, of what "makes it tick," at the specific point of time and space he's interested in—whether it be the present or some time in the past—and make an accurate description of it, at least for his own use and preferably published for others' use as well. Such a work is called a *descriptive grammar*. He can then go ahead and study the variations from any particular dialect which are found either in space (*linguistic geography*) or in time (*historical grammar*). In any of these kinds of study, the analyst adopts certain divisions which fit his subject-matter. Just as the chemist, say, classes certain phenomena under organic chemistry and others under inorganic chemistry, so the linguistic analyst divides his work into three main branches: the study of 1) sound, 2) form and 3) meaning.

STUDY QUESTIONS AND EXERCISES

1. Explain the difference between the descriptive and the prescriptive linguists' attitudes toward such locutions as "Sure, the window's broke, but it ain't my fault; Jack done it." To convey meaning, are such substandard utterances as useful as "Father, I cannot tell a lie; I did it with my little hatchet"? In the first example, where does the "incorrectness" of the separate words lie: in the word itself or in the form of the word in its syntactical context? Is there any word in this example that would never be used by an educated person?

2. Which would provide the prescriptive linguist with more material for a study of "correct" spoken English, the dialogue in a novel by J. P. Marquand about upper-class Bostonians or that in J. D. Salinger's *Catcher in the Rye* or Mark Twain's *Huckleberry Finn*? Of what value to the descriptive linguist would be the dialogue in realistic fiction dealing with uneducated characters?

3. Without overstressing the analogy, compare the botanist's interest in weeds with the descriptive linguist's interest in substandard speech. To whom and why are weeds or substandard elements in speech undesirable? What functions do weeds serve in nature and substandard speech in society?

4. With which of the four aspects of language represented by the main divisions of this book would the linguistic analyst be concerned? Which would he disregard as a basis for value judgments? Which would he consider in relation to spoken and written language?

3

The Nature and History of Linguistics

William G. Moulton

In this essay Professor Moulton of Princeton University explains some of the specialized terms used by students of language to describe fundamental linguistic processes. His essay appears as a chapter in Linguistics Today *(1969), edited by Archibald Hill.*

The ability of human beings to talk—to use language in order to communicate with one another—is so universal and seems so natural that most of us never bother to think much about it. We take it for granted that every normal human being can talk, just as we take it for granted that he can eat, sleep, or walk. This common attitude toward language is in part entirely correct: every normal human being beyond infancy *can* use language to communicate with his fellow human beings. It is precisely this ability that distinguishes man as "the talking animal" most sharply from all other beings. This is not to say that other living beings do not communicate with the other members of their species. They do of course; and a few of them have communication systems that are complex and flexible enough to deserve the name "language." The research of recent decades has shown us, for example, a great deal about the remarkable language of bees; and we are just beginning to realize that dolphins use a language that is perhaps even more remarkable. Nevertheless, none of these animal languages even remotely approaches the complexity, flexibility, and elegance of every human language. Man's ability to use language far surpasses that of any other living being.

Though it is true that every normal human being is able to use language, it is misleading to compare this with his ability to eat, sleep, or walk. All of these abilities are passed on to us by genetic transmission: we receive them by way of the genes that we inherit from our parents. In the case of language, however, it is only the *ability* to talk and understand that we inherit genetically; the particular language or languages that we speak are passed on to us not by genetic transmission but by cultural transmission. That is to say, a language is something that we learn and are taught, not something that we know by instinct.

When we say that a language is culturally transmitted—that it is learned and not inherited—we mean that it is part of that whole complex of learned and shared behavior that anthropologists call "culture." This might lead us to believe that a simple culture would make use of a simple language, that a complex culture would make use of a complex language, and so on. In fact, this does not seem to be true at all, except in a very trivial sense. There are so-called primitive cultures in the jungles of the Amazon and on the island of New Guinea, and there are so-called advanced cultures in Europe, Asia, and Africa; but the languages of these cultures are all equally "advanced" and complex. The trivial sense in which some languages are simpler than others concerns only matters of vocabulary: it is obvious that a language whose speakers talk about philosophy and science will contain more words than a language whose speakers are engaged primarily in hunting and fishing. With this one exception, it is quite wrong to suppose that a "simple" culture will also have a "simple" language. The grammar and sound system of such a language may turn out to be more complex than that of many an "advanced" culture; and even its vocabulary will run to many thousands of words and may include subtle distinctions which strike outsiders as very complex indeed.

Linguistics is the branch of learning which studies the languages of any and all human societies: how each such language is constructed; how it varies through space and changes through time; how it is related to other languages; and how it is used by its speakers. Fundamental to all branches of linguistics is the basic question: What *is* language? How does it work? What happens when a speaker says something and a hearer understands him? If we look at a typical act of communication by means of language, two aspects seem quite clear. First, it is obvious that language makes use of *sound*. Second, this sound is used to convey *meaning* from speaker to hearer. We might therefore be tempted to say that a language is a communication system consisting merely of sound and meaning.

If we look a little further, however, it becomes clear that this is not even a first approximation of the way language works. Language does indeed involve sound and meaning; but it clearly involves much more than this since we can easily think of situations in which we can hear the sound and know the meaning and yet really understand nothing of the language. Consider the following example. Suppose that we are in Japan and that we see two people talking together. The first one makes the sounds "Nañ-zi desu ka?" whereupon the second pulls out his watch, looks at it, and then makes the sounds "Ni-zi desu." Here two messages have been transmitted. We have heard all the sounds in each message, and we can easily guess at the meanings: the first speaker was surely asking what time it is, and the second speaker almost surely answered that it is two o'clock—since our own watch tells us that this is the time. Yet though we have heard the sound and know the meaning, we do not yet really understand anything of the Japanese language. To learn this we must investigate the connection between sound and meaning. We must find out what parts of the sound correspond to what parts of the meaning, how the first sentence is marked as a question and the second as a statement, and so on. Sound and meaning are not language, but only the external, observable aspects of language. Language itself, in the narrower sense, is neither of these observable things but rather the connection between them—which can be observed only indirectly, by inference.

In order to understand a little better how sound and meaning are connected so as to yield language, let us consider a typical speech event in which a speaker says something and is understood by a hearer. How does the speaker formulate his message? How is it transmitted to the hearer? And how does the hearer understand it? There seem to be 11 different stages in the whole process, and we can consider them briefly one by one.

1. *Semantic encoding.* The first thing the speaker must do is to formulate his message in the semantic units his language uses. Since this is like putting a message into proper shape to fit the code in which it is being sent, we can call this stage "semantic encoding." If the situation we have just described had taken place in an English-speaking country, we would have heard the sounds "What *time* is it?"—"It's two *o'clock.*" In the question we use the semantic unit *time,* the same unit that also occurs in such sentences as "I don't have *time*" and "I saw him last *time*"; and in the answer we use the curious unit *o'clock,* which occurs only in sentences of this sort. Where we must use two different semantic units, *time* and *o'clock,* a Frenchman can use the same semantic unit in both the question and the answer: "Quelle *heure* est-il?"—"Il est deux *heures*" (with singular *heure* and plural *heures*). This semantic unit *heure* is the one which corresponds in other sentences to English *hour,* a unit of time. A German would also use the same semantic unit in both the question and the answer: "Wieviel *Uhr* ist es?"—"Es ist zwei *Uhr,*" though his semantic unit *Uhr* does not correspond to English *hour* (for this the Germans use the unit *Stunde*), but rather to what we call a *clock* or a *watch.* A Dutchman handles the matter still differently. He says: "Hoe *laat* is het?"—"Het is twee *uur.*" His word *laat* corresponds in other sentences to our English *late;* that is to say, his "Hoe *laat* is het?" corresponds to the English question "How *late* is it?" The semantic unit *uur* he uses in his answer is similar to French *heure* in that it corresponds in other sentences to English *hour;* but, unlike French *heure,* it can be used only in the answer and never in the question. A Japanese uses the same semantic unit, *-zi,* in both the question and the answer: "Nañ-*zi* desu ka?"—"Ni-*zi* desu." This unit, however, is quite different from English *time,* French *heure,* German *Uhr,* and Dutch *uur:* it is never used *except* in asking or telling time, and has no other uses.

As the above examples show, each of these five languages encodes the same situation in ways that are semantically quite different. Metaphorically speaking, every language gathers together various bits and pieces of the things people talk about and symbolizes them with its own particular set of semantic units. In English we use the same unit, *time*, in such sentences as: "What *time* is it?" "I don't have *time*," and "I saw him last *time*."

On the other hand, in equivalent sentences, French employs three different semantic units: "Quelle *heure* est-il?" "Je n'ai pas le *temps*," and "Je l'ai vu la dernière *fois*." Any instrument used for telling time can be referred to in German by the semantic unit *Uhr*. In English, however, we make a sharp distinction depending on whether the instrument is usually portable: if it is, we call it a *watch*; if it is not, we call it a *clock*. Every language, in short, has its own particular set of semantic units; and any message which is to be sent must first be encoded into the particular semantic units of that language.

2. *Grammatical encoding.* Once a speaker has chosen the proper semantic units for the message he wants to send, his next task is to find the corresponding grammatical units and to arrange them in the way required by the grammar of his language. For example, if we want to make an English message out of the semantic units *boy*, *buy*, and *watch*, we can encode them grammatically—among other ways—as *The boy buys the watch*. As we do so, our language forces us to add some further elements of meaning to the message—the kind of meaning that is customarily called "grammatical meaning." In English we are forced to specify whether *boy* and *watch* are singular or plural: *boy* vs. *boys*, *watch* vs. *watches*. We are also forced to classify both units as either definite or indefinite: *the boy* vs. *a boy*, *the watch* vs. *a watch*. And we are forced to specify whether the buying takes place in the present or the past: present, *The boy buys the watch*; past, *The boy bought the watch*. Further, if we make *boy* singular, we must add the grammatical element *-s* to the unit *buy*. *The boy buy-s the watch*—though English does *not* force us to do this if we choose past *bought* rather than present *buy*.

What name should we select for the grammatical units that are used at this stage of the encoding process—for example, for the six units in the sentence *The boy buy-s the watch?* The customary name for each such minimal grammatical unit is, in English, the term "morpheme" (from Greek *morphē*, meaning "form"). Some morphemes are words: *the, boy, buy, watch*; others are smaller than words: the *-s* of *buy-s*, or the *-ing* of *buy-ing*. Some morphemes clearly correspond to semantic units: *boy, buy, watch*; with others the semantic connection is far less clear: *the, a*, or the *-s* of *buy-s*; still others do not seem to have any semantic connection at all, such as the *to* of *The boy wants to buy a watch*.

Where the basic *unit* of grammar is the morpheme, the basic *device* of grammar is that of *construction*: putting two (or more) grammatical forms together so as to produce a larger form. For example, if in English we put the morphemes *boy* and *the* together in the order *boy the*, we have added nothing: the whole is no greater than the sum of the parts. But if we put them together in the order *the boy*, something *is* added and the whole *is* greater than the sum of the parts. Put together in this way they form a construction; and the added element of meaning is the constructional meaning.

A very striking feature of human language is the fact that all grammars are so designed that a speaker can say and a hearer can understand sentences that they have never said or heard before, and that there is no theoretical limit to the number of sentences that can be produced. How do human languages attain this marvelous flexibility? All of them seem to do so by means of a number of very ingenious grammatical devices. First, every language groups its words into a number of different classes—traditionally called "parts of speech"—which are specialized in certain specific grammatical functions. In English, for example, nouns function (among other ways) as the subject of a sentence, and verbs as the main element in the predicate. This means that, given 1,000 nouns like *fire, water, snow,* and 1,000 verbs like *burn, boil, melt,* we can make 1,000 × 1,000—one million—sentences like *Fire burns, Water boils, Snow melts.* The only limitations are semantic ones. At the moment we can make no use of the sentence *Snow boils,* though some day we shall perhaps need it. If so, we shall be able to say and understand it, even though we have never heard it before.

Though all languages use specialization in this way, they also have devices for avoiding the dangers of overspecialization. English, for example, permits a noun like *girl* to function not only as the subject of a sentence, as in *The girl sings,* but also as the object of a verb, as in *The boy loves the girl.* This means that, given only 1,000 nouns and 1,000 verbs that can take an object, we can form not just 1,000 × 1,000 sentences, but 1,000 × 1,000 × 1,000, or one billion, sentences—since every noun can function in either of two ways. Of course, if we allow a noun to fill more than one grammatical function, we must then add something to the grammar that tells us when it is functioning in which way. In the example just given, English does this by means of word order. In *The boy loves the girl,* word order tells us that *the boy* is functioning as the subject of the sentence; but in *The girl loves the boy,* word order tells us that *the boy* is functioning as the object of the verb.

Another device through which languages gain flexibility is that of *embedding*: arranging morphemes and words not just in simple sequence, with one merely following the other, but rather in successive layers of construction, with one inside the other—theoretically without limit. Even so simple a sentence as *The boy loves the girl* contains three layers of embedding. At the highest level this is a construction made up of *the boy* + *loves the girl*; at the next level these consist, respectively, of the constructions *the + boy* and *loves + the girl;* and at the third level these latter consist of the constructions *love + -s* and *the + girl:*

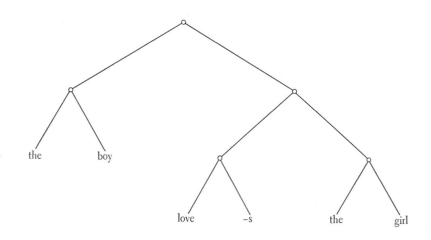

Still another device which all languages seem to use to gain flexibility has recently come to be called *transformation.* Consider, for example, the grammatical structure which underlies the sentence *The boy buys the watch.* If to this underlying structure we apply a passive transformation, we get *The watch is bought by the boy.* An interrogative transformation gives *Does the boy buy the watch?* A negative transformation gives *The boy does not buy the watch.* A combination of interrogative and negative gives *Doesn't the boy buy the watch?* One type of embedding transformation gives *(the boy) who buys the watch.* Another type of embedding transformation gives *(the watch) that the boy buys.* Still another type of embedding transformation gives *(it was easy) for the boy to buy the watch.* Since successive embeddings, theoretically without limit, can be added to a sentence, there is no such thing as a "longest sentence": no matter how long it is, we can always add more to it by means of further transformations.

3. *Phonological encoding.* Once a speaker has given the proper grammatical encoding to his message, we can assume that it consists simply of a string of morphemes. (We know, of course, that this "string of morphemes" may show a complex internal structure in terms of layers of embedding; but at least on the surface the morphemes merely follow one another.) What the speaker must now do is to convert this string of morphemes into sound so that the message can be transmitted to his listener. The simplest way of doing this would be to go directly

from morpheme to sound, converting each unit of grammar (each morpheme) into a unit of sound. A sentence such as *Boy loves girl* would then require four different units of sound: one each for the morphemes *boy, love, -s,* and *girl.* If a language had only thirty or forty morphemes, this would be a delightfully simple way of sending messages. In actual fact, of course, every language has many thousands of morphemes, and a more ingenious method of sending has to be used. What every language does is to convert each unit of grammar (each morpheme) not into *one* unit of sound but rather into *one or more* units of sound. Such units of sound are customarily called *phonemes* (from Greek *phōnē,* meaning "sound"). For example, in English we encode the morpheme *if* into two phonemes, /if/; the morpheme *cough* into three phonemes, /kof/; *shift* into four phonemes, /šift/; *thrift* into five phonemes, /θrift/; *glimpse* into six phonemes, /glimps/; and so on. A few morphemes, by chance, are encoded into only one phoneme—for example, the /-z/ of /baiz/ *buys,* or the /-t/ of /koft/ *coughed;* but this is not a necessary part of the system.

This device of encoding each grammatical unit (each morpheme) into *one or more* phonological units (one or more phonemes) is extraordinarily efficient and economical. If each morpheme were encoded into only one phoneme, then the number of morphemes in a language would be limited by the number of sounds that the human ear can easily distinguish from one another. But when each morpheme is encoded into one or more phonemes, the number of available morpheme shapes is far larger than will ever be needed in any language. If a language has, for example, thirty phonemes (a relatively modest number as the languages of the world go), and if it permits morphemes no larger than five phonemes in length (again a modest limitation), it would allow—theoretically—for over 25 million different morpheme shapes.

When we examine the way the phonemes of any language are turned into audible sound, and the way they are used in encoding morphemes, we find that they show two types of structure. First, no language permits its phonemes to occur in any and all possible sequences. In English, for example, we find that morphemes can begin with /pl-/ (*play*), or /bl-/ (*blow*), or /sl-/ (*slow*); but English does not permit us to encode morphemes beginning with /tl-/, or with /dl-/, or with /θl-/, or with any of many other possible sequences of phonemes. Every language shows strict limitations of this sort. As a result, no language allows its speakers to use more than a small fraction of the morpheme shapes that are theoretically available. At the same time, every language also provides for far more morpheme shapes than its speakers actually use or need. In English we use the shapes *tab, tube, tub;* but we have not yet made use of such further permitted shapes as *teeb, tib, tabe, teb, tob, tobe, tibe,* and *toyb.* They are there, ready and waiting, whenever we should want them.

Every language also shows a great deal of structure in the ways in

which it converts its phonemes into audible sound. Our English phoneme /p/, for example, is phonetically a voiceless labial stop. Corresponding to it we also have a voiced labial stop, /b/; a voiceless labial
fricative, /f/; a voiced labial fricative, /v/; and a labial nasal, /m/. That
is to say, these five phonemes are not converted into sound in a random way; instead, they form a tightly structured system composed of
the features "voiceless" (/p/ and /f/), "voiced" (/b/ and /v/),
"stop" (/p/ and /b/), "fricative" (/f/ and /v/), and "nasal"
(/m/). The English dental consonants show a similar structure: voiceless /t/ and /θ/; voiced /d/ and /ð/; stops /t/ and /d/; fricatives /θ/
and /ð/; and dental /n/. Very often this sort of neat and economical
symmetry occurs in only part of the system. The English velar consonants, for example, include only the two stops, voiceless /k/ and voiced
/g/, plus the nasal /ŋ/ (as in *sing*); there are no corresponding voiceless and voiced fricatives.

4–8. *Sending, transmission, receiving.* The first three stages in
our typical speech event have now been completed: the message has
been encoded (1) semantically, (2) grammatically, and (3) phonologically. We are now ready for the next five stages: two for sending, one
for transmission, and two for receiving. As encoded thus far, the message
consists of a sequence of phonemes. At stage (4) the speaker sends
instructions from his brain to his speech organs, telling them what
movements to make for each phoneme. At stage (5) the speech organs
make these movements and thereby set the air molecules into vibration,
producing audible sound. At stage (6) these vibrations fan out from
the speaker's mouth and are transmitted to any listener within hearing
distance. At stage (7) the vibrations produce corresponding vibrations
in the hearer's middle and inner ear. And at stage (8) the energy of
these vibrations is carried from the hearer's ear to his brain.

9–11. *Phonological, grammatical, semantic decoding.* At this
point the process of decoding begins. As the hearer receives the energy
of the message in his brain, he must decode it (9) phonologically, (10)
grammatically, and (11) semantically. This, of course, is possible only
if he possesses, somewhere inside his head, the same total code as the
speaker—that is, if he knows the same language. We shall assume this
to be true.

How is this decoding accomplished? To answer this question in detail
we would have to look inside the hearer's brain, and this is obviously
impossible. Nevertheless, we can make a number of useful indirect observations. Basically what the hearer seems to do is to match what he
hears against his own knowledge of the language. In doing this he does
not decode the entire message first phonologically, then grammatically,
then semantically; instead, he seems to race back and forth from one
part of the total code to another, picking up all the clues he can. Let us
suppose that he hears, in American English, the partial sentence "He
was writing/riding . . . ," with a sound halfway between a /t/ and a

/d/. From the phonological code he knows that such a halfway sound is not acceptable; it must be decoded as either a /t/ or a /d/ because the code does not provide for any halfway items. The grammatical code tells him that the word can be either *writing* with /t/ or *riding* with /d/, since both of these verbs occur in English. To settle the matter he must refer it on to the semantic code. If the sentence continues "He was writing/riding *a letter*," he knows that it must be the word *writing* with /t/; but if it continues "He was writing/riding *a horse*," he knows that it must be the word *riding* with /d/.

When a speaker sends a message, it consists of a linear sequence of morphemes which have been converted into a linear sequence of phonemes. It is of course this latter which the hearer hears and tries to interpret. At the same time, because he also knows the grammar of the language, he is able to reconstruct and interpret the nonlinear structures which lie behind what he hears. Suppose, for example, that he hears such a sentence as: "The man is horrified by his son's being accused of stealing." In terms of surface structure, this is a passive sentence consisting of *the man* as subject, *is horrified* as verb, plus the complement *by his son's being accused of stealing*; and this latter consists of the passive expression *being accused* with the modifier *his son's* and the complement *of stealing*. At the level of deep structure, however, this sentence has been put together by transformation from four different active sentence structures: *Something horrifies the man, The man has a son, Someone accuses the son of something,* and *The son steals.* Because the hearer also knows the language, he is able to reconstruct this series of deep structure sentences; and, from them, he derives the proper semantic interpretation of the surface structure.

In the preceding paragraphs we have described a typical speech event in order to show the various aspects of language with which linguistics is concerned. *Semantics* is the study of the semantic code. *Lexicology* studies the total stock of morphemes—the "lexicon"—of a language, particularly those items which have clear semantic references (e.g., *boy, buy, watch,* as against *the, a, -s, to*). (Note the difference between *lexicology,* the study of the lexicon of a language, and *lexicography,* the art of making dictionaries of various sorts.) *Grammar* is the study of the grammatical code. *Phonology* (or, in American usage, *phonemics*) is the study of the phonological code. *Articulatory phonetics* studies the movements of the vocal organs in producing the sounds of speech (the way the sounds of speech are "articulated"); *acoustic phonetics* studies the vibrations of the air molecules; and *auditory phonetics* studies the way the sounds of speech are perceived by the human ear.

Further branches of linguistics are concerned with variations within language, changes in language, and relationships among languages. *Linguistic geography* deals with the way in which a language varies through geographical space—the fact, for example, that the pronunciation *barn* (with /r/) in western New England corresponds to the pronunciation *bahn* (without /r/) in eastern New England—and how this difference in pronunciation came about. Traditionally, linguistic geography also deals with the variations in linguistic usage of different social classes, though work of this type has recently come to be called *sociolinguistics*.

All of these branches of linguistics are commonly referred to as *synchronic linguistics*—the study of a given language at a given period in time. Opposed to this is *diachronic linguistics*—the study of language change through time. Here the two chief branches are *historical linguistics*, which studies the historical development of a language; and *comparative linguistics*, which studies the historical relationships among languages and attempts to group them into families, subfamilies, and so on.

Because language is such a unique possession of human beings, and because it is of such obvious importance to the functioning of human society, it is not surprising that it has been studied for many centuries in many parts of the world. One of the greatest linguistic achievements of all time was also one of the earliest: the highly detailed Sanskrit grammar attributed to the Hindu scholar Pānini, which is dated about 300 B.C. Every language changes in the course of time; and this grammatical description—like so many later ones—was written in order to preserve unchanged the language of sacred writings. Many centuries later this same motivation led to the descriptions of Classical Arabic written by Arab grammarians and to works on Classical Hebrew written by Jewish scholars.

Though modern linguistics has been influenced by these early writings, especially those of the Sanskrit grammarians, it is based primarily on the scholarly traditions of Europe. Like so many other branches of modern science, it had its origins in the philosophical speculations of the ancient Greeks. As early as the fourth century B.C. the philosopher Plato raised one of the basic questions of linguistics: Is there any necessary connection between the words we use and the things they name? Though Plato seems to have believed that there is such a connection, his most distinguished pupil, Aristotle, took the opposite point of view: that the connection between the form and the meaning of a word is a matter of convention and of tacit agreement among the speakers of a language. This is the view we accept today. There is no necessary reason why the same animal should be called in English *dog*, in German *Hund*, in French *chien*, in Spanish *perro*, in Russian *sobaka*, and so on.

The Greeks were not interested in foreign languages but confined their studies almost exclusively to Greek; they seem to have taken it for granted that their language represented universal forms of human thought. Though their observations on language were made almost exclusively in abstract philosophical terms, many of their ideas are still accepted in modern linguistics—for example, the theory of parts of speech, the division of the sentence into subject and predicate, and such inflectional categories as gender, number, case, person, tense, and mood.

The Greek approach to language was taken over by the Romans and applied with little change to their language, Latin. Once again grammars were written in order to preserve highly valued forms of language which had already become archaic. Two outstanding examples are the Latin grammars of Donatus in the fourth century A.D. and of Priscian in the sixth century—both written long after Classical Latin had ceased being spoken in everyday use. Even after the fall of the Roman Empire, Latin continued for many centuries to be *the* language of learning in all of western Europe; and the approach to language used in these late Latin grammars constituted for centuries the "linguistics" of the western world.

It is customary to date modern linguistics from the late eighteenth and early nineteenth century, when scholars for the first time worked out detailed scientific methods for establishing relationships among languages—notably those of the Indo-European family. Most of nineteenth-century linguistics was devoted to historical–comparative studies of this sort. Toward the end of the century there were rapid advances in both phonetics and linguistic geography, though scholarly interests were in both cases still in large part historical. Modern synchronic linguistics traditionally dates from the *Cours de linguistique générale* of the Swiss scholar Ferdinand de Saussure, a work published posthumously from lecture notes in 1916. Because Saussure showed for the first time the great importance of structure within language, this approach to the study of language has often been called "structural linguistics." Similar ideas were developed or taken over in many other parts of the world during the following decades, notably by such scholars as the German-American Franz Boas, the Americans Edward Sapir and Leonard Bloomfield, and the expatriate Russian N. S. Trubetzkoy. It is significant that these scholars also extended their studies to many languages which had never been investigated before.

What should we say of linguistics today? First, we find that the diachronic and synchronic traditions have been united in the works of such scholars as the Russian-American Roman Jakobson and the Frenchman André Martinet. Second, there has been renewed interest in the building of comprehensive linguistic theories, notably in the works of the Dane Louis Hjelmslev and the American Noam Chomsky. The latter has done us the special service of reuniting modern grammar with the traditional Greco-Roman grammar of past centuries. Finally, perhaps the most striking development in modern linguistics is the extent to which it has been carried over into related fields. We find this in such joint fields of study as psycholinguistics, anthropological linguistics, and mathematical linguistics; in the new interest which philosophers have taken in linguistics and linguists in philosophy; and in the application of the findings of linguistics to such fields as machine translation and foreign-language teaching. Great strides have been taken in the past decades; but, as with so many other fields of study, the more we learn of our subject, the more we realize how little we yet know.

STUDY QUESTIONS AND EXERCISES

1. In a brief history of the English language, such as that by Harold Whitehall in the first or second edition of *Webster's New World Dictionary* or that by Kemp Malone in *The Random House Dictionary*, what evidence do you find, in the account of Anglo-Saxon (Old English) to illustrate the idea stated by Moulton that a "simple" culture may have a more complex language—although a more limited vocabulary—than a complex culture? Has the simpler grammar of modern English limited our power of expression, in comparison with that of Anglo-Saxon or of modern German? How do you suppose the learned Anglo-Saxons of early England regarded the dropping of word endings?

2. Compare Moulton's definition of language with Hill's: what is the genus in Moulton's definition? Look up *linguistics* in the *Random House Dictionary*: is Moulton defining descriptive or historical linguistics? What details given by Moulton would apply to only one kind of linguistics and thus are differentiae?

3. For further illustration of semantic encoding, assemble as many "encodings" in other languages of "How are you?" and "It is a fine day" as you can. How do these compare with Moulton's example? (This exercise might be a class project.)

4. Look up *morpheme* in *Webster's Third* and *Random House* unabridged dictionaries: compare definitions and etymologies for this word and for related terms beginning with or containing *morph-*, and labeled as Linguistics. Also compare definitions and etymologies for *phoneme, semantics, lexicology.*

5. To illustrate the flexibility of English sentences, have each member of a group state, in one sentence, what a given cartoon depicts.

6. How would you know that a proper name beginning with *Ng* or *Tm* is not a name in the English language? In *Random House Dictionary*, look up each combination: what language does permit the combination of these consonants at the start of a word?

7. Read the last three pages of Chapter 3 in Aldous Huxley's *Point Counter Point.* What literary use is made of a detailed description of the "sending, transmitting, receiving" process? What do you consider significant about Huxley's and Moulton's concern, in such different contexts, with similar phenomena?

8. Often the hearer's interests and his knowledge are factors in

determining the message he receives. Mark Twain's small daughter heard his statement that he was "going to write an anecdote" as "going to ride a nanny goat." Can you think of similar errors in understanding? Of what importance is careful enunciation, with attention to stress, pitch, and juncture, in preventing "messages" from being garbled by a hearer?

9. How is the change in the description of the English language since that of the Latin-based grammars of the seventeenth and eighteenth centuries analogous to that in the description of matter by physicists during the same period? How has knowledge in both fields been advanced by modern inventions and technology?

NOTE: The discussion of word order, classes of words, and word functions refers to aspects of language dealt with by structural grammar. For a select bibliography of basic sources in modern linguistics cited by Moulton and others, see the Bibliography in this text.

4

The Current Scene in Linguistics:
Present Directions

Noam Chomsky

Professor Chomsky of the Massachusetts Institute of Technology, one of the most innovative of present-day linguistic theoreticians, summarizes developments in a rapidly changing field. His essay appeared in College English *for May, 1966.*

The title of this paper may suggest something more than can be provided. It would be foolhardy to attempt to forecast the development of linguistics or any other field, even in general terms and in the short run. There is no way to anticipate ideas and insights that may, at any time, direct research in new directions or reopen traditional problems that had been too difficult or too unclear to provide a fruitful challenge. The most that one can hope to do is to arrive at a clear appraisal of the present situation in linguistic research, and an accurate understanding of historical tendencies. It would not be realistic to attempt to project such tendencies into the future.

Two major traditions can be distinguished in modern linguistic theory: one is the tradition of "universal" or "philosophical grammar," which flourished in the seventeenth and eighteenth centuries; the second is the tradition of structural or descriptive linguistics, which reached the high point of its development perhaps fifteen or twenty years ago. I think that a synthesis of these two major traditions is possible, and that it is, to some extent, being achieved in current work. Before approaching the problem of synthesis, I would like to sketch briefly—and, necessarily, with some oversimplification—what seem to me to be the most significant features in these two traditions.

As the name indicates, universal grammar was concerned with general features of language structure rather than with particular idiosyncrasies. Particularly in France, universal grammar developed in part in reaction to an earlier descriptivist tradition which held that the only proper task for the grammarian was to present data, to give a kind of "natural history" of language (specifically, of the "cultivated usage" of the court and the best writers). In contrast, universal grammarians urged that the study of language should be elevated from the level of "natural history" to that of "natural philosophy"; hence the term "philosophical grammar," "philosophical" being used, of course, in essentially the sense of our term "scientific." Grammar should not be merely a record of the data of usage, but, rather, should offer an explanation for such data. It should establish general principles, applicable to all languages and based ultimately on intrinsic properties of the mind, which would explain how language is used and why it has the particular properties to which the descriptive grammarian chooses, irrationally, to restrict his attention.

Universal grammarians did not content themselves with merely stating this goal. In fact, many generations of scholars proceeded to develop a rich and far-reaching account of the general principles of language structure, supported by whatever detailed evidence they could find from the linguistic materials available to them. On the basis of these principles, they attempted to explain many particular facts, and to develop a psychological theory dealing with certain aspects of language use, with the production and comprehension of sentences.

The tradition of universal grammar came to an abrupt end in the nineteenth century, for reasons that I will discuss directly. Furthermore, its achievements were very rapidly forgotten, and an interesting mythology developed concerning its limitations and excesses. It has now become something of a cliché among linguists that universal grammar suffered from the following defects: (1) it was not concerned with the sounds of speech, but only with writing; (2) it was based primarily on a Latin model, and was, in some sense "prescriptive"; (3) its assumptions about language structure have been refuted by modern "anthropological linguistics." In addition, many linguists, though not all, would hold that universal grammar was misguided in principle in its attempt to provide explanations rather than mere description of usage, the latter being all that can be contemplated by the "sober scientist."

The first two criticisms are quite easy to refute; the third and fourth are more interesting. Even a cursory glance at the texts will show that phonetics was a major concern of universal grammarians, and that their phonetic theories were not very different from our own. Nor have I been able to discover any confusion of speech and writing. The belief that universal grammar was based on a Latin model is rather curious. In fact, the earliest studies of universal grammar, in France, were a part of the movement to raise the status of the vernacular, and are concerned with details of French that often do not even have any Latin analogue.

As to the belief that modern "anthropological linguistics" has refuted the assumptions of universal grammar, this is not only untrue, but, for a rather important reason, could not be true. The reason is that universal grammar made a sharp distinction between what we may call "deep structure" and "surface structure." The deep structure of a sentence is the abstract underlying form which determines the meaning of the sentence; it is present in the mind but not necessarily represented directly in the physical signal. The surface structure of a sentence is the actual organization of the physical signal into phrases of varying size, into words of various categories, with certain particles, inflections, arrangement, and so on. The fundamental assumption of the universal grammarians was that languages scarcely differ at the level of deep structure—which reflects the basic properties of thought and conception—but that they may vary widely at the much less interesting level of surface structure. But modern anthropological linguistics does not attempt to deal with deep structure and its relations to surface structure. Rather, its attention is limited to surface structure—to the phonetic form of an utterance and its organization into units of varying size. Consequently, the information that it provides has no direct bearing on the hypotheses concerning deep structure postulated by the universal grammarians. And, in fact, it seems to me that what information is now available to us suggests not that they went too far in assuming universality of underlying structure, but that they may have been much too cautious and restrained in what they proposed.

The fourth criticism of universal grammar—namely, that it was misguided in seeking explanations in the first place—I will not discuss. It seems to me that this criticism is based on a misunderstanding of the nature of all rational inquiry. There is particular irony in the fact that this criticism should be advanced with the avowed intention of making linguistics "scientific." It is hardly open to question that the natural sciences are concerned precisely with the problem of explaining phenomena, and have little use for accurate description that is unrelated to problems of explanation.

I think that we have much to learn from a careful study of what was achieved by the universal grammarians of the seventeenth and eighteenth centuries. It seems to me, in fact, that contemporary linguistics would do well to take their concept of language as a point of departure for current work. Not only do they make a fairly clear and well-founded distinction between deep and surface structure, but they also go on to study the nature of deep structure and to provide valuable hints and insights concerning the rules that relate the abstract underlying mental structures to surface form, the rules that we would now call "grammatical transformations." What is more, universal grammar developed as part of a general philosophical tradition that provided deep and important insights, also largely forgotten, into the use and acquisition of language, and, furthermore, into problems of perception and acquisition of knowledge in general. These insights can be exploited and developed. The idea that the study of language should proceed within the framework of what we might nowadays call "cognitive psychology" is sound. There is much truth in the traditional view that language provides the most effective means for studying the nature and mechanisms of the human mind, and that only within this context can we perceive the larger issues that determine the directions in which the study of language should develop.

The tradition of universal grammar came to an end more than a century ago. Several factors combined to lead to its decline. For one thing, the problems posed were beyond the scope of the technique and understanding then available. The problem of formulating the rules that determine deep structures and relate them to surface structures, and the deeper problem of determining the general abstract characteristics of these rules, could not be studied with any precision, and discussion therefore remained at the level of hints, examples, and vaguely formulated intentions. In particular, the problem of rule-governed creativity in language simply could not be formulated with sufficient precision to permit research to proceed very far. A second reason for the decline of traditional linguistic theory lies in the remarkable successes of Indo-European comparative linguistics in the nineteenth century. These achievements appeared to dwarf the accomplishments of universal grammar, and led many linguists to scoff at the "metaphysical" and "airy pronouncements" of those who were attempting to deal with a much wider range of problems—and at that particular stage of the development of linguistic theory, were discussing these topics in a highly inconclusive fashion. Looking back now, we can see quite clearly that the concept of language employed by the Indo-European comparativists was an extremely primitive one. It was, however, well-suited to the tasks at hand. It is, therefore, not too surprising that this concept of language, which was then extended and developed by the structural and descriptive linguists of the twentieth century, became almost completely dominant, and that the older tradition of linguistic theory was largely swept aside and forgotten. This is hardly a unique instance in intellectual history.

Structural linguistics is a direct outgrowth of the concepts that emerged in Indo-European comparative study, which was primarily concerned with language as a system of phonological units that undergo systematic modification in phonetically determined contexts. Structural linguistics reinterpreted this concept for a fixed state of a language, investigated the relations among such units and the patterns they form, and attempted, with varying success, to extend the same kind of analysis to "higher levels" of linguistic structure. Its fundamental assumption is that procedures of segmentation and classification, applied to data in a systematic way, can isolate and identify all types of elements that function in a particular language along with the constraints that they obey. A catalogue of these elements, their relations, and their restrictions of "distribution," would, in most structuralist views, constitute a full grammar of the language.

Structural linguistics has very real accomplishments to its credit. To me, it seems that its major achievement is to have provided a factual and a methodological basis that makes it possible to return to the problems that occupied the traditional universal grammarians with some hope of extending and deepening their theory of language structure and language use. Modern descriptive linguistics has enormously enriched the range of factual material available, and has provided entirely new standards of clarity and objectivity. Given this advance in precision and objectivity, it becomes possible to return, with new hope for success, to the problem of constructing the theory of a particular language—its grammar—and to the still more ambitious study of the general theory of language. On the other hand, it seems to me that the substantive contributions to the theory of language structure are few, and that, to a large extent, the concepts of modern linguistics constitute a retrogression as compared with universal grammar. One real advance has been in universal phonetics—I refer here particularly to the work of Jakobson. Other new and important insights might also be cited. But in general, the major contributions of structural linguistics seem to me to be methodological rather than substantive. These methodological contributions are not limited to a raising of the standards of precision. In a more subtle way, the idea that language can be studied as a formal system, a notion which is developed with force and effectiveness in the work of Harris and Hockett, is of particular significance. It is, in fact, this general insight and the techniques that emerged as it developed that have made it possible, in the last few years, to approach the traditional problems once again. Specifically, it is now possible to study the problem of rule-governed creativity in natural language, the problem of constructing grammars that explicitly generate deep and surface structures and express the relations between them, and the deeper problem of determining the universal conditions that limit the form and organization of rules in the grammar of a human language. When these problems are clearly formulated and studied, we are led to a conception of language not unlike that suggested in universal grammar. Furthermore, I think that we are led to conclusions regarding mental processes of very much the sort that were developed, with care and insight, in the rationalist philosophy of mind that provided the intellectual background for universal grammar. It is in this sense that I think we can look forward to a productive synthesis of the two major traditions of linguistic research.

If this point of view is correct in essentials, we can proceed to outline the problems facing the linguist in the following way. He is, first of all, concerned to report data accurately. What is less obvious, but nonetheless correct, is that the data will not be of particular interest to him in itself, but rather only insofar as it sheds light on the grammar of the language from which it is drawn, where by the "grammar of a language" I mean the theory that deals with the mechanisms of sentence construction, which establish a sound-meaning relation in this language. At the next level of study, the linguist is concerned to give a factually accurate formulation of this grammar, that is, a correct formulation of the rules that generate deep and surface structures and interrelate them, and the rules that give a phonetic interpretation of surface structures and a semantic interpretation of deep structures. But, once again, this correct statement of the grammatical principles of a language is not primarily of interest in itself, but only insofar as it sheds light on the more general question of the nature of language; that is, the nature of universal grammar. The primary interest of a correct grammar is that it provides the basis for substantiating or refuting a general theory of linguistic structure which establishes general principles concerning the form of grammar.

Continuing one step higher in level of abstraction, a universal grammar—a general theory of linguistic structure that determines the form of grammar—is primarily of interest for the information it provides concerning innate intellectual structure. Specifically, a general theory of this sort itself must provide a hypothesis concerning innate intellectual structure of sufficient richness to account for the fact that the child acquires a given grammar on the basis of the data available to him. More generally, both a grammar of a particular language and a general theory of language are of interest primarily because of the insight they provide concerning the nature of mental processes, the mechanisms of perception and production and the mechanisms by which knowledge is acquired. There can be little doubt that both specific theories of particular languages and the general theory of linguistic structure provide very relevant evidence for anyone concerned with these matters; to me it seems quite obvious that it is within this general framework that linguistic research finds its intellectual justification.

At every level of abstraction, the linguist is concerned with explanation, not merely with stating facts in one form or another. He tries to construct a grammar which explains particular data on the basis of general principles that govern the language in question. He is interested in explaining these general principles themselves, by showing how they are derived from still more general and abstract postulates drawn from universal grammar. And he would ultimately have to find a way to account for universal grammar on the basis of still more general principles of human mental structure. Finally, although this goal is too remote to be seriously considered, he might envision the prospect that the kind of evidence he can provide may lead to a physiological explanation for this entire range of phenomena.

I should stress that what I have sketched is a logical, not a temporal order of tasks of increasing abstractness. For example, it is not necessary to delay the study of general linguistic theory until particular grammars are available for many languages. Quite the contrary. The study of particular grammars will be fruitful only insofar as it is based on a precisely articulated theory of linguistic structure, just as the study of particular facts is worth undertaking only when it is guided by some general assumptions about the grammar of the language from which these observations are drawn.

All of this is rather abstract. Let me try to bring the discussion down to earth by mentioning a few particular problems, in the grammar of English, that point to the need for explanatory hypotheses of the sort I have been discussing.

Consider the comparative construction in English; in particular, such sentences as:

(1) I have never seen a man taller than John
(2) I have never seen a taller man than John

Sentences (1) and (2), along with innumerable others, suggest that there should be a rule of English that permits a sentence containing a Noun followed by a Comparative Adjective to be transformed into the corresponding sentence containing the sequence: Comparative Adjective—Noun. This rule would then appear as a special case of the very general rule that forms such Adjective-Noun constructions as "the tall man" from the underlying form "the man who is tall," and so on.

But now consider the sentence:

(3) I have never seen a man taller than Mary

This is perfectly analogous to (1); but we cannot use the rule just mentioned to form

(4) I have never seen a taller man than Mary.

In fact, the sentence (4) is certainly not synonymous with (3), although (2) appears to be synonymous with (1). Sentence (4) implies that Mary is a man, although (3) does not. Clearly either the proposed analysis is incorrect, despite the very considerable support one can find for it, or there is some specific condition in English grammar that explains why the rule in question can be used to form (2) but not (4). In either case, a serious explanation is lacking; there is some principle of English grammar, now unknown, for which we must search to explain these facts. The facts are quite clear. They are of no particular interest in themselves, but if they can bring to light some general principle of English grammar, they will be of real significance.

Furthermore, we must ask how every speaker of English comes to acquire this still unknown principle of English grammar. We must, in other words, try to determine what general concept of linguistic structure he employs that leads him to the conclusion that the grammar of English treats (1) and (2) as paraphrases but not the superficially similar pair (3) and (4). This still unknown principle of English grammar may lead us to discover the relevant abstract principle of linguistic structure. It is this hope, of course, that motivates the search for the relevant principle of English grammar.

Innumerable examples can be given of this sort. I will mention just one more. Consider the synonymous sentences (5) and (6):

(5) It would be difficult for him to understand *this*
(6) For him to understand *this* would be difficult.

Corresponding to (5), we can form relative clauses and questions such as (7):

(7) (i) something which it would be difficult for him to understand
      (ii) what would it be difficult for him to understand?
But there is some principle that prevents the formation of the corresponding constructions of (8), formed in the analogous way from (6):
(8) (i) something which for him to understand would be difficult
      (ii) what would for him to understand be difficult?
The nonsentences of (8) are formed from (6) by exactly the same
process that forms the correct sentences of (7) from (5); namely, pro-
nominalization in the position occupied by "this," and a reordering operation. But in the case of (6), something blocks the operation of the
rules for forming relative clauses and interrogatives. Again, the facts
are interesting because they indicate that some general principle of
English grammar must be functioning, unconsciously; and, at the next
level of abstraction, they raise the question what general concept of
linguistic structure is used by the person learning the language to enable him to acquire the particular principle that explains the difference
between (7) and (8).

Notice that there is nothing particularly esoteric about these examples. The processes that form comparative, relative, and interrogative
constructions are among the simplest and most obvious in English
grammar. Every normal speaker has mastered these processes at an
early age. But when we take a really careful look, we find much that is
mysterious in these very elementary processes of grammar.

Whatever aspect of a language one studies, problems of this sort
abound. There are very few well-supported answers, either at the level
of particular or universal grammar. The linguist who is content merely
to record and organize phenomena, and to devise appropriate terminol-
ogies, will never come face to face with these problems. They only arise
when he attempts to construct a precise system of rules that generate
deep structures and relate them to corresponding surface structures. But
this is just another way of saying that "pure descriptivism" is not fruitful, that progress in linguistics, as in any other field of inquiry, requires
that at every stage of our knowledge and understanding we pursue the
search for a deeper explanatory theory.

I would like to conclude with just a few remarks about two problems
that are of direct concern to teachers of English. The first is the problem of which grammar to teach, the second, the problem why grammar
should be taught at all.

If one thinks of a grammar of English as a theory of English structure, then the question which grammar to teach is no different in principle from the problem facing the biologist who has to decide which
of several competing theories to teach. The answer, in either case, is
that he should teach the one which appears to be true, given the evidence presently available. Where the evidence does not justify a clear
decision, this should be brought to the student's attention and he
should be presented with the case for the various alternatives. But in

the case of teaching grammar, the issue is often confused by a pseudo-problem, which I think deserves some further discussion.

To facilitate this discussion, let me introduce some terminology. I will use the term "generative grammar" to refer to a theory of language in the sense described above, that is, a system of rules that determine the deep and surface structures of the language in question, the relation between them, the semantic interpretation of the deep structures and the phonetic interpretation of the surface structures. The generative grammar of a language, then, is the system of rules which establishes the relation between sound and meaning in this language. Suppose that the teacher is faced with the question: which generative grammar of English shall I teach? The answer is straightforward in principle, however difficult the problem may be to settle in practice. The answer is, simply: teach the one that is correct.

But generally the problem is posed in rather different terms. There has been a great deal of discussion of the choice not between competing generative grammars, but between a generative grammar and a "descriptive grammar." A "descriptive grammar" is not a theory of the language in the sense described above; it is not, in other words, a system of rules that establishes the sound-meaning correspondence in the language, insofar as this can be precisely expressed. Rather, it is an inventory of elements of various kinds that play a role in the language. For example, a descriptive grammar of English might contain an inventory of phonetic units, of phonemes, of morphemes, of words, of lexical categories, and of phrases or phrase types. Of course the inventory of phrases or phrase types cannot be completed since it is infinite, but let us put aside this difficulty.

It is clear, however, that the choice between a generative grammar and a descriptive grammar is not a genuine one. Actually, a descriptive grammar can be immediately derived from a generative grammar, but not conversely. Given a generative grammar, we can derive the inventories of elements that appear at various levels. The descriptive grammar, in the sense just outlined, is simply one aspect of the full generative grammar. It is an epiphenomenon, derivable from the full system of rules and principles that constitutes the generative grammar. The choice, then, is not between two competing grammars, but between a grammar and one particular aspect of this grammar. To me it seems obvious how this choice should be resolved, since the particular aspect that is isolated in the descriptive grammar seems to be of little independent importance. Surely the principles that determine the inventory, and much else, are more important than the inventory itself. In any event, the nature of the choice is clear; it is not a choice between competing systems, but rather a choice between the whole and a part.

Although I think what I have just said is literally correct, it is still somewhat misleading. I have characterized a descriptive grammar as one particular aspect of a full generative grammar, but actually the concept "descriptive grammar" arose in modern linguistics in a rather different way. A descriptive grammar was itself regarded as a full account of the language. It was, in other words, assumed that the inventory of elements exhausts the grammatical description of the language. Once we have listed the phones, phonemes, etc., we have given a full description of grammatical structure. The grammar is, simply, the collection of these various inventories.

This observation suggests a way of formulating the difference between generative and descriptive grammars in terms of a factual assumption about the nature of language. Let us suppose that a theory of language will consist of a definition of the notion "grammar," as well as definitions of various kinds of units (e.g., phonological units, morphological units, etc.). When we apply such a general theory to data, we use the definitions to find a particular grammar and a particular collection of units. Consider now two theories of this sort that differ in the following way. In one, the units of various kinds are defined independently of the notion "grammar"; the grammar, then, is simply the collection of the various kinds of unit. For example, we define "phoneme," "morpheme," etc., in terms of certain analytic procedures, and define the "grammar" to be the collection of units derived by applying these procedures. In the other theory, the situation is reversed. The notion "grammar" is defined independently of the various kinds of unit; the grammar is a system of such-and-such a kind. The units of various kinds are defined in terms of the logically prior concept "grammar." They are whatever appears in the grammar at such-and-such a level of functioning.

The difference between these two kinds of theory is quite an important one. It is a difference of factual assumption. The intuition that lies behind descriptive grammar is that the units are logically prior to the grammar, which is merely a collection of units. The intuition that lies behind the development of generative grammar is the opposite; it is that the grammar is logically prior to the units, which are merely the elements that appear at a particular stage in the functioning of grammatical processes. We can interpret this controversy in terms of its implications as to the nature of language acquisition. One who accepts the point of view of descriptive grammar will expect language acquisition to be a process of accretion, marked by gradual growth in the size of inventories, the elements of the inventories being developed by some sort of analytic or inductive procedures. One who accepts the underlying point of view of generative grammar will expect, rather, that the process of language acquisition must be more like that of selecting a particular hypothesis from a restricted class of possible hypotheses, on the basis of limited data. The selected hypothesis is the grammar; once accepted, it determines a system of relations among elements and inventories of various sorts. There will, of course, be growth of inventory, but it will be a rather peripheral and "external" matter. Once the child has selected a certain grammar, he will "know" whatever is predicted by this selected hypothesis. He will, in other words, know a great deal about sentences to which he has never been exposed. This is, of course, the characteristic fact about human language.

I have outlined the difference between two theories of grammar in rather vague terms. It can be made quite precise, and the question of choice between them becomes a matter of fact, not decision. My own view is that no descriptivist theory can be reconciled with the known facts about the nature and use of language. This, however, is a matter that goes beyond the scope of this discussion.

To summarize, as the problem is usually put, the choice between generative and descriptive grammars is not a genuine one. It is a choice between a system of principles and one, rather marginal selection of consequences of these principles. But there is a deeper and ultimately factual question, to be resolved not by decision but by sharpening the assumptions and confronting them with facts.

Finally, I would like to say just a word about the matter of the teaching of grammar in the schools. My impression is that grammar is generally taught as an essentially closed and finished system, and in a rather mechanical way. What is taught is a system of terminology, a set of techniques for diagramming sentences, and so on. I do not doubt that this has its function, that the student must have a way of talking about language and its properties. But it seems to me that a great opportunity is lost when the teaching of grammar is limited in this way. I think it is important for students to realize how little we know about the rules that determine the relation of sound and meaning in English, about the general properties of human language, about the matter of how the incredibly complex system of rules that constitutes a grammar is acquired or put to use. Few students are aware of the fact that in their normal, everyday life they are constantly creating new linguistic structures that are immediately understood, despite their novelty, by those to whom they speak or write. They are never brought to the realization of how amazing an accomplishment this is, and of how limited is our comprehension of what makes it possible. Nor do they acquire any insight into the remarkable intricacy of the grammar that they use unconsciously, even insofar as this system is understood and can be explicitly presented. Consequently, they miss both the challenge and the accomplishments of the study of language. This seems to me a pity, because both are very real. Perhaps as the study of language returns gradually to the full scope and scale of its rich tradition, some way will be found to introduce students to the tantalizing problems that language has always posed for those who are puzzled and intrigued by the mysteries of human intelligence.

STUDY QUESTIONS AND EXERCISES

1. Note the reference to Chomsky by Moulton in the last paragraph of his article (selection 3). Explain the synthesis of "two major traditions" that constitutes Chomsky's "special service" to "comprehensive linguistic theories." How is it related to Moulton's discussion of deep and surface structures?

2. What was the concern of universal grammar? What kind of theory was the ultimate goal of universal grammarians?

3. Which of the "defects" of this tradition of grammar were identified by Hill (in selection 1) and by Moulton (in selection 3)? Which "defects" were falsely ascribed to this tradition?

4. What previous developments in linguistic study produced, as a direct outgrowth, structural linguistics and descriptive grammar?

5. How has the major achievement of structural linguistics been reflected so far in this text?

6. What advantages does the modern linguist have in reporting data accurately? Which ones help to explain the emphasis on "sound-meaning" in language?

7. How do descriptive and generative grammar differ? What are the different intuitions behind these grammars? Which intuitions reflect the facts of a child's acquisition of language? Why is an understanding of those facts essential in effective teaching?

5

Editor's Choice—You Couldn't Do Woise

Bergen Evans

In a speech before the Managing Editors Association of The Associated Press, Professor Evans of Northwestern University outlines some of the concepts of language, grammar, and usage derived from unbiased observation and analysis.

I am greatly honored at being asked to address so august and influential a body as the Managing Editors of The Associated Press and I would be embarrassed at the flippant aggressiveness of the title of my talk were it not that first, it was selected from among more dignified titles by one of your own officers, and second, the press itself exploits sensationalism and stirs up aggressiveness so consistently and recklessly that it can't complain if a little of it bounces back, but most of all because the absurdity of the title makes it plain, I hope, that I do not regard myself as a Delphic oracle or intend to do any thundering out of Zion.

I want to lay down a few postulates or axioms just to save time. First, speech is the most important thing life has produced. The brilliance of speech, the amazingness of it is something that those of us who use it don't bother to stop to think about. There are no organs of speech. Man invented speech. It is purely parasitic upon organs that have other physiologic functions. Second, speech is spoken. This is so basic, so fundamental to any discussion of speech that, although it seems almost idiotic to state it, it has to be stated over and over again. The ordinary person will talk more in one good, gabby, excited day when he has some real dirt to dish out and meets enough people to listen, or he is angry about something, than he will write in his entire lifetime. Now this doesn't apply to people who, like ourselves, make a living of writing, but we'll do pretty well.

Man's speech is a living thing; hence, it is constantly changing. Speech is organic and hence, in relation to speech, the word *correct*, which one so often hears, and so often asks about, is utterly meaningless. If you found a mouse, and took it to a mousologist of some kind, and you said to him, "Is this a correct mouse?" he would think you were balmy or something. He would say, "It is a mouse of this species, it seems to be a mouse of this age, it's a mouse of this sex, it's a mouse of this weight, it seems to have had a hard winter." He could go on talking about it all day, but he can't tell you that it's a correct mouse or an incorrect mouse.

The third postulate is that grammar is simply a description of any language. This is not obvious immediately in your own language where status is so much involved and one's ego is at stake, but all you have to do is to translate it to another language to see this at once. Suppose you and I decide for some reason that we want to write an Eskimo grammar. All we can do is go where Eskimos are and write down what they say. If somebody is with us who takes correctness very seriously and he says to you, "Yeh, yeh, yeh, but is this correct Eskimo?" the answer is "I don't know." He says, "Well, look, this is the way they talk here in Baffin Bay but over in Greenland I heard different sounds." All you can say is, "This is Baffin Bay Eskimo—that's Greenland Eskimo," and in your grammar, if somebody is willing to finance a hundred-volume grammar on Eskimo, then you will make these distinctions.

The fourth postulate is that use and custom alone—and here I know many people disagree—determine what each generation and each locality finds acceptable. If in the South they say *clean* and in the North they say *clear*—you went *clean through town* and so on—you cannot say one is wrong and one is right. Forty million people have a right to speak their own language, whether it be southern, French, Romanian, or anything else. And incidentally, everybody used to say *clean*. Many of the things that people find wrong are old forms. They never recognize the really new as wrong at all. They are so much a part of it that they don't really realize the language has been actually changed.

The last postulate I want to state is that there are many forms of English. And no one of them can be unconditionally claimed to be good English to the total exclusion of the others. What passes for rules of grammar—this phrase we often hear—is usually simply half a dozen shibboleths that assert status. That is, they simply are part of the great game of oneupmanship. Somebody learns half a dozen forms—when he hears any deviation from them, he likes to pull rank and usually it terrifies people.

Now there is no way you can scare a man quicker than by using such horrendous words as *pluperfect, future indicative, hortatory subjunctive, nonrestrictive clause, mood, passivals,* and the like. The minute you hit a man with something like this, he crumbles. He heard stuff like this in high school. But he wasn't listening, and in the innocence of his heart, he assumes that other people were listening. And it doesn't enter his mind that for the most part they were meaningless and the teacher herself hadn't the faintest idea what they meant, and that not listening to them was a highly salutary exercise.

The ordinary man is annoyed and he says, "Come on, you guys, cut it out." He has employed two colloquialisms, a verb in the imperative, the third person singular pronoun and he's made an idiomatic application of an adverb. Well, he'd be startled to be told all this, because all of these horrendous words merely describe what this man is doing.

Speech is incredibly subtle. You just don't know how clever you are to be able to speak. Speech is infinitely more subtle than writing. Writing is a poor, numb, stumbling, inadequate, approximate thing compared to speech, and always must be. The only way you could hope to equate speech and writing would be if you could orchestrate writing. So much of our meaning in speech is conveyed by emphasis, pause, rising or falling voice, and so on and so on. "He gave her *dog biscuits*." "He gave her *dog* biscuits." I've exaggerated a bit there. In ordinary speech you wouldn't even make that sharp an emphasis to make two wholly different meanings. "The car stopped with a jerk at the wheel." The very slightest emphasis conveys totally different meaning.

This year I teach a course at Northwestern in Literature and in the course we read from the Bible and I had been lecturing about the Beatitudes. In reading an examination paper of an otherwise intelligent boy, I found a reference to the "B attitudes." Now this boy must have thought, "What are the A attitudes?" That is, he must have gone on, you know, on a totally different thing. The slightest shift of emphasis could reduce meaning to nonsense.

Now people get very excited about problems of grammar. They're not really problems of grammar at all; they are actually very excited about the challenging of their own status somewhere or they're determined to pull rank, and I just want to go into one or two of these statements with you.

Here is a nervous explosion from the *Christian Science Monitor* quite recently entitled "Cheap and Childish." It's objecting to the use of what they call incorrect English and attacking some wicked place called Madison Avenue. The *Monitor* is blowing up because the language is being corrupted. Says the *Monitor*: "To read or to listen, in advertisements in particular, one would get the impression that the American people is a race of semi-illiterates that neither speaks correct English nor is interested . . . . The ineffable monstrosity of Madison Avenue is the substitution of *like* for *as*; we are now told that a certain type of bread is baked just like Mother baked it." Then the editorial concludes by saying: "It is a fact, long noted by Europeans and a fact which has done nothing to increase their opinion of American cultural standards, that the United States is one of the few countries in the world in which public indignation is not stirred by offenses to the language. In most European countries quick and strong resentment is shown whenever the priceless heritage of the national speech is abused." You couldn't get more balderdash in fewer words.

Let me for a moment go into this business of *like* as a conjunction, since not only the *Monitor*, but many other papers, including the *New*

York Times made an issue of this. Most half-educated people, or three-quarters-educated, well, I'll be generous, $\frac{9}{10}$-educated people, will tell you with very great assurance, that *like* cannot be used as a conjunction when introducing a clause and they look you right in the eye when they say this. And most people, not being quite sure what a conjunction is, usually wilt at this point.

But let me show you how complex the problem really is by giving you four examples of the use of *like* as a conjunction in sentences each one of which has a status different from the other. "He takes to it like a duck to water." Here the clause verb *does* has been suppressed. Now sentences of this kind are not only acceptable but preferable. If anyone said, "He takes to it as a duck to water," you'd move your seat over a few inches away from him. This is a little lofty for my taste at least.

Now take what we are told is the most monstrous debauch of the English language ever known. "Winstons taste good like a cigarette should." Madison Avenue, that wicked place, couldn't believe its luck when they got so much mileage out of that. Here where the clause verb is actually expressed, *like* and *as* have long been competing forms.

When this advertisement was stirring up all this furor that it caused, my sister and I were completing our book on the American language and we amused ourselves by questioning and cross-questioning people who got excited about things like this. I met one of my colleagues one day who said, "By God, I'll never smoke another Winston." "Why?" "They're corrupting the language." Then I said to him, "What's wrong with it, what's wrong with 'Winstons taste good like a cigarette should'?" And the answer almost invariably was the same "What's wrong with it? My God, what's wrong with it?" "Yep, what's wrong with it?" "What do you mean, what's wrong with it?" "What's wrong with it?" Then they start to splutter. Finally they may be trapped into saying *like* should not be used as a conjunction. We found many people, when you press them, thought in some way something was wrong with *good*.

Now, what are the facts? *Like* is found in sentences of this kind as far back as 1579. For 300 years some people have used *like* and some have used *as* and steadily and consistently, and within this century in a very rapidly ascending curve, *like* has dominated. About the middle of the 19th century, not until then, somebody decided that the use of *as* in these constructions marked you as a very superior person. This person and his or her followers, whom I call the *ases*, have been very militant on this point, and if they could have done you in any time they would.

However, for the moment, *like* is certainly in the ascendency. The use of *as* in constructions like "He takes to it as a duck to water" puts you in the minority. You may say you are the correct minority, but if you are enough of a minority, you cannot go on even claiming to be correct. I would say at the moment that the *ases* have lost the battle and that the *likeables* have won.

Now take another use of *like* as a conjunction. "Life is hard for a girl like I." This is from Anita Loos' *Gentlemen Prefer Blondes*. The use of the nominative *I*, implying the suppressed *am* makes this *like* a conjunction. Had it been *me*, it would have been a preposition. Now this sentence differs from "He takes to it like a duck to water" only in the fact that *like* is here followed by a pronoun instead of a noun. Yet nonetheless this construction is substandard. That is, the use of this construction would mark you as an uneducated person. You could not hold a job requiring a normal education if you used this construction. Why? Because usage says accept one, not the other.

Then take a fourth. "You act like you are a combination of Socrates and Napoleon." Is this right or wrong? You try it on people and they are puzzled. They don't know—they are uneasy. What it is, actually, is a regional matter. You will hear this in the South. This is acceptable in the South—it is not acceptable in the North and East.

All I meant with these *likes* is to demonstrate that the use of *like* as a conjunction is a very involved matter. If you just arbitrarily say you can't use it as a conjunction, you're not representing the English language as it is spoken and has been spoken for centuries. You cannot say, "Well, everybody was wrong for 400 years and I'm right." Well, you can say it, but you don't earn vast respect by saying that.

When I did, with Mr. John Mason Brown, a TV show called *The Last Word*, which ran on the Columbia network for three years, by giving away a Britannica among other bait, we got an enormous amount of mail—we got 2,000 letters a day. We got over a million and a half letters, and I read well over 50,000 to 60,000 letters myself.

One of the things that emerged was how passionately the North disapproves of the South's speech, and how supremely indifferent to the North the South is. I don't believe we got a single letter from the South saying "Why do these ignorant damnyankees talk this way?" I think the feeling is they are scum anyway and what does it matter—why do you expect people like that to talk English? But the North is very much on the defensive. We got more angry letters because people said "It's real hot today" instead of saying *very*. *Real* simply means "very." *Very* simply means "real." "Thou art the very God," the Bible says. Yet nonetheless, people assumed in the North the one thing was absolutely criminal and you better call out the militia again.

Now people who talk about rules of grammar, unless they are grammarians, are talking for the most part pretentious nonsense. You cannot understand the rules of English. English is so enormous a language. So amazingly complex. You can't understand it by rules. Fortunately, you have to understand it before you can even go to the kindergarten. You couldn't be admitted to kindergarten if you were not already fairly conversant with the English language; and the great place for learning English in the school system is the schoolyard. This teaches you a great deal more than you get in school. One sneer in the schoolyard will do more to correct the deviation from the norm of that group than any amount of parental thundering.

My children both said *tooken*, and I never correct anybody's speech unless he pays me, and they didn't pay, and we let them go, and they don't say *tooken* now. They are grown up; they are both in college. Somewhere along the line somebody snickered, or some one of their contemporaries in the schoolyard said "yea, yea, yea, tooken, tooken, tooken." That'll do it—that'll do it far better than talking about regular past forms, the present, or gerundive, believe me.

When we were on the air in *The Last Word*, a schoolteacher wrote from Atlanta. She was obviously on the verge of a complete nervous breakdown and needed a sedative very badly. She wrote: "Can you give me some simple rules for teaching my students to use the word *the* properly?" Well, obviously, she had reached the point that all teachers and parents reach, the feeling of getting nowhere. You pick out some trifle like, "You will pick up your clothes tonight," or "You will close the garage door." Concentrate on this one or you are always licked— you never get anywhere. She decided apparently she couldn't teach them anything, but she could pick one simple word and some way they would learn to use that.

Well, I wrote her a letter—I felt rather sorry for her—and pointed out that in Jespersen's *Modern English Grammar*, which is a great English grammar, seven thick volumes in small print and double columns, 75 closely printed, double column pages are devoted to the word *the*, and at the end of this, Jespersen throws in the towel. He says that he knows this treatment is superficial and inadequate, but he has to move on. Three score and ten years is all a man has.

The idiomatic uses of T-H-E—we pronounce it three different ways, depending whether or not it is followed by a stressed vowel or whether it is followed by a consonant—the idiomatic uses of T-H-E are beyond bewildering. We go *to college, to the university*; we go *to church*, but *to the hospital*. The British don't. They go *to hospital*. We go *to town*, but *to the city*. Americans look *out of the window*; British look *out of window*. We may be found *at home, at the house*; we catch *typhoid*, but *the smallpox*; we catch *a cold*, but *the flu*; we have *diphtheria*, but *the measles*. And this goes on and on and on.

Now, suppose this woman decided, nonetheless, she was going to carry on. Let's assume she becomes deeply paranoid and is determined to teach *the*. Let's suppose she gets a year off with pay in order to understand Jespersen, to codify, to make up rules, and subdivisions, and exceptions, and all the other stuff. With fire in her eye and with Jespersen in her hand, she meets the class the next year and she means it. This is the first grade. She puts the rules down and, by God, they shall memorize them. What would she do? She would utterly frustrate the education of those children. Boys would stutter and stammer all the rest of their lives, all of them would be ill at the sight of a book, none of them would ever learn to read. I'm serious about this. She would produce a class of complete and absolute illiterates, with nervous breakdowns.

What's the alternative? The alternative is very simple. Never in my life have I heard a native-born speaker misuse the word *the*. Leave them alone, since they learn it anyway, enormously complicated as it is. No American says "I am going to hospital." And no Englishman says "I'm going to the hospital." And no American says, "I caught the cold." He says *a cold*, if he is a native-born speaker. Since he does all this, amazing as it is, since his ear taught him all this and he will do it anyway and I've never known anyone who didn't, just let him alone. Don't try to teach the use of *the* by rules.

Now writing cannot equal speech. It cannot be the exact reproduction of speech. The language is changing so rapidly. We pick up so many new words. You know the much attacked *Webster's Third New International* had to add 100,000 words to the list they had in 1934. It seems incredible to think that in 1934 people simply didn't have, therefore had no words for, the atom bomb, baby-sitters, coffee breaks, electronic computers, astronauts, nylons, parking meters, antibiotics, and so on and so on. New experiences are bringing floods of new words. And what's more, they are changing old words.

Many of the letters that we got on the show asked us, "Can this word mean that?" Almost anytime anyone asks you that question, the answer is yes. Otherwise, he wouldn't have asked you the question. Nobody asks, "Can *hippopotamus* mean 'pumpkin pie'?" Nobody's ever heard it used that way. You don't ask this question until you have heard the word used and by the time you have heard the word used, and your ear notices it enough so that you don't think it is an idiotic aberration of some kind, then that probably means that, incredible as it may seem, that has become the meaning of that word.

The most common meaning, for instance, of *silo*, that one reads in the papers now, is the concrete pit in the ground from which a missile is being launched. The other word, my idea of silo, a thing sticking out of the ground in which you put food for cattle, is still known, is still used, but the word is completely changed. And this is the meaning, which by the way, I see all of the time in the *New York Times*.

The *New York Times* wrote a very silly editorial on the appearance of the Third Webster, in which they stated that they were not going to use it—they were going to stick to the good old Second Webster. If they were, they would be out of business right now. You can't publish a newspaper in '63 or '61 with the language of 1934. Poor Webster, they had very poor public relations, but in their bleating, Webster pointed out that the largest single source they had drawn from was the *New York Times*. Obviously, the editors don't read their own paper.

Incidentally, I happened to be in the hospital at the time this came out, just convalescing. I had a little time on my hands, and I took that issue, the issue of the *Times* in which they made this bold and lunatic announcement and there were over 170 usages in that issue which were countenanced by the Third Webster which they said they wouldn't use, and were not countenanced by the Second, which they said they would use, and in the very editorial there were two of them.

People often hurl at me the word *permissive*. They say, "You are permissive." What do you mean "permissive"? There are 300 million who speak this language. What am I to do? Club them all on the head? What have I got to do with it? I permit Niagara Falls to go over, too. I don't know what to do about it. I permit the Grand Canyon to remain just where it is. To talk about people being permissive of what 300 million people do every day—back of this is an incredibly arrogant assumption that we who have to do with observing and using speech in some way control it. We don't. The masses control speech. And all we do, ultimately, is follow on.

Now some people believe that words have only one meaning. Of course words have, as we all know, many meanings. And only the context will show you, but the context will show you very clearly. The verb *run* is listed in the *Oxford English Dictionary*, which is now 100 years out of date, as having 265 clearly distinguishable verbal meanings. Now we don't have all those meanings in our vocabulary, but I expect any educated person has maybe 30 meanings of the word *run* in his vocabulary. Well, how do you know which one you mean? You never falter. It's like using *the*. You know. The context almost always tells you.

For instance, what does the word *locks* mean? Well, it means one thing to a locksmith, it means another thing to a delicatessen, it means another thing in a missile base. Anybody who says in a missile base "put some lox in the missile" and finds he's stuffing salmon into it—this isn't likely to happen. Nor is a locksmith likely to shove liquid oxygen through the keyhole.

Words in context almost always define their own meaning. People get unnecessarily agitated about these things. People who believe that words have only one meaning also seem to think they have only one function and they will get very angry and they will say, "You can't use that as a verb, it's a noun." Verbs and nouns are just words which describe what the word is doing at the time you are using it. A verb doesn't mark a species like a dinosaur as against a rabbit.

I have some stuff here from the *Washington Post*, which has gotten very agitated about the English language and isn't always justified in its agitation. The *Washington Post* was very upset about the Third Webster. And, after the usual discharge of rage in such phrases as "abdication of authority," "barbarism" they then accused the dictionary of pretentious and obscure verbosity and illustrated the accusation by referring to the Third Webster's definition of so simple an object as a door.

The editor seemed to think that a door is a door, and that any damn fool ought to knew that it is a door, and why do you have to take 94 words to tell someone what a door is? The point is that doors have changed like anything since 1934. We have more strange closing contraptions today. Are they doors or aren't they?

This word has come into the courts. I have a little article here from the *Boston Globe* in which a gentleman too eager to leave a modernistic post office walked through a glass partition to his own damage and then sued the United States government on the grounds that he thought it was a door. And this had to come into court and the judge had to decide not only what is a door, but what is a reasonable man in a reasonable hurry, leaving a reasonable post office, reasonably likely to think is a door? And the judge's decision was that there was no ground for suit here, that, damn it all, you ought to look at least for a handle, a knob, or something, before you start walking out of modern buildings.

But in 1963 the problem of defining a door is a much more difficult thing than it was in 1934. Take these accordion sort of things that slide shut in apartments. Your apartment rent is based on the number of rooms; the landlord may look you right in the eye and tell you that that thing marks a room, because it's a door. You may go to court—and people have gone to court on this, and the courts have ruled it's a door all right. So the dictionary has to take cognizance of this.

Now a more serious charge against the *Post.* I am in a way sorry to single out any paper, because a great many did this, but one has to deal with specific instances. The *Post*, having got its blood pressure up on the matter of usage, ran another editorial. It got very agitated, because it had come across the word *trimester.* Some college was going to go on a trimester system and the editor, huffing and puffing about this, said: "Beginning next fall, state universities will operate on three equal terms each year instead of the present semester system. Incidentally, they are calling the plan a 'trimester system' which implies a miraculous improvement indeed, for *semester* derives from the Latin word *semestris* meaning 'half-yearly'. And trimester, by analogy, must mean 'three halves'. That will be crowding it, even for Florida."

Unfortunately, that isn't what *semester* means at all. Now there is no reason to expect the editor to know Latin, but before he states what Latin means, he ought to look it up. *Semester* is based on *sex mensis,* "six months, a six months period." *Semester* has been in the language very long. *Trimester* has been in the language over a hundred years. All *trimester* means is a "three month period." This is no great crime, except that the indignation is simply unjustified and it is uninformed. And if a man is going to write editorials, scorning the dictionary, and invents facts to his fancy, then he shouldn't get too excited about the incorrect use of words.

Many words pass in the language simply as errors. We have many established errors. Once an error is fixed by usage, it will stay and you have to use it. For instance, if a child said *gooder, knowed, me am* or *girlses,* he would agitate his parents deeply. Most children do something like this and most parents are agitated. Nonetheless, we all use words like that every day because we don't know that they are corruptions. *Lesser* and *nearer* and even the word *more* are historically exactly the same as *gooder*.

The historical word, which didn't change until Shakespeare's time, is *moe*. When Macbeth says "Send out moe horses, skirr the country round," he is not talking Dixie talk—this is the old English word. The *r* was then added by somebody who didn't perceive that *moe* was an irregular comparative. *Me am* would seem unthinkable to anybody, yet we all say *you are*, which is exactly the same, exactly the use of the accusative for the nominative and fairly recent. *Girlses* sounds awful, but we all say *children*, which is even more awful: *children* is a triplication of a plural.

Let me call your attention to some real changes that are taking place in the language that don't bother these people at all because they simply go on using them. There has been a great increase in empty verbs, that is, where people used to say "Let's drink, Let's swim," they are now inclined to say "Let's have a drink, Let's take a drink, Let's have a swim, Let's take a swim." Where our fathers said "It snowed heavily," we're likely to say "There was a heavy snow." Our fathers "decided," we "reach a decision." Why we put these extra verbs in, I don't know. I have only some theories and won't bother you with them, but this again is a marked change in the language.

There is a great increase in the use of the passive, which probably reflects a civilized or degenerate—the two things are often the same— awareness of the fact that we are being acted on. The barbarian is never aware of this; he is acted on, but he is too aggressive to know it. The barbarian lives in the active present indicative. "I eat," "I steal," "I rob," "I rape," and eventually he drops dead. But the civilized man knows that the forces are working on him. The Greeks had a very elaborate passive, Romans didn't have much of a passive, our language has very little passive.

There is an increased use of the subjunctive in modern American English for some reason. The true subjunctive has now retreated almost entirely. Among illiterate Negroes you will hear the proper use of the subjunctive. "Be he there, see him I will." This would sound very strange, but I heard our laundress the other day, who comes right out of the Delta, say she was going back to see her grandpappy, "Be he still living." This is good, good, good, fine old historical English.

The new subjunctive you hear in such phrases as "I wouldn't know." In the quiz shows, if someone says "Who was George Washington?" instead of saying "The first president," the quizee says "That would be the first president." There seems to be a feeling that the subjunctive gives a touch of gentility in some way or protects you in some way. I don't know exactly why it's used.

Well now, most people don't know anything about grammar and

there's no earthly reason why they should. You don't have to know any more about grammar to speak effectively than you have to know about physics to drive a car. The one is the theory of the other, but you don't have to know the theory. The people who get agitated usually fall back on logic, and there they are on completely false grounds because language isn't logical.

Language knows no logic except itself. You cannot apply mathematics to language. Classical Latin is logical, but classical Latin is a mandarin language; nobody ever spoke it. Spoken Latin was quite different from what Cicero and Virgil wrote. If language were logical, for instance, *unloose* ought to mean "tie up," but it doesn't. If language were logical, an outlaw ought to be the opposite of an inlaw. But it isn't.

One of the commonest charges people make who get logical about languages, for instance, is that you cannot use the plural with *none*. You say, "Well, none of them are coming" and they seem to think you should say "None of them *is* coming." They base this on the triumphant grounds that *none* doesn't include *one*. Well, if it doesn't include one, then you can't use the singular either if you want to be logical. I don't know what to do at that point.

Nonetheless, the simple fact is that people use the plural increasingly. Most people would say "None of them are coming," rather than say "None of them *is*." When our *Dictionary of Contemporary American Usage* was published, the *Chicago Tribune* did us the honor of ten separate attacks. The thing seemed to agitate them very deeply, and they picked on this. We had said that contemporary usage countenances plural with *none* more often than the singular. This doesn't mean that either one is wrong. They said absolutely no, and I wrote them a letter, pointing out Shakespeare used *none* with the plural, though I didn't expect that to bother them much, but I thought I had a real topper—I pointed out that God uses *none* with the plural in the very first commandment, as in Deuteronomy 5:7—but I guess my authority was regarded at the *Tribune* as secondary and they weren't impressed.

We've all heard the business of double negatives—we're all taught in school that you mustn't use two negatives. That's all right if you want to say to a class, "If you use two negatives in a certain way, you will mark yourself as a part of a certain level of education and social position." "But I was told two negatives make a positive." A more absurd statement in relation to language was never made. Two negatives may make a positive in algebra, but they don't in any Teutonic language. In every Teutonic language, the duplication of the negative simply heightens the negation. When Chaucer says of his Knight that he "hadn't never yet said nothing nasty to no man in all his life," you would be feebleminded to say "well, did he or didn't he"? Chaucer has knocked himself and the language out trying to tell you this man never said anything nasty to people. You ought to know that by that time.

Furthermore, if you want to be logical, if you want to say logic does not countenance a double negative and you say two negatives make a positive, then three negatives make a negative again. So that if it is wrong to say "It doesn't make no difference," then it must be all right to say "It don't never make no difference."

But it isn't all right to say either of these simply because neither is accepted by educated people in either America or England today, though they were in the past. Not because of logic, but simply because custom doesn't countenance them, either one.

Usage is capricious and illogical, but it is tyrannical. Many times the charge has been brought: "Well, then you are saying anything goes." Oh, no, anything does not go at all. There is no activity of human life in which less goes. In speech you are not permitted to deviate one iota from the customs of your group without being severely punished. Consider what was made of Al Smith's pronunciation of what other people call *radio* and he called *raddio*. Maybe his constituents called it *raddio*. I don't know. Actually, *radio* is an artificial word made up from Latin. *Raddio* is nearer what we know of Latin than *radio*. Nonetheless, when I was a boy and the campaign was going on, I heard nothing about his career as governor of New York—all I heard was *raddio*. This man said *raddio*, just as today you hear another man say *Cuber* over and over. If you have any doubt that society will punish you for a deviation, go into a cheap restaurant in Chicago and ask for *tomahto* soup. You will feel public disapproval very quickly. If you can afford the Pump Room, they will furnish you with *tomahto* soup; don't try it in Joe's Beanery. It won't go.

All *idiom* means is something we do in this language which doesn't make any sense, but we do it all the same. And the very people who get so upset about English idioms, because idioms don't conform to some preconceived theory, are proud of their use of idioms in another language. We say *a couple of dollars*, but we say *a dozen eggs*. Our great grandfathers said *a dozen of eggs* and I suspect in backward rural parts today you would hear *a dozen of eggs*. We say that we *adore* God, but we would be shocked if someone would say that he is *adorable*. But centuries ago, this was said quite seriously in very solemn words. We say *later on*. This sounds all right to us. The English say *early on* and *earlier on* and this baffles us.

Suppose for instance, you want to be an innovator in language and you just decided that you would say *squoze*. Why *squeezed*? *Squoze* sounds better. We say *freeze, froze*, and so on—why not say *squoze*? What would happen if you decided on just that one little thing? You are going to change the language. You come down to the office and say "Well, I squoze some oranges for breakfast this morning." The general look would be, "Very funny very early in the morning," and nobody would be vastly amused and they would say, "He thinks he's a card." But suppose you keep up. Day after day you're going to be a "squoze" man. You keep at it. People would begin to say, "Look, this guy has a screw loose. He says *squoze*. What's the matter with him?" And they would be right. That would cost you advancement. I'd be willing to swear that in any organization if you stuck to *squoze*, they wouldn't promote you, and they'd be right. "This guy, there is something wrong with this guy." And there is something wrong with everyone who would deliberately deviate that way.

We have deviations, but usually they are not deliberate. Men have been driven out of public life for deviating one syllable. In our speech, for instance, one of the signs of what we regard as supreme illiteracy is making stops of certain *th* sounds. That is, instead of saying *th-*, saying *dese, dem, dose*. This is supposed to mark you as a person absolutely outside the pale. Yet these sounds don't bother us if we all agree. It doesn't bother us in the least if we all say *bedlam* instead of *Bethlehem*, which is the proper word. We all say *murder* instead of *murther*, as it used to be. We say *burden* instead of *burthen*, as it used to be, and so on.

Certainly Mr. Kennedy, who is a highly educated man and speaks very effectively, has come in for plenty of criticism for that Boston pronunciation of the last syllable of *Cuba*. I don't know whether he does it deliberately or whether it was necessary in the early parts of his career that he might identify himself with East Boston. I don't know. If it comes natural to him, why shouldn't he speak his own language?

I speak Ohio-ese overlaid with the speech of England where I got my early and later education, plus considerable personal idiosyncrasy as a result of adenoids, I guess. At any rate, that's the way you speak. No man ought—I would mistrust a man who changed his speech much more than I would mistrust one who went right ahead.

Truman is a wonderful speaker. Truman's voice is purely American, western Missouri.

Well, in conclusion, what are we supposed to do about all this? Are you just to drift? Are you to permit anybody to write the way he wants to? Well, you can't do much about it. You are not going to hire illiterates. You are not likely to hire them as teachers or editorial writers or reporters, though they might make very good ones. That is, there might be a freshness in their speech.

What you have to do is admit that there is a very wide range in this great language we speak. There are many local ways of speaking. There are different ways of speaking at different levels. Everybody has several languages. You couldn't possibly speak at home as you would speak in public. We have highly formal ways of speaking on highly formal occasions, and then we have relaxed ways of speaking with our friends and then you have ways of usually grunting within the family. This conveys your feeling and you shift without any trouble from one level to another.

When you're dealing with the public as with a class or as in a newspaper or an editorial, naturally you conform to whatever the usage of that group is and I mean naturally. And I don't mean naturally in the sense that you make an effort to do it. It doesn't occur to you to do anything else.

Rules, good rules, are those which state as best they can what cultivated, sensitive people who want passionately to express their meaning now say. Bad rules are those which state what such people used to do. Very bad rules are those which state what somebody thinks they ought to do, but don't. And anyway, all rules are simply a means to an end and the end is being understood, expressing ourselves exactly and completely and expressing our emotions as well as our thoughts.

I read, as you probably do also, "Winners and Sinners," put out by Mr. Bernstein of the *New York Times*. I find it very fascinating, and it is high on my list of preferred reading. I often disagree with Mr. Bernstein on questions of grammar, but I don't disagree with him for one moment—indeed I am usually wracked with admiration for the subtlety of his perceptions—that this word in this context is loaded, that you colored this statement by putting this word in there. That is very fine editing indeed. That helps make the *Times* the very great paper it is. What you want to do is express the exact meaning. If you want to color it, fine, but you've got to know that you are coloring. The only sin is not to know this is a loaded word, not to know this word conveys something else to the average reader because you have to know what the average reader means by these words.

All writing is a form of communication and all communication is a form of translation from one man's observation and experience into another's and when you are translating, the important one is the language into which you are translating. You have to know it, of course—reporters do. The advantage of newspaper writing, the reason it is often fascinating reading, is that it has to be written with great haste. You have to meet a deadline. The thing happens, you want to beat another man with an account of it. This compels you to write in contemporary —as close to contemporary as you can, because you haven't time to think of how Shakespeare would have done it, very fortunately. Shakespeare never took time off to think how anyone else would have done it, he just did it his way.

The difficulty seems to be, the reason you get these editorials of the kind I quoted, is that only superannuated reporters become editors. You are far advanced, apparently, into the vale of arteriosclerosis by the time you become an editor. And as you are not aware of the change in the language, all you see in it is corruption whereas it isn't corrupt at all, it's very live.

The English language isn't made in classrooms; it isn't made in dictionaries, it isn't made in grammar books, it isn't made in editorials. The English language is made by the three hundred million people who speak it, who are living, who are angry, who are excited, who are greedy, who are passionate about something, and out of this enormous vocabulary that time and fate has given us, put these wonderful words together. I don't believe I've ever heard a remark in a faculty meeting that has suddenly excited me with glory and wonder, at the brilliance, the humor, the aptness of it. You don't hear that sort of thing in faculty meetings, but you do hear it on the street. Suddenly you hear a phrase, you hear something in a bus or somewhere and your heart will leap up and dance with the daffodils.

I remember at a football game—a referee who was introduced as the head of the YMCA league or something. He made a number of decisions which angered one side very much, and when he finally blew the whistle and the whole thing was over, I remember a guy behind me just yelling at the top of his voice:

"Goodbye for good, you Sunday School son of a bitch."

That was good language for that man's purposes at that moment, I thought.

STUDY QUESTIONS AND EXERCISES

1. Bergen Evans is an authority on usage, rather than a linguist. How does his title reflect both his audience and his attitude toward them and himself?

2. What five postulates does Evans set down? Do they agree with the principles set forth in the previous selections? In what sense does he use *grammar*?

3. What does *shibboleth* mean? Why is it useful in referring to those inside and those outside a dominant culture? What does *oneupmanship* mean? Look up the works of Stephen Potter, such as *Oneupmanship*, *Gamesmanship*, and *Lifemanship*, for humorous use of the term.

4. Look up *stress*, *pitch*, and *juncture* as grammatical terms. What terms does Evans use for these in the paragraph beginning "Speech is incredibly subtle" (page 47)? How does he illustrate these characteristics of speech? Give similar examples. How does writing attempt to convey these speech devices?

5. Look up *beatitude* in *Webster's Third*, unabridged or collegiate, *Random House* or the *American College*, *American Heritage*, and *Webster's New World* dictionaries. Look at the words that precede it. In which ones might Mr. Evans' student have easily stumbled on the meaning of the root word, explaining *beatitude* and related words?

6. What general point is illustrated by the discussion of *like* and *as*? What one example of *like* as a conjunction is definitely substandard? Why? Examine Evans' own practice—does he use *like* as a conjunction? Look up *like* as an adverb in the *American Heritage* and

Random House dictionaries. In light of the usage notes there and of reactions like that quoted from the *Christian Science Monitor,* why might a Northern college student be wise to use *like* carefully in formal contexts? See the interview with William Faulkner in *Writers at Work** for Faulkner's use of *like, as, than, ain't,* in a formal interview, one of the best that has been published. How many times does he use *like* as a conjunction? How many times does he use *as,* with and without the following verb? Is his attitude on language strict or relaxed? Is it significant that he was a Southerner, of a locally eminent family? What differences between North and South in class structure and social tradition might explain Northern anxiety over "correctness" and Southern upper-class complacency?

7. How and when does a person really learn basic patterns, forms, and idioms? Compare Evans with Chomsky on this point, referring to selection 4, question 7.

8. If you are studying a foreign language that contains the equivalent of *the,* can you tell when to use this article in an English translation?

9. Look up *run* in a recent unabridged dictionary. How many meanings do you find? Which meanings are new to you and why?

10. What basic relationship between meaning and usage of words does Evans present? What examples are given of how usage converts errors into correct usage?

11. Is the rule about double negatives violated by such sentences as: "It is not unlikely that it will rain tomorrow"? Do these two negatives make an affirmative? Look up "double negative" in Bergen Evans and Cornelia Evans, *Dictionary of Contemporary American Usage* or in Margaret Bryant, *Current American Usage.*

12. What is an idiom? Why are idioms the most difficult elements to learn in a foreign language? Give comparable idioms in two languages.

13. "Everybody has several languages." What does this statement imply for the student whose native speech is not the standard English dialect: should he discard his natural speech? Should he resist learning standard English? Should he learn standard English to use when occasion requires and relax into the old speech habits for familiar use?

14. Of what vital and practical significance to an educated young person are the facts that employers, like editors, belong to older generations and believe that "naturally you conform" to the usage of the group you are dealing with?

---

* Malcolm Cowley, ed. (New York: Viking Press, 1959).

SUBJECTS FOR BRIEF PAPERS
OR WRITTEN REPORTS

1. In Lewis Carroll's *Alice Through the Looking Glass* look up

'Twas brillig, and the slithy toves
Did gyre and gimble in the wabe.

In the "frames" of this nonsense poem substitute words that make sense. What do you discover about basic English sentence patterns and structure as distinct from meaning? Write a brief report on how position, word forms—tense, person, number, etc.—and structure words—articles, prepositions, and conjunctions—signal sentence patterns independent of lexical meaning.

2. After studying Chapter 8, "The Poetry in Our Daily Speech," in Harry Warfel, *Language: A Science of Human Behavior*, analyze a poem of your own choice and write a report on how meaning and rhythm are related to structure words.

3. What limits a speaker's "possibility of making a linguistic response to any experience"? What limitations are you most conscious of in your own responses? In what ways can those limitations be reduced and your own possibilities of making linguistic responses be extended? How can knowledge of the basic principles of language and the characteristics of English contribute to your skill in making linguistic responses? Rewrite a paragraph of your own in which you strive for effective use of variety in sentence beginnings and endings; subordination by word, by phrase, by clause; emphasis by inversion; emphasis by climactic series; balanced sentence; periodic sentence; parallel participial phrases; clearing out of dead wood; precise diction.

4. How does Aldous Huxley's *Brave New World* show the arbitrary meaning and the conventional character of language? What familiar English words have different meanings or different connotations? How have these been developed? Write a short theme explaining the language process by which one group of words, such as those dealing with motherhood, acquire connotations opposed to our present ones.

5. Noam Chomsky's article "The Current Scene in Linguistics" (selection 4) defines and presents a choice between generative and descriptive grammar. Using some of the techniques of definition, comparison, and contrast that Chomsky uses, define and explain the difference between descriptive and prescriptive grammar.

6. "Words are conventional signs." * Study the word *conventional* and the related words near it in an unabridged dictionary. What

---

* James B. Greenough and George Lyman Kittredge, *Words and Their Ways in English Speech* (New York: Macmillan, 1961).

different meanings of the root *ven* can you identify? Classify and illustrate them. How do the meanings of *convention* illustrate both the literal and figurative meanings? Is the original meaning wholly lost in any words in the group? In a short paper present your findings and your generalizations from them.

7. Examine a recent college English handbook or a freshman composition textbook and determine whether the author follows the scientific or the prescriptive point of view toward language. Write a short paper in which you classify your evidence and draw your conclusions from it.

8. Examine Jacques Barzun's *The House of Intellect,* summarize Barzun's main objections to the scientific linguists, and evaluate his objections on the basis of your readings in Part 1.

9. On the basis of your study of Part 1 and of the Preface of *Webster's Third New International Dictionary,* show what linguistic principles the compilers of that dictionary were following in their work. Examine one of the later dictionaries—*Random House, Webster's New World,* 2nd ed., or *American Heritage*: what principles are stated? What linguistic principles are represented in the two dictionaries examined? Write a short report on your findings.

10. Write a short paper on William Faulkner's "Barn Burning" as representing Fries's four "Differences in Language Practice," † showing how historical differences have become substandard regional, how other regional differences are reflected in words and pronunciation, how literary language and colloquial language are used, and how dialogue reflects difference in social levels.

11. In Evans' *Comfortable Words* look up *albatross* and browse through and collect other examples of words which have no "real" meaning according to Evans. Write a brief report on the language processes represented in Evans' book.

12. Using Archibald Hill's "What Is Language" (selection 1) as a model, write an inductive definition of one of the key elements in linguistics, such as *word, lexicon, phoneme,* or *morpheme.*

---

† Charles C. Fries, *American English Grammar* (New York: Appleton-Century-Crofts, 1940). See the introductions to Parts 2, 3, 4, and 5 of *Aspects of American English.*

part **2**

Historical Aspects

This section deals with some of the historical aspects of language. As Charles C. Fries states, in American English Grammar:

> *The language forms of each age have differed in some respect from those of any other time. Constant change is the outstanding characteristic of a live language used by an intellectually active people. The historical changes do not come suddenly, nor do they affect all the users of a language equally. Thus at any time there will be found those who cling to the older methods and those who use the newer fashion. Many of the differences we note in the language today find their explanation in this process of historical change.*

In dictionaries, the changes in the meaning and pronunciation of words are carefully recorded. Once a student understands the pattern which the dictionary uses in dealing with these changes, he can easily trace the different stages of word history. A study of two different editions of the same dictionary or an examination of the citations in the Oxford English Dictionary *will reveal how the characteristics of words change with the passage of years. (Although linguists look upon this function as the primary one many other people regard the dictionary as an absolute authority which decides questions of usage, pronunciation, meaning, and appropriateness.) With the aid of the dictionary, then, the student can acquire a sense of historical perspective about words and their role in human communication.*

Many place-names also function historically. Like fossils, they often reflect the prevailing characteristics of a bygone era. The reading, the peculiar interests, the ethnic and religious backgrounds, the prominent personages of a community are a few of the historical implications preserved in place-names long after the nature of the community has otherwise changed completely.

The history of words shows the significance of language as a living, dynamic force. The study of language changes provides information about the flexibility of language—the leveling of inflections, the simplification of sentence patterns, and the tendency toward monosyllabism. Investigation of the history of a language also discloses that new words are added when they become necessary for effective communication and that old words atrophy and drop out of normal usage when they no longer serve a useful function. This process of growth, development, and change, common to all languages, is most easily perceived when words are examined in their historical context.

Since word history is so basic in the study of language, it will reappear in later sections, often masquerading as an element of the regional quality of words or as a determining factor in the literary or social implications of words. This overlapping and fusion serves to stress the basic historical quality inherent in words. In fact, it is the historical element which makes words so flexible and, at times, so perplexing.

6

American Linguistic Traits Compared with Standard British

Margaret Schlauch

In her study of The English Language in Modern Times (since 1400) *Professor Margaret Schlauch of the University of Warsaw analyzes some of the elements that differentiate British from English.*

The phenomena of differentiation separating British from American English, and the signs of influence exercised by the latter on the former, have been the subject of considerable discussion in recent years. Attention has been called to the problem by the achievements of American novelists and playwrights who abundantly make use of vernacular idiom for literary expression. The discussion has become lively, and at times even acrimonious, in proportion as technical advances in communication (besides military and economic relations) have fortified the American impact on contemporary culture in other English-speaking countries.

Differences in standard vocabulary are among the most obvious elements of contrast.[1] They are also the most readily studied and explained. Visitors in England and America find themselves obliged to substitute back and forth between word pairs such as the following:

British	American	British	American
biscuit	cracker	lorry	truck
book (as verb)	reserve, order	perambulator, pram	baby carriage
braces	suspenders	public house, pub	saloon
chemist's shop	drugstore	reel of cotton	spool of thread
drawing-pin	thumb-tack	spanner	monkey-wrench
goods waggon	freight car	sweets	candy
ironmongery	hardware	tin (container)	can

---

[1] The reference dictionary of standard American English is Sir William Craigie and James R. Hulbert, *A Dictionary of American English on Historical Principles*, 4 vols. (University of Chicago Press, 1938–44). See also M. M. Mathews, *Dictionary of Americanisms* (Chicago, 1951).

However, though these distinctions[2] may assume crucial importance in a given practical situation, they are hardly significant enough to support the claim, advanced by H. L. Mencken, that a quite new language has been developed in the United States. Nor are the strictly morphological differences very great between English and American, when viewed on the level of standard usage. Certain strong and weak verbs do show somewhat different forms, with the American fairly often though not always the more conservative: U.S. *gotten* versus English *got; proven* versus *proved; wakened* versus *woke; swelled* versus *swollen; sheared* versus *shorn,* etc. These and other such deviations are conspicuous because they have to do with some of the few surviving inflections in the English language.

Perhaps it may be said that linguistic differences between the two communities are to be noticed primarily in the ways in which they make use of the common linguistic heritage, both in word formation and in certain patterns of syntactic usage. Even here, of course, many of the distinctions tend to be obliterated with time. American neologisms are quickly conveyed to England and become familiar to readers, theatre-goers and film enthusiasts. In some cases they are finally adopted. Others die out on both sides of the Atlantic. Neologisms are frequent in both domains, and it is interesting to observe how they arise.

In both countries, new terms arise from the native stock by a method of compounding an uninflected verbal root with an adverbial particle, either preceding or following it. The former method produces words like: *income, inset, inlay, outlay, overpass, output, underwrite(r).* These are current on both sides of the Atlantic. But insofar as new formations are created with postpositional particles, the greater activity appears to be carried on in the United States. The coinages may not be far more numerous, but their use appears to be more prevalent. Nouns formed in this way have a strong stress on the verbal element but none on the particle, as distinguished from the similarly constituted verbs which have more evenly distributed stress on the two elements. Thus among the nouns we have: *set-up* (a term with many meanings), *run-around, check-off, check-up, run-in, feed-back, feed-in, fall-out* (applied to radioactive substances), *knock-out, sit-down, lock-out, pay-off, showdown, build-up, walk-away* (easy victory), *brush-off, work-out,* and many others. These are sometimes found inflected for plural number by adding -(e)s to the attached particle: *set-backs, check-offs, flare-ups,* etc. The verbs formed from these same elements are given a more even accentuation, being treated as a complex of two stressed elements: to *'check 'off* (as opposed to *'check-off*); to *'set 'back* (as opposed to *'set-back*), etc.

---

[2] A classified list of such Anglo-American synonyms is given by Hans Galinsky, *Die Sprache des Amerikaners* (Heidelberg, 1951–52), II, pp. 7–44. Mencken also provided a list in his *American Language.*

American usage not only inclines to the somewhat wider use of such newly minted (or re-minted) terms, but also displays a greater freedom —shall we say license?—in the use of them, as compared with contemporary British English. By placement before another noun these become adjectival in function, for instance: *a knock-down, drag-out fight; a try-out performance; a sit-down strike; a walk-away success.* A stylistic change is effected when these nouns derived from verbs are used to convey the notion of activity which in conventional sentences would be conveyed by the verb itself, while the verb is reduced to something colourless like *is, have, give,* etc. Thus an American speaker will say: They *gave him the run-around* or *the brush-off,* instead of: They *evaded him* or *thrust him aside;* His press-agent *gave him a build-up,* instead of: *praised him* and his accomplishments for commercial purposes; They *had a show-down,* instead of: *settled the matter finally;* There *was a try-out performance,* instead of: The actors *performed* the play as a test; Let's *have a check-up,* instead of: Let's *verify* our results. If the tendency here noted were to prevail, the predicate would cease to be the part of a sentence conveying a message of activity, while this function would be discharged by a noun object. It is still too early, however, to decide whether such a shift is occurring in American English. The probability is that the tendency will be held in check by competing tendencies in the linguistic system.

American English takes certain freedoms with grammatical categories which are avoided or infrequently used in British English. Nouns appear as verbs in expressions like: to *chair* a meeting (to act as chairman), to *author* a book (to write it), to *pressure* (exert pressure upon) someone; to *vacation* (spend one's holidays), to *radio* a message, to *captain* a team. Conversely, verbs appear as nouns: a big *push;* a good *buy;* an *assist;* an athletic *meet.* There are adjectives freely employed as nouns, sometimes with the nominal inflection for plural number added; young *hopefuls, comics, funnies, empties* (empty bottles), *Reds* (loosely applied to Communists and other militant progressives), *flimsies* (thin sheets of paper used for making carbon copies), *uppers* and *lowers* (berths in a train or ship). Adjectival participles may even be inflected like nouns: *marked-downs* (merchandise reduced in price). Whole phrases appear from time to time in adjectival position before the nouns modified: *portal-to-portal* pay; an *on-the-spot* conference; an *off-the-record* speech; an *out-of-town* district; *down-the-line* support; a *round-the-clock* watch. Another conspicuous nominal construction is what has been called the block compound by a recent commentator.[3] This type

[3] Gustav Kirchner, "Recent American Influence on Standard English: The Syntactical Sphere," *Zeitschrift für Anglistik,* V (1957), 29–42. On general usage see Margaret Nicholson, *A Dictionary of American-English Usage* (Oxford, 1957); and especially B. and C. Evans, *A Dictionary of Contemporary American Usage* (New York, 1957).

arises by the placement of two or more nouns in series so that each one modifies the meaning of the following one and serves in place of a prepositional phrase. The simpler type is represented by sets like: *pupil activities* (in place of a subjective genitive), *child guidance* (in place of an objective genitive), and *sex appeal* or *eye appeal* (in place of a modifying phrase). More complicated types are represented by: *Natural Resources Committee Report* (i.e., report of the committee concerned with natural resources); *election reform law* (law for the reform of elections); *price control board* (board dealing with the control of prices). Similar in its effect of concentration is the combination of a noun followed by an adjective or perfect passive participle, when the noun stands in place of a modifying phrase: *space-minded* (thinking in terms of space); *fashion-conscious; union-interlocked finances* (finances interlocked with those of a union); *land-hungry peasants* (those hungry for land), etc.

Journalistic writing in the United States has fostered such linguistic creations in great numbers. They do not, to be sure, represent a complete innovation. Older compounds were made on the same pattern: *bed-ridden, care-free, war-weary*, etc. But such forms are especially favoured in journalism because they, like the block compounds, permit the shifting of a concrete image from a postponed dependent position to the leading position in a phrase. The same impulse to placement in head position leads, in journalistic writing, to the use of inflected genitives where normal usage calls for *of*-phrases. The total effect is of a crowding of information into the limited space available before the subject of a sentence: *North Carolina's* Democratic Senator Sam Erwin (*Newsweek*, 6 May 1957), *Chicago's* week-long centenary celebration (*ibid.*). Besides being challenging in a strident sort of way, this type of construction also saves words. The drive for economy of space, especially in headlines, has led to the choice of less usual short words in place of ordinary long ones: *probe* for *investigation, wed* for *married.* Yet these special devices of journalism, consciously thought out for specific stylistic purposes, do not appear in normal American discouse, whether oral or written.

Nor is space-saving the only motive of journalistic abbreviations. Some of them result from linguistic playfulness and the desire to attract attention. Portmanteau words launched by newspaper writers, a few of which gain a limited currency, are primarily designed for entertainment. Thus a luminary of the social world is called a *socialite* (a term fairly often found in "gossip columns" of the press); a matron who has just received a divorce in the capital city of Nevada is said to be *Renovated*; slang is referred to as *slanguage*, and elocution as *yellocution*.

American slang[4] is of course very striking in respect to the number and

---

[4] Maurice H. Weseen, *A Dictionary of American Slang* (New York, 1934); Berrey and van den Bark, *American Thesaurus of Slang* (New York, 1942 and 1947).

range of its creations. Because of the wide prevalence today of American films and light fiction, this esoteric vocabulary has become familiar far beyond the borders of the United States. It is baffling to outsiders, not only because of the special circumstances of its origin, but also because of its rapid changes. When Krapp wrote his book on American English, he mentioned the following words as typical of slang in the 1920's: *oodles, flabbergasted, mollycoddle, blooey, foozle, frazzle, woozy, dotty.* Most of them are now out of date if not completely dropped. Among those now current, many are expressions substituting a concrete image for the more abstract or colourless expressions of ordinary speech:

Term	Meaning:	Term	Meaning:
bone orchard	— cemetery	lift the elbow	— take a drink
brass tacks	— essentials	pound the sidewalk	— walk
coffin-nail	— cigarette	put the finger on	— betray
cut a melon	— divide profits	scare the pants off	— terrify
flatfoot	— policeman	squeal on someone	— inform to the police
flat tire	— boring person	stick-in-the-mud	— a conservative
gum shoe	— detective	wooden overcoat	— a coffin

Many such terms combine vivid imagery with sound effects such as alliteration, assonance and rime: *face lace* for whiskers, *hot squat* for electric chair, *rock 'n' roll, city slicker, hush money, live wire, slow poke, slush fund* (money used for corrupt political practices). Humorous prolixity gives rise to metaphors like: *ball and chain* for wife; *yesterday, today and forever* for hash; *bats in the belfry* for insane. But abbreviations also gain currency: *D. A.* for District Attorney, *M. C.* for master of ceremonies, *pen* for penitentiary, and so on. Many single standard words substitute for others in slang parlance. Among the terms for a girl or woman are: *baby, dame, doll, femme, fluff, frail, frill, jane, mouse, skirt, tomato.* There is an imposing list of terms also to designate a condition of intoxication: *blotto, canned, cock-eyed, corned, flooey, fried, pickled, plastered, stewed, stiff.*—It will be noticed that metaphors from cooking are well represented here.

Despite its vividness and gamesomeness, however, the terminology of slang is seldom adopted in serious writing, save in passages of realistic dialogue, and seldom achieves a long life, whether in England or America.

Another problem connected with the American vocabulary is its infiltration with foreign loan words of recent date, due to the influx of immigrants from various European countries in the late 19th and early 20th century.[5] Of permanent loan-words into English there are relatively

---

[5] On the contacts of English with these other languages in America, H. L. Mencken has collected much material, both in his original book and the Supplements to it. There are also a number of special studies in this field.

few, and these are restricted to a narrow field, notably that of the kitchen: *sauerkraut, leberwurst, ravioli, smörgaas, egg foo young, matzoh, borsch, chile con carne*. The influence of alien grammatical constructions on American English is negligible, and when apparent is frequently humorous in intention, for instance in the unidiomatic inversions: *food* I have to cook for him; *dresses* he says I can buy, etc. Here the intonation also undertakes to imitate a foreign model, thus emphasising the humorous tone.[6]

It would be hazardous to attempt any prophecy now concerning the future relations of British and American English. The fate of the language as a whole is of course bound up with factors lying outside of the sphere of pure linguistics. In general it may be said that despite the persistence of regional dialects in both countries, the tendency in both is towards a single national language. This condition is in turn dependent for both on the extension of advanced education to the utmost possible and the abolishment of class barriers. Notwithstanding the divergencies manifest between American and British speech on certain levels, the language of cultured communication still resists any marked separation of the two; notwithstanding the attachment to native linguistic conservatism in both England and America (probably more conscious in England than in America), modern technology in communication may be counted on to bring closer these two important parts of the English-speaking world and to level out the differences between them. There was a time when American patriots deplored the servile imitation of British models; there is a time now when British purists deplore the influx of Yankee phraseology. It is possible that the roles may be reversed once more, and then ultimately the reasons for deploring one way or the other may disappear as peoples draw closer together in a cultural exchange where spatial separation means very little. But these are purely speculative matters for the present. We can do no more at the moment than indicate their existence and record the situation as we see it now.[7]

STUDY QUESTIONS AND EXERCISES

1. Examine the dialogue in two current detective stories, one British and one American, that "use vernacular idiom for literary ex-

---

[6] On standard American intonation see Kenneth Pike, *Intonation of American English* (University of Michigan Press, 1946).

[7] In addition to authorities already cited, the student should consult W. N. Francis and R. I. McDavid, Jr., *The Structure of American English* (New York, 1958).

pression"; note and classify the differences between the two vernaculars. (Detective stories are likely to represent a range of social classes and to make much use of lively, realistic dialogue.)

2. To the British and American word pairs listed, add others from: (a) other selections in this text, (b) your own observation and experience, (c) acquaintances native to or familiar with England. Does your evidence confirm Mrs. Schlauch's view or H. L. Mencken's claim? From the same sources indicated above, what additional examples of differences in British and American inflected verbs can you provide, to supplement Mrs. Schlauch's list?

3. What are the "many meanings" of *set-up* at the present time, according to a recent dictionary? Compare these meanings with those given in an earlier edition of the same dictionary or a different dictionary of earlier date. How have new meanings or the dropping of meanings reflected social changes and language needs?

4. Which of the root-particle compounds listed are used figuratively but in their literal sense reflect such contexts as sports, occupations, or natural phenomena? Look up several of these terms or similar ones for which you recognize the literal meanings and several others for which you have no idea as to origin: which ones most frequently retain some of the literal sense in the figurative use (such as *knock-down, drag-out* applied to a political contest), and which ones have largely lost the literal significance? Can you arrive at any generalizations based on the specific examples?

5. Compare recent British and American news magazine entries dealing with the same event: what differences do you discover in: (a) basic vocabulary, (b) forms of words, (c) choice of words (formal or colloquial)? Which of the specific categories of linguistic traits cited by Schlauch do you observe? What specific problems, if any, did you have in understanding British English?

6. Supply further examples, in current American usage, of: (a) nouns as verbs, (b) verbs as nouns, (c) adjectives as nouns, singular and plural, (d) phrases as adjectives, (e) two or more nouns as a phrase, and (f) noun-adjective phrases.

7. Collect examples of space-saving constructions and word choice from a recent newspaper or news magazine. Which of your examples would not be used "in normal American discourse, whether oral or written"?

8. What are the current slang terms for the meanings listed by Schlauch? Are any of the slang terms she lists still current? Which ones, if any, would not be understood at present by your generation? Can you arrive at any generalization about the current slang terms, in comparison with the older ones listed? (Slang is further dealt with in Part 4.)

9. What factors in England and America contribute to the tendency toward "a single national language" in each country?

7

The Hallmarks of American

H. L. Mencken and Raven I. McDavid, Jr.

*In the following essay, H. L. Mencken describes the distinctive character-
istics of the English language as used in the United States. This selection is
from* The American Language *(1963) as abridged by Raven I. McDavid of
the University of Chicago. Mencken employs examples of usage gleaned
from his reading and from the reports of informants.*

The characters chiefly noted in American English are, first, its
general uniformity throughout the country; second, its impatient disregard for grammatical, syntactical and phonological rule and precedent;
and third, its large capacity (distinctly greater than that of the English
of present-day England) for taking in new words and phrases from outside sources, and for manufacturing them of its own materials.

The first of these characters has struck every observer, native and foreign. In place of the discordant local dialects of nearly all the other
major countries, including England, we have a general *Volkssprache* for
the whole nation, conditioned only by minor differences in pronunciation and vocabulary and by the linguistic struggles of various groups of
newcomers. No other country can show such linguistic solidarity, not
even Canada, for there a large minority of the population resists speaking English altogether. The Little Russian of the Ukraine is unintelligible to the citizen of Moscow; the northern Italian can scarcely follow a conversation in Sicilian; the Low German from Hamburg is a
foreigner in Munich; the Breton flounders in Gascony. Even in the
United Kingdom there are wide divergences. There are some regional
peculiarities in American English, and they will be examined in Chapter
VII, but all Americans use pretty much the same words in the same
way.

Of the intrinsic differences that separate American from English the
chief have their roots in the disparity between the environment and
traditions of the two peoples since the Seventeenth Century. The English have lived under a relatively stable social order, and it has impressed
upon their souls their characteristic respect for what is customary and
of good report. Their whole lives are regulated by a regard for precedent.

[Until the 1950s] the Americans felt no such restraint and acquired no such habit of conformity. They plunged to the other extreme, for life in their country put a high value upon the qualities of curiosity and daring, and so they acquired that character of restlessness, that disdain for the dead hand, which still broadly marks them. The American is not, of course, lacking in a capacity for discipline; he submits to leadership readily, and even to tyranny. But, curiously, it is not the leadership that is old and decorous that commonly fetches him, but the leadership that is new and extravagant [—even when, as in the demagogue-infested South, it purports to defend tradition]. He will resist dictation out of the past, but he will follow a new messiah with almost Russian willingness, and into the wildest vagaries of economics, religion, morals and speech. A new fallacy in politics spreads faster in the United States than anywhere else on earth, and so does a new revelation of God, or a new shibboleth, or metaphor, or piece of slang. The American likes to make his language as he goes along. A novelty loses nothing by the fact that it is a novelty, particularly if it meets the national fancy for the terse, the vivid and, above all, the bold and imaginative. The characteristic American habit of reducing complex concepts to the starkest abbreviations was already noticeable in colonial times, and such typical Americanisms as *O.K.*, *N.G.* and *P.D.Q.* have been traced back to the early days of the Republic. In so modest an operation as that which has evolved *bunk* from *buncombe* there is evidence of a phenomenon which the philologian recognizes as belonging to the most lusty stages of speech.

But more important than the sheer inventions, if only because more numerous, are the extensions of the vocabulary by the devices of rhetoric. The American, from the beginning, has been the most ardent of recorded rhetoricians. His politics bristles with pungent epithets; his whole history has been bedizened with tall talk; his fundamental institutions rest far more upon brilliant phrases than upon logical ideas. He exercises continually an incomparable capacity for projecting hidden and often fantastic relationships into his speech. Such a term as *rubberneck* is almost a complete treatise on American psychology; it has precisely the boldness and contempt for ordered forms that are so characteristically American. The same qualities are in *roughhouse, has-been, lame duck* and a thousand other such racy substantives, and in all the great stock of native verbs and adjectives. There is, indeed, but a shadowy boundary in these new coinages between the various parts of speech. *Corral*, borrowed from the Spanish, immediately becomes a verb and the father of an adjective. *Bust*, carved out of *burst*, erects itself into a noun. *Bum*, coming by way of an earlier *bummer* from the German, becomes noun, adjective, verb and adverb. Verbs are fashioned out of substantives: *to engineer, to stump, to hog, to style.* Others are made by torturing nouns with harsh affixes, as *to burglarize* and *to itemize*, or by groping for the root, as *to resurrect* and *to jell*. Yet others are changed from intransitive to transitive: a sleeping car *sleeps* thirty passengers.

All these processes are to be observed in the history of the English of England; at the time of its sturdiest growth they flourished. More than one observer has noted the likeness between the situation of American English today and that of British English at the end of the Sixteenth Century. The Englishmen of that time had not yet come under the yoke of grammarians and lexicographers, and were free to mold their language to the throng of new ideas that marked an era of adventure and expansion. Their situation closely resembled that of the American pioneers who swarmed into the West following the War of 1812, and they met linguistic needs with the same boldness. By a happy accident they had a group of men who could bring to the business of word-making a degree of ingenuity and taste far beyond the common; above all, they had the aid of a really first-rate genius, Shakespeare. The result was a renovation of old ways of speech and a proliferation of new and useful terms that has had no parallel, to date, save on this side of the Atlantic [and, to a lesser degree, in Australia]. Standard English, in the Eighteenth Century, succumbed to pedants whose ignorance of language processes was only equaled by their impudent assumption of authority: Swift, Horace Walpole, Thomas Gray of the oft-misquoted "Elegy" and, above all, Samuel Johnson. No eminent lexicographer was ever more ignorant of speechways than he was. In his Dictionary of 1755 he thundered idiotically against many words that are now universally recognized as sound English, e.g., to wabble, to bamboozle and touchy. To wabble he described as "low, barbarous," and to bamboozle and touchy as "low," and at other times he denounced to swap, to coax, to budge, fib, banter, fop, fun, stingy, swimmingly, row (in the sense of a disturbance), chaperon and to derange. Under the influence of Johnson and his Nineteenth Century apes, the Standard Southern dialect of English has been arrested in its growth and burdened with irrational affectations. Its tendency is to combat all that expansive gusto which made for its pliancy and resilience in the days of Shakespeare. In place of the old loose-footedness there is a preciosity which, in one direction, takes the form of clumsy artificialities in the spoken language, and in another shows itself in the even clumsier Johnsonese of so much current English writing—the jargon denounced by Sir Arthur Quiller-Couch in his Cambridge lectures [and more recently by Sir Ernest Gowers, of Her Majesty's Stationery Office[1]].

American has so far escaped such suffocating formalism. Of course, we have our occasional practitioners of the authentic English jargon [and have seen some weird mutations develop under the green thumbs of federal bureaucrats, educationists, literary critics and the gray-flanneled admen of Madison Avenue]. "Once upon a time," says Jacques

---

[1] [Plain Words, London, 1948; The ABC of Plain Words, London, 1951; The Complete Plain Words, London, 1954.]

Barzun, of Columbia University, "American speech was really known for its racy, colloquial creations—*barnstorm, boom, boost, bulldoze, pan out, splurge* and so on. Now it is the flaccid polysyllable that expresses the country's mind. *Pioneer* has yielded to *pedant*, and one begins to wonder whether the German word-order had better not be adopted to complete the system."[2] What fevers Barzun, of course, is the artificial pseudo-English that schoolma'ams, whether in panties or in pantaloons, try to foist upon their victims, and the even worse jargon that Dogberrys in and out of office use for their revelations to the multitude. But in the main our faults lie in precisely the opposite direction. That is to say, we incline toward a directness of statement which, at its greatest, lacks restraint and urbanity altogether, and toward a hospitality which often admits novelties for the mere sake of their novelty, and is quite uncritical of the difference between a genuine improvement in succinctness and clarity, and mere extravagant raciness.

This revolt against conventional bounds and restraints is most noticeable, of course, on the lower levels of American speech. But even in the upper regions there are rebels aplenty, some of such authority that it is impossible to dismiss them. A glance through the speeches of Woodrow Wilson, a conscientious purist and Anglomaniac, reveals in a few moments half a dozen locutions that an Englishman in like position would certainly hesitate to use, among them *we must get a move on*,[3] *to gumshoe*,[4] and *that is going some*.[5] John Dewey, the country's most respectable metaphysician, unhesitatingly used *dope* for *opium*.[6] In recent years certain English magnificoes have shown signs of going the same route, but whenever they yield they are accused, and rightly, of succumbing to American influence.

Let American confront a novel problem alongside English, and immediately its superior imaginativeness and resourcefulness become obvious. *Movie* is better than *cinema* [—though the English *telly* excels *video* or even *TV*]. *Billboard* is better than *hoarding*. *Officeholder* is more honest, more picturesque, more thoroughly Anglo-Saxon than *public servant*. Turn to the terminology of *railroading* (itself, by the way, an Americanism): its creation fell upon the two peoples equally, but they tackled the job independently. The English, seeking a figure to describe the wedge-shaped fender in front of a locomotive, called it

---

[2] How to Suffocate the English Language, *Saturday Review of Literature*, Feb. 13, 1943, p. 3.

[3] Speech before the Chamber of Commerce Convention, Washington, Feb. 19, 1916.

[4] Wit and Wisdom of Woodrow Wilson, comp. by Richard Linthicum; New York, 1916, p. 54.

[5] *Ibid.*, p. 56.

[6] *New Republic*, Dec. 24, 1919, p. 116.

a *plough*; the American gave it the pungent name of *cowcatcher*. So with the casting which guides the wheels from one rail to another. The English called it a *crossing-plate*; the Americans, more responsive to the suggestion in its shape, called it a *frog*. One pictures the common materials of English dumped into a pot, exotic flavorings added, and the bubblings assiduously and expectantly skimmed. "When we Americans are through with the English language," says Mr. Dooley, "it will look as if it had been run over by a musical comedy."

All this boldness of conceit, of course, makes for vulgarity. It flowers in such barbaric inventions as *tasty, goof* and *semi-occasional*. But vulgarity, after all, means no more than yielding to natural impulses in the face of conventional inhibitions—the heart of all healthy language-making. The history of English, like the history of American and of every other living tongue, is a history of vulgarisms that, by their accurate meeting of real needs, have forced their way into sound usage, and even into the lifeless catalogues of the grammarians. In our own case the greater conservatism of the English restrains our native tendency to go too far, but the process itself is as inexorable in its workings as the precession of the equinoxes, and if we yield to it more eagerly than the English, it is only a proof, perhaps, that the future of what was once the Anglo-Saxon tongue lies on this side of the water.

Attempts to force the language into a strait jacket all come to grief in America, though the schoolma'am to this day clings to the doctrine that there is such a thing as "correct English," that its principles have been laid down for all time by the English purists and that she is under a moral obligation to inculcate it. But not many American grammarians above the level of writers of school texts subscribe to any such idea. They have learned by their studies that every healthy language has ways of its own, and that those of vernacular American are very far from those of Johnsonese English. Said Robert G. Pooley in his presidential address to the National Council of Teachers of English in 1941:

> American English may be derided by conservative critics for the readiness with which neologisms become accepted and flash overnight to all parts of our land, but the fact itself is a sign of health. The purpose of a language is to communicate; if a new word or a new phrase carries with it a freshness of meaning, a short cut to communication, it is a desirable addition to our tongue, no matter how low its source, or how questionable its etymology. We need not fear word creation as harmful; what we must fear is crystallization, the preservation of a conventional vocabulary by a limited minority who resent the normal steady changes which inevitably must take place within a language. . . . We need not fear exuberance. What we must fear and guard against is senility, the complacency of old age, which is content with things as they are and mockingly derisive of change.[7]

---

[7] One People, One Language, *EJ*, Vol. XXXI, Feb. 1942, pp. 110–20.

2. What is an Americanism?

As we have seen, Americanisms were first defined by the Rev. John Witherspoon in 1781 as "ways of speaking peculiar to this country." Pickering in turn divided them into three categories:

1. "We have formed some new words."
2. "To some old ones, that are still in use in England, we have affixed new significations."
3. "Others, which have been long obsolete in England, are still retained in common use among us."

The other early writers on the subject did not attempt to define categories of Americanisms.[8] Noah Webster omitted all discussion of them from his "Dissertations on the English Language" (1789), and not before the preface of his American Dictionary of 1828 did he undertake any formal consideration of them:

> Language is the expression of ideas; and if the people of one country cannot preserve an identity of ideas they cannot retain an identity of language. Now, an identity of ideas depends materially upon the sameness of things or objects with which the people of the two countries are conversant. But in no two portions of the earth, remote from each other, can such identity be found. Even physical objects must be different. But the principal differences between the people of this country and of all others arise from different forms of government, different laws, institutions and customs.

The other lexicographers of the Webster era attempted no categories of Americanisms: David Humphreys, whose glossary of 1815 has been noticed; and Theodoric Romeyn Beck, whose "Notes on Mr. Pickering's Vocabulary" was published in 1830. Robley Dunglison, in the articles headed "Americanisms" in the *Virginia Museum* for 1829–30, contented himself with setting up two classes—"old words used in a new sense," and "new words of indigenous origin." He excluded old words preserved or revived in America in their original sense. Also, he frowned upon native inventions that were not absolutely essential. The English travelers who denounced Americanisms were negligent about defining them. William C. Fowler, in his brief chapter on "American Dialects" in

---

[8] One of them, the Rev. Jonathan Boucher, alleged in the preface to his Glossary of Archaic and Provincial Words (2nd. ed., London, 1832, p. xlix) that the only additions the Americans had made to the English vocabulary were "such as they have adapted either from naval or mercantile men, with whom, on their first settlement, they were principally connected, or else from the aboriginal inhabitants," but the evidence offered by a poem from his hand, printed in the same volume, was strongly against him.

"The English Language" (1850), offered the following formidable classification, the first after Pickering:

1. Words borrowed from other languages.
   a. Indian, as *Kennebec, Ohio, sagamore, succotash.*
   b. Dutch, as *boss, stoop.*
   c. German, as *spuke* [?], *sauerkraut.*
   d. French, as *bayou, cache, levee.*
   e. Spanish, as *calaboose, hacienda, rancho.*
   f. Negro, as *buckra.*
2. Words "introduced from the necessity of our situation, in order to express new ideas."
   a. Words "connected with and flowing from our political institutions," as *selectman, presidential, mass meeting, lynch law, help* (for *servants*).
   b. Words "connected with our ecclesiastical institutions," as *associational, to fellowship.*
   c. Words "connected with a new country," as *lot, squatter.*
3. Miscellaneous Americanisms.
   a. Words and phrases become obsolete in England, as *talented, off-set* (for *set-off*), *back and forth* (for *backward and forward*).
   b. Old words and phrases "which are now merely provincial in England," as *hub, to wilt.*
   c. Nouns formed from verbs by adding the French suffix *-ment*, as *publishment, requirement.*
   d. Forms of words "which fill the gap or vacancy between two words which are approved," as *obligate* (between *oblige* and *obligation*) and *variate* (between *vary* and *variation*).
   e. "Certain compound terms for which the English have different compounds," as *bookstore* (*bookseller's shop*), *bottom land* (*interval-land*), *clapboard* (*pale*), *seaboard* (*seashore*).
   f. "Certain colloquial phrases, apparently idiomatic, and very expressive," as *to cave in, to fork over, to hold on, to stave off.*
   g. Intensives, "often a matter of mere temporary fashion," as *dreadful, powerful.*
   h. "Certain verbs expressing one's state of mind, but partially or timidly," as *to calculate, to expect* (*to think* or *believe*), *to guess, to reckon.*
   i. "Certain adjectives, expressing not only quality, but one's subjective feelings in regard to it," as *clever, grand, smart, ugly.*
   j. Abridgments, as *stage* (for *stagecoach*), *spry* (for *sprightly*).
   k. "Quaint or burlesque terms," as *to tote, humbug, loafer, plunder* (for *baggage*), *rock* (for *stone*).
   l. "Low expressions, mostly political," as *locofoco, hunker, to get the hang of.*
   m. "Ungrammatical expressions, disapproved by all," as *do don't, used to could, there's no two ways about it.*

John Russell Bartlett, in the second edition of his "Glossary of Words and Phrases Usually Regarded as Peculiar to the United States" (1859), offered nine classes:

1. Archaisms, *i.e.*, old English words, obsolete, or nearly so, in England, but retained in use in this country.

2. English words used in a different sense from what they are in England. "These include many names of natural objects differently applied."

3. Words which have retained their original meaning in the United States, though not in England.

4. English provincialisms adopted into general use in America.

5. New-coined words, which owe their origin to the productions or to the circumstances of the country.

6. Words borrowed from European languages, especially the French, Spanish, Dutch and German.

7. Indian words.

8. Negroisms.

9. Peculiarities of pronunciation.

Alfred L. Elwyn confined his "Glossary of Supposed Americanisms" (1859) to archaic English words surviving in America, and sought only to prove that they had come down "from our remotest ancestry" and were thus undeserving of English scorn. Schele de Vere's "Americanisms" (1872) followed Bartlett, concentrating on borrowings from the Indian languages and from the French, Spanish and Dutch. But John S. Farmer, in his "Americanisms Old and New" (1889), ventured upon a new classification, prefacing it with the following definition:

> An Americanism may be defined as a word or phrase, old or new, employed by general or respectable usage in America in a way not sanctioned by the best standards of the English language. . . . However, the term has come to possess a wider meaning, and it is now applied not only to words and phrases which can be so described, but also to the new and legitimately born words adapted to the general needs and usages, to the survivals of an older type of English than that now current in the mother country, and to the racy, pungent vernacular of Western life.

He then proceeded to this classification:

1. Words and phrases of purely American derivation, embracing words originating in:
   a. Indian and aboriginal life.
   b. Pioneer and frontier life.
   c. The church.
   d. Politics.
   e. Trades of all kinds.
   f. Travel, afloat and ashore.
2. Words brought by colonists, including:
   a. The German element.
   b. The French.
   c. The Spanish.
   d. The Dutch.

   e. The Negro.
   f. The Chinese.
  3. Names of American things, embracing:
   a. Natural products.
   b. Manufactured articles.
  4. Perverted English words.
  5. Obsolete English words still in good use in America.
  6. English words, American by inflection and modification.
  7. Odd and ignorant popular phrases, proverbs, vulgarisms and colloquialisms, cant and slang.
  8. Individualisms.
  9. Doubtful and miscellaneous.

Sylva Clapin's "New Dictionary of Americanisms" (1902) reduced these categories to four:

  1. Genuine English words, obsolete or provincial in England, and universally used in the United States.
  2. English words conveying, in the United States, a different meaning from that attached to them in England.
  3. Words introduced from other languages than the English: French, Dutch, Spanish, German, Indian, etc.
  4. Americanisms proper, *i.e.*, words coined in the country, either representing some new idea or peculiar product.

Richard H. Thornton's "American Glossary" (1912) substituted the following:

  1. Forms of speech now obsolete or provincial in England, which survive in the United States, such as *allow, bureau, fall, gotten, guess.*
  2. Words and phrases of distinctly American origin, such as *belittle, lengthy, lightning rod, to darken one's door, to bark up the wrong tree, blind tiger, cold snap.*
  3. Nouns which indicate quadrupeds, birds, trees, articles of food, etc., that are distinctively American, such as *ground hog, hangbird, hominy, live oak, locust, opossum.*
  4. Names of persons and classes of persons, and of places, such as *Buckeye, Hoosier, Old Hickory, Dixie, Gotham,* the *Bay State,* the *Monumental City.*
  5. Words which have assumed a new meaning, such as *card, clever, fork, help, penny, plunder.*

In addition, Thornton added a provisional class of "words and phrases of which I have found earlier examples in American than in English writers; . . . with the *caveat* that further research may reverse the claim"—a class offering specimens in *alarmist, capitalize, horse of another colour* [sic!], *the jig's up, omnibus bill* and *whitewash.*

Gilbert M. Tucker's "American English" (1921) attempted to reduce all Americanisms to two grand divisions:

>   1. Words and phrases that originated in America and express
> something that the British have always expressed differently if they
> have mentioned it at all.
>   2. Words and phrases that would convey to a British ear a dif-
> ferent meaning from that which they bear in this country.

To this he added seven categories of locution *not* to be regarded as
Americanisms:

>   1. Words and phrases stated by the previous compiler himself
> to be of foreign (*i.e.*, chiefly of English) origin, like Farmer's *hand-
> me-down*.
>   2. Names of things exclusively American, but known abroad
> under the same name, such as *moccasin*.
>   3. Names of things invented in the United States, like *drawing-
> room car*.
>   4. Words used in this country in a sense hardly distinguishable
> from that they bear in England, like *force* for a gang of laborers.
>   5. Nonce words like Mark Twain's *cavalieress*.
>   6. Perfectly regular and self-explanatory compounds, like *office-
> holder, planing machine, ink slinger* and *flytime*.
>   7. Purely technical terms, such as those employed in baseball.

A glance at these discordant classifications shows that they hamper
inquiry by limiting its scope. They leave out of account some of the
most salient characters of a living language. Only Bartlett and Farmer
establish a separate category of Americanisms produced by phonological changes, though even Thornton is obliged to take notice of such
forms as *bust* and *bile*, and even Tucker lists *buster*. Obviously many
words and phrases excluded by Tucker's *Index Expurgatorius* are genuine Americanisms. Why bar *moccasin* because it is also known in England? So is *caucus*, which he includes. He is also too hostile to characteristic American compounds like *officeholder* and *flytime*. True enough,
their materials are good English, with no change in the meaning of
their component parts, but they were put together in the United States,
and an Englishman always sees a certain strangeness in them. *Pay dirt,
passageway, night rider, know-nothing* and *hog wallow* are equally compounded of pure English metal, and yet he lists them all. Again, he is
too ready to bar archaisms. It is idle to prove that Chaucer used *to
guess*. The important thing is that the English abandoned it centuries
ago, and that when they happen to use it today they are conscious that
it is an Americanism. *Baggage* is in Shakespeare, but not often in the
London *Times*. Here Mr. Tucker's historical principles run away with
his judgment. His book, the labor of nearly forty years, is full of shrewd

observations and persuasive contentions, but is sometimes excessively dogmatic.

James Maitland did not categorize Americanisms in "The American Slang Dictionary," [9] nor did Brander Matthews in his "Americanisms and Briticisms," [10] nor did George Philip Krapp in "The English Language in America." [11] The editors of "A Dictionary of American English," when they brought out their first volume in 1938, contented themselves with saying in their preface that "the different types of words and phrases" listed in it could "be more readily ascertained by inspection than by any attempt at classification," but their chief, Sir William Craigie, went into rather more detail in a paper published in 1940.[12] After excluding loan words, the topographical terms derived from them, and "composite names of plants and trees, animals, birds and fishes, of the type *black alder, black bear, black bass,* etc.," he listed the following categories:

> 1. Words showing "the addition of new senses to existing words and phrases."
> 2. "New derivative forms and attributive collocations or other compounds."
> 3. "Words not previously in use, and not adapted from other languages of the American continent."

[Finally, in the Preface to the "Dictionary of Americanisms," M. M. Mathews defines an Americanism as a word or expression or meaning that originated in what is now the United States. He is less concerned than the DAE with American survivals of words or meanings that have disappeared in England. And like his predecessors he avoids the complicated problem of the difference in status of the same word or meaning.]

The most scientific and laborious collection of Americanisms, before the DAE, was Thornton's. It presents an enormous mass of quotations, carefully dated; but its very dependence upon quotations limits it chiefly to the written language, and so the enormously richer materials of the spoken language are passed over, particularly the materials evolved during the past generation. In vain one searches for *buttinski, sure* as an

---

[9] Chicago, 1891.

[10] First published in *Harper's Magazine,* 1891, pp. 214–22; republished in Americanisms and Briticisms, With Other Essays on Other Issues; New York, 1892, pp. 1 ff.

[11] Two vols.; New York, 1925. In the chapter on Vocabulary in Vol. I, Krapp discussed Americanisms at great length, but did not undertake a formal classification of them. He was greatly inclined to pooh-pooh them.

[12] The Growth of American English, I, *SPE Tract,* No. LVI; Oxford, 1940, p. 204.

adverb, and *well* as a sort of general equivalent of the German *also*. These grammatical and syntactical tendencies lay beyond the scope of Thornton, and some of them lie outside the field of the DAE and DA, but they are prime concerns of any student who essays to get at the inner spirit of the American language. Its difference from Standard English is not merely a difference in vocabulary, to be disposed of in an alphabetical list; it is also a difference in pronunciation, in intonation, in conjugation and declension, in metaphor and idiom, in the whole fashion of using words. The vocabulary, of course, must be given first attention, for in it the earliest American divergences are embalmed, and it tends to grow richer and freer year after year, but attention must be paid to materials and ways of speech that are less obvious, particularly to tendencies in vulgar American, the great reservoir of the language, and perhaps the forerunner of what it will be on higher levels in the years to come.

STUDY QUESTIONS AND EXERCISES

1. Why and how has the American language resisted the formalism often found in British English?

2. Look up *character* in the dictionary. Does Mencken use the term in a standard way in his first two paragraphs? What related word might seem preferable?

3. Summarize the characteristics of American English that Mencken discusses and evaluate his attitude toward each of them.

4. Check several of Mencken's examples of the extension of American vocabulary in the *Dictionary of Americanisms, Dictionary of American English,* and *Webster's Third New International Dictionary* to determine when the changes took place and how long it took for them to be accepted as standard usage.

5. Examine Mencken's *The American Language* and its *Supplements* for pertinent illustrations of the unconventionality of the grammar and vocabulary of American English. On the basis of your findings discuss the various aspects of unconventionality in the language.

6. What is Mencken's attitude toward the prescriptive grammarians? Although Mencken is more concerned with vocabulary than with grammar, which words or group of words that he discusses involve questions of grammar?

7. Does Mencken's style illustrate the "hallmarks of American"? Are American words and idioms prominent in this selection? Check the etymology of his most notable words.

8. Except in the terms cited as examples, would a British reader have any difficulty in understanding Mencken? Considering the

context of Mencken's article and the context in which most of the italicized words would be used, what generalization can you make about British and American literary language and British and American colloquial language?

9. What, according to Robert Pooley, should be feared in language and what need not be feared? Compare his attitude with that of Bergen Evans. Is there evidence in Evans to show that Pooley's fears are not groundless? Explain.

10. Examine carefully the definitions and classifications of Americanisms cited here from William C. Fowler to Gilbert M. Tucker. Why are they "discordant classifications"? Consult a text on expository writing for discussion of principles of sound classification; then work out a classification that will cover the various categories of Americanisms represented in the classifications Mencken cites, without omissions or overlapping.

11. What are the implications of the concluding sentence as to the sources and the process of language growth and enrichment?

8

Language on the American Frontier

Frederic G. Cassidy

The settling and extension of the American frontier by hardy pioneers have contributed much to our language. Professor Cassidy of the University of Wisconsin illustrates various ways that speakers and writers on the frontier have enriched the language. This essay appeared in Walker D. Wyman and Clifton B. Kroeber, eds., The Frontier in Perspective *(1957).*

It is currently fashionable, and has been for some years, to refer to the language we speak in the United States as "the American language." This phrase may, of course, be produced in several tones of voice—a patriotic tone, a tone vibrating with manifest destiny, a naïve tone, or a chauvinistic one. Our most recently published dictionary has rushed forth with the clamorous title of the *New World Dictionary of the American Language*—betraying clearly the tone of voice of its business office, which is out to make Americanism pay.

The student of language, however, uses this phrase in the tone of voice indicating quotation marks. By no acceptable *linguistic* definition can our language be called "the American language"; it is not a separate speech unintelligible to speakers in the British Isles, Australia, or Canada; it is merely one variant form of the language which already has an established name: the English language. Not even the sturdiest isolationist can deny the historic connections.

The term "the American Language" was given currency, as we all know, by the great popular success of H. L. Mencken's book, first published in 1919, of which it was the title. Mencken was nothing if not bold; he had an ax to grind; he enjoyed telling the English where to get off *at*. Evidently this struck a note of welcome to many American ears, for his book became surprisingly a best seller. Scholars, therefore, even while rejecting the linguistic validity of his phrase, owe Mencken a considerable debt of gratitude for at last making the public intelligently aware—as many a better scholar before him had failed to do—that among the most interesting achievements of our new nation has been a characteristically different idiom. The colony which grew away from the homeland politically and has since come of age has also developed its own ways of speech. It is fair to say that if the English language had only one pole or center a hundred years ago, today it has two. And this bipolarity is the direct result of what happened on the American frontier.

To begin with, of course, America itself was the frontier: so are all colonies with respect to their parent lands. The most striking characteristic of a frontier society is its fluidity. True enough, there is considerable carry-over of habits, customs, institutions, ideals from the homeland, insofar as these are desirable and possible under the new conditions. But the important thing is that the fixity, the settled and confining structure of society in the old country, is shaken loose. Thus the new country gives a new chance. It demands fresh ways—and it makes fresh ways possible.

The migrations of humanity that take place from time to time, seen through the long eye of history, are like the flowing of a stream of volcanic lava. Driven by an outburst from a center of pressure, this stream pours out, running wherever it may, over the unresisting flats, around the rockier protuberances, picking up and incorporating many things in its path, ever cooling and hardening as it goes, but always with that glowing, fluid edge. This edge is the frontier.

So in the past three centuries the pressures of Europe flung out the crowd of adventurers and refugees, the rebellious and the ambitious, the disinherited and the farsighted. To America they flowed, thinly at first, spreading along the coast, trickling inland in the lower places, slowed by the mountains and resistance of Indians, but always with the hot edge rising and creeping on. At last, after a century and a half the lava stream broke into the plains and rolled westward ineluctably. In some places it eddied to a stop, cooled and became sluggish; but there was always the hot edge, the frontier, flowing on and on, taking many new shapes, swallowing many things that it came upon, some of its own currents mingling with others or overflowing them wholly—molten, hungry, seething with bubbles of humanity.

What of language in all this? It would be impossible to imagine such a movement of peoples as taking place without the use of language. Language is at once the exclusive and the most characteristic property of human beings: in the movement to the world frontiers, language went along. The first comers, of course, spoke some variety of their European tongue as it existed at the time. Limiting ourselves to English, we may say that on the ships of the explorers probably every sort of local or dialectal speech could have been heard. Settlements, when those were made, were sometimes less miscellaneous linguistically, but they were never "pure." Mixture, a characteristic of the frontier, was present too in the settlers' speech.

In a valuable study of New England pronunciation published in 1927, Professor Anders Orbeck looked into the places of origin of some 680 early English-speaking settlers of the towns of Plymouth, Water-

town, and Dedham, Massachusetts.[1] He discovered that among the
number there was one settler each from Scotland, Wales, and the Isle
of Man; less than ten each from nineteen shires of England; and that
the greatest number clearly came from Norfolk, Suffolk, Essex, and
London. Stated in terms of the major language areas of England, this is
to say that 7 per cent came from the North, 4 per cent from the West
Midlands, 9 per cent from the Southwest, 5 per cent from the South-
east, and 75 per cent from the East Midlands. If this may be generally
taken as representing the early settlement of New England, it means
that the pronunciation and usage which furnished the basis of standard
British English clearly predominated also on the New England frontier.

Evidence for the Virginia colony is not as satisfactory, but the language of the East Midlands seems also to have predominated there. Nevertheless, there was the other 25 per cent not from the East Midlands—
an admixture which left its effect—and the compromise speech of the
colonies was thus begun with elements deriving from the homeland
even before elements newly acquired by the settlers could make themselves felt.

As this first flow of settlement in eastern New England began to
cool, there came another of a somewhat different sort, deriving more
from the North and West of England than from the East Midlands.
Since lands along the coast were by now taken up, the new settlers
moved inland, and eventually their speech became dominant in New
England west of the Connecticut River, in the upper Hudson River
Valley, and in eastern Pennsylvania. Then this current spread out farther to the south and west, and so the speech differences of these later
comers took their place on the new frontier and rolled across the plains
and mountains to the Pacific.

To note only the most striking linguistic effect of this, one may look
at the loss or retention of post-vocalic *r* in such words as *bar* and *barn*
in the United States today. Following the pattern of London and British standard pronunciation, the Atlantic coastal strip both north and
south generally drops the *r*—*baa, baan*. The inland area, following the
pattern of the North of England, which eventually covered most of the
rest of the country, retained the *r*—*bar, barn*. This latter wave has
flowed so strongly that there appears to be a backwash today toward
the East. It may even be that within a few generations the *r*-usage of
the country at large may engulf the *r*-less areas of the East.

The American colonies, then, were the linguistic frontier of the
motherland, with two main currents of regional influence flowing in.
And from a mingling of these, the colonies soon produced their own
linguistic frontier. The development of the language in the old country

---

[1] *Early New England Pronunciation as Reflected in Some Seventeenth Century
Town Records* (Ann Arbor, Mich., 1927), 119 *ff*.

and in the new seems indeed to have moved, for a time, in opposite directions. In Britain, a certain local type of speech—that of London and the near-by shires—was becoming more and more accepted as a standard for educated, literary, and official use, emerging steadily as the upper-class language in a very class-conscious society. In contrast, in America generally and especially on the frontier, the dominant speech was of middle-class origin, and in its relatively classless society, there was nothing really parallel to British upper-class speech. The language has been refined and spread by education—and that not without continuing British influence—but the historic differences established in colonial days have not disappeared.

The separation between American English and British English did not go unnoticed. Travelers had commented on the colonial ways of speech before the Revolution, but the emotions which that event aroused brought the matter into greater prominence. The first list of Americanisms, that of John Witherspoon, appeared in 1781; the next, collected by John Pickering, in 1816.[2] Rather than quote from these, however, I turn to the Diary kept by the English novelist, Captain Frederick Marryat, who visited the new United States in 1837–38. Marryat's account shows keen observation of features which we still use daily. He writes:[3]

> Many English words are used in a very different sense from that which we attach to them; for instance: a *clever* person in America means an amiable good tempered person, and the Americans make the distinction by saying, I mean English clever.
> Our clever is represented by the word *smart*.
> The verb *to admire* is also used in the East, instead of the verb *to like*.
> "Have you ever been at Paris?"
> "No; but I should *admire* to go."
> A Yankee description of a clever woman:—"Well, now, she'll walk right into you, and talk to you like a book"; or, as I have heard them say, "she'll talk you out of sight."
> The word ugly is used for cross, ill-tempered. "I did feel so *ugly* when he said that."
> *Bad* is used in an odd sense: it is employed for awkward, uncomfortable, sorry:—
> "I did feel so *bad* when I read that"—awkward.
> "I have felt quite *bad* about it ever since"—uncomfortable.
> "She was so *bad*, I thought she would cry"—sorry.
> And as bad is tantamount to *not good*, I have heard a lady say,

[2] H. L. Mencken, *The American Language* (4th rev. ed., New York, 1936), Ch. II; *Supplement I* (1945), Ch. II.

[3] *A Diary in America, with Remarks on its Institutions* (Philadelphia, 1839), II, 33–38.

"I don't feel *at all good*, this morning."

Mean is occasionally used for ashamed.

"I never felt so mean in my life."

"We reckon this very handsome scenery, sir," said an American to me, pointing to the landscape.

"I consider him very truthful," is another expression.

"He stimulates too much."

"He dissipates awfully."

And they are very fond of using the noun as a verb, as—

"I *suspicion* that's a fact."

"I *opinion* quite the contrary."

The word *considerable* is in considerable demand in the United States. In a work in which the letters of the party had been given to the public as specimens of good style and polite literature, it is used as follows:—

"My dear sister, I have taken up the pen early this morning, as I intend to write *considerable*."

The word *great* is oddly used for fine, splendid.

"She's the *greatest* gal in the whole Union."

"Are you cold, Miss?" said I to a young lady, who pulled the shawl closer over her shoulders.

"Some," was the reply.

The English *what?* implying that you did not hear what was said to you, is changed in America to the word *how?*

"I reckon," "I calculate," "I guess," are all used as the common English phrase, "I suppose." Each term is said to be peculiar to different states, but I found them used every where, one as often as the other. . . .

The verb "to fix" is universal. It means to do any thing.

"Shall I fix it right away?"—*i.e.* "Shall I do it immediately?" . . . . brush your coat, or *get ready* your breakfast first?"

Right away, for immediately or at once, is very general.

"Shall I fix it right away?"—*i.e.* "Shall I do it immediately?" . . . .

"I'm a *gone 'coon*" implies "I am distressed—or ruined or lost." I once asked the origin of this expression, and was very gravely told as follows:—

"There is a Captain Martin Scott in the United States army who is a remarkable shot with a rifle. He was raised, I believe, in Vermont. His fame was so considerable through the State, that even the animals were aware of it. He went out one morning with his rifle, and spying a raccoon upon the upper branches of a high tree, brought his gun up to his shoulder; when the raccoon, perceiving it, raised his paw up for a parley. "I beg your pardon, mister," said the raccoon very politely; "but may I ask you if your name is *Scott?*"—"Yes," replied the captain.—"*Martin Scott?*" continued the raccoon.—"Yes," replied the captain.—"*Captain* Martin Scott?" still continued the animal.—"Yes," replied the captain, "Captain Martin Scott."—"Oh! then," says the animal, "I may just as well come down, for I'm a *gone 'coon*."

Marryat sums up his impressions by saying that in provincial use the language has become "debased"—which is not surprising. Even the upper classes of Americans, however, he remarks, "do not . . . speak or pronounce English according to our standard; they appear to have no exact rule to guide them. . . . In fact, every one appears to be independent, and pronounces just as he pleases.

"But it is not for me to decide the very momentous question, as to which nation speaks the best English. The Americans generally improve upon the inventions of others; probably they may have improved upon our language."

Judging by his general tone, I do not think that Marryat is sneering here. Certainly there were plenty of Americans, flushed with revolutionary ardor, who believed that they *could* improve on the English language. One of these, of course, was the man who taught America to spell, the great lexicographer, Noah Webster. In 1789, Webster proclaimed his eagerness for a new language in the following words:[4]

> As an independent nation our honor requires us to have a system of our own, in language as well as government. Great Britain, whose children we are, and whose language we speak, should no longer be *our* standard; for the taste of her writers is already corrupted, and her language on the decline. But if it were not so, she is at too great a distance to be our model and to instruct us in the principles of our own tongue.
>
> Several circumstances [he continues] render a future separation of the American tongue from the English necessary and unavoidable. [These he next discusses, then concludes:] We have therefore the fairest opportunity of establishing a national language and of giving it uniformity and perspicuity, in North America, that ever presented itself to mankind. Now is the time to begin the plan.

Webster's prediction, of course, has not come true. The separation between British and American speech has grown no greater than it was in his time, at least at the standard level. If anything, modern communication and cultural interchange have reduced the breach. What the prediction signified in its time, however, was that the differences had become too striking to ignore; that the newly independent nation was in no disposition to imitate what now seemed a foreign model; that, on the contrary, some fruits of the linguistic frontier seemed desirable and defensible. Webster's separatism is a rationalization of a real situation.

We may now look in some detail at the elements of which the new American English was formed. When the words which the colonists had brought proved inadequate to the new environment, they responded in three chief ways: they borrowed from the Indians or from

---

[4] *Dissertations on the English Language* . . . (Boston, 1789), I, Introduction.

other Europeans, they gave new meanings to old words, they made new combinations. It is interesting to notice at what time the various Indian words, for example, came in. Naturally enough, the first of these were the names of animals and plants of the new world, especially those valuable for food.

Even before 1620, *moose, raccoon, opossum, terrapin, persimmon, moccasin, tomahawk,* and *totem* had entered the English language. Within the next thirty years, by the middle of the century, *muskrat, sachem, papoose, quahog, hominy, powwow, skunk, squash, squaw, wampum,* and *wigwam* had followed. Still other seventeenth-century borrowings were *hickory, manitou, woodchuck,* and *Tammany.* Eighteenth-century additions are *pecan, muskellunge, Catawba, succotash, catalpa, caucus;* and the nineteenth century saw the adoption of *chipmunk, sequoia, tamarack, mugwump, mackinaw, teepee, cayuse,* and climactically, at the very end of the century, *hooch.*

Some of these Indian words did not come directly: both *bayou* and *cisco* came through French—*bayou* in Louisiana from Choctaw *bayuk,* and *cisco* in the Great Lakes area. The name of this fish, *cisco,* is in fact an abbreviation of French *ciscoette,* itself an abbreviation of the Ojibwa *pemitewiskawet.* Thus, these Indian words have been naturalized first into French, then into English, the *-ette* suffix probably due to analogy with the common suffix that we have also borrowed in such words as *cigarette* and *quartette,* and the first syllable of *bayou* probably recalling French *baie.* The French habit of abbreviating long Indian words for simplicity is seen not only in *ciscoette,* but also in *caribou,* which they reduced from Algonkian *buccarebou.* They also shortened Indian tribal names: *Sioux* is all that they left of *Nadouessioux,* and the *ark* of *Ozark* is their abbreviation of *Arkansas.*

Another thing to notice is the succession of borrowings as the moving frontier brought the whites into contact with different tribes. Early loans were mostly from Algonkian languages, a few from Iroquois; across the Mississippi, more words were taken from the Sioux; still later the languages of the Northwest and Southwest were levied upon. We have two well-known words for an Indian dwelling: *wigwam* taken before 1628 from Algonkian, and *teepee* taken before 1872 from Siouan. *Hooch* is a western word, abbreviated from Tlingit *hootsnuwu.*

Indian terms have entered strikingly into our political language. The *powwows* of the red men, with their big meetings, deliberations, oratory, and dances—aided often enough by the white men's firewater— struck a responsive chord. Not only *powwow,* but *mugwump, Tammany, sachem,* and others testify to this influence. Nor should we forget that from Indian sources have come into the language a host of American place names, some euphonious, like *Ohio* and *Missouri,* others that fall less comfortably upon the ear, like *Ogunquit, Walla Walla, Keokuk, Puyallup,* and the now proverbial *Podunk.*

In the process of naturalization, words are not only abbreviated and otherwise simplified in pronunciation, but many are frankly made over and suited to English word patterns. The notorious example of this process is *woodchuck*, which makes us think of an animal which lives in the *woods*, and *chucks*. Everybody knows, of course, *what* it chucks, though nobody is certain how much it would if it could. All this accretion of nursery lore is due entirely to the naturalization of the word by speakers of *English:* its original in Algonkian has no such implications —it is simply the name for a kind of weasel, *wejack,* mistakenly applied.

As to the words which English-speakers on the American frontier borrowed from other Europeans, the chief sources were, of course, French and Spanish, though Dutch and German have also added their bit. The far-flung French outposts and colonies in the Great Lakes and Mississippi system have furnished several geographical terms: *butte, coulee* (probably first adopted in Wisconsin), *sault* (*Sault Ste. Marie* is the best known), *rapids, prairie.* From the intrepid *voyageurs* and *coureurs de bois* who made first contacts with the Indians of the interior come *portage* and *cache, calumet* and *lacrosse.* But the French loans have entered at every cultural level from the most homely upward: *shivaree* and *sashay, pumpkin* and *chowder, bureau* and *depot, cent, dime,* and *picayune,* and the word that has become utterly American in atmosphere of song and story—*levee.*

The direct Spanish influence came somewhat later but has been very marked and is still continuing. Few of our state names show the influence of French—*Vermont, Louisiana, Illinois,* possibly some others; many more are Spanish—*Florida, California, Nevada, Colorado, Arizona, Montana.* From Spanish have come the topographic terms *arroyo, mesa, canyon, sierra,* and *savannah,* to say nothing of *tornado.* Spanish names for plants and animals are particularly numerous: *alfalfa, marijuana, mosquito, bonito, palomino, armadillo, alligator* are purely Spanish, but the Spaniards have also passed on to us such originally Indian words as *avocado, yucca, mesquite, coyote,* and now *peyote.* We have discarded the name of the fish *tunny,* which came into British use through French, and have substituted the American word *tuna,* which came to us from the Spanish—who, by the way, got it from the English to begin with!

I will not attempt to go through the whole list of Spanish loans—it is too long; but let me at least suggest the fields to which these words belong. Food and drink—*tamale, barbecue, chili con carne, cafeteria;* building—*adobe, patio, plaza, pueblo;* clothing—*chaps, poncho, sombrero,* ten *gallon* hat; ranch life—*rodeo, stampede, corral, lariat, bronco, buckaroo, mustang;* legal and penal—*hoosegow, calaboose, desperado, vigilante;* mining—*bonanza* and *placer.*

Let me touch next, rapidly, on the Dutch and German loans. The Dutch, of course, had a successful colony centrally placed in the lower Hudson valley. From this point, their influence spread into southeastern New England, up the Hudson, and into New Jersey. Overrun by superior numbers, they nevertheless left several words that are essential to American English—some of which, indeed, have gone around the world—so *Yankee, boss,* and *Santa Claus.* Others in daily use are *cookie, cole slaw, caboose, scow, snoop,* and *spook.* German loans came considerably later and mostly refer to foods—*delicatessen, frankfurter, hamburger, wiener, noodle, pretzel, sauerkraut,* and so on; but some relate to education—*kindergarten, semester, seminar;* and to various other things less uplifting—*loafer, bum, dumb* (in the sense of stupid), *pinochle,* and *spiel.* Even the exclamation *ouch* is German, and the new suffix *-fest,* used in popular combinations such as *slug-fest* in boxing, *run-fest* in baseball, and *talk-fest,* which may be found at any *coffee-clutch.*

So much for foreign elements—there is no time to mention others taken from the Africans, the Irish, the Chinese, the Jews. All were incorporated in the flowing lava of the frontier and have become an inseparable part of it. We turn next to the English words which acquired a new meaning under frontier conditions. One remarkable example is the word *lumber.* In England it had meant, and still means, castoff material of any sort—what most Americans would call *junk.* The first task of the settlers in the new land, however, was to make clearings in the forest primeval. Trees were in the way; when cut down, they lay about everywhere. The wood from them, in fact, was so much lumber, in the old sense of the word. So it naturally acquired the new sense of *wood,* and by now *lumber* has displaced *timber* as the general term.

One other notorious example: *corn* in the old country had meant grain of any sort—wheat, barley, oats. On the American frontier, the new grain which was the most accessible and best suited to the climate, upon which the Indians depended and which they taught the white man to grow, was *maize.* The settlers began by calling it *Indian corn,* but that was immediately abbreviated to plain *corn.* From it was made *pone, hominy, suppawn, succotash.* American settlers adopted all of these—they even made it the basis of a drink. In Dr. Mitford Mathews' *Dictionary of Americanisms,* published in 1951, are listed no less than 151 words and phrases in which corn is used in its new sense—*cornbread, cornsilk, corn belt, cornbird, corn-cracker* are just a few of the commoner ones.

Then there is the third way in which the vocabulary has been increased: by forming new combinations. These too are very numerous, but a few of the more striking may be offered in approximately the order of their creation. From the seventeenth century: *log house, snowshoe, pine knot, bayberry;* from the eighteenth century: *salt lick, mountain laurel, horse-thief, minuteman, cotton gin;* and from the nineteenth century: *cocktail, gerrymander, sod fence, Indian giver, know-nothing, stern-wheeler, cowboy, mail order,* and *sideburns.*

The intimate connection of language with the frontier cannot be better demonstrated, however, than by showing the additions made in the course of a single exploration. Fortunately, the most famous one has been studied in Dr. E. H. Criswell's work entitled *Lewis and Clark: Linguistic Pioneers*.[5] The expedition lasted some twenty-eight months, from May, 1804, till September, 1806, and went from St. Louis through the Louisiana Territory to the Pacific and back. Of the 29 regular members of the group, nine are believed to have kept journals, and seven of these journals survive. Dr. Criswell has digested these painstakingly and offers the following conclusions: The seven writers, among them, used 1,107 Americanisms of all kinds, of which 583 were unrecorded before. In addition, their use of 301 words, meanings, and combinations is the earliest on record. As to the source of the words, 143 were new adoptions, 86 were words that were going out of use in Britain, and 91 were survivals of words already obsolete in Britain but still alive in America. A large number are names of fauna and flora newly encountered, and many relate to Indians, but there are all kinds. Examples of fresh combinations are *beaver pond, council lodge, tow-cord, Indian mush, melon-bug*. Some old words that acquire new meanings are *goldfinch, apron, button, run, bear claw*. The additions to the language made by this one expedition are impressive. Yet they represent only one small record, one small insight into what was a continuous, ebullient language activity by millions of others—scouts, Indian fighters, trappers, miners, settlers —a vast part of which went *un*recorded. There can be no question that hundreds of the verbal creations that bubbled up along the hot fringe of the frontier are now irrecoverably lost.

So far, we have been treating of the language chiefly in terms of words. But this is not enough. Language is not a mere collection of single items—it is an articulate thing varying in its style of expression; and this style as much as anything else goes to reflect the fluidity of the frontier, its infinite variety and unceasing change. In the general flow, some currents become strong enough to gain at least a temporary identity. They follow a course and leave a definite impress. The regional types of American English today reflect such larger currents, though time, widespread education, easy transportation and communication, and the restlessness of our population have done much to level out differences in the last fifty years. Only in the more isolated places where industrial society has not yet triumphed, where national broadcasting, national distribution of movies and reading materials have not swept everything before them, are local characteristics strongly preserved in present speech. Fortunately, however, American literature can furnish us quite accurate representations of some of the local types of language that mingled on the frontier a hundred years ago.

For New England, the *Biglow Papers* of James Russell Lowell may

---

[5] *University of Missouri Studies*, XV (April, 1940), 2.

be taken.[6] Lowell describes what he was attempting in them as follows: "I imagined to myself such an up-country man as I had often seen at anti-slavery gatherings, capable of district-school English, but always instinctively falling back into the natural stronghold of his homely dialect when heated to the point of self-forgetfulness. . . . To me the dialect was native, and spoken all about me when a boy."

Hosea Biglow has written a poem against war. His father, Ezekiel, writes an explanatory letter to the editor of the *Boston Courier*, to whom he is submitting the poem for publication. This is part of the letter:

> MISTER EDDYTER:—Our Hosea wuz down to Boston last week, and he see a cruetin Sarjunt a struttin round as popler as a hen with 1 chicking, with 2 fellers a drummin and fifin arter him like all nater. the sarjunt he thout Hosea hed n't gut his i teeth cut cos he looked a kindo's though he'd jest com down, so he cal'lated to hook him in, but Hosy would n't take none o' his sarse for all he hed much as 20 Rooster's tales stuck onto his hat and eenamost enuf brass a bobbin up and down on his shoulders and figureed on to his coat and trousis, let alone wut nater hed sot in his featers, to make a 6 pounder out on.
>
> wal, Hosea he com home considerabal riled, and arter I'd gone to bed I heern him a thrashin round like a short-tailed Bull in fli-time. The old Woman ses she to me ses she, Zekle, ses she, our Hosee's gut the chollery or suthin anuther ses she, don't you Bee skeered, ses I, he's oney amakin pottery, ses i, he's ollers on hand at thet ere busynes like Da & martin, and shure enuf, cum mornin, Hosy he cum down stares full chizzle, hare on eend and cote tales flyin, and sot rite of to go reed his varses to Parson Wilbur bein he haint any grate shows o' book larnin himself, bimeby he cum back and sed the parson wuz dreffle tickled with 'em as i hoop you will Be, and said they wuz True grit.
>
> Hosea ses taint hardly fair to call 'em hisn now, cos the parson kind o' slicked off sume of the last varses, but he told Hosee he didn't want to put his ore in to tetch to the Rest on 'em, bein they wuz veery well As they wuz, and then Hosy ses he sed suthin a nuther about Simplex Mundishes or sum such feller, but I guess Hosea kind o' didn't hear him, for I never hearn o' nobody o' that name in this villadge, and I've lived here man and boy 76 year cum next tater diggin, and thair aint no wheres a kitting spryer 'n I be.

The most characteristic quality of the pronunciation, as we can see, is a sort of choppiness, an emphatic accentuation which reduces words

---

[6] Quotations are from the preface to the second series of the *Biglow Papers* and from Paper No. 1 of the first series. Horace E. Scudder (ed.), *The Complete Poetical Works of James Russell Lowell* (Boston, 1924).

to their essentials, unstressed syllables tending to disappear entirely—
thus *recruiting* becomes *cruetin; calculated* becomes *cal'lated; always* is
ollers; dreadful, dreffle; ∼*mething, suthin; potato, tater;* and so on.
Present participles "drop their g's," but by compensation they usually
have the syllable "a" prefixed: *a drummin, a bobbin, a thrashin.* This
syllable "a" is used in other places too; it serves as a link between
strongly stressed words: "he looked *a* kindo's though. . . ."

The old pronunciation—it goes back to Shakespeare's day—of "ar"
where we would say "er" is found here in such words as *varses,* book
larnin, and of course *parson,* where, however, it has become standard.
Other old pronunciations are *riled* for *roiled,* and *nater* and *feater* for
nature and *feature.* Final "a" becomes "y" in *chollery* for *cholera,* and
Hosy for *Hosea.* "E" becomes "ee" in *skeered, eend, veery.*

But more characteristic even than details of pronunciation or the
choppy emphatic delivery is the use of lively popular metaphor, usually
drawn from the immediacies of life, often becoming almost proverbial,
and often with a dry irony: "as poplar as a hen with 1 chicking," "hed
n't gut his i teeth cut," "a thrashin round like a short-tailed Bull in fli-
time," "woud n't take none o' his sarse," and of course such words as
spry, eenamost, sot, hisn, hearn for *heard.* This then is the down-East
Yankee manner of speech that went west with the frontier, and which
in a milder form can be heard still in Wisconsin from the oldest generation in a few places where the strong New England settlements were
made.

By way of comparison, let us turn to the South. Following is part of
a conversation from *Woodcraft,* a novel of William Gilmore Simms,
first published in 1856.[7] It represents the speech of a South Carolinian
named Millhouse, who is helping Captain Porgy to rehabilitate his
plantation after the Revolution. Millhouse is urging the Captain to
marry the widow Eveleigh, who, he says, is *willing.* The Captain speaks
first:

> "Ha! ha! ha! Delightful! 'Pon my soul, Millhouse, you put the
> case in quite a new and striking point of view. You think I should
> speak in time to prevent the widow from addressing me, and so
> spare her blushes."
>
> "In course, I does! That's jest the thing—spar' her blushes!"
>
> "But, suppose she were to propose to me, and I were to—refuse
> her?"
>
> "Lord love you, cappin, and be merciful to your onderstanding;
> but you wouldn't be so onkind and outright redickilous, as to do
> that—and arter all that she's been a-doing for you."
>
> "It would be rather hard-hearted, I confess."
>
> " 'Twould be most monstrous redickilous! But, cappin, you mus'n't

---

[7] Quotation is from Ch. LVI, "The Sheriff in Limbo."

wait for her to do the axing. It mout-be she'd come arter awhile, and when she couldn't stan' keepin' in her feelin's any longer; but then it mout-be—it would be—too late, then, to help your sarcumstances. Ef the property was to be sold by the sheriff, what would it bring, I want to know, now, when thar's so little money guine about. Not enough, by half, to pay this warmint, M'Kewn. But, ef 'twas only on account of the lady, it's your business to speak quick. The man has no right to keep the poor woman a-waiting on him. He has no right to keep a-thinking, with pipe in his mouth, while she's a-weeping and pining away a-most to nothin'."

"But I don't see that Mrs. Eveleigh shows any such signs of suffering, Millhouse."

"It's all innard, cappin. She's got too proud a stomach, to show outside, in her flesh and sperrits, how much she suffers innardly. Many's the woman that's looked fat and hearty, while her heart's been a-breaking in her buzzum. . . ."

There are many obvious similarities here to the speech of the Biglows, though the rendering of Millhouse's speech is somewhat less accurate: Simms has given it a literary turn. Nevertheless it contrasts clearly with the language of the educated Captain and shows a few local characteristics. In common with the Yankee speech, we find the "dropping of g's" and the prefixing of "a": *keepin', feelin's, a-waiting, a-thinking, a-weeping*. There is the Elizabethan "ar" in *sarcumstances* and *warmint*. There are such pronunciations as *ef* for *if, jest* for *just*, and such reduced forms as *arter* for *after, a-most* for *almost, innard* for *inward,* and so on—none of these specifically local, but merely indicating the general character of uneducated speech at the popular level.

Local features, in the selection read, are few, but one may point to *spar'* for *spare* and *thar* for *there,* which Zekle and Hosy Biglow would not have said. *Mout-be,* repeated twice, is still a notable South Carolina feature today, and *ax* for *ask* and *monstrous* as an emphatic adverb were probably more favored in this region than elsewhere.

Let us next skip to the frontier itself, to Nevada in the "flush times" of the silver fever, and read a bit out of Mark Twain's *Roughing It,*[8] first published in 1872. Of this time and place, Twain has written: "As all the peoples of the earth had representative adventurers in Silverland, and as each adventurer had brought the slang of his nation or his locality with him, the combination made the slang of Nevada the richest and most infinitely varied and copious that had ever existed anywhere in the world, perhaps, except in the mines of California in the early days. Slang was the language of Nevada."

Our scene depicts a rough named "Scotty," whose fellow rough, Buck Fanshawe, has died, attempting to tell the minister about it and to get

---

[8] Quotation is from Vol. II, Ch. VI.

him to preach Buck's funeral. Scotty's slangy talk is put side by side with the sober formality of the clergyman.

But to return to Scotty's visit to the minister. He was on a sorrowful mission, now, and his face was the picture of woe. Being admitted to the presence, he sat down before the clergyman, placed his fire-hat on an unfinished manuscript sermon under the minister's nose, took from it a red silk handkerchief, wiped his brow and heaved a sigh of dismal impressiveness, explanatory of his business. He choked, and even shed tears; but with an effort he mastered his voice and said in lugubrious tones:

"Are you the duck that runs the gospel-mill next door?"

"Am I the—pardon me, I believe I do not understand?"

With another sigh, and half-sob, Scotty rejoined:

"Why you see we are in a bit of trouble, and the boys thought maybe you would give us a lift, if we'd tackle you—that is, if I've got the rights of it and you are the head clerk of the doxology-works next door."

"I am the shepherd in charge of the flock whose fold is next door."

"The which?"

"The spiritual adviser of the little company of believers whose sanctuary adjoins these premises."

Scotty scratched his head, reflected a moment, and then said:

"You ruther hold over me, pard. I reckon I can't call that hand. Ante and pass the buck."

"How? I beg your pardon. What did I understand you to say?"

"Well, you've rather got the bulge on me. Or maybe we've both got the bulge somehow. You don't smoke me and I don't smoke you. You see, one of the boys has passed in his checks and we want to give him a good send-off, and so the thing I'm on now is to roust out somebody to jerk a little chin-music for us and waltz him through handsome."

"My friend, I seem to grow more and more bewildered. Your observations are wholly incomprehensible to me. Cannot you simplify them in some way? At first I thought perhaps I understood you, but I grope now. Would it not expedite matters if you restricted yourself to categorical statements of fact unencumbered with obstructing accumulations of metaphor and allegory?"

Another pause, and more reflection. Then, said Scotty:

"I'll have to pass, I judge."

"How?"

"You've raised me out, pard."

"I still fail to catch your meaning."

"Why, that last lead of yourn is too many for me—that's the idea. I can't trump nor follow suit."

The clergyman sank back in his chair perplexed. Scotty leaned his head on his hand and gave himself up to thought. Presently his face came up, sorrowful but confident.

"I've got it now, so's you can savvy," he said. "What we want is a gospel-sharp. See?"

"A what?"

"Gospel-sharp. Parson."

"Oh! Why did you not say so before? I am a clergyman—a parson."

"Now you talk! You see my blind and straddle it like a man. Put it there!"—extending a brawny paw, which closed over the minister's small hand and gave it a shake indicative of fraternal sympathy and fervent gratification.

"Now we're all right, pard. Let's start fresh. Don't you mind my snuffling a little—becuz we're in a power of trouble. You see one of the boys has gone up the flume—"

"Gone where?"

"Up the flume—throwed up the sponge, you understand."

"Thrown up the sponge?"

"Yes—kicked the bucket—"

"Ah—has departed to that mysterious country from whose bourne no traveler returns."

"Return! I reckon not. Why, pard, he's *dead!*"

This is, of course, a "set piece" in which exaggeration has had its role. One should not fail to notice, however, that the speech of the minister is also under scrutiny. His unctuous polysyllabism, his unbending rejection of even the most ordinary conversational informality—he refuses to say "can't" or "I'm"—and withal his repeated use of the "How?" rather than "What?" on which, we recall, Captain Marryat commented—all these Mark Twain has observed quite as carefully as he has the slang.

We conclude with another selection from Mark Twain, *Life on the Mississippi*, published about 1852.[9] It is an example of the very tall talk of a boaster of a type that had his day on the frontier a hundred years ago. Mark Twain is not the only writer to depict this kind of hyperbolic blowhard, but his picture is an eloquent one. The speaker is winding himself up verbally for a fight with all comers, if he is to be believed, and seeks to warn the beholders of the devastation which he will wreak:

Whoo-oop! I'm the original iron-jawed, brass-mounted, copper-bellied corpse-maker from the wilds of Arkansaw! Look at me! I'm the man they call Sudden Death and General Desolation! Sired by a hurricane, dam'd by an earthquake, half-brother to the cholera, nearly related to the small-pox on the mother's side! Look at me! I take nineteen alligators and a bar'l of whiskey for breakfast when I'm in robust health, and a bushel of rattlesnakes and a dead body when I'm ailing. I split the everlasting rocks with my glance, and

---

[9] Quotation is from Ch. III.

> I squench the thunder when I speak! Whoo-oop! Stand back and give me room according to my strength! Blood's my natural drink, and the wails of the dying is music to my ear. Cast your eye on me, gentlemen, and lay low and hold your breath, for I'm 'bout to turn myself loose!

These few short samples cannot possibly give a balanced view of the state of language on the frontier. Suffice it to say that there was to be heard every *local* type of pronunciation and idiom which had become established in the more settled parts of the country, that the contacts of these variant types led forever to compromises of one kind and another, that interlingual contacts with Indians and non-English-speaking Europeans were ever-present, that certain types of adventurers—the roaring boys, the crackers and bullies and slingers of extravagant talk—were loosing their tongues on all sides. On the seething frontier, everything went—the turbulence of life in general was inevitably reflected in language. There was an enormous appetite for words, an admiration for words: a man who could bring out a salty phrase or an apt comparison would smash the cracker-barrels.

Reflections of this ebullience are with us still. Americans pay less attention to "rules" of language, written or unwritten, than devoted schoolteachers would like them to. Our authors are less afraid of linguistic innovation than those of many other nations; we set more value upon vigor of expression than upon control. These things, no doubt, are reflections of the recency of the frontier experience. In addition to this, the language we speak, while not "the American language," is definitely our own, a type of English enlarged and, in general, enriched by the retention of older elements, the development of many new meanings and combinations, and the seasoning of numerous foreign acquisitions. It has a smack of its own, a strength of its own. It is no longer a semiattached colonial speech: it has achieved autonomy, even polarity, side by side with the original pole of British English. A great deal—the fundamental part—these two poles share in common; their difference has come about as a direct result of the tremendous experience that made this nation. And in that experience, a most vivid and creative part was played by the frontier.

STUDY QUESTIONS AND EXERCISES

1. Examine the 1968 edition of *Webster's New World Dictionary of the American Language*: do any features and characteristics justify the title? (*Webster's New World Dictionary*, Encyclopedic Edition, was published in 1952, the College Edition in 1953.)

2. Although this essay is included under "Historical Aspects," time and space are inseparable in American language of the frontier.

Why? During the same period, would British English present the same fusion of two aspects of language or would language there "hold still" geographically for a chronological study in rural areas? Would the situation be different in urban areas? If so, why?

3. According to Cassidy, what is the most striking characteristic of a frontier society? Throughout Cassidy's article, trace his use of the lava flow image. What was the most striking characteristic of British rural society before the Industrial Revolution? (In George Eliot's *Adam Bede*, for example, successive generations of the Poyser family had been tenants on the same farm.)

4. Do Cassidy's details about the origins of New England settlers confirm or disprove the generalizations by Pyles about New England speech? What was the second main current of regional influence from England?

5. What differences between English and colonial society contributed to separation of English and American speech?

6. Suggest specific reasons why Noah Webster's prediction of a separate American language did not come true. How does your access to spoken and written British compare with that of your grandparents when they were your age? Would this "generation gap" be greater or less as one moved backward to earlier generations?

7. Outline Cassidy's classification and compare it with those cited by Mencken.

8. Milwaukee in 1970 proclaimed a "Summerfest." Can you give recent similar examples of new coinages in your own community that illustrate Cassidy's categories and add to his examples?

9. A common British term is *lumber room*. See the section on *store room* in Hans Kurath's essay (p. 185) for that term and its equivalents in American English. Where and why does *lumber room* appear in the United States?

10. Look up the entries under *corn* in Mathews, *Dictionary of Americanisms*. What "hallmarks of American" do they exhibit?

11. What aspects of language besides vocabulary does Cassidy consider? What periods and what geographical frontiers are represented in the literary examples?

12. Why has the expression "true grit," from Lowell's *Biglow Papers*, been revived in 1970? "Simplex Mundishes" is a misspelling of "simplex munditiis." Look this term up in a dictionary of quotations and explain the humor. Why would Lowell expect his educated readers to understand the joke?

13. The passage from Mark Twain represents the same kind of satire on pompous language as that in the scene between Hamlet and Osric (V. ii.), except that Hamlet understands and is making fun of Osric by imitating him. How does Hamlet's concluding comment apply to any inflated language?

14. What stylistic features grew out of frontier life?

9

Mark Twain and the Dictionary

C. Merton Babcock

As even a cursory look at Mark Twain's writing reveals, he is a master of word and phrase. He has contributed color, freshness, and vigor to the American language. Professor Babcock of Michigan State University examines Mark Twain's interest in language and reports his findings in an essay that first appeared in Word Study *for October, 1966.*

The English critic Geoffrey Moore called the author of *Huckleberry Finn* "the father of the American natural style." Bernard De Voto acclaimed Mark Twain's use of an American vernacular as "a triumph in technique." H. L. Mencken believed that widespread interest in the celebrated "Jumping Frog" story was primarily instrumental in bringing about the popular shift from Yankee dialect to frontier dialect as "the typical American patois." These and other critical judgments pay highest tribute to the linguistic achievements of a one-time Mississippi River ragamuffin who made wild excursions into the unexplored frontiers of language, and who came away with a heterogeneous and nondescript collection of mutilated verbs and torn and bleeding forms of speech, not realizing that he had actually discovered "gold."

Mark Twain had an ingenious way with words. He understood the dynamic, shifting, mercurial dimensions of language, and he was not above adapting it to suit his own purposes. Not for a moment did he suppose that all the words of a language were corralled in the dictionary. When he and his brother Orion headed west during gold-rush days, Orion insisted on lugging a copy of Webster's Unabridged along. "It weighed about a thousand pounds," Mark wrote in the *Autobiography*, "and was a ruinous expense." "We could have kept a family for a time," he said, "on what that dictionary cost in the way of extra freight —and it wasn't a good dictionary, anyway—didn't have any modern words in it—only had obsolete ones that they used when Noah Webster was a child." In *Roughing It*, he added the comment that there could not have been found in a whole library of dictionaries language sufficient to tell how tired those mules were at the end of the journey.

The author, himself, was such an innovator that no dictionary could possibly have kept up with his startling creations. Living at a time in the history of the country when hundreds of new words were vying with each other for a place in the lexicon, he introduced a number which have become standard American expressions: *forty-niner, barbed wire, wild west, hay-ride, billiard parlor, ex-convict, press notice, race-prejudice, dust-storm, cussword.* He also experimented with some which have not survived: *typewriter copyist, type girl, mental telegraphy, sodasquirter, accidental insurance.* Incidentally, Mark Twain, not Walter Winchell, introduced *whoopee* into the American vocabulary, and he, not Franklin D. Roosevelt, first used *new deal* in the political sense for which it has become so famous.

Some of Mark Twain's words have an ultramodern twist, having anticipated the form of our own verbal novelties: *psychologizer, quintessential, telelectrophonoscope, Shakesperiod, poundiferous, preforeordestination, uncledom, disenthuse, religiouswise, vinegarishly, millinerize, humanbeingship, perhapser, mumble 'n screechograph.* Many of his contributions to the American language were doubtless words that he picked up from others, words like *gospel sharp, flea pasture, lunkhead, dollface, rat's nest, phrase juggler.* Others were pure inventions, manufactured for specific humorous or satirical effects: *hypothenuse, wombat, jumbulacious, clapperdudgeon, superimbrication, hogglebumgullop.*

Of 7802 of Mark Twain's words listed in the Ramsay-Emberson *Mark Twain Lexicon* (1938), 3400 are not listed in the *Oxford English Dictionary*, and more than 3500 are not in *Webster's New International, Second Edition.* For words from the author's vocabulary that are cited in the OED, Mark Twain's usage, in nearly 1000 instances, antedates the earliest evidence recorded. No wonder the *Dictionary of American English* and *Dictionary of Americanisms* leaned so heavily upon Mark Twain's vocabulary for examples of bona fide Americanisms.

Speaking of the British-American conflict over the property rights of the English language, Mark Twain bluntly denied that there is such a thing as Queen's English. "The property has gone into the hands of a joint stock company," he said, "and we own the bulk of the shares." While visiting in England, the famous humorist was once complimented on his excellent use of English. He hastened to explain that he wasn't entitled to the compliment, for, he said, "I don't speak English at all—I only speak American." Then he listed a number of English words which he claimed are not in American use: *'ousemaid, 'ospital, 'otel, 'istrionic.* Don't try to pronounce an English name," he advised, "till some native shows you how. The common Welch name Bzjxxllwcp is pronounced Jackson."

In order to understand properly Mark Twain's attitudes toward grammar, punctuation, spelling, and usage, one must be aware of a certain ambivalence in the author. He lived a double life. As a Western frontiersman he felt awkward and insecure in the face of Eastern literary opulence. As a member of the literary illuminati who were making an impression on the American mind, he was ashamed of his "crude" manners and lack of education. Mark Twain of Hannibal, Missouri, and Mark Twain of Hartford, Connecticut, were at war with each other and both were at war with the world and the "damned human race." The author tried desperately, with the aid of his wife "Livy" and his friend Howells, to polish his homely speechways and make them "respectable," while at the same time he insulted and belittled the very people whose position in society he ostensibly envied and coveted.

A letter Mark Twain wrote to Howells in connection with one of his manuscripts explains his predicament: "Should the language be altered?" he asked, "or the hyphens taken out? Won't you please fix it the way it ought to be, altering the language as you choose, only making it bitter and contemptuous?" When he wrote *damned* in the copy, Howells changed it to *deuced*, and Mark Twain complained: "*Deuced* was not strong enough; so I met you half way with *devilish*."

On another occasion, he wrote, "I mustn't stop to play now, or I shall never get those *helfiard* letters answered. (That is not my spelling, but Mrs. Clemens's: I have told her the right way a thousand times, but it does no good. She cannot remember.)" The irony here is unmistakable. Mrs. Clemens, of course, was morally opposed to such "profanity" and forbade its use around the house. "Consound my cats" was the absolute limit of her swearing vocabulary, and this expression she employed only when "roused to ferocity." Mark Twain, on the other hand, employed 123 cusswords without impunity, besides a sizable number of unsavory epithets charged with vigor and venom which have never found their way into the dictionary.

The author's difficulty in replacing his native vulgarisms with his wife's genteel expressions is one of the subjects of "Eve's Autobiography" in *Letters from the Earth*. "We are starting at the very bottom of things," Eve wrote, "at the very beginning; we had to learn the ABC of things. . . . There was no dictionary, and we couldn't know whether we used our words correctly or not." "Building a dictionary is exceedingly interesting work," Adam said, "but tough." Eve had to assist. "Adam wakes up," she reported, "asks me not to forget to set down those four new words. It shows that he has forgotten them. But I have not. For his sake I am always watching. They are down. It is he that is building the Dictionary—as *he* thinks—but I have noticed that it is I who do the work."

In an article published anonymously in the June, 1880, issue of *Atlantic Monthly* (and later mentioned in a letter to Howells), Mark Twain commented on a note he allegedly received from "A Boston Girl," (See *Harper's*, June, 1961) who took him to task for his ruptured grammar and glaring solecisms. The opening line of the piece reveals the author's intention: "This note comes to me from the home of culture—." Quite clearly the Boston Girl is Eve, or Livy Clemens, created by Mark Twain himself to represent the "civilized" side of his two-faced linguistic nature. Once he had created the target he could fire away to his heart's content with all the fury of his pent-up unrefinement.

After calling attention to some of the girl's own errors in English, the author proceeded to set forth a functional and operational theory of language which rejected all the forms of linguistic piety which his self-appointed tutors approved. "Some people were not born to punctuate," he told the girl, "these cannot learn the art. They can learn only a rude fashion of it; they cannot attain to its niceties, for these must be *felt*; they cannot be reasoned out. Cast-iron rules will not answer, here, anyway; what is one man's comma is another man's colon. One man can't punctuate another man's manuscript any more than one person can make the gestures for another person's speech."

He expressed an equally nonprescriptive attitude toward grammar. In his *Autobiography* he wrote: "Perfect grammar—persistent, continuous, sustained—is the fourth dimension, so to speak. Many have sought it, but none has found it. . . . I know grammar by ear only, not by note, not by the rules. A generation ago I knew the rules—knew them by heart, word for word, though not their meanings—and I still know one of them: the one which says—which says—but never mind, it will come back to me presently."

The same with spelling. "I have been a correct speller, always," he assured his critics, "but it is a low accomplishment, and not a thing to be vain of. Why should one take pride in spelling a word rightly when he knows he is spelling it wrongly? *Though* is the right way to spell "though," but it is not *the* right way to spell it. Do I make myself understood?" Recognizing the meaninglessness of words in isolation, he argued that no one can tell what a word spells when he sees it off by itself. Using the word *bow* as an example, he said, the only way you can tell what it spells is "by referring to the context and finding out what it signifies,—whether it is a thing to shoot arrows with, or a nod of one's head, or the forward end of a boat."

The author considered the English alphabet "pure insanity." "It can hardly spell any word in the language with any degree of certainty," he said. "When you see the word *chaldron* in an English book no foreigner can guess how to pronounce it; neither can any native. The reader knows that it is pronounced *chaldron*—or *kaldron*, or *kawldron*—but neither he nor his grandmother can tell which is the right way without looking in the dictionary; and when he looks in the dictionary the chances are a hundred to one that the dictionary itself doesn't know which is the right way, but will furnish him all three and let him take his choice."

One of Mark Twain's boyish linguistic pranks in the text of *Huckleberry Finn* reveals the author's pugnacious attitude toward overregulated, overregimented, and overdisciplined ways with words. In a note prepared by Tom and Huck and signed "Unknown Friend," a startling ambiguity lies half concealed in the toils of a misplaced modifier. "I am one of the gang," the note reads, "but have got relliggion and wish to quit it and lead a honest life again, and will betray the helish design." The passage may well indicate the author's own determination to "quit religgion" (including all varieties of dogmatism) and its puristic, pedagogical, and puritanical rituals and pronouncements.

The author's attitude toward accuracy of diction was a horse of another color. If anything the frontier linguist was more meticulous than any of his critics. He had a veritable mania for the right expression. "It tingles exquisitely around through the walls of the mouth," he said, "and tastes as tart and crisp and good as the autumn-butter that creams the sumac-berry." Speaking of Bret Harte's deplorable use of dialect, he said: "Mr. Harte can write a delightful story; he can describe the miner and the gambler perfectly,—as to gait and look and garb; but no human being, living or dead, ever had experience of the dialect which he puts into his people's mouths."

Calling attention to the dialect in *Huckleberry Finn*, he defended its authenticity in a note to Howells in which he mentioned some perplexities he had encountered: "I had difficulty with the negro talk, because a negro sometimes (rarely) says 'goin'' and sometimes 'gwyne,' and they make just such discrepancies in other words—and when you come to reproduce them on paper they look as if the variation resulted from the writer's carelessness. But I want to work at the proofs and get the dialect as nearly right as possible."

The "Washoe giant" abominated big words—afraid they might give him the lockjaw. He took endless delight in belittling the German custom of hooking bits and pieces of words together *en tandem* in order to produce larger and larger specimens of the lexicographer's art—"crisp and noble words" like *daybeforeyesterdayshortlyaftereleveno'clock*. In *Letters from the Earth*, he depicts the trouble Adam had trying to manhandle the unwieldy *ratiocination*, which got completely out of hand, blew up the lexical works, and wrecked the "vocabulary mill." Mark Twain took no stock in such "insipid messes of verbal asininity" as legal briefs, ecclesiastical textuary, or languorous literary elucidations. For his own transactions, he much preferred the loose change of linguistic currency. The artificialities of so-called literary giants reminded him of "a cat having a fit in a platter of tomatoes."

Opie Read recalls a story Mark Twain used to tell about Jim Watrous, who wanted to be a representative in the state legislature, but who used such big words whenever he made a speech that his farmer neighbors couldn't understand what he was saying. One evening, while milking a cow, Jim began practicing one of his speeches. The cow, not accustomed to such high-flown lingo, kicked him in the jaw causing him to bite off the end of his tongue. After that he used only words of one syllable, and it made such a hit with the farmers that they rallied to his support, and he won the election.

Life was Mark Twain's lexicon. His words, collected during his childhood and youth along the margins of the Mississippi, were deeply rooted in experience. They have about them the "mystery of the deep woods, the earthy smells, the faint odors of wild flowers, the sheen of rain-washed foliage." Despite the author's incongruous announcement that *Joan of Arc* was his greatest work, it is *Huckleberry Finn,* and its absence of ponderous syllables, for which he is remembered. This classic constitutes an irrefutable argument for linguistic freedom. It has immortalized the idiom of democracy. De Voto was surely right in his judgment that Mark Twain's greatest accomplishment with words was his "superb adaptation of vernacular to the purposes of art."

STUDY QUESTIONS AND EXERCISES

1. In light of Cassidy's article, develop the metaphor "wild excursions into the unexplored *frontiers* of language." What analogy can you discover between geographical and linguistic frontiers—in general, and in writers like Mark Twain?

2. In a short biography of Mark Twain, such as that in the *Dictionary of American Biography,* find out what frontiers Mark Twain knew, and when. Which of these are reflected in the words Babcock cites?

3. To understand Mark Twain's jest about pronunciation of English proper names, look up the derivation of *maudlin* and *bedlam* and if possible such names as *Cholmondely* and *Featherstonehaugh.* (There is a story about some Americans, irritated by weird British pronunciations, who retaliated by telling some British friends that Americans pronounce *Niagara Falls* "Niffles.")

4. Mrs. Clemens is said to have attempted to cure her husband of swearing by repeating, in a dull monotone, the curses he poured into a badly-functioning telephone. He once replied—"Oh, Livy, you know the words but you don't know the tune." What aspects of the spoken language was he referring to?

5. How does Babcock's term "two-faced linguistic nature" describe the American people? Consider the language as it is recorded in modern dictionaries, reflecting impatience with tradition and restraints, versus the striving for "correctness" and the desire for authorities to define correctness. On this point, refer also to Evans (selection 5), and the articles by Walter Ong and Philip Gove that follow.

6. Study the punctuation in the Mark Twain passage in the Cassidy essay. How does the punctuation convey stress, pitch, and juncture in speech? (Note Twain's analogy between punctuation and gestures.)

7. Look up the pronunciations and meanings of *bow,* in the *Random House Dictionary.*

8. On several occasions, Mark Twain satirized the differences

between English and French and German. In *The Family Mark Twain* (Harper & Row, 1935) compare the French version of "The Jumping Frog," and Twain's literal retranslation of it into English. Read his essay "The Awful German Language." In the latter, note in "Tale of the Fishwife and Its Sad Fate" the capitals and genders—"Hear the rain, how he pours." (Twain's genders do not always agree with those in German.)

9. Note Babcock's metaphor, "the loose change of linguistic currency." Develop the suggested analogy to show significant ways in which language resembles money.

10

Hostility, Literacy, and Webster III

Walter J. Ong, S. J.

*Father Ong of St. Louis University considers some of the factors that con-
tributed to the negative reactions to* Webster's Third International Dictionary *upon its publication in 1961. The essay appeared in* College English *for*
November, 1964.

The cultural lag in attacks launched against *Webster's New International Dictionary*, Third Edition, by nonprofessional reviewers has
been beautifully and circumstantially shown by Karl W. Dykema in a
recent article in the *AAUP Bulletin*.[1] Dean Dykema has laid the blame
at the door of the right persons. He has indicted first the reviewers themselves for their dated "medieval" linguistic outlook and failure to know
what they are talking about, and secondly those of us who should see
to it that college and university graduates (including these same reviewers) are properly informed concerning the nature of lexicography
and who have not done so. He has suggested possible causes for the
heat in the attacks on this monumental lexicographical achievement:
the greater anxieties of our present age (this cause he discounts, rightly,
I believe, for want of evidence that our anxieties are "greater" than
those of earlier man), the uncompromising presentation of "upsetting"
information which had been hidden away or muted in editions before
this third, the choice of reviewers for nonscholarly journals who could
write well or simply entertainingly rather than reviewers who knew the
field they were writing about, and the acceleration of linguistic change
among "cultivated groups" due to the accelerated upward mobility of
persons whose linguistic habits were not formed in the social environment from which earlier "cultivated groups" came.

There appears to be, however, a further reason for the heat in the
attacks. This reason deserves mention, for in some ways it is more basic
than any of those Dykema lists. It relates to the psychological structures
which alphabetic literacy fosters and on which a dictionary builds.

---

[1] Karl W. Dykema, "Cultural Lag and Reviewers of *Webster III*," AAUP *Bulletin*, 49 (1963), 364–369.

To see what this reason is, we must understand the relationship of alphabetic writing and alphabetic typography to speech. Writing and print propose to be records of sound. But they are so only in a forced and permanently imperfect sense. Sound is of itself an event in time, one-directional and evanescent as time itself is. Sound exists only when it is passing out of existence. In the word "existence," by the time I get to the "-tence," the "exis-" must have disappeared. I cannot hold all of a sound or any part of a sound permanently in existence. I can stop an object in the field of vision to see it more clearly. If I stop a sound, I get not sound but silence. If I think of sound as quiescent, I am not thinking of sound but of something else.

To reduce sound to the alphabet is to do just this: to think of sound as something else by converting it (and, with it, time itself) into space. Picture writing, to which the alphabet appears to have been at first deviously related, operates essentially on another principle, as does Chinese character writing. Picture writing does not put sound as such into space. A picture of a bird will call forth different sounds from different speakers—for example, V*ogel, pájaro, oiseau, bird.* The alphabet, however, converts sound itself into non-sound. With the alphabet, one pretends that entire words are present all at once, that they can be cut up into little spatial parts which can be reassembled independently of the one-directional flow of time. This, of course, is to pretend the impossible. I can write the letters in the word "over" in the sequence "o—v—e—r." I can write them also in the sequence "r—e—v—o." If I do so, but read them in reverse sequence, as I can do, I get again the same word "over." The timing of the production of letters in space does not necessarily coincide with the timing of their equivalent production in sound and time. Letters admit of curious other reversals, too. I can write "part" backwards and get "trap." But if I pronounce "part" on a recording tape and then reverse the tape, I do not get "trap" but only a different sound. I have not reversed the sound, only the tape.

There is no way to reverse sound. Pretended reversals of sound, like pretended reversals of time (commonplace in science fiction), work in a simple fashion: one establishes a spatial equivalent of sound or time and reverses the spatial equivalent, considering this to be a reversal of sound or time itself. The pretence is convincing and hardly noticeable, since we are elsewhere so used to spatializing time (on clocks, calendars, in our countless expressions, standard in English and many other Western European languages, which bring us to think of a "long" time or a "short" time by analogy with long objects or short objects in space, since these languages are impoverished in qualifiers derived directly from time, such as "old" and "young" or "enduring" or "permanent"). Physics itself treats sound in terms of space, measuring it by wave "lengths" and visible oscillograph patterns. In these cases, too, we are of course not measuring sound directly, although we are measuring it more accurately than we could otherwise—sound, to be measured accurately, must not be handled directly! It is a phenomenon of itself resistant to measurement, and hence "indefinite." Persons deaf from youth can operate with the physics of sound waves and with oscillograph patterns quite as effectively as anyone else, although they have no direct knowledge at all of what sound is. Physics, as we know it, will never tell you.

Many and perhaps all languages make possible a certain amount of conversion of time phenomena into spatial analogies—after all, the analogies are there to be exploited by anyone who wishes to avail himself of them. But the kind of conversion which makes the alphabet is radical and weird, setting up strains within the psyche to a degree difficult for us today to grasp, conditioned to the alphabet, as we are, from infancy. How uncongenial this conversion is can be seen from the fact that the alphabet was invented only once, every alphabet in the world being derived, in one way or another, from the primitive alphabet which arose in the Mediterranean region somewhere in the years around 2000–1500 B. C.[2] If man has been on earth some 400,000 years—a fairly firm working figure—it has taken him almost this entire time to come upon this device, which to us appears so inevitable.

Alphabetic letterpress typography, too, was a nonce invention in the fifteenth century.[3] The invention—or, better, development—consisted essentially of a process of printing from alphabetic types cast from matrices made by being struck with a punch. One first cut a set of punches in hard metal—iron or an alloy of iron—with a raised letter on the head of each, like the letter on a typewriter key. Then one struck these punches into a softer metal, generally brass, to form a mold. To

---

[2] The nonce origin of the alphabet is a fact which, curiously, escapes the notice of a great many scholars, even some in language and literature. It is readily documented from encyclopedia articles and the references they give. A definitive treatment of the subject is found in David Diringer, *Writing* (New York, 1962), pp. 104–184. The Ugaritic alphabet is only a seemingly independent development: it apparently does not model the forms of its letters on previous alphabetic forms, but its inventor or inventors, who lived in the alphabetized Mediterranean area, approached their undertaking with a knowledge of other alphabetic writing. See William Foxwell Albright, *The Archaeology of Palestine* (Harmondsworth, Eng., 1951), pp. 187–88.

[3] See Thomas Francis Carter, *The Invention of Printing in China and Its Spread Westward*, rev. by L. Carrington Goodrich (2d ed.: New York, 1955). Carter explains how surprisingly close the Uigur Turks and the Koreans came to movable alphabetic type without being able to cross the threshold: the Uigurs used alphabetic writing and movable type, but the only known Uigur movable type "consists entirely of word-type, in slavish imitation of the Chinese system" (p. 218). The Koreans also had the alphabet and movable type, but their movable type consisted of pieces even more complicated than those of the Uigurs: each type contained not only an alphabetized Korean word but also the Chinese character to which it corresponded (p. 228). There is of course a large literature on the development of letterpress printing in fifteenth-century Europe.

this mold one brought a still softer metal, molten, generally an alloy of lead with antimony (to assure expansion rather than contraction on cooling), casting large numbers of types for each letter of the alphabet. These types were stored in a case or font. To this the compositor came with his composing stick, on which he set up lines of type from copy. This set type was moved to a galley for proof, then, corrected, put into a form, which was locked up and moved on to a press, where it was locked further into position. (These steps, given here more or less as they occur today, were slightly curtailed in the early days of printing.) Then the form was inked, paper brought into contact with it, the platen of the press squeezed into close contact with the paper, removed, and the paper removed. By this time, one is a dozen or so steps away from the spoken word, which has receded into the background so far as to make it unnecessary for those engaged in the typographical operation to know the language they are dealing with or even be able to speak it at all. The reduction of sound to space imitated by the alphabet has reached truly monumental proportions. The voice has been swallowed by something like a huge Rube Goldberg machine. What was once a living operation in sound has become a matter of local motion.

Here not only are we far from the spoken word, the free-flowing world of oratory and epic: we are in a new world of pressure and constraint, where exactitude can become an obsession. The analogy, loose at least, between the progression from the oral word to the controlled, constrained, written or printed word and the Freudian succession oral-to-anal is sure to be adverted to here, although what to make of the analogy is not clear since it must be remembered that here the oral is not, as in the Freudian sequence, basically receptive but rather diffusive (it is the ear which receives the word, not the mouth). This is the awesome world out of which the dictionary was born.

The world out of which the dictionary was born has another relevant trait: it is the product of the cultivation of Latin (with some Greek, and a tiny dash of Hebrew) as a basically chirographic language. From the time between the sixth and the ninth century, when Learned Latin was separated from the vernacular dialects of the tongue which became the modern Romance languages, Learned Latin had been the language of all learning in the West—of grammar, rhetoric, logic, physics, medicine, law, theology, and the other academic subjects. By the eighteenth century, the great germinal age for the modern dictionary, Latin was in a curious condition. For roughly a millennium, although it was spoken by millions, it had been spoken by no one who did not know how to write it. The language was far from "dead," for new terms had been formed by the thousands in Latin since antiquity (they still are being formed), but it was subject to total chirographic (and latterly typographic) control. Within Learned Latin there was no properly phonetic development at all. The sound was controlled out of space. What was primary (voice) was being totally controlled by its derivative (writing). The only way to learn a language of this sort is to match everything to written models. Writing and print by definition constitute regularity.

It is a commonplace that the early approaches to the vernaculars were through the Latin and Greek. The efforts of dictionary-makers, like those of earlier devotees of the vernaculars,[4] were powered by a desire to raise the vernaculars to the regularity of the classical tongues—a regularity due to their curious domination by chirography. Dr. Johnson, as Dykema points out, learned to qualify his original desire to see a dictionary as a means of establishing utter regularity in English comparable to that in Latin and classical Greek. He finally owned that his ambition to "fix" the language was one "which neither reason nor experience can justify." [5] But he was unable to forget entirely the regulatory approach.

So were most of his successors before *Webster III*. Even when lexicographers protested that they were registering usage and not prescribing rules, they took as their norm for usage the practice of persons in the community who were, more or less, professional or semiprofessional *writers*. Oral influence was discounted. The new *Webster III* reverses this stand. As never before, what falls on the ear is recorded: pronunciation variants, words chiefly heard, seldom written. Most telling about the dictionary's orientation is the fact that persons whose influence on the language is primarily oral, such as Willie Mays, are cited among those whose usage is recorded. (Of course, Willie Mays's oral usage will have to get itself recorded somewhere in writing—this much concession to writing must always be made by the best-intentioned lexicographers.)

Webster III represents one more instance—a monumental one—of the breakthrough to a more oral-aural culture which marks our day, characterized by the electronic media of communication, telephone, telegraph, radio, television (more oral-aural than visual—the weather chart is always accompanied by a commentator), and the beep-beep of orbiting spacecraft. The breakthrough manifests itself in language study by the development of linguistics, of which *Webster III* is a product and which approaches language as basically an aural-oral phenomenon, whereas traditional grammar had taken language basically as written (*gramma* is the Greek word for a letter of the alphabet).

It is this breakthrough from quiescent to vibrant, temporally fluid sound [6] which, I believe, constitutes the most deep-seated source of anxiety in reactions to *Webster III*. Space is the great symbol of order,

---

[4] See Richard Foster Jones, *The Triumph of the English Language* (Stanford, 1953).

[5] Quoted by Dykema, "Cultural Lag . . . ," p. 364, from Johnson's Preface to his dictionary.

[6] For further discussion of the role of voice and other media in communication see Walter J. Ong, *The Barbarian Within* (New York, 1962), esp. pp. 49–67, 164–229.

and its primacy is now being compromised. The alphabet and print had made language as never before an instrument of constraint rather than openness, and had thereby reorganized man's life world. To learn the alphabet is to impose on oneself a sense of control which we are only beginning to understand. We have yet to assess the terrible strain on the psyche which the learning of alphabetic writing always entails, although studies of the different psychotic syndromes of literates, as compared to illiterates, have begun to alert us to the state of affairs.[7] Any teacher of a foreign language knows some of the depths which are affected by literacy: how difficult it is, for example, to re-establish among literates an awareness of sounds as sounds—a sense, for example, that the "p" in French is not the "p" in English, and the ability to *hear* a French "p" rather than to *see* an English-sounding "p" when a French word is uttered.

The investment of psychic energy in the mastery of writing (and of typography) is jealously guarded by the psyche, which does not wish to yield an inch of the ground it has so laboriously occupied. Writing has been such an achievement that the psyche feels compelled to over-value it, to believe that writing, which reduces restless, unpredictable, evanescent sound to the quiescent order of space, *must* control all speech, and, moreover, that speech must normally have the kind of utter regularity which can become an obsessive dream once the threshold has been crossed from the fluid (and real, living) world of sound to the static (and unreal, dead) world of alphabetic space. The alphabetically conditioned psyche, in other words, is terrorized by the fact that *Webster III* has abandoned the solid world of space for the uncertainties of time. Wyndham Lewis, who proclaimed himself a "space" man and hated "time" men, wouldn't have liked it at all.

This additional reason for the heat in the attacks on *Webster III* ties in directly with Dykema's analysis at two points. First, it lends some meaning to a modified version of his first reason, which has to do with the purported anxieties of our present age and which he thought no real reason as it stood, since it is not at all evident how our anxieties as a whole compare with those of earlier ages. The present account does not contradict Dykema here, for it does not imply that anxieties today as a whole are either greater or less than they have been in the past—only that some of them are different. Just because our anxieties, about which we have lately become so reflective and so articulate, press us very hard does not mean that other persons in earlier cultures were not pressed as hard or harder by other anxieties which to us now appear only exotic. One can hardly measure with great assurance the overall anxieties of

---

[7] See the work reported on in J. C. Carothers, "Culture, Psychiatry, and the Written Word," *Psychiatry*, 22 (1959), 307–320; and Marvin K. Opler, *Culture, Psychiatry, and Human Values* (Springfield, Ill., 1956).

vanished cultures as one can at least hope to measure one's own. And, in fact, strangely enough, a recent study of present-day cultures appears to show that the society (the United States) most technologically advanced and thus presumably most unequivocally belonging to the present world, produces, contrary to expectation, personality structures with the least anxiety.[8] The phenomena here described, however, do point to a particular source for some particular anxieties of our age, identifying them as the result of a sequence of communications developments terminating in our day: the shift from oral-aural media to chirographic media to typographic media, and now to a new kind of oral-aural media which electronically transforms the old kind.

Secondly, the perspectives here suggested give new relevance to the term "medieval" which Dykema uses as a descriptive label to cover a state of mind among critics of *Webster III*. He styles these critics medieval because, like medieval (and Renaissance and later) grammarians, they opt for the view that the study of language is basically a normative matter, a quest for and enforcement of "rules." The present account suggests one of the reasons why medieval man was so beset by the need for rules. Medieval culture, by contrast with the earlier rhetorical culture of antiquity, was a manuscript culture, deeply committed to textual commentary and to exactitude—and thus ultimately committed, incidentally, to the quest for verification which helped form the modern scientific mind. The typical scholar of medieval times would probably not have liked *Webster III*. The atypical scholar—of which there were not a few—probably would have. But even the typical medieval scholar was enough under the influence of a two-sided dialectic not to have given *Webster III* such short and vengeful shrift as its uninformed reviewers have accorded it.

STUDY QUESTIONS AND EXERCISES

The title of this selection refers to the controversy between lexicographers and reviewers occasioned by the publication of *Webster's Third New International Dictionary*, 1961. The two sides of this controversy, reflecting attitudes that still exist though the specific issue is dead, are well represented in a casebook for freshman English courses: *Dictionaries and That Dictionary*, James Sledd and Wilma R. Ebbitt, eds. (Glenview, Ill.: Scott, Foresman and Company, 1962).

1. Read the article by Karl Dykema cited by Ong. How do the readers Dykema addresses differ from those for whom Chomsky (selec-

---

[8] Raymond B. Cattell, "The Nature and Measurement of Anxiety," *Scientific American*, Vol. 208, No. 3 (March 1963), pp. 96–104.

tion 4) and Ong write in *College English* and from Evans' (selection 5) audience? How are these articles suited to the groups they address?

2. In the *Random House Dictionary*, or the *American Heritage Dictionary*, examine the charts at the beginning of each letter section, showing the evolution of that letter, both capital and small forms. In *Webster's Third* or the *American Heritage*, look up, under *alphabet*, the chart of English and related alphabets. Why does Ong specify alphabetic writing: what other kinds are there? How do they differ? Approximately when and where did the sole primitive alphabet originate?

3. What connections can you see between the invention of printing, the discovery of America, the Protestant Reformation, and the colonization of America? What notable advantage did American English, as a vernacular, have over English and all other Indo-European languages?

4. What difference between Learned Latin and vernacular dialects did dictionary-makers and grammarians overlook in viewing Latin as a model language?

5. Dictionaries record the development of language through time and thus show the historical aspect of language. The *Oxford English Dictionary* traces the history of each word from its first recorded use to the present, with dated illustrative quotations. *Webster's Third* presents all of the modern meanings of a word but generally does not include obsolete or archaic ones. How does *Webster's Third* differ radically from earlier English dictionaries? What developments in modern culture between *Webster's Second* and *Webster's Third* made a new approach necessary and feasible?

6. According to Ong how are psychic anxieties derived from writing and new media of communication?

7. It has long been known that young children can learn to pronounce a foreign language more rapidly and far better than adults. What claims does Ong make in his essay that might explain this greater flexibility on the part of children?

8. Look up the derivation of the two adjectives in "rhetorical culture" and "manuscript culture." Why are *medieval* and *Middle Ages* sometimes extended to 1500?

9. Compare Ong's and Evans' attitudes toward nonprofessional critics and reviewers of *Webster's Third*.

11

Telling the Truth About Words

Philip B. Gove

Philip Gove, the editor-in-chief of the Webster's Third International Dictionary, *asserts that a dictionary today should describe usage rather than prescribe it. Dr. Gove's comments appeared in* Word Study, *April, 1968.*

"The function of grammars and dictionaries," writes Professor Robert A. Hall, Jr., of Cornell University, "is to tell the truth about language. Not what somebody thinks ought to be true, not what somebody wants to ram down somebody else's throat, nor what somebody wants to sell somebody else as being the 'best' language, but what people actually do when they talk and write. Anything else is not the truth, but an untruth" (*Quarterly Journal of Speech*, December, 1962, p. 434).

Suppose you want to find out about the reading habits of the English-speaking people. Would you consider that these habits could be described by simply writing down the titles of all the best books you could think of? Would you accept as evidence what people say they ought to read or intend to read? Or would you consult libraries and publishers and booksellers to find out what they actually do read? Ideally you'd want to see them reading. Since that is impracticable, you'd need some reliable next-best evidence.

A dictionary should be based on what educated people actually do write and say. Its maker must find this out, not by asking how they think they ought to use words or think they would use them in imagined situations. Its maker must get hold of some real evidence. There are at least two kinds of evidence, subjective and objective.

A dictionary maker should be someone who has studied his language carefully and has read in it widely. Such a person can give opinions on how certain words are used because over the years he has become accustomed to seeing and hearing them used in the same way. These opinions are evidence, but this kind of evidence is subjective. The opinions have been stored by the learning process. They need verification. A dictionary based on only subjective evidence without immediate verification is sure to be weak and even defective. No one person and no editorial staff can have read and stored away enough to be sure about

117

all the details of usage which must be recalled and set forth in a dictionary that is to have any valid claim to scholarly merit.

For example, do educated users of English speak about a *chronic* deficit? Does a leerer *give* leers to the object of his attention? Do you speak of a magazine's *passing*? If you promise to pay in the fall, do you omit the preposition when you specify *next* fall? Do educated writers use *contact* as a transitive verb? Was the acquitted Andrew Johnson *impeached*? Does any careful writer refer to losing *some* $737.52 or report that *some* 35,492 people saw the baseball game? "She hated every minute she was there," but can one *hate* a minute? Or is *hate*, perhaps, intransitive? Is *hall of fame* generic? Could an African nation *abolish* polygamy? Can you *stop* ignorance by becoming a Big Brother? Is a harp player a *harper* (compare *drummer*) or a *harpist* (compare *violinist*)? What is the difference between *adjudication, negotiation, mediation, conciliation,* and *arbitration* as methods of settling the Arab-Israeli problem today? How do English-speakers pronounce *Kuwait?* Does donating a heart for a human transplant constitute a *gift* of life? Is starvation something that can become *obsolete* by production of enough food? Does the work of the *psychiatrist* overlap that of the *psychoanalyst?* Can you have a *proclivity* for not dropping things? What is a coffee shop that gives away matchbooks with the word *notorious* on them trying to say? Does "we will give you a lot of dollars" sound like the English of a native English speaker? Can a marihuana smoker become *addicted?* Is it true that few people under forty would write "we do not know *to* which of our dictionaries you refer"? Who uses *so* as a coordinating conjunction? Is it *Jennie's* hat or *Jenny's* hat? What does *by* mean in "he's a lawyer by profession"? Is it six *people* or six *persons?* What is a *module* in today's English? How do you straighten this statement out: "I mention this only to justify the departure from the traditional socalled overview in which I intend to indulge myself"? What is a *scarehead?* Is man *suctorial?*

No one can authoritatively answer a hundred thousand questions like these—and this is not an exaggeration; the number is limited only by the number of hours you can stay awake each day—day after day, month after month, year after year in the course of making a dictionary. No one can recall the whole truth about the hundred thousand and up words that must go into a desk dictionary. (And it doesn't follow that ten editors can each be assigned the responsibility for ten thousand words, in an alphabetical sequence or otherwise, for language cannot be fragmented in that way.) The indispensable here is objective evidence. This is to be found in real examples of actual usage, in filed quotations taken from thousands and thousands of writers. The dictionary maker goes to his files to find out who uses *chronic* to modify nonhuman things like deficits and who uses *contact* as a transitive verb. Only when he can rely on this kind of objective evidence can he feel sure that he is making his dictionary serve its proper function.

The Empire State Building pays a two-cent entertainment tax on every paid admission to the tower. That adds up to well over $100,000 a year which is turned over to the tax office under protest, on the grounds that the view is education, not entertainment. The Court said no and pointed to the words in its own advertising that call it "the world's most spectacular view" (Springfield, Mass., *Union*, November 9, 1967, p. 41). When can education be entertainment? Can a spectacular be education?

Anyone can think about the terms *rest home, convalescent home,* and *nursing home* and conclude that they designate, in order, a home for someone who needs rest, someone who is convalescing, and someone who needs the care of a nurse. This looks logical, in fact indisputable, but how do people actually use these terms? Do people use one when another is meant? The nature of people implies they often do, not simply because people are often imprecise but more significantly because there may be no need to make careful discriminations. A situation which calls for saying "I hear his father is in a ———— home" probably does not require one of the three modifiers instead of either of the other two. Any of the three will do. But if the speaker says "I really ought to put my father in a ———— home right away," he will apply the appropriate modifier because he knows his father's condition, what kind of care he needs, and how long he is probably going to stay. From this real-life situation, accurately recorded, we can extract the precise sense of at least one of these three terms. If the reading for the files has been wide enough, the files will yield the necessary objective evidence.

Every teacher of English knows that a handbook of composition needs objective evidence more than prescription. From time to time an excellent one comes along to delight the teacher and enlighten the student. The excellent handbook reveals on every page that it has been carefully based on objective evidence, the kind that can teach a student control over words. The control of language, as of any established cultural system, comes from within. It is not imposed from without by manipulation of the symbols. The last few decades have brought a surfeit of hastily prepared handbooks based on subjective evidence. ("It's a lucrative business and I've certainly taught English long enough to turn out a handbook. Heaven knows I've seen all the errors possible.") The distribution of some handbooks suggests that dictionaries can be made in the same way. And indeed they have been.

Who now uses *contact* transitively in the sense of "to get into communication with (a person or agency)"? If we had all the evidence, we could answer "just about everybody—under forty years of age." We don't have it all, but we have enough to justify putting this sense in today's dictionary without a deprecating label. The vehement attacks of the 1930s on this use of *contact* probably explain why many still alive among us—and over forty—will go to the grave without ever once saying, "Contact the office as soon as you arrive." Among us presumably will be the senior manuscript editor at a large university press who said in 1967 that if an applicant uses *contact* as a verb (among other heinous offenses) "forget him" (*Publishers' Weekly*, July 17, 1967, p. 45).

Sometime in November of 1931 F. W. Lienau, tariff expert of the Western Union Telegraph Company, wrote in a letter to his general managers: "Somewhere there cumbers this fair earth with his loathsome presence a man who for the common good should have been destroyed in early childhood. He is the originator of the hideous vulgarism of using *contact* as a verb." Such vehement extremism made news, of course, and was kept alive for months by letters to the editors; both the *New York Times* and the *Herald Tribune* wrote approving editorials. The latter said, "It is the latest and one of the blackest in the lengthening list of similar crimes attributable to the illiterate authors of business correspondence" (May 18, 1932). Quixotically, the earliest example known to us could hardly escape being called a vulgarism: "Men are divided in thought and feeling. They are no longer satisfied to be either churchmen or atheists, but are beginning to *contact* God vaguely, uncertainly, in many ways" (Springfield, Mass., *Union*, January 14, 1926). That is four years older than the *OED Supplement* citation, which is marked *U.S.*, probably rightly so, but its 1929 citation is taken from a book titled *America Challenged*, published in London, and written by an Englishman, Lewis F. Carr.

The new sense of *contact* had to be put into *Webster's New International Dictionary, Second Edition* (W2) in 1934, but because of the word's notoriety, it was labeled *slang*. Gradually the controversy did die down, the word does fill a need, and by midcentury it had forced its way into acceptableness except by those who had been indelibly affected by the controversy of the 1930s. A new word or a new sense of an old word gets into a dictionary because it is used by a large number of educated people in a lot of places and usually over a period of time. Record of the usage lies mostly in the written language (unless the dictionary maker wants to hear how a word is spoken). Books of all kinds (mostly expository), journals (learned, professional, trade), magazines (literary and popular), newspapers (mostly daily), reports, reviews, catalogs, house organs, menus, timetables, instruction manuals—just about everything in English that is written down for the practical end of conveying information and keeping our culture and economy from falling apart contributes to a mass of writing that moves across the desks of Merriam editors daily to be read, marked, and reduced (by copying or cutting) to 3 x 5 slips, each containing a quoted passage. When these slips from various sources are filed alphabetically, all the quotations for any one word eventually come together.

Some words, instead of forcing their way, come into prominence suddenly and may not require overwhelming evidence. For example, when most of the airlines began to call the passenger who doesn't show up a *no-show* and when they put up signs reading "don't be a no-show" and printed notices and pleading requests on their timetables and ticket covers, the word was here to stay. (It could disappear, too, but not suddenly.) Millions of air travelers read it and said it (at least to themselves). One ticket cover in our files represents all the passengers who have thrown theirs away, just as one quotation from a daily newspaper represents a usage frequency equal to the estimated readership of the one issue containing it. Even more sudden and unusual is the new word *cosmonaut*. This word, translated into English from a Russian dispatch, was used within the course of a few hours in English newspapers throughout the world. We do not have to pile up evidence for it, because millions have seen and used it.

The dictionary maker's claim to accurate analyses of meaning and usage does not rest only on the amount of the evidence. It must derive from the interaction of a unique citation file with an editorial staff highly trained in the study of language behavior and highly specialized in various fields of knowledge. If the file incorporates a valid cross section of the entire language, the interaction of staff and file makes possible a dictionary that presents the truth about language, that presents the language as a plastic living thing as vigorous as the culture from which it stems.

The commonplace but complex verb *come* is covered in the files used in the making of *Webster's Third New International Dictionary* (W3) by over 5000 citations representing usage extending from the 16th century to the present. Before this one word can be defined, its various occurrences must be studied by various editors who (among them) have studied (among other fields) agronomy, animal husbandry, botany, education, engineering, food technology, metallurgy, printing, religion, and seamanship. The senses must then be coordinated to formulate a definition genuinely reflecting usage and duly supplemented by appropriate labels, guide phrases, usage notes, and illustrative matter designed to bring the word alive for the dictionary user. Nor does the process end here, for before being released for publication the whole sequence is reviewed by separate editors.

In the planning stages the editorial staff must decide what needs to be included in its unabridged dictionary and in its college desk dictionary. Are there functions to be performed by one that are not performed by the other? How must they differ from their counterparts of a generation ago in order to serve today's users best? In short, what are the functions of a dictionary? The intentions of those who make dictionaries should be governed by the needs of those who use dictionaries. To be sure, there are whole classes of information that the user of W2 could find out that the user of W3 cannot, or if so only incidentally. W3's user cannot find the population in the commune of Oostdongeradeel in the Netherlands. He cannot find that François Magendie was a pioneer early 19th-century French physiologist well known to today's heart surgeons or how to pronounce his name. He cannot learn that

Nydia is a blind flower girl in Bulwer-Lytton's *Last Days of Pompeii* (Is this on your students' reading list today?). He cannot find that Mannus is "according to Tacitus, the divine ancestor of the Germanic peoples." He cannot, unless he reads the etymology at W3's entry *man on horseback*, find that the original was General Boulanger.

We know a lot more about military dictators today than in the early 1930s. Compare W3's entry at *man on horseback:*

> **man on horseback**   [after the *Man on Horseback*, nickname of Georges E. J. M. Boulanger †1891 Fr. chauvinistic general and demagogue; fr. his frequent appearance before the Paris crowds mounted on a black horse] **1**: a man typically a military figure whose ambitions, personal popularity, and pretensions to be destined to save the nation or lead it to greatness mark him as a potential dictator <endangered by *men on horseback* or rabble-rousers—Telford Taylor> <used to advantage by the first rascally *man on horseback* who comes along—*New Yorker*> **2**: DICTATOR, CAUDILLO; *esp*: a military dictator <the *man on horseback* . . . comes to power by way of a coup, usually with army support—Bruce Bliven b. 1889>

with W2's:

> **Man on Horseback**   General Boulanger (1837–91);—so called because he usually appeared mounted.

Which dictionary serves the user better? Did you even know that real people have actually used this esoteric phrase often enough in the 20th century to make it more a generic than an epithet? This is what the dictionary user needs and wants. There are four basic questions a dictionary user expects to find answered: how a word is spelled, how it is pronounced, how it originated, and how it is used. *Man on horseback* is a three-word combination whose elements are pronounced at their own single places of entry. At the entry for the term itself the user can find its spelling (without hyphens), its origin, its meaning, and its range of usage.

The largest category of matter not found in W3, then, consists of proper nouns, names of one-of-a-kind items. (See for a detailed list and fuller explanation "The Nonlexical and the Encyclopedic," *Names*, June, 1965, pp. 103–15.) In an age of expanding vocabulary, of wider and different ranges of interest, and of rapid shifts in political entities, it is a small loss considering the wider availability of more specialized reference works, atlases, almanacs, biographical dictionaries of every description that are more easily kept current than a formidably time-consuming unabridged dictionary. Such information is not the province of an unabridged dictionary anyway. If it were in W3, it would be at the expense of a large number of words now in. Individuals need a larger vocabulary now than in the 1930s. Whether there is more or less stratification of vocabulary now need not be settled, but every speaker in a culture in which princesses, babysitters, presidents, and baseball players are exposed to the same language by film, radio, and television needs access to more language strata. He wears more hats. As Prof. Arnold B. Larson of Stanford University has written: "In our society we speak as we live: according to our roles. Our roles are many, and the ways we use speech are as numerous. One may be a physicist, gardener, husband, father, lover, do-it-yourselfer . . . birder, surfer, hiker, biker, piker, Scout leader, discussion-group chairman, and much more, all more or less contemporaneously and with no trouble at all. And each of these roles requires a different use of language if the role-player is 'with it' " (*Science*, January 18, 1963, p. 245 f.).

Critical opinion says that a dictionary should disregard objective evidence and *set* a standard. The W3 editors say that a dictionary must describe the objective evidence and *show* a standard. The editors' view is not revolutionary or even new. Samuel Johnson in the preface to his great dictionary of 1755 said, "this uncertainty [about the meaning of words] is not to be imputed to me, who do not form, but register the language; who do not teach men how they should think, but relate how they have hitherto expressed their thoughts" (C^{1v}). Such was the viewpoint of the editors of W2, and such is the viewpoint of the editors of W3. Each staff assumed in its own time the responsibility for telling the truth about the English language. The editors of W3 were well aware of the standing of its predecessor as an arbiter, even as they are aware today of the role their book will assume in the eyes of their successors of the next generation. But the W2 editors did not attempt to present their own opinions as an arbitrary standard. The merits of W2 are those of a distillation of the behavior of English-speaking writers in an earlier quarter of the 20th century. W3 professes to do the same for midcentury writers, and W4 will do it for a later group.

The developments in language use during the twenty-seven years between W2 and W3 seemed to call for some fairly basic changes in the dictionary presentation of objective evidence. One is the inclusion of illustrative quotations on a large scale—identified by the author or publication for the purpose of placing the word defined in a typical and genuine language context. The illustrative quotations in W3 are there for one reason, to show the user how a particular sense of an entry word has actually been used by a typical user. The definer of that sense of that word may find the opinion expressed in that quotation unacceptable to him, and he may find the style something he would never put his name to. Nevertheless, if he finds that a particular quotation best fits the sense which covers it, he selects it for an example. If the author quoted happens to be one commonly held in high esteem, so much the better. Although hardly a column in W3 is without the names of some well-known contemporary writers of good quality, being contemporary was not an overriding criterion. Still at the top of the list of the most quoted sources are Shakespeare and the Bible, and well represented are names like Milton, Meredith, Jane Austen, Sir James G. Frazer, Dryden, Dickens, and Shelley. The search for illustrative quotations was not for the new or the ephemeral but for the most useful to the dictionary user.

Because the English language has added many new words and meanings to its vocabulary as a result of increasing knowledge as the century advances, W3 has been required to show even greater selectivity than W2 in its choice of entries. This was made mandatory by the decision to allot more space to illustrative quotations than ever before. The editors scrutinized more closely the technical vocabularies while taking into account the dissemination of mechanical and technical knowledge to a wider segment of the informed reading public than was true at the time of W2. The most stringent tests of entry were applied to the new terms of the general vocabulary. As has been said in many ways, W3 is a dictionary for the 1960s and must—its most important function— show today's user today's language. It can show only a selection, a selection intended to be of value now and of value for a few decades, until superseded. A new entry deserves entry when the evidence shows frequency, scope of currency, spread of time, and a strong likelihood of staying in the language. Usefulness may or may not be criterional; innumerable useful words have been introduced, sometimes with trumpets, only to remain unused. As an instance of the principles guiding selection of a new entry, consider the cases of *rock 'n' roll* and *rockabilly*. Rock 'n' roll it may be fondly wished, is not here to stay, but the word *rock 'n' roll* is a longtime addition to the English vocabulary. The word *rockabilly*, however, though supported by some evidence, turns out to be ephemeral and omissible.

Another change is the dropping of the label *colloquial*. Of course there are distinguishable levels of usage, but in situations in which words vary from one extreme to another, attempting to fix them on one level without context would inevitably result in being more often misleading than helpful. W3 employs the labels *slang, substandard, dialect, obsolete,* and *archaic,* when there is a fair chance of being informative, as well as such usage guide phrases as "not often in formal use" and "usu. considered vulgar." For instance, on the slightly more than five pages extending from *logistics* through *loose,* chosen at random on the basis of the fact that they come near the middle of the dictionary, there are sixty such labels, including not only *archaic* and *obs* but also *dial, slang,* and a considerable variety of labels indicating regionally restricted use, such as *Brit* (for "British"), *West, South, North, New Eng* (for "New England"), and *Scot* (for "Scottish"). In the same section of the alphabet—*logistics* through *loose*—there are instances of the dropping of the label *slang* from W2 (*so long, looker* as in "a good looker"), of the retention of a label (*long green* for "paper money"), and of the addition of a label (as in the new entries *looey* for "lieutenant" and *long-sleever*, an Australian term for a large drink of beer); similarly, there are instances of the dropping of the label *dial* (*London pride*, the popular name of two different flowers), of the retention of the same label (*long dog* for "greyhound"), and of the addition of the label (*look* in the transitive-verb sense of "to count (as sheep) to determine whether any have strayed"). These are only a few samples, but they afford glimpses of responsible editors applying themselves, word by word and sense by sense, and always on the basis of genuine records of usage, to the task of giving a clear, detailed, and undistorted picture of our current language.

There has, it is true, been a considerable drop in the frequency of use of *slang* as a label, but this reflects only evidence that the language of the sixties employs informal English to a greater degree than did the language of the thirties. An influence equally important is the observation that certain technical terms, such as those of baseball, formerly labeled *slang*, are in reality not slang but the original and appropriate terms for what they designate. W3 and *Webster's Seventh New Collegiate Dictionary* both distinguish levels of usage according to a consistent set of criteria.

In line with the editors' determination to more consistently describe usage rather than prescribe it, W3 attempts to make the definitions and their illustrative quotations themselves show their level of usage to the intelligent consultant. Too often in past dictionaries a usage note has been a crutch for a limping definition. The dropping of the label *colloquial* is in line with these policies. Whether or not the true glories of the English language lie in some ceremonious tongue reserved for special occasions and pronouncements, the bulk of the English language quantitatively is a stock of words whose use is governed by immediate need, by personal taste and education, by culture and reading, by prominence in current broadcasts, in journals, or in newspapers. It is often easy enough to decide that such-and-such a word of this stock is or is not formal, is or is not colloquial. But most speech and writing today is colloquial. There is no longer such a wide gap between the kind of natural unforced language that people usually use in oral discussion of a serious subject and the kind of language they use in writing about the same subject as there was a generation or two ago. Examples such as *long face* and *look down one's nose*, labeled *colloquial* in W2, illustrate the point: to exclude such items from written English is to imply that written English cannot be correct unless it is devoid of all color. To stigmatize a particular word from this stock as "colloquial" too easily gives the impression that there is something linguistically bad about it, when actually it may be pure linguistic coin of the realm. There are situations in which a person would not use *okay*, but there are also situations in which one would not use *sesquipedalian* or *photosynthesis*. The definitions in W3 with their illustrative quotations give some hint as to what these situations are. The rest is a matter of the consultant's own linguistic sense. If that sense is lacking, the label *colloquial* cannot replace it.

Both *Webster's Third New International Dictionary* and *Webster's Seventh New Collegiate Dictionary* respect the intelligence of the dictionary user and challenge him to bring all of his word-sense to the dictionary. With the backing of the largest assemblage of ordered objective evidence in existence these dictionaries undertake to tell the truth about the English language. It is for the most part up to the dictionary user to apply his intelligence and education to the truth before him and decide on whether a particular word in a particular context fits. For, as has been said of the law, a word is not the same at morning and at night.

STUDY QUESTIONS AND EXERCISES

1. Look up the Robert Hall article to which Gove refers and compare it with the articles in this text on usage and dictionaries. (See also the selection by Hall at the end of this text.)

2. Explain the differences between the two kinds of evidence used by a dictionary maker. Why is either kind by itself inadequate?

3. In *Webster's Third* and one other dictionary look up six or eight of the italicized words that Gove uses as examples in paragraph 5. What answers can you give to Gove's questions? What differences do you find between the dictionaries? Is there any pattern in the differences?

4. Where would the writer of a handbook on composition get objective evidence: in other handbooks? in the most complete and recent dictionaries? in Margaret Bryant's *Current American Usage?* In a recent handbook of composition select some "rule" of usage and see what objective evidence *Webster's Third* gives as to the validity of that rule as representing usage of educated people.

5. Secure biographical data on the panel of 100 who judged questions of usage in the *American Heritage Dictionary.* What are the extremes of age represented? What is the average age? What was their verdict on the transitive verb *contact?* Get the verdict on *contact,* v. tr., of twenty-five instructors or assistant professors (likely to be under forty) in various academic fields. How does their verdict compare with that of the panel of 100? Do you regard the *American Heritage* use of *contact* as unsuitable for contexts in which the word is likely to occur? Where usage differs, why may usage notes be helpful to young people seeking positions in a profession? (This exercise might be a class project.)

6. Can you cite any recent words which have been immediately

accepted, as was *cosmonaut?* What classes of words are most likely to be immediately accepted?

7. In *Webster's Third* look up *go* or *get.* How many different meanings do you find? How many idiomatic phrases? How many synonyms? Compare with the *Random House Dictionary.* Are there any notable differences?

8. What kinds of information are excluded from *Webster's Third?* Compare the table of contents, as well as specific sections in the vocabulary, with those of *Random House, American Heritage,* and *Webster's New World* dictionaries. How do concepts of what a dictionary is differ from Gove's as represented in *Webster's Third?* Is there any agreement, total or partial, with Gove?

9. What are the four basic questions of the dictionary user? Why does *Webster's Third* list the etymology of a word after the pronunciation: is there any relation between spelling and pronunciation and derivation? between the literal meaning in the derivation and the present meanings? Is there any advantage in putting the etymology where it may be noted in passing? Look up *dexterous* and *sinister* in *Webster's Third:* of what interest and value is the literal meaning?

10. What did Samuel Johnson finally decide was the function of a lexicographer? What was his original ambition as a lexicographer? (See Ong, selection 10.)

12

A Linguistic Look at Aerospace English

Donald A. Sears and Henry A. Smith

With the exploration of new frontiers, the need to express new concepts and new values more precisely arises. Professor Donald A. Sears of California State College at Fullerton and Henry A. Smith, Publications Project Coordinator of North American Rockwell Corporation, discuss some of the effects of aerospace activities upon the English language. Their article appeared in Word Study *for April, 1969.*

There has been extremely little written on the subject of this paper.[1] None of the standard technical writing books deals with language as affected by aerospace science and technology. Linguists, except for the few referred to and the mathematical/electronic communication specialists, have not treated aerospace or scientific English.

Yet some of the linguistic aspects of aerospace English are both interesting and worthy of study for the light they shed on broader problems of language. In order to clarify our approach to these problems, it is first necessary to distinguish levels of aerospace English.

One level is that found in the usage guides and technical writing handbooks employed within the industry. They are concerned strictly with written language in its final printed form. The scientific language reflected in them is "concrete, specific, simple, direct, precise, generally more active than passive, concise, clear, and readable."[2]

Another level is that of the raw, crude language of a rough draft re-

---

[1] Alfred M. Bork, *Science and Language* (Boston, 1966), Walker Gibson, ed., *The Limits of Language* (New York, 1962), and Mario Pei, *Language of the Specialists* (New York, 1966) are perhaps the most useful.

[2] These possibly redundant terms are taken from Theodore A. Sherman, *Modern Technical Writing* (New Jersey, 1966). He says, "Our style becomes readable when we choose our words intelligently, write sentences of suitable length, develop such qualities as simplicity and directness and conciseness—in fact do all the things that have been recommended" (p. 23). This approach to language is something like that of a foreign-traveling English lady quoted by H. Allen Smith, *How To Write Without Knowing Nothing* (New York, 1950): "I don't see why, if one speaks slowly and distinctly, English should not be understood by everybody."

flecting "birdworks"[3] conversation. This paper is a consideration, from the standpoint of linguistics, of birdworks prose of this unedited sort. Specifically we wish to investigate the words and the language patterns peculiar to aerospace technology in order to discover to what extent the evolution of aerospace technology has influenced the language generally. Has the hardware affected the words; have the programs, with all of their economic, political, and cultural implications, affected American language patterns?

The Words

Imbedded in our everyday speech are words that evidence the once pervasive influence of the predecessor of modern astronomy, astrology. The extent of these vestiges of old astrology is greater than we usually realize. The heavenly bodies have caused us to be *jovial, mercurial, saturnine, martial,* and *venereal* (an ironic tribute to the goddess of love). Something of the original "value" of some astrological terms is still maintained: *disaster* (an evil star) retains a superlative graveness, and *consider* (to be with the stars) still denotes a very high form of mental deliberation.*

Well may we ask, then, if modern aerospace technology exerts such an etymological influence. And if so, what effect does such a vocabulary have on American speech? The American linguist Leonard Bloomfield has stated:

> The connotation of technical forms gets its flavor from the standing of the trade or craft from which they are taken. Sea terms sound ready, honest, and devil-may-care: *abaft, aloft,* the *cut of his jib, stand by*; legal terms precise and a bit tricky: *without let or hindrance, in the premises, heirs and assigns. . . .*[4]

Similarly, aerospace terms have a confident devil-may-care tone from historical air-force sources (the mission is *A-OK*), but there is an added tinge of mystery drawn out of the deep, adventurous, and unknown "space" which we are approaching: *space probe, acculation, neutrosphere, primary body, translunar, weightlessness, earth-escape trajectory.*

Economy of effort is a strong influence on aerospace words, and it can be seen in the tendency to abbreviate (*recirc* is widely used for *recirculation, conbud* is official for contractural budget) and in the tendency to make new words from the abbreviations, as in the case of acro-

---

[3] *Bird* is "a colloquial term for a rocket, satellite, or spacecraft." (Mario Pei, *Language of the Specialists*, p. 375.) A *birdworks* is an aerospace corporation.

* The asterisk is also an astrological effect.

[4] Leonard Bloomfield, *Language* (New York, 1933), p. 152.

nyms. NASA / næsə / started as *The National Aeronautics and Space Administration*, then became *The N-A-S-A*, then *the NASA*, and finally NASA. Problems arise: one company which has two large NASA contracts uses both *LOX* and *LO₂* in written reports as abbreviations for *liquid oxygen* depending on which program is being reported because of the preferences of the particular NASA project managers. All engineers, of course, say *LOX*. Editors in the Publications Department, of course, say *LOX* or *LO₂* as a matter of habit, depending on which program group they are in, since it is their duty to maintain the integrity of final report language. (The last three words themselves form part of the jargon of the trade.)

Some acronyms have strange histories and also exert an interesting influence. For example, a Saturn booster rocket must be tested and checked before it is delivered to NASA. However, such a rocket is a rather complex set of systems encased in an aerodynamic structure, and the testing and checking process involves the performance of some 30 to 40 separate and combined tests, which have to be reported in written form to NASA. In the original contract, these reports were originally referred to as *system test and checkout reports*. Soon an abbreviation arose, but it was phonetically clumsy: *STCR*. It then became redundantly an *STCR report*. Eventually, just as if *STCR* were a Hebrew tetragrammaton, the engineers added vowel points, and the word *streetcar* emerged as a reference for *system test and checkout report*. It proves that words are arbitrary. Once in a while an engineer from another part of the program will ask in complete puzzlement: "What the hell is a streetcar?" However, this problem has had the good effect of causing more careful linguistic planning by the people who control acronyms in additions to the contract. Some of the latest are the *failure effect analysis report* (FEAR), *special materials and special handling* (SMASH), the *electronic ground automatic destruct sequencer* (EGADS) button.

A few words, of course, are not arbitrary. An editor recently encountered a *POGO* program and could not figure out the acronymic referents. It turned out that *POGO* was not an acronym even though it had been capitalized. *POGO* is the accordion-like squeeze and stretch oscillation that occurs along the central axis of a launch vehicle during liftoff and flight. The expression was meant to be the same as for the movement involved in using a pogostick. This type of cultural reference could have unfortunate consequences, since it is idiomatic and confusing to a non-American audience. It proves that language is better left alone to be arbitrary so that it can be understood by all.

Sometimes a word resists being stretched to fit an expanded meaning. Until recently, the verb *slave* was used for one unit being *slaved* (or tied into the function of) another mechanically (in the manner of gears) and also, in an extended meaning, for gyros being *slaved* to electrical potentials in closed loop systems. However, the latter was a new concept, and *slaving* was not really meant. The verb *slew* has now replaced *slave* for gyros or for gears electrically *slewed* to each other.

The level of usage of words used in space technology is in an unusually chaotic state, mainly because there is never sufficient time for usage to settle into a stable body of "Standard Aerospace English." To start with, English is a highly assimilative language; aerospace English, because of its encounter with new scientific concepts and technical possibilities, becomes radically assimilative. As a result, "standard" is hard to find; "correct" usage is often impossible. Language purists who find themselves in aerospace organizations can never completely adjust to the situation. Numerous lists and documents of "preferred" usage are issued, but these are seldom followed and often not even read by technical writers. Most competent writers see an allomorphic range of intelligible forms (e.g., LOX and LO_2), make selections, and use them consistently within specific areas of documentation.

When a piece of equipment is delivered to NASA, the first information reported back to the contractor is *squawks*. These are not *complaints*, which would be a word too strong in connotation; not *discrepancies*, which is too weak and concerned mainly with basic design problems of principal interest to the contractor before the item has completed its manufacturing cycle; and certainly not *mistakes*, the contractor, by means of advanced inspection techniques, already knowing about them. They are simply *squawks*. Purists have tried for years to find a succinct but pure alternative to this word, but have so far been unsuccessful, and the term has become standard aerospace English. Other examples of standard slang are *debugging* and *boilerplate* (used in regard to formula-type language standard for all reports), both of which are also examples of transferred meaning.

Taboo Words. A technical aerospace editor was asked what he felt his main job to be. He replied facetiously, "When I edit a report, my first job is to change all of the *errors* to *malfunctions* and all of the *failures* to *partial successes*." This was a standard practice and the editor was the official keeper of the euphemisms. The reliability engineers, on the other hand, did not want to avoid taboo words; they were chiefly interested in alarming the program to potential failures. To alarm, of course, they needed to use taboo words, like *dangerous* and *catastrophic failures*, which the good editor would, in turn, change to *catastrophic partial successes*. During the early stages of a large booster-rocket contract, all of the companies serving as subcontractors had to be referred to as *suppliers* rather than as *vendors*, because *vendor* implied a poor, blind beggar *vending* pencils. Editors were expected to correct all deviations. Eventually, according to linguistic laws, the disyllable won out, and the trisyllabic *supplier* was eliminated, except when used in the alliterative phrase *supplier support*.

The Patterns

The physicist Percy Bridgman has said that on the printed page, he was

> . . . compelled to express . . . nonverbal emergence in verbal terms. The words in which the physicist defined the meaning of such concepts as "length" must be of the type that have nonverbal referents—no more can be demanded. We have to get back onto the verbal level if we wish to communicate the results of our non-verbal operations.[5]

Bridgman basically wanted *verbalized* language in order to avoid metaphysical and moral problems in expression of reality as seen by science.

In everyday aerospace English, there are two areas of "reality" that the writer must verbalize:

1. Technical facts
2. The meaning (often nontechnical) he wishes the reader to draw from the facts

The communication in writing of these two items is the problem of the aerospace writer. The patterns of aerospace English result from the linguistic encounter with this problem. Engineers often say and believe that the meaning is more important than the English. To the extent that it is true, the hardware and the programs have influenced the language for their own purpose. Also, to the extent that it is true, there are specific patterns of aerospace English.

Technical Factors. The aerospace writer sits down before an accumulation of data. He must present the data verbally and give it meaning in a report. Is his problem one of merely choosing the correct, the preferred words and in making his language "concrete, specific, simple, direct, precise, generally more active than passive, concise, clear, and readable?" Or must he pattern his language in certain ways? Benjamin Lee Whorf, an engineer and a linguist, said,

> Reference is the lesser part of meaning, patternment the greater. . . . It is certain that scientific terms like "force, average, sex, allergic, biological" are . . . no more certain in reference than "sweet, gorgeous, rapture, enchantment, heart and soul, stardust." [6]

---

[5] Percy W. Bridgman, "Words, Meanings, and Verbal Analysis," in Bork's *Science and Language*, pp. 23–43.

[6] Benjamin Lee Whorf, *Language, Thought, and Reality* (Cambridge: MIT Press, 1956), p. 261.

If Whorf's thesis be true, we should expect pattern to supersede reference (or words) as the determiner in aerospace English.

One example of this is the use of redundancy and exaggeration. There are such word groups as the *Specific Specification Control Board* and documents such as the *Logistics Support Plan.* For years, all revisions of reports of a large booster program carried a notice on the cover: "This reissue completely supersedes and replaces all previous issues of this document." The "pattern" of this notice resulted from the strong desire to prevent anyone from using outdated information. Rocket boosters must contain, by pattern of design, hundreds of redundant systems to preclude failure and to provide reliability; they are overdesigned, well beyond what is necessary for normal function. The same overdesign appears in much of the prose. The following sentence, taken from a printed document, is a good example:

> The reliable acquisition of accurate biomedical data on animals has become increasingly important with the use of animals in space flight programs.

It is a long way of saying that measurements must be more accurate and reliable for biomedical data than for other data. "Acquisition of data" should be understood to involve reliability and accuracy. The *degree* of reliability and accuracy is something else. And "biomedical data" on something besides animals would constitute some kind of radical breakthrough worthy of a book of its own.

This type of making assurance doubly sure through redundancy is, of course, never recommended in style guides and should not appear in final printed form. Nevertheless, it does appear often enough in rough copy to be no accident but the manifestation of the techniques of overdesign on language.

The popular concept of a *countdown* being merely a "count" like "one, two, three, go" was changed as the public witnessed actual countdowns on television. The real meaning or referent of the word is a long, difficult, technical checkout with many *holds* and frequent *postponements.* The obvious referent was the wrong one. Now the public language has adjusted itself to the real pattern. Words like *hold* instead of *stop* or *pause* and even *GO/NO GO* have entered the language. Similar qualifications are *memory* (often a device), *noise* (to include non-sounds), the verb *optimize,* and new concepts of measurement such as *g's* (gravities) and *Machs* (times the speed of sound).

Paradoxically, *quality* is now measured *quantitatively.* NASA defines *quality* as

> A measure of the degree to which it conforms to specification or workmanship standards. Its *numerical rating* (our italics) is ob-

tained by measuring the percentage defective of a lot or population at a given time.[7]

Aerospace English does not distinguish between *quality* and *quantity* in the same way that standard English does.

Since our national space program is tied in with our economy and with international and domestic politics, scheduling is an ever-changing thing. The shifting nature of schedules influences the pattern of language. A plan of action for a program change contained the following order:

> Reconfigurate equipment container base drawing to reflect new insert requirement at vehicle 5.

Vehicle 5 is the fifth production model of a booster rocket. The prepositional phrase *at Vehicle 5* would normally terminate an action: *Look at Vehicle 5* for example. But here it is used as a time reference because of the ever-changing schedule. Other usages stemming from the flexible nature of aerospace schedules are *critical path* (the sequence of events on a charted schedule which will take the longest and ultimately govern the accomplishment of other phases of the overall schedule), and *PERT* (and the verb *perted,* from *program evaluation review technique,* a scheduling system).

The verb *reconfigurate* from the aforementioned order is also a term of aerospace writing. A nonengineer might be satisfied with "Change the base drawing," but since the engineer knows that the drawing is a *configuration,* any modification to it is naturally a *reconfiguration.* In this case, there could be too strong an emphasis upon the referent rather than the meaning intended: *change* certainly supplies the pattern, does not curtail the meaning, and is much more economical.

Another aspect of pattern of aerospace English can be seen in the same order in the phrase *equipment container base drawing.* Noun clusters such as this appear frequently enough in aerospace language to constitute a pattern. They are caused by the necessity to describe complicated equipment, and they cause aerospace English to be more agglutinative in certain respects than is standard English. Other noun clusters are *explosive devices simulator set, net positive suction head,* and *stage systems design parameters.* From two of these, the "galloping plural," a technical-age phenomenon, can also be observed. In the last example, singular *system* would suffice; but there are many *systems,* so that the plural must be *built into* the phrase. This technical pattern, a mechanistic result of engineer-built language, is gaining wider usage, into popular technical language, as in *sports* car.

---

[7] NASA, *Apollo Terminology* (Washington, D.C., 1963).

Another minor type of patterning is observable in the use of adjectival subordinate elements as adverbial modifiers.

> Acoustic testing on the forward skirt was accomplished during the first two weeks of December, which completes all testing on the forward skirt.
> Also, this addition allows the facility recorders and cameras to be slaved to the countdown programmer, thereby preventing a premature run out of paper or film during critical firing times.

This practice serves to control the level of reference just because it is not too precise.

Aerospace writing is free, in a sense, of some inhibitions, and often the exigencies of pattern bring to life ancient meanings and produce new meanings. The phrase,

> Responsibility for safing the camera capsule for all pyrotechnics prior to departure from the recovery ship. . . .

was taken from a plan of action for correct processing of cameras recovered after the flight of a large booster rocket. The cameras were ejected from the booster by means of an explosive wire, and they were picked up in the ocean. To avoid having any unused explosive going off in the faces of members of the post-recovery team, the capsule must be disarmed or *safed*. Webster's *Third New International*, liberal and up-to-date as it is, still calls *safed* obsolete. But the word is quite handy and economical for the space program (similar to the slang *debug* and *squawk*). *Pyrotechnics* is really the art of making firecrackers or even an eloquent display of wit. In this case, it is something that, through error or failure (*partial success*), could cause a delayed explosion. The assimilation of new meanings and the renascence of obsolete terms allows great elasticity of expression for conveying specifically chosen levels of technical meaning; in this case, the company was not to be blamed for anyone's getting injured by leftover explosives on the ejected camera.

Nontechnical Factors. The language generally has had its own impact on the patterns of aerospace communications. This can be seen in the romantic tendency to name every rocket or spacecraft after a Greek or Roman god (*Jupiter, Atlas, Hercules, Saturn, Apollo, Thor* [Norse], *Mercury, Gemini,* etc.). These names seem to connote a secular or pagan overseriousness regarding man's ability to conquer the unknown universe by means of "godlike" man-made vehicles, sort of a heresy of technique. Such naming breeds an overconfidence, a sign of which is the gravity of disappointment and the serious economic implications of failure or even poor performance. But it is hard to believe that a "god" could die, even a god of technology. Therefore, the "answer" to any problems of failure always seems to be with the "organization" or the "management" of the program. There seems to be no room for what the poet Paul Roche has called "the rank obstinancy of things." We seem more to be following the thought that Norbert Wiener was so fond of, "God may be subtle, but he is not plain mean," and that might be an example of scientific heresy caused by our linguistic overconfidence.

Confidence in the face of the reality of failure and hardship as seen, for instance, in the military linguistics of World War II:

> Though there's one motor gone
> We will still carry on
> Coming in on a wing and a prayer

and of such realistic names as *The Ruptured Duck* as opposed to *Apollo* or *Jupiter* is a sharp linguistic contrast to the present mentality. If there is one motor gone from a major space vehicle and the astronaut comes in "on a wing and a prayer," someone will be in serious trouble.

The international and domestic political aspects of the *race for space* bring about a linguistic atmosphere of "hard sell." By means of the space program, the United States can make a favorable impression on the "uncommitted" nations; the Democrats could win votes; California representatives want to bring more money into the state in the form of more big contracts; individual companies want the contracts. Consequently, there is a lot of selling, and the language tends to be persuasive, overpositive, and rigged, much like the language and art of socialist realism in which nothing ever really goes wrong and certain negative facts or realities are nearly hidden in the positive perspective. "Factual" data must always be interpreted in the right light. In a program in which an expensive experimental package was placed in a space pod and put into orbit, the costly pod and package failed to separate from the spacecraft and were destroyed upon reentry. In the final report to the customer, the opening paragraph read like a bulletin from *Pravda*:

> The objectives of this program were accomplished. The test results demonstrated that such experiments are feasible for use in space flight research. Sufficient information was obtained to permit recommendations to be made for future efforts.
>
> All equipments functioned properly with the exception of the scientific pod, which failed to eject from the missile prior to reentry. Thus, the pod and experimental package were not recovered.

Note the *positive* tone given to the conclusion. Objectives were accomplished. All *equipments* (the galloping plural) functioned *properly*, except. . . . The linguistic-semantic (meaning control) communicative necessities override any dry, objective listing of the simple facts. The taboo notion of the failure of the expensive recovery system was euphemized: "The . . . package were *not recovered.*" This positive *pattern* or *stylistic* is seen in many aerospace reports; there is a high frequency of positive words (*accomplished, successful, on-schedule, functioned properly, partial success*) and a tabooing of negative words (*failure, error,* etc.).

Conclusion

One might compare the linguistic aftermath of the Biblical effort to step beyond our sphere by means of a tower with the linguistic effects of the similar contemporary efforts at Cape Kennedy. In the first case, the result is best described by the etymological depth of the very name of the effort. The United States' space program is no legend, however, and the linguistic *spin-off* from it can be more accurately defined than that of Babel. It seems that when the engineers use English, they change it to suit their advantage. But that is really the same thing as using English, assimilative and adaptable as it is. Where English cannot be used, other languages are developing.[8]

The engineer who said that the meaning is more important than the English still had to make his meaning meaningful (control its loss) to an English-speaking readership. Perhaps we should say that the meaning (or the language) is more important than the preferred usage.

In a recent, nationally televised lift-off, the smooth, articulated voice from mission control said, in a relaxed Southern dialect, "The pitch and roll program are in." Not many listeners know what the pitch and roll program is, and the speaker does not know that the program *is in.* There is a language gap between advanced technical aerospace English and the standard language of the common man.

There is a semantic problem. For instance, *input* has replaced *put into* in computer parlance; the noun has become the verb again. But the preposition has been retained, and many computer documents now contain *input into.* (The data were input into the program.) The strictly technical computer man is not affronted by this: the "field" of language in which he moves will provide him with the basis for satisfactory comprehension; *input into* forms part of the area of his meaning. This is a sign of a language gap.

The existence of the gap is further verified by the fairly recent development in the aerospace industry of a high-priced group of technical editors (not writers). This field is new, and its personnel are drawn mainly from other language-related fields: journalism, teaching, advertising, the ministry. The race for space has created an urgency in aero-

---

[8] For nonverbal communication, see, for instance, J. R. Pierce, *Symbols, Signals, and Noise* (New York, 1961).

space technical development which has to be reported to nontechnical industrial executives and government officials. At its root the problem may be an educational one. In many universities, engineering majors are required to take few English or foreign language courses; therefore, they do not develop competence in formal composition even though some might be gifted at self-expression. But, in today's communicative world, they have to write; they have to report to the nontechnical sponsoring community. In the current moon project, it is estimated that the paper work, if put in a stack, would reach deeper than the space probe itself.

As the paper mounts, technical editors are astounded, day after day, as they labor through reams of rough copy. They rewrite; they interview the engineer-writers; they key in references to illustrations and tables; they have the book typed and printed nicely, with a well-designed cover. Then a copy is sent to the engineer and he reacts like the actor quoted by H. Allen Smith: "My God, what a swell book I've written!"

STUDY QUESTIONS AND EXERCISES

1. What is the importance of this kind of study of a special vocabulary?

2. What are the levels of aerospace English as identified by Sears and Smith? Would these levels be found in most comparable special vocabularies?

3. What qualities of aerospace English are noted? (See LOX, Evans, selection 5, page 52.)

4. What are acronyms? What examples can you cite from other sciences? from advertising? from government bureaucracy? Why is this kind of word formation now a vital element in neologisms? A campus building was humorously dubbed EPSASH because it housed the departments of Economics, Political Science, Anthropology, Sociology, and History. Why was the term more useful than a conventional name?

5. Why is usage unstable in aerospace English? What practice is followed by competent writers in the field? Look up *squawks, debugging, boilerplate:* would the aerospace meanings be clear, in context, from the dictionary meanings?

6. Look up *euphemism.* Can you cite examples from other dangerous or unpleasant occupations? Consider death and burial and the terminology of morticians.

7. Why does aerospace English have specific patterns? Explain *reference* as used in the quotation from Whorf.

8. Why is redundancy a pattern in aerospace English?

9. If you have some knowledge of French and German, explain

why word clusters are more suitable additions to technical English (with its Germanic origin) than they would be to French.

10. How does the naming of rockets show a return to pre-space-age classical tradition, as the word clusters do to Anglo-Saxon word-formation? At what points in this article is this earlier classical tradition referred to? (The Greek term for superhuman aspiration and overconfidence is *hybris*. Look up the most pertinent classical examples of *hybris*, the stories of Phaeton and Icarus.)

11. In a passage from a current article on the space program, analyze the characteristics of the language, as it is analyzed in the paragraph preceding the *Conclusion*.

12. Why is the allusion to "Biblical effort" in the *Conclusion* particularly suitable?

13. Note the examples of language gap: what principles of grammar are involved?

13

The Vernacular of Space

Mary C. Bromage

In Word Study *for December, 1966, Professor Mary C. Bromage of the University of Michigan describes some of the linguistic peculiarities in the speech of astronauts while in space, and proposes reasons for these peculiarities.*

As the first generation of astronauts, Project Mercury's six pilots pioneered in the language field as well as in space itself. Nobody had seen the same sights or undergone the same sensations as those which these explorers had to report to the waiting world. Language is a frail vehicle, even for communicating the known and the familiar. In reporting the unknown, did the Mercury men succeed—as they so spectacularly succeeded in probing it?

Each had to report verbally and instantly whatever circumstances confronted him and had to do so through a microphone inside his helmet as he lay strapped to his couch: "only man as a living computer system," according to the House of Representatives Subcommittee on the Selection of Astronauts, "can certify to the validity of the data gathered in flight . . . Only he can evaluate the hitherto unsuspected or [un]known . . ." Familiar or at least calculable circumstances which normally supply our instinctive choices in words were, for the first spacemen, without precedent. In spite of a few rifts, the astronauts' ability to communicate showed rapid adaptation to their environment.

Their observations were replete with specialized terminology, much of it scientific: *perigee, telemetry, ionosphere, tropopause, absolute zero, albedo.* Commander Alan B. Shepard, whose flight lasted only fifteen minutes, was precise and terse: "Disarm." "Auto retro jettison circuit." "Cap sep is green." In the interchange of crucial instructions between ground and space, the spacemen's vocabulary was generally technical, the grammatical structure tight: "Clock is started." "Start the sequence."

Major Leroy G. Cooper, in space, heard Lieutenant Colonel John H. Glenn, on the ground, calling:

"Are you ready for a block command?"

Major Cooper: "I am."

Colonel Glenn: "Command on."

The code that developed as in any highly specialized enterprise drew upon existing words, syllables, or letters to meet new needs: *g-pulse, retro rockets, suborbital, capsule, yaw, horizon scannery inputs.* Standard words acquired new senses—*capsule,* for example—senses that may or may not be retained.

The new terms were manufactured to deliver specific messages in minimum time, often alphabetical abbreviations. Colonel Glenn, while in flight, sent back instructions by calling, "Beco, beco," meaning "B(ooster) E(ngines) C(ut) O(ff)." There was no risk of ambiguity here. The private astronautic shoptalk quickly moved over into common parlance because of the status accorded the men and the project.

In reality, their adaptations of phraseology (as in "fly-by-wire") reflect an oral, casual, slangy idiom, easy for most people to follow, underlined with humor, brevity, brotherliness. "Everyone I think sort of gets go-fever," Colonel Glenn was heard to remark at his news conference. Commander Walter M. Schirra while in flight, used the phrase "chimp configuration," meaning he had his spacecraft on an automatic basis as when the monkeys had been sent up. Upon being told he had brought his spaceship down on target, Major Cooper was heard to exclaim: "Right on the old bazoo." Some thought the colloquialism was *kazoo* and others *gazola.* "I'll be doggone if I know what it means," said one of the ground-support men who, nevertheless, got the point: "It's just an old expression I've heard for years."

In addition to their predilection for colloquial words, the space crews habitually used a colloquial syntax. Sentences were talk-built, producing both fragments and pileups with constant variety in length and structure. Verbs became nouns, adjectives became adverbs, as the least of the liberties that were taken: "We were treating this pretty blasé . . ." Again: "I slept too sound to have dreams." And: "I was just laying there minding my own business when—pow! the hatch went . . ." Grammarians reacted critically. For such style, the *Manchester Guardian* coined a word: "Canaveralese." An American critic characterized it as a "blend of launching-pad slang and slovenly syntax." Certainly there was no false elegance, no linguistic "side," in the way the Mercury men communicated under stress.

Expressions familiar in the United States from the level of ordinary conversation were repeated: "First off" was the way Colonel Glenn began his press commentary. "How long did I control on fly-by-wire?" he repeated from a newsman's query. "This is something we want to total out." Later he explained that, while in space, he could not pick out things like a bridge from "this type distance." *Real* was used as an adverb; "sort of," "lots of," "a human," "gotten," "different than" were common parlance. Speaking of the pleasantness of the weightless sensation, Colonel Glenn said: ". . . it sounds like I was an addict to it . . ." Expressions entirely conversational were naturally frequent: "Wow," "yeah," "Ha, ha, ha," "How bout that," "Well," "Ah," "You bet." Colonel Glenn exclaimed in recalling his reentry: "Boy, what a ride." Major Virgil I. Grissom sent back from space this impression: "Boy, that sun is real bright."

The personal characteristics of the astronauts which had led to their selection overall for the pioneer space mission provide the first clue to the way they reported. All were found to possess stability, intelligence, physical stamina, pertinent experience, and personal motivation. Born and raised in different regions of the United States, they were family men in their thirties or earliest forties. All had college training (none, as it happened, with concentration in English); all were members of the armed forces with outstanding records as jet test pilots, plus three-year training in simulated space flight.

As to practice in making themselves clear, their military service had involved dealing with individuals at many different levels. In addition, contacts had been numerous with people outside their own occupation through their religious, civic, social, and athletic affiliations and through the hobbies they listed: archery, boating, fishing, golf, hunting, photography, shooting, skating, skiing, and woodwork. In their general makeup idealism, intrepidity, and enthusiasm seem indisputably to have been present; all had volunteered for Project Mercury. Of all the explorers in history, few if any made their adventurous journeys unaccompanied, as did the Mercury men.

Words they relayed back reflected this solo status in a paradoxical fashion. Commander Shepard repeatedly employed the pronoun "we" while aloft and he continued to do so after his landing. ". . . we actually—I actually—controlled in this case the vehicle, its position during the retrofiring," he stated at his press conference. "We controlled it during the reentry."

"To whom are you referring," reporters wanted to know, "when you say 'we'?" Commander Shepard replied that he felt he was only one of a team which had worked to make this trip a success. Lindbergh's plane, We, suggests an earlier analogue.

The plural constituted linguistic defiance of the sensation of isolation from the rest of humankind. As Colonel Glenn put it, the traveler in space was someone who was "alone where no one has been before," someone who "will need a confidence only experience can give him." Instinctive need to maintain kinship with the known world as suggested in the continuing use of "we" by the earliest astronauts seemed to prove less necessary on the later flights. As experience accumulated, the plural became less noticeable in the running commentaries. Commander Schirra, the fifth to go into space, and Major Cooper, the sixth, reported almost entirely in the first person singular.

As an increment of loneliness, fear was present though not put into words during the flights. Afterward, it was objectively acknowledged:

"Well, I must say there was some apprehension, yes," Commander Shepard was to reply at his press conference. "But," he added significantly, "there's no real point in worrying anyhow. It just messes you up." These were men "who have trained themselves not to think," one listener felt, "but to act and react instantaneously." In the task of conveying quick, lucid comments, fear is usually a minus, not a plus agent. The second suborbital flier, Major Grissom, equaled his predecessor in frankness when he recalled that he "was scared a good deal of the time."

Colonel Glenn described his feelings during reentry this way: "The sensation . . . during the fireball—I guess you'd say cautious apprehension or something like that. Now this is an unknown area, of course." Later, in another connection, he said: "You fear the least what you know the most about," a remark that has to be taken conversely, too: you fear the most what you know the least about.

Only less hard to handle than fear of the unknown was the glare of publicity. The whole universe seemed to be listening in on the flight. "All of a sudden during the middle of the period of weightlessness," explained Commander Shepard afterward, "I realized that somebody was going to ask me that question [i.e., how he felt]. So I said to myself, you'd better figure out an answer." He and his fellows were conscious of being the focal point of world interest: "We had very few secrets about our plans," he remarked ". . . , but I think we all rationalize with the thought that the free democratic society which produced us . . . had a right to be presented [sic] in such a fashion."

In counterbalance to the sense of public exposure, frequent banter between the spaceman and his ground control betokened a sense of intimate rapport. As with much humor, theirs was often based on tacit allusion to common bonds and on common recognition of danger. One astronaut was described as coming "through the radio link easygoing and full of humor." The same could have been said of them all. Much of the space wit that flew back and forth sprang from the sheer matter of incongruity. While orbiting over Australia, Colonel Glenn radioed: "Hey, Gordon, I want to send a message. Tell the Marine Corps commander I have four hours of required flight time and request that a flight chit be prepared for me." He meant that he had qualified for the monthly bonus based on elapsed hours aloft. Out of their jesting arose the image of the spaceman as "cool," "hepped," "in."

Though they could and did switch back instantly into total seriousness, repartee abounded in the capsule-to-tower dialogues. Commander Schirra struck the note of comic relief even before he was aboard his vehicle. En route to the launch pad in the early-morning dark, he explained to a technician watching him pass: "Well, I didn't have much to do today, so I thought I'd go out and take a flight," something of an understatement.

Though humor was not a source of miscommunication for the astronauts, one bit of ambiguity did cause trouble. Dubious meaning, if not quickly detected and rectified, starts a snowballing that soon places the intended sense beyond retrieval. Anxiety arose over Colonel Glenn near the end of his final orbit. Ground telemetry had picked up signals indicating that the heat shield on his Friendship 7 might have come loose. The astronaut about the same time radioed that he was going to "black out." Silence ensued. Had he lost consciousness?

Actually, two things were happening. First, in an emergency decision a radio pack was kept in position so the heat shield could not come loose. Second, in the normal flight plan the Friendship 7 was put into the zone where the atmosphere was so heavily ionized by the shock of reentry that radio messages could not get through for four minutes. ". . . a communication blackout is what we were referring to in this case," explained Colonel Glenn at his news conference, in answer to questions as to "when I regained consciousness and a few things like that." "And," he continued, in one of the rare comments on use of the language in space exploration, "we probably should reterm this a *comloss* or something like that, so that we don't confuse it . . ." Creation of a specialized word is often the only way to pin down new and unmistakable meaning. *Blackout* has, however, now established itself in space lingo, even if only by reason of its notoriety, and *comloss* has not superseded it. Seldom does language follow a planned path of conscious determination.

An accelerated kaleidoscope of nature—the changing horizon, the high-colored sunrises and sunsets, the moon's chiaroscuro—moved the spacemen to graphic wording. "I don't know what you can say [of a day] in which you see four beautiful sunsets," Colonel Glenn reported. "As the sun goes down it's a very white, brilliant light, and as it goes below the horizon and you get your light coming to you then through the atmosphere, it's a very bright orange color; down close to the surface it pales out into sort of a blue, a darker blue, and then off into black."

The most dazzling phenomenon proved to be the particles sighted on several Mercury flights. Since neither Colonel Glenn nor the others knew what the luminescent beams or motes outside their portholes were, they had to compare them to something familiar in order to transmit any idea of what they were like. The similes and metaphors used by the astronauts attested to their early memories of nature.

"At the first light of sunrise—the first sunrise I came to—my initial reaction was that I was looking out into a complete star field," reported Colonel Glenn. "But this wasn't the case, because a lot of the little things that I thought initially were stars were actually a bright yellowish-green about the size and intensity of looking at a firefly on a real dark night." He could only guess at their origin: "I was moving very slowly through this field . . . perhaps water vapor was turning to little snowflakes . . . Occasionally one would come drifting up by the capsule window very close in the shade from the sun."

The next man in orbit, Lieutenant Commander Malcolm S. Carpen-

ter, saw the same spectacle: "they look exactly like snowflakes to me."
Soon after came Commander Schirra's encounter: "I have a delightful
report for John Glenn. I, too, see fireflies! White—they look like ice
crystals." Star fields, fireflies, snowflakes, ice crystals all served as points
of reference for describing the unknown, all drawn from the natural
universe. Aesthetic sensitivity had certainly not been inculcated as part
of space training, nor is it usually inherent in the language of techni-
cally oriented engineers and pilots. Yet the astronauts' reports took on
color and imagery in conveying their pristine observations while en-
circling the earth.

Between the waiting public and each returning space explorer, the
cleavage that had opened was vast. The unknown was still shining
through his eyes and ringing in his ears; to communicate all this meant
that he had to speak without assumptions of familiarity on the part of
his audience. The sense of aloneness, the degree of apprehension, the
consciousness of worldwide exposure, an evanescent vision of ultima
thule, were at work within him.

The Mercury men's idiom proved natural, unpretentious, colloquial,
flexible, fluent, and graphic. All expressed themselves with ease, rapidity,
accuracy, and economy, and at times with vividness. Except for the
formal tone adopted for the ritual of the president's welcome-back
telephone call, the astronauts' vernacular was devoid of traditional
niceties both in word choices and in word relationships. It was the
style best known to Americans from radio and television, a language
pattern induced within a close-knit group whose slang echoed the
World War II generation. These individuals became laboratory models
in the use of words under unprecedented conditions.

Overnight the vernacular of space became a popular idiom: "A-OK,"
"Go-fever," "All signals go," for instance. One critic commented wryly,
"We take their high school verbalisms as perfectly fine and dandy.
They're heroes and astronauts, aren't they?" But another critic of the
style of the space chatter acknowledged, "These men are very typically
American, admirable in candor."

As Colonel Glenn told the House of Representatives' Subcommittee
on Selection of Astronauts: " . . . the human being brings an adapta-
bility, certainly, in his ability to make observations that instruments
and other equipment cannot make." Gemini and Apollo fliers may seem,
in contrast to their Mercury forebears, to be quiet men. Their use of
language is likely to grow more technical and less spontaneous as the
elements of uncertainty decrease and the duties of operational piloting
increase. But as long as discovery is part of the space mission, the wording of the spacemen is not likely to be sterile. The movement of language is the movement of life itself, of circumstances both physical and
psychological attendant upon the communicator. Use of language is,
after all, a form of human behavior. The more who engage in a space
mission, the longer they remain, the farther they go, the stranger the

surroundings they penetrate, the greater the demand placed upon human as well as on mechanical systems of communication.

STUDY QUESTIONS AND EXERCISES

1. Which of the language patterns analyzed by Sears and Smith are represented by the technical terms used by the astronauts and the ground support? (Look up *astronaut*: how is it typical of both new scientific terminology and traditional, familiar language?)

2. What are the characteristics of vocabulary and style of the space crews? What are their personal characteristics? Should their language be seriously considered as illustrating acceptable American usage?

3. What language processes are illustrated by *blackout* and *comloss*?

4. Compare the concluding quotation from Commander Glenn with previous quotations from him and the other astronauts. What differences do you note in vocabulary and style? How do you explain these differences?

14

Words and Meanings

Thomas Pyles

Communication is a complex process, and our response is affected by several factors that Professor Pyles examines in this selection from The Origin and Development of the English Language *(1964).*

In considering meaning, we cannot here be concerned with those larger philosophical aspects of language which have increasingly in recent years engaged the attention of scholars like Rudolf Carnap, Charles W. Morris, I. A. Richards, Ernst Cassirer, and Susanne K. Langer, nor with the "general semantics" of Alfred Korzybski, whose disciples with evangelical zeal unwittingly made *semantic* a vogue word meaning little more than 'verbal.' These approaches are certainly of great interest and value, but are not directly connected with such changes in meaning in the course of the development of the English language as we shall examine in this chapter.

Devices for Signaling Meaning

The educated man or woman is by long tradition expected to possess what is frequently referred to as "a good command of language." Actually . . . a child of five or so already has a "good command," in the sense that he uses without effort practically all the devices by which meaning is signaled vocally, sometimes with the aid of gestures. No normal child of even tenderer years would fail to understand, and to make an appropriate response to, such an utterance as "Is your mother busy?" or to distinguish it from the utterances "Your mother is busy" and "Your mother is busy?" It will be noted that the words in these utterances are identical in form and in meaning. What, then, are the linguistic devices by which the child distinguishes any one of these utterances from the others? Word order and intonation do the trick; in "Your mother is busy?" intonation alone (the rising tone beginning on the first syllable of *busy*) does it.

After we have mastered the use of such devices—we did so more or less unconsciously, of course, long before we could make any analysis of what we do or how we do it—about all that we acquire, except for a few more or less sophisticated "literary" constructions, are vocabulary items. Though we should as educated persons be able to analyze the linguistic devices by which we communicate with one another, we actually acquire these devices without formal instruction. But in the process we acquire only the most useful, everyday words—usually words which have been a part of the English language from the earliest times (*mother, moon, busy, ready, good, run, have, to, and*), along with some words of foreign origin which have been a part of it for a very long time (*giant, chase, catch*) or which for some other reason have been thoroughly naturalized—more or less homely words which continue for all our lives to provide our basic word hoard. But such equipment, common to all speakers of a language, does not comprise what is meant by "a good command of language."

Why Study Words?

The fact is that, if we are going to be able to talk about anything very far beyond our day-to-day, bread-and-butter living, if we are going to associate in an easy manner with cultivated people, if we are going to read books which such people have found to be important and significant, then we must have at our command a great many words that the man in the street and the man with the hoe neither know nor use. This is not to imply that there is anything wrong in being a common man; his name is Legion, he is the salt of the earth and "a man for a' that." But it is assumed that most people, even though they may have no real intellectual aspirations, want to be—or at least to pass for—something more than, or at least different from, common men and women.

To begin the study of language with an examination of its word stock is, however, to put the cart before the horse, for words come later to us in our linguistic development than sentences—even the child's first meaningful utterances are sentences, though many of them may consist of only a single word each. But the fact remains that most people find the study of words and their meanings interesting and colorful. Witness in newspapers and magazines the number of "letters to the editor," usually sadly misinformed, which are devoted to the uses and misuses of words. These are frequently etymological in nature, like the old and oft recurring wheeze that sirloin is so called because King Henry VIII (or James I or Charles II) liked a loin of beef so well that he knighted one, saying "Arise, Sir Loin" at the conferring of the accolade.

Why Meaning Varies

The attribution of some sort of meaning to combinations of distinctive speech sounds and in a few instances to single sounds is a matter of social custom, and like other customs may vary in time, place, and situation: thus *tonic* may mean 'soft drink made with charged water' in parts of eastern New England, though elsewhere it usually means 'liquid medicinal preparation to invigorate the system' or in the phrase *gin and tonic*, 'quinine water'; in the usage of musicians the same word may also mean the first tone of a musical scale. It is also true that many words in frequent use, like *nice, God*, and *democracy*, have among speakers and writers of the same intellectual and social level meanings which are more or less subjective, and hence loose. All meanings of what is thought of as the same word have, however, certain elements in common—elements which may be said to operate within a certain field of meaning. If this were not true, there would be no communication.[1] But this is quite different from assuming the existence of "fixed," or "real," meanings.

Even though words do not have such inflexible meanings as we might prefer them to have, but only a field of meaning in which they operate and which may be extended in any direction or narrowed likewise, it is possible to be irritated at what we may consider a too-loose use of words. For instance, after relating that he had seen a well-dressed man take the arm of a blind and ragged beggar and escort him across a crowded thoroughfare, a rather sentimental man remarked, "That was true democracy." It was, of course, only ordinary human decency, as likely to occur in a monarchy as in a democracy, and by no means impossible under a totalitarian form of government like, say, that of Oliver Cromwell or Adolf Hitler. The semantic element of the word *democracy* which was in the speaker's mind was kindness to those less fortunate than oneself. He approved of such kindness, as indeed we all do; it was "good," and "democracy" was also "good." Hence, as soft-minded people are quite prone to do, he equated "democracy" with goodness.

We are defeating the purpose of accurate communication when we use words thus loosely. It is true that some words are by general consent used with a very loose meaning, and it is very likely that we could not get along without a certain number of such words—*nice*, for instance, as in "She's a nice girl" (meaning that she has been well brought up, is kind, gracious, and generally well-mannered, or, with the word

---

[1] It is neither appropriate nor necessary here to go into the vexed philosophical question of what constitutes meaning—the "meaning" of *meaning*—which belongs in the realm of general semantics.

stressed, merely that she is chaste), in contrast to "That's a nice state of affairs" (meaning that it is a perfectly awful state of affairs). There is certainly nothing wrong with expressing pleasure and appreciation to a hostess by a heartfelt "I've had a very nice time," or even "I've had an awfully nice time." To seek for a more "accurate" word, one of more limited meaning, would be self-conscious and affected.

A large number of educated speakers and writers, for whatever reason, refuse to use *disinterested* in the sense 'uninterested,' a sense which it previously had and lost for a while, and reserve the word for the meaning 'impartial, unprejudiced.' The meaning 'uninterested' has gained ground at a terrific rate, and it is possible that before long it will completely drive out the other one. There will have been no great loss to language *qua* communication. We shall merely have lost a synonym for *impartial* and acquired on all levels another way of saying 'uninterested.' Educated readers of the future will be no more annoyed by the change than they are by similar changes that have given some of the words used in, say, the plays of Shakespeare and in the King James Bible different meanings for us from those which they had in early Modern English. Uneducated readers will be baffled and misled, to be sure; but simple people today frequently misinterpret the King James Bible (the only literature in early Modern English which they are likely ever to read) with complete satisfaction to themselves. It is hardly feasible to expect language to stand still for the sake of ignorant people, who as a matter of fact manage quite well enough, as do the rest of us so long as our less informed fellows are restrained from forcibly imposing their interpretations of what they read, whether sacred or profane, upon us. How long they can be so restrained in a democracy, where numbers are all-important, is a very important question, but it is outside the scope of the present discussion.

Etymology and Meaning

There is a widespread belief, held even by some quite learned people, that the way to find out what a word means is to find out what it previously meant—or, preferably, if it were possible to do so, what it originally meant—a notion similar to the Greek belief in the etymon. Such is the frequent method of dealing with borrowed words, the mistaken idea being that the meaning of the word in current English and the meaning of the non-English word from which the English word is derived must be, or at any rate ought to be, one and the same. As a matter of fact, such an appeal to etymology to determine present meaning is as unreliable as would be an appeal to spelling to determine modern pronunciation. Change of meaning—semantic change, as it is called—may, and frequently does, alter the so-called etymological sense (that is to say, the earliest sense we can *discover*, which is not necessarily the very earliest sense), which may have become altogether obsolete. The study of etymologies is of course richly rewarding. It may, for instance, throw a great deal of light on present meanings, and it frequently tells us something of the workings of the human mind in dealing with the phenomenon of meaning, but it is of very limited help in determining for us what a word "actually" means.

Certain popular writers, overeager to display their learning, have asserted that words are misused when they depart from their etymological meanings. Thus Ambrose Bierce once declared that *dilapidated*, because of its ultimate derivation from Latin *lapis* 'stone,' could appropriately be used only of a stone structure.[2] Such a notion if true would commit us to the parallel assertion that only what actually had roots could properly be eradicated, since *eradicate* is ultimately derived from Latin *rādix* 'root,' that *calculation* be restricted to counting pebbles (Lat. *calx* 'stone'), that *sinister* be applied only to leftists, and *dexterous* to rightists. By the same token we should have to insist that we could *admire* only what we could 'wonder at,' inasmuch as the English word comes from Latin *ad* 'at' plus *mīrāri* 'to wonder,'[3] or that *giddy* persons must be divinely inspired, inasmuch as *gid* is a derivative of *god*.[4] Or that only men may be virtuous, because *virtue* is derived from Latin *virtus* 'manliness,' itself a derivative of *vir* 'man.' Now, alas for the wicked times in which we live, *virtue* is applied exclusively to women. *Virile*, also a derivative of *vir*, has retained all of its earlier meaning, and has even added to it.

From these few examples, it must be obvious that we cannot ascribe anything like "fixed" meanings to words. What we actually encounter much of the time are meanings that are variable, and that may have wandered from what their etymologies suggest. To suppose that invariable meanings exist, quite apart from context, is to be guilty of a type of naïveté which may vitiate all our thinking.

How Meaning Changes

Change of meaning—a phenomenon common to all languages—while frequently unpredictable, is not wholly chaotic. Rather, it follows cer-

---

[2] In his *Write It Right* (New York, 1928), cited in Stuart Roberston, *The Development of Modern English*, 2nd ed., rev. Frederic G. Cassidy (New York, 1954), p. 234.

[3] Compare Hamlet's use of *admiration* in the sense 'wonderment, amazement' in "Season your admiration for a while/With an attent eare" (I.ii. 192–93).

[4] Compare *dizzy*, which may in very early times have had the same meaning. See Henry Bradley, *The Making of English* (New York, 1904), pp. 198–200. *Enthusiastic*, from the Greek, also had this meaning.

tain paths which we might do well to familiarize ourselves with. Much, probably most, of the illustrative matter which is to follow, like that which precedes, has come from many books read over a long period of years. Some of the examples are by now more or less stock ones, but they make their point better than less familiar ones would do, and hence are used without apology, but with gratitude to whoever first dug them out. It is likely that many of them will be found in James Bradstreet Greenough and George Lyman Kittredge's old, but still good, *Words and Their Ways in English Speech* (New York, 1901).

Generalization and Specialization

An obvious classification of meaning is that based on scope. This is to say, meaning may be generalized (extended, widened) or it may be specialized (restricted, narrowed). When we increase the scope of a word, we reduce the elements of its contents. For instance, *tail* (from OE *tægl*) in earlier times seems to have meant 'hairy caudal appendage, as of a horse.' When we eliminated the hairiness (or the horsiness) from the meaning, we increased its scope, so that in modern English the word means simply 'caudal appendage.' The same thing has happened to Danish *hale*, earlier 'tail of a cow.' In course of time the cow was eliminated, and in present-day Danish the word means simply 'tail,' having undergone a semantic generalization precisely like that of the English word cited; the closely related Icelandic *hali* still keeps the cow in the picture. Similarly, a *mill* was earlier a place for making things by the process of grinding, that is, for making meal. The words *meal* and *mill* are themselves related, as one might guess from their similarity. A mill is now simply a place for making things: the grinding has been eliminated, so that we may speak of a woolen mill, a steel mill, or even a gin mill. The word *corn* earlier meant 'grain' and is in fact related to the word *grain*. It is still used in this general sense in England, as in the "Corn Laws," but specifically it may mean either oats (for animals) or wheat (for human beings). In American usage *corn* denotes maize, which is of course not at all what Keats meant in his "Ode to a Nightingale" when he described Ruth as standing "in tears amid the alien corn." The building in which corn, regardless of its meaning, is stored is called a barn. *Barn* earlier denoted a storehouse for barley; the word is in fact a compound of two Old English words, *bere* 'barley' and *ærn* 'house.' By elimination of a part of its earlier content, the scope of this word has been extended to mean a storehouse for any kind of grain. American English has still further generalized by eliminating the grain, so that *barn* may mean also a place for housing livestock.

The opposite of generalization is specialization, a process in which, by adding to the elements of meaning, the semantic content of a word is reduced. *Deer*, for instance, used to mean simply 'animal' (OE *dēor*) as its German cognate *Tier* still does. Shakespeare writes of "Mice, and Rats, and such small Deare" (*King Lear* III.iv.144). By adding something particular (the family *Cervidae*) to the content, the scope of the word has been reduced, and it has come to mean a specific kind of animal. Similarly *hound* used to mean 'dog,' as does its German cognate *Hund*. To this earlier meaning we have in the course of time added the idea of hunting, and thereby restricted the scope of the word, which to us means a special sort of dog, a hunting dog. To the earlier content of *liquor* 'fluid' (compare *liquid*) we have added 'alcoholic.' But generalization, the opposite tendency, has occurred in the case of the word *rum*, the name of a specific alcoholic drink, which in the usage of those who disapprove of all alcoholic beverages long ago came to mean strong drink in general, even though other liquors are much more copiously imbibed today. The word has even been personified in *Demon Rum*.

Meat once meant simply 'food,' a meaning which it retains in *sweetmeat* and throughout the King James Bible ("meat for the belly," "meat and drink"), though it acquired the meaning 'flesh' much earlier and had for a while both the general and the specialized meaning. *Starve* (OE *steorfan*) used to mean simply 'to die,' as its German cognate *sterben* still does.[5] Chaucer writes, for instance, "But as hire man I wol ay lyve and sterve" (*Troilus and Criseyde* I.427). A specific way of dying had to be expressed by a following phrase, for example "of hunger, for cold." The *OED* cites "starving with the cold," presumably dialectal, as late as 1867. The word came somehow to be primarily associated with death by hunger, and for a while there existed a compound verb *hunger-starve*. Usually nowadays we put the stress altogether on the added idea of hunger and lose the older meaning altogether. Although the usual meaning of *to starve* now is 'to die of hunger,' we also use the phrase "starve to death," which in earlier times would have been tautological. An additional, toned-down meaning grows out of hyperbole, so that "I'm starving" may mean only 'I'm very hungry.' The word is of course used figuratively, as in "starving for love," which, as we have seen, once meant 'dying for love.' This word furnishes a striking example of specialization and proliferation of meaning.

Pejoration and Amelioration

Change in meaning is frequently due to ethical, or moral, considerations. A word may, as it were, go downhill, or it may rise in the world; there is no way of predicting what its career may be. *Politician* has had a downhill development in American English; in British English it is

---

[5] An even earlier meaning may have been 'to grow stiff.'

still not entirely without honor. *Knave* (OE *cnafa*), which used to mean simply 'boy'—it is cognate with German *Knabe*, which retains the earlier meaning—is another example of pejorative (from Lat. *pējor* 'worse') development; it came to mean successively 'serving boy'[6] (specialization), like that well-known knave of hearts[7] who was given to stealing tarts, and ultimately 'bad human being,' so that we may now speak of an old knave, or conceivably even of a knavish woman. On its journey downhill this word has thus undergone both specialization and generalization. *Boor*, once meaning 'peasant,'[8] has had a similar pejorative development, as has *lewd*, earlier 'lay, as opposed to clerical,' and thereafter 'ignorant,' 'base,' and finally 'obscene,' which is the only meaning to survive.[9] The same fate has befallen the Latin loan-word *vulgar*, ultimately from *vulgus* 'the common people'; the earlier meaning is retained in *Vulgar Latin*, the Latin which was spoken by the people up to the time of the early Middle Ages and was to develop into the various Romance languages. *Censure* earlier meant 'opinion.' In the course of time it has come to mean 'bad opinion'; *criticism* is well on its way to the same pejorative goal, ordinarily meaning nowadays 'adverse judgment.' The verbs *to censure* and *to criticize* have undergone a similar development. *Deserts* (as in *just deserts*) likewise started out indifferently to mean simply what one deserved, whether good or bad, but has come to mean 'punishment.' A few more examples of this tendency must suffice. *Silly* (OE *sǣlig*), earlier 'timely,' came to mean 'happy, blessed,' and subsequently 'innocent, simple'; then the simplicity, a desirable quality under most circumstances, was misunderstood (note the present ambiguity of *a simple man*), and the word took on its present meaning. Its German cognate *selig* progressed only to the second stage, though the word may be used facetiously to mean 'tipsy.'

Like *censure* and *criticize*, *praise* started out indifferently; it is simply *appraise* 'put a value on' with loss of its initial unstressed syllable (aphesis). But *praise* has come to mean 'value highly.' Here what has been added has ameliorated, or elevated, the semantic content of the word. Amelioration, the opposite of pejoration, is well illustrated by *knight*, which used to mean 'servant,' as its German relative *Knecht*

---

[6] Cf. French *garçon* 'boy,' which in a similarly specialized use means 'waiter.'

[7] Actually a further specialization: the jacks in card games are called the knaves in upper-class British usage.

[8] Its cognate *Bauer* is the usual equivalent of *jack* or *knave* in German card-playing, whence English *bower* (as in *right bower* and *left bower*) in certain card games such as euchre and five hundred.

[9] The development of *nice*, going back to Latin *nescius* 'ignorant,' has been just the opposite. The Old French form used in English meant 'simple,' a meaning retained in Modern French *niais*. In the course of its career in English it has had the meanings 'foolishly particular' and then merely 'particular' (as in *a nice distinction*), among others.

still does.[10] This particular word has obviously moved far from its earlier meaning, denoting as it usually now does a very special and exalted man who has been signally honored by his sovereign and who is entitled to prefix *Sir* to his name. *Earl* (OE *eorl*) once meant simply 'man,' though in ancient Germanic times it was specially applied to a warrior, who was almost invariably a man of good birth, in contrast to a *ceorl* (*churl*), or ordinary freeman. When under the Norman kings French titles were adopted in England, *earl* failed to be displaced, but remained as the equivalent of the Continental *count*.

Changes Due to Social Class

The meaning of a word may vary even with the group in which it is used. For all speakers *smart* has the meaning 'intelligent,' but there is a specialized class usage in which it means 'fashionable.' The meaning of *a smart woman* may thus vary with the social level of the speaker; it may, indeed, have to be inferred from the context. The earliest meaning of this word seems to have been 'sharp,' as in *a smart blow*. It is interesting to note that *sharp* is also used nowadays in the sense 'up-to-date, fashionable,' as in *a sharp dresser*, by certain groups of speakers who admire this particular type of "sharpness."

Similarly, a word's meaning may vary according to the circumstances under which it is used. *Hall* (OE *heall*), for instance, once meant a very large roofed place, like the splendid royal dwelling-place Heorot in which Beowulf fought Grendel. Such buildings were usually without smaller attached rooms, though Heorot had a "bower" [11] (*būr*), earlier a separate cottage, but in *Beowulf* a bedroom to which the king and queen retired. For retainers the hall served as meeting-room, feasting-room, and sleeping-room. Later *hall* came to mean the largest room in a great house, used for large gatherings such as receptions and feasts, though the use of the word for the entire structure survives in the names of a number of manor houses such as Little Wenham Hall and Speke Hall in England. There are a number of other meanings, all connoting size and some degree of splendor, and all a far cry from the modern American use of *hall* as a narrow passageway leading to rooms.[12] The meaning of *hall* must be determined by the context in which it occurs.

---

[10] It must not be supposed that, because German cognates have frequently been cited as still having meanings which have become archaic in English, German words are necessarily less susceptible to semantic change than English ones. With different choices of examples it is possible that a contrary impression might be given.

[11] Note that this word survives only in the sense 'arbor, enclosure formed by vegetation.'

[12] In British English the reduced meaning of *hall* refers to the vestibule or entrance passage immediately inside the front door of a small house.

Akin to what we have been considering is modification of meaning as the result of a shift in point of view. *Crescent*, from the present participial form of Latin *cresco*, used to mean simply 'growing, increasing,' as in Pompey's "My powers are Cressent, and my Auguring hope/Sayes it will come to'th'full" (*Antony and Cleopatra* II.i.10–11). The new, or growing, moon was thus called the crescent moon. There has been, however, a shift in the dominant element of meaning, the emphasis coming to be put entirely on shape, specifically on a particular shape of the moon, rather than upon growth. *Crescent* has thus come to mean 'new-moon-shaped.' Similarly, in *veteran* (Lat. *veterānus*, a derivative of *vetus* 'old'), the emphasis has shifted from age to military service, though not necessarily long service: a veteran need not have grown old in service, and we may in fact speak of a *young veteran*. The fact that etymologically the phrase is self-contradictory is of no significance as far as present usage is concerned. The word is of course extended to other areas, for instance *veteran politician*; in its extended meanings it continues to connote long experience and usually mature years as well.

The Vogue for Words of Learned Origin

When learned words acquire popular currency, they almost inevitably acquire at the same time new, less exact, meanings, or at least new shades of meaning. *Philosophy*, for instance, earlier 'love of wisdom,' has now a popular sense 'practical opinion or body of opinions,' as in "the philosophy of salesmanship," "the philosophy of Will Rogers," and "homespun philosophy." An error in translation from a foreign language may result in a useful new meaning, for example *psychological moment*, now 'most opportune time,' rather than 'psychological momentum,' which is the proper translation of German *psychologisches Moment*, the ultimate source of the phrase. The popular misunderstanding of *inferiority complex*, first used to designate an unconscious sense of inferiority manifesting itself in assertive behavior, has given us a synonym for *diffidence, shyness*. It is similar with *guilt complex*, now used to denote nothing more psychopathic than a feeling of guilt. The term *complex* as first used by psychoanalysts more than half a century ago designated a type of aberration resulting from the unconscious suppression of more or less related attitudes. The word soon passed into voguish and subsequently into general use to designate an obsession of any kind—a bee in the bonnet, as it were. Among its progeny are *Oedipus complex, herd complex*, and *sex complex*. The odds on its increasing fecundity would seem to be rather high.

Other fashionable terms from psychoanalysis and psychology, with which our times are so intensely preoccupied, are *subliminal*, which has been widely used in reference to a very sneaky kind of advertising technique; *behavior pattern,* meaning simply 'behavior'; *neurotic,* with a wide range of meaning, including 'nervous, highstrung, artistic by temperament, eccentric, or given to worrying'; *compulsive* 'habitual,' as in *compulsive drinker* and *compulsive criminal;* and *schizophrenia* 'practically any mental or emotional disorder.'

It is not surprising that the newer, popular meanings of what were once more or less technical terms should generally show a considerable extension of the earlier, technical meanings. Thus, *sadism* has come to mean simply 'cruelty' and *exhibitionism* merely 'showing off,' without any of the earlier connotations of sexual perversion, as in fact the word *psychology* itself may mean nothing more than 'mental processes' in a vague sort of way. An intense preoccupation in the mid-twentieth century with what is fashionably and doubtless humanely referred to as *mental illness*—a less enlightened age than ours called it *insanity,* and people afflicted with it were said to be *crazy*—must to a large extent be responsible for the use of such terms as have been cited. Also notable is the specialization of *sick* to refer to mental imbalance.

The greatest darling among the loosely used pseudoscientific vogue words of recent years is unquestionably *image* in the sense 'impression that others subconsciously have of someone.' A jaundiced observer of modern life might well suppose that what one actually is is not nearly so important as the image of oneself that one is able—to use another vogue word—to project. If the "image" is phony, what difference does it make? Everyone must get along; all must be allowed to have what the political orators refer to as human dignity, whatever the phrase means.

From an interview with two eminent psychiatrists syndicated by the Women's News Service,[13] one may learn that Governor Nelson Rockefeller's campaign headquarters before the political conventions of 1960 "had an 'image division,' set up to help project a favorable impression." One of the sages being interviewed declared, after consulting his badly clouded crystal ball: "There is no doubt that Mr. Kennedy appeals to women. He is the image of their little boy. . . . But they will not vote for him because they do not want a boy in the White House. Women want a father image as president—especially if they have weak husbands." "Many psychologists have said," according to the same gentleman, "that President Eisenhower's great personal hold on the public is due to the fact that he creates a strong father image" and moreover "has nurtured this image by never taking a single act not compatible with the subconscious concept of the ideal father." Images do not necessarily have to be those of persons, for a quarterly report of the Standard Oil Company of New Jersey states that "a current advertising campaign featuring the skillful, courteous service available at

---

[13] Published in the Jacksonville *Florida Times-Union,* February 9, 1960, p. 10.

Esso stations is proving remarkably effective not only at building a favorable dealer service image in the public mind but also at encouraging and stimulating dealers and service station attendants to measure up to this image." [14]

The awesome prestige of science and technology in our day is indicated by the diversion of terms previously associated with them to humbler activities. A Reading *Clinic*, for instance, is a department of a college or university for the "diagnosis" and correction of the reading difficulties of students (why not "patients"?) who have not hitherto learned to read—at least, not without moving their lips. A Retail Hardware Salesmanship *Clinic* is, as far as the layman is able to determine, nothing more than a conference of hardware salesmen. An Auto *Clinic* is a hospital for ailing cars. The exact nature of the "second annual Evangelism Clinic at the Pine Grove [Florida] Baptist Church," [15] with the pleasantly alcoholically named Rev. Tom Collins as "principal inspirational speaker," is difficult to determine. A Writing *Laboratory* (or *Lab*) is a classroom with chairs, tables, and dictionaries where students of what used to be unassumingly called Freshman English write themes under the supervision of graduate assistants, who in due time will probably wish to be regarded as "lab assistants." Similarly, an *intern* may nowadays just as well be a beginning teacher in a public school as an M.D. serving in a hospital. By a sort of inverted snobbery, *workshop*, sharing much the same range of meaning as *laboratory*, has become quite voguish, for instance *Writers' Workshop*.

There are a good many special types of transfer of meaning. *Long* and *short*, for instance, are on occasion transferred from the spatial concepts to which they ordinarily refer and made to refer to temporal concepts, as in *a long time, a short while*; similarly with such nouns as *length* and *space*. Metaphor is involved when we extend the word *foot* 'lowest extremity of an animal' to all sorts of things, as in *foot of a mountain, tree,* and so forth. The meaning of the same word is specialized or restricted when we add to its original content something like 'approximate length of the lowest extremity of the male human animal,' thereby making the word mean a unit of measure; we do much the same thing to *hand* when we use it as a unit of measure for the height of horses.

Transfer from One Sense to Another

Meaning may be transferred from one sense to another (synesthesia), as when we apply *clear*, with principal reference to sight, to hearing, as

---

[14] Quoted in the *New Yorker*, December 3, 1960, p. 100.
[15] Gainesville, Florida, *Sun*, February 10, 1960, p. 14.

in *clear-sounding*. *Loud* is transferred from hearing to sight when we speak of *loud colors*. *Sweet*, with primary reference to taste, may be extended to hearing (*sweet music*), smell ("The rose smells sweet"), and to all senses at once (*a sweet girl*). *Sharp* may be transferred from feeling to taste, and so may *smooth*. *Warm* may shift its usual reference from feeling to sight, as in *warm colors*, and along with *cold* may refer in a general way to all senses, as in *a warm (cold) welcome*.

Abstract meanings may evolve from more concrete ones. Latin *cantus* 'the act of singing' came to acquire the more abstract meaning 'song.' The compound *understand*, as Leonard Bloomfield points out, must in prehistoric Old English times have meant 'to stand among, that is, close to'—*under* presumably having had the meaning 'among,' like its German and Latin cognates *unter* and *inter*.[16] But this literal, concrete meaning gave way to the more abstract meaning which the word has today. Bloomfield cites parallel shifts from concrete to abstract in German *verstehen* ('to stand before'), Greek *epistamai* ('I stand upon'), Latin *comprehendere* ('to take hold of'), and Italian *capire*, based on Latin *capere* 'to grasp,' among others.

The first person to use *grasp* in an abstract sense, as in "He has a good grasp of his subject," was coining an interesting metaphor. But the shift from concrete to abstract, or from physical to mental, has been so complete that we no longer think of this usage as metaphorical: *grasp* has come to be synonymous with *comprehension* in such a context as that cited, though the word has of course retained its physical reference. It was similar with *glad*, earlier 'smooth,' though this word has completely lost the earlier meaning (except in the proper name *Gladstone*, if surnames may be thought of nowadays as having meaning) and may refer only to a mental state. Likewise, meaning may shift from subjective to objective, as when *pitiful*, earlier 'full of pity, compassionate,' came to mean 'deserving of pity'; or the shift may be the other way round, as when *fear*, earlier 'danger,' something objective, came to mean 'terror,' a state of mind.

STUDY QUESTIONS AND EXERCISES

1. What kinds of information given in a dictionary are relevant to meaning and changes of meaning? How do general dictionaries differ from the *Oxford English Dictionary* in providing word history?

2. What does the child chiefly acquire, in language, after his earliest years? What does a good command of language involve beyond what is gained by ordinary, everyday experience?

3. Note that both time and place are factors in word meanings. To *tonic*, cited by Pyles as used in New England, for a soft drink,

[16] *Language* (New York, 1933), pp. 425, 429–30.

may be added *dope,* used in the South. In the Midwest, either term would be badly misunderstood. Can you give other such examples?

4. What is the value of the study of etymology? Consider the examples given by Pyles: of what interest and value are the earlier meanings?

5. Using the first two paired categories in Pyles' classification of changes in meaning, choose significant words in a passage of prose or poetry of an earlier period, such as the Elizabethan Age, and trace the etymology and changes in meaning of the words down to the present.

6. Note that class aspects of language extend to meaning. How is this analogous to slang uses of common words among special groups? Give examples.

7. The importance of the concept of *image* in modern life is the theme of a satiric two-volume novel, *The Image Makers,* by J. B. Priestley, which is worth studying for the use of colloquial, pseudo-scientific, academic, and political British English. Pyles' account of the "image-division" of a political campaign has its fictitious equivalent in the novel.

8. What specific categories are included under "transfer of meaning"?

9. Another category Pyles deals with in the remainder of the chapter from which this selection is taken is "Taboo and Euphemism." What observations can you make on taboo words as representing sexuality and physical functions and on those subjects and death and burial as contributing to euphemisms? Are common words for death and killing taboo, as words for procreation and birth are or have been? Give examples in which taboos in language are related to dress. Victorian women used *limb* for *leg,* put ruffles on legs of furniture, and used euphemisms for *pregnant.* How has language accommodated to such changes in dress and manners as are symbolized by the miniskirt? Are these changes as likely to be reversible as is the length of skirts?

SUBJECTS FOR BRIEF PAPERS
OR WRITTEN REPORTS

1. Compare and contrast Wilson Follett, "Sabotage in Springfield," with Bergen Evans, "But What's a Dictionary For?" * Deal with basic assumptions about the functions of a dictionary and specific criticisms of *Webster's Third International* and arrive at your own conclusions as to the reasoning and tone used in each argument.

---

* Follett's article is in *Atlantic Monthly* (January, 1962), pp. 73–77; Evans' is in *Atlantic Monthly* (May, 1962), pp. 57–62.

2. Look up the editorial comment on *Webster's Third International* in *Life* (October 27, 1961), p. 4. Check every major word in the sentence "concocted from words found in Webster's." Which words would *not* be so used by a person seriously concerned with correctness in written English? Look up the same words in *Webster's Second New International*. Which ones do you find? Classify your findings—words designated as nonstandard, words not found in the form used, and so forth—and report your conclusions as to the soundness of the basic criticism that *Webster's Third* does not "distinguish between good and bad usage." Comment on the validity of the implication that the "concocted" sentence represents only expressions that *Webster's Third* presents as unquestionably used by the most eminent modern writers in the precise sense in which *Life* uses them.

3. Look up the review of *Webster's Third International* in *Time* (October 6, 1961), p. 49. Write a review of the review, considering the writer's concept of what dictionaries should be and have been, his purpose, his method, and his style, giving your own evaluation of each point.

4. Examine the issues of *Time* and *Life* cited above and report on the use of words, constructions, and meanings that are not given in *Webster's Second International*. Does *Webster's Third International* describe the usage found in *Time* and *Life*?

5. Compare the Prefaces of *Webster's Second* and *Webster's Third New International*: what differences are apparent? Are there any innovations in basic principles? In techniques? Why?

6. Bergen Evans is not only an authority on American English usage but also a versatile speaker and writer of American English. Study his two selections (5 and 25) and analyze the "hallmarks of American" exhibited in his style.

7. Analyze the "hallmarks of American" which you recognize in one of Mencken's critical articles in any of the six series of *Prejudices*, in the Vintage selection from *Prejudices* (1959), or in *The American Mercury* during the 1920's.

8. Study Mencken's "American" version of the "Declaration of Independence," in *Parodies* (Random House, 1960), and discuss how it differs from the English of the original, distinguishing between standard and nonstandard American. What "hallmarks" do you find? Is Mencken's version an example of "current standard American"?

9. Read Robertson and Cassidy on Mencken, in *The Development of Modern English*. What criticism do they make of Mencken's comparison between British and American English? On the basis of "The Hallmarks of American," decide whether their criticism is justified and in a short paper state their views, your opinion, and your reasons.

10. In an essay on Ring Lardner, Mencken comments on how "magnificently" Lardner handles the American vulgate. Read Lardner's

"Haircut" or one of his "You know me, Al" baseball stories and write a paper on the unconventionality of grammar and vocabulary.

11. Mencken alludes to the great conservative influence of Lindley Murray and Joseph E. Worcester. Investigate the linguistic activities of either one and write a brief report of your findings.

12. Analyze the differences between British and American English in the dialogue in Harry Leon Wilson's *Ruggles of Red Gap*.

13. In a brief paper present your own scheme of classification of place-names in your home county. Illustrate with examples, and arrive at a conclusion as to dominant trends exhibited.

14. In a subject in which you are competent, write a paper based on both research in language and an examination of writing in the field. Use the Sears and Smith selection as a model but work out your own analysis of significant vocabulary and patterns.

15. Using as sources several news articles dealing with a person or persons comparable with the astronauts for representing distinguished achievement in a special field, write a short paper analyzing and evaluating the language of the person(s). Use the selection by Mary C. Bromage as a model.

16. Compare and contrast the dialogue in two similar short stories published in the *Atlantic Monthly*, one of recent date and the other about a hundred years earlier. What similarities and differences do you find in vocabulary, grammar and idiom, and sentence structure? Which differences can be accounted for chiefly by the difference in time? Which are evidence of cultural differences?

17. Compare the dialect in a short story by Mark Twain with one by Bret Harte, taking care that the stories offer some points of similarity in time and, if possible, in place. Is Mark Twain's criticism of Bret Harte's dialect (see selections 8 and 9 in Part 2 by Cassidy and Babcock) justified?

18. In Dickens' *Martin Chuzzlewit*, study the dialogue of the American characters, applying Mencken's characteristics as given in "Hallmarks of American." Compare the characters in Dickens with characters in Mark Twain who also represent humorous and satiric exaggeration: in what respects does Mark Twain present authentic dialect and Dickens a distortion of it?

19. Write a short paper on survivals of the frontier in the language of a specific locality, considering: place names, words for flora and fauna, words for topographical features, and words for common objects and processes. What layers of history appear in the combinations of terms and names from different national origins or from earlier settlements in America?

part 3

Geographical Aspects

In his classification of language differences in American English Grammar, Charles C. Fries includes the regional peculiarities of pronunciation, grammar, and usage: "Some of the differences we note in the language practices of those about us find their explanation in the fact that the fashions in one community or section of the country do not necessarily develop in others." A traveler going from Chicago to Boston or New Orleans quickly recognizes marked differences in the way people in various sections of the United States use language. In order to have a record of the distinctive sectional characteristics, investigators have been making field surveys of the language patterns before their distinctive elements are changed as a result of the homogenizing process caused by today's radio, television, and rapid transportation. These investigators are interested merely in recording scientifically the facts of language that they discover; they are not interested in judging the social acceptability of the pronunciation, vocabulary, grammar, or syntax of a particular area. This latter task they leave to the arbiters of manners and behavior.

In this section we shall consider some of the objective aspects of language in a region: the gathering of evidence, the study of dialects and usage, and the generalizations about them. The social or class implications of these regional aspects of language will be treated more fully in Part 5.

15

American Regionalisms

John Nist

American speech falls into three general regional patterns: Northern, Midland, and Southern. Professor John Nist of Auburn University describes the distinguishing characteristics of each in this passage of A Structural History of English *(1966).*

George P. Krapp declared in 1919 that "Relatively few Americans spend all their lives in one locality, and even if they do, they cannot possibly escape coming into contact with Americans from other localities. . . . We can distinguish with some certainty Eastern and Western and Southern speech, but beyond this the author has little confidence in those confident experts who think they can tell infallibly, by the test of speech, a native of Hartford from a native of Providence, or a native of Philadelphia from a native of Atlanta, or even, if one insists on infallibility, a native of Chicago from a native of Boston." Despite some minor regional vocabulary differences, a leveling of speech habits has been a primary factor in the similarity of American regionalisms. The reasons for that leveling, according to Mencken, are "The railroad, the automobile, the mail-order catalogue, the movie and, above all, radio and television. . . ." As a present-day indication of regional leveling in American English, the omitted *r* in the pronunciation of Eastern New England, New York City, and the South is beginning to reassert itself.

Regionalisms do, nevertheless, exist. They now constitute three major speech areas in the United States: Northern, Midland, and Southern. These speech areas foster their own regional subdivisions, which at times have little to do with geographical location. Thus the pronunciation habits of the Southwest area of Arizona, Nevada, and California are generally of Northern derivation, whereas the speech patterns of the Northwest (Montana, Idaho, Oregon, and Washington) are basically of Midland origin. West Texas speech shows the dominance of Appalachian; East Texas speech is an outgrowth of Southern. Since Appalachian is a regional version of Midland, the differences between the pronunciations of East and West Texas are marked.

American English, then, is characterized by three major speech areas that have generated ten leading regionalisms:

Northern

1) *Eastern New England.* This Atlantic seaboard regionalism, with Boston as its center, lengthens the vowel /a/ to compensate for the loss of r in a word like *barn* /bahn/; tends to use the broad British /a/ in words like *ask, dance, path, aunt,* and *rather;* interjects a final r in words like *idea* and *Cuba;* distinguishes the low-central vowel of *cot* /kat/ from the low-back vowel of *caught* /kɔt/; prefers /æ/ as the stressed vowel of *barren;* lowers the stressed vowel of *hurry* to /ə/; often interjects the glide /y/ after /d/ in a word like *due* /dyuw/; centers the low-back vowel of *log* to /a/; either lengthens or *schwa*-glides the vowel of *horse* and *hoarse* to compensate for the loss of r: /hɔhs/ or /hoəs/; pronounces *greasy* with an /s/.

2) *North Central.* This regionalism extends from Western New England across the Champlain and Great Lakes basins to the central Dakotas; Hartford, Syracuse, Cleveland, Detroit, Chicago, and Minneapolis are centers. North Central American English pronounces its medial and final r's; prefers the flat /æ/ in words like *ask;* does not interject a final r in words like *idea;* also distinguishes *cot* from *caught;* usually prefers /e/ as the stressed vowel of *barren;* heightens the stressed vowel of *hurry* to /I/; does not interject the glide /y/ into the pronunciation of *due* /duw/; employs the low-back vowel /ɔ/ in the word *log;* uses r in both *horse* and *hoarse* so that they sound alike: /hɔrs/; pronounces *greasy* with an /s/.

3) *Southwest.* This regionalism covers Arizona, Nevada, and California; Phoenix, San Francisco, and Los Angeles are centers. Southwest American English is almost identical with North Central. A higher incidence of Mexican Spanish vocabulary constitutes the primary difference.

Midland

1) *New York City.* This regionalism covers a small area (southern New York, southwestern Connecticut, and northeastern New Jersey), but it is big in importance because of the population and prestige of its center. Agreeing with Eastern New England in many of its pronunciation patterns, New York City American English is different in several major respects, for it often articulates medial and final r's; does not interject a final r after a terminal vowel; makes a clearer phonemic distinction between the /a/ of *cot* and the /ɔ/ of *caught;* and refuses

to employ the glide /ə/ in any actualization of *hoarse*. Known for its heavy nasal quality and Yiddish influence, this regionalism is often hard and metallic in intonation; it also permits such variants as /c/ for /j/, /t/ for /θ/, /d/ for /ð/. Brooklyn versions of /ɔy/ and /Ir/ are notorious.

2) *Middle Atlantic.* Extending from New Jersey to Maryland and from Delaware to the mountains of Pennsylvania, with Philadelphia as center, this regionalism does not permit the complex /ah/ to replace the *r* in *barn*; allows /z/ as a phonemic variant of /s/ in the pronunciation of *greasy*; often rounds and elevates the /ɔ/ of *horse* to /o/; permits both /lag/ and /lɔg/ for *log*; and resembles New York City in the use of either /e/ or /æ/ as the stressed vowel of *various*.

3) *Western Pennsylvania.* This small regionalism covers western Pennsylvania, the eastern tip of Ohio, and the northern portion of West Virginia. With Pittsburgh as center, Western Pennsylvania American English is noted for its "Pennsylvania Dutch" vocabulary and idioms. Much like Middle Atlantic, Western Pennsylvania differs in that it backs the /a/ in *orange* to /ɔ/; it makes absolutely no distinction between *cot* and *caught*; it does not permit /æ/ as the stressed vowel of *various*; it consistently pronounces *log* as /lɔg/.

4) *Central Midland.* This vast regionalism covers the heartland of the United States from Ohio to Utah and from west Texas to Wyoming, with such centers as Cincinnati, Indianapolis, St. Louis, Kansas City, Denver, Albuquerque, and Salt Lake City. Because it dominates such a large area of the country and is the immediate progenitor of Northwest American English, Central Midland is perhaps the best candidate for the office of Standard American, the outstanding characteristics of which are the articulation of medial and terminal *r*; the distinction between the vocalic phonemes of *cot* and *caught*; the preference for /e/ over /æ/ as the stressed vowel of *barren*; the universal use of the flat /æ/ in words like *ask* and *path*; the tolerance of /s/ and /z/ as phonemic variants in the pronunciation of *greasy*; the preference for /I/ over /ə/ as the stressed vowel of *hurry*; the rejection of interjectional /y/ in words like *due* /duw/; the interchangeability of /ɔ/ and /o/ as the stressed vowel of *hoarse*; and the exclusive use of /ɔ/ as the stressed vowel of *log*.

5) *Northwest.* With Seattle as center, this regionalism covers Washington, Oregon, Idaho, and Montana, and small portions of northern California, Nevada, Utah, of northwestern Wyoming, and of western North Dakota and South Dakota. In most respects, Northwest American English is identical with Central Midland. It differs slightly by permitting a higher-tongued and tenser pronunciation of the stressed vowel in *various* and by allowing /lag/ as a variant of /lɔg/.

6) *Appalachian.* Commonly referred to as "hillbilly" American English, this regionalism covers the eastern area of the United States

known as Appalachia (most of West Virginia, Kentucky, Tennessee, and portions of eastern Virginia, North Carolina, South Carolina, and northern Georgia, Alabama, and Mississippi). Noted for the archaic features of its grammar and the substandard usage of its "folk speech," Appalachian partakes of certain Midland characteristics that distinguish it from Southern—especially in retaining *r* in words like *barn;* in refusing to add the breaking glide /ə/ to diphthongs; in maintaining /æ/ as a simple vowel without tension and in adding the breaking glide /I/; in backing Southern /a/ to /ɔ/ in words like *orange;* in permitting /e/ as a phonemic variant of /æ/ in the pronunciation of *barren;* and in the preference for /duw/ over /dyuw/. Appalachian is like Southern in its distinction between *cot* and *caught;* in its use of flat /æ/ in words like *ask* and *path;* in its complete use of /z/ in the pronunciation of *greasy;* in its universal preference for /ə/ as the stressed vowel of *hurry* and for /ɔ/ as the stressed vowel of *log.*

Southern

A complex of various subregionalisms, this vast speech variety extends from Virginia through most of the old Confederacy to western Texas. With centers in Richmond, Charleston, Atlanta, Miami, Montgomery, New Orleans, and Houston, Southern American English is famous for its loss of final *r;* for its conversion of *r* to either the breaking glide /ə/ or the offset glide /h/ when the *r* is followed by another consonant or by a juncture; for its transmutation of simple vowels to diphthongs, as in *dog* /dɔəg/ and *class* /klæIs/; for reducing complex narrow vowels to complex wide vowels, as in *time* /tahm/ and *oil* /ɔhl/, so that words like *Mike* and *Mark* sound identical: /mahk/; and for a generally slower rate of speech that gives the intonation a "honey-and-molasses" effect.

The characteristics for each of these regionalisms are merely representative and not exhaustive. Both Hawaiian and Alaskan American English, furthermore, need detailed study. But the ten major regionalisms listed above are *speech varieties;* they are not confined within arbitrary borders. From the migration of munitions workers during World War II, for example, Appalachian gained an entrance into, and thus an influence upon, North Central American English. Appalachian, as a matter of fact, spills way beyond its traditional confines—into Texas as far east as the Brazos River, into southern Missouri, Illinois, Indiana, and Pennsylvania. Some of the most interesting phonemic features of American English have to do with Southern pronunciations. The nasalizations of the South tend to raise the preceding vowel; hence it is that *pin* is articulated as /piyn/, *pen* as /pin/, and *pan* as /pen/. Southern American English shows several signs that a major sound shift is taking place within its area of dominance: 1) back vowels tend to be fronted whenever possible; 2) checked "short" vowels generally develop a high-central glide before voiceless consonants and a mid-central glide before voiced consonants: /I/ and /ə/ respectively; 3) the /I/ glide tends to form before post-apical consonants, as in /θIŋk/ for *thank*, /bæIs/ for bass, and /puĬš/ for *push*; 4) tense vowels, therefore, tend to break into two segments (or syllables) at points of pitch change—hence the Southern *drawl*, as in /rihəst/ for *wrist*.

Far more important than the phonemic features of Southern speech habits, however, is the gradual wearing away of pronunciation differences among the four regionalisms that cover most of the land mass of the continental United States: North Central, Southwest, Central Midland, and Northwest. Because of the vast increase in population mobility and the immense impact of the mass media, at present these four regionalisms constitute an Emerging General American, which in time may become the accepted American Standard. The resultant seven major speech varieties of present-day American English are distributed as shown in Map 3.

STUDY QUESTIONS AND EXERCISES

1. What are the three major speech areas in the United States? Of what area and what regional subdivision are you a native? In what area do you now live? Of what areas were your parents natives? (In rural England even now the answer to all three questions would frequently be the same.) How many members of your class belong to the third generation of their family living in the same area? To the second? To the first?

2. What new influences in the twentieth century have accelerated the leveling influence of the nineteenth? Compare your opportunities to hear the speech of other areas in the United States with the opportunities of your grandparents in their youth and with those of the settlers who carried the frontier to the Pacific Ocean.

3. What is the relation between the three major speech areas, as identified by Nist, and the historical facts presented in the articles by Schlauch and Cassidy in Part 2?

4. Of the three major areas, which subdivision has the best claim to be considered Standard American? Why? Which regional pronunciation is that represented in recent dictionaries? How can you tell?

5. Can you identify, among your associates, representatives of the three major speech areas? Can you identify subdivisions of those areas?

6. Write a speech profile of yourself: the speech areas from

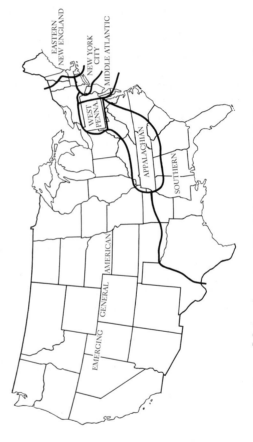

MAP 3. Major American English Speech Varieties, ca. 1965.

which your parents came, the places you have lived, the pronunciations and vocabulary that identify your specific combination of speech influences.

7. As a modest experiment, make tape-recordings of several acquaintances reading aloud a passage containing a number of the "test" words cited by Nist. (Do not reveal the significant words: self-consciousness can affect pronunciation.) From the recordings try to identify the region of which each person is a native: check with the facts and, if there are nontypical pronunciations, try to discover possible explanations.

8. In John Steinbeck's *The Grapes of Wrath*, a migratory worker comments that "ever'body says words different," Arkansas folks and "Oklahomy folks says 'em different," and a Massachusetts "lady . . . said 'em differentest of all." How do the facts given in the selections in Parts 2 and 3 explain these differences, especially the superlative difference of Boston speech?

16

The Linguistic Atlases:
Our New Resource

Harold B. Allen

Professor Allen's observations about linguistic fieldwork result from many years of close association with the Linguistic Atlas *project. This discussion of some of the applications of* Linguistic Atlas *data originally appeared in the* English Journal *for April, 1956.*

A few years ago a teacher in South Carolina was pushing her less than enthusiastic pupils through a grammar drill book, painfully but relentlessly. The class struggled on to an exercise intended to teach the correct use of the negative of *ought.* Here the students found sentences with the approved construction *ought not.* But they found also some sentences with a construction they were supposed to cross out, *hadn't ought.* This the pupils had never seen or heard before, and they were delighted with it. True, the book said it was wrong, and teacher, as always, agreed with the book. But there it was—in the book —as plain as anything could be; and somehow it seemed marvelously sensible. *He hadn't intended to do it: He hadn't ought to do it. I hadn't wanted to go: I hadn't ought to go.* Why not? So within a week or two the puzzled teacher began to find more and more of her pupils using *hadn't ought,* pupils who up until then had used *ought not* with unconscious ease.

Such an incident cannot happen in the future if teachers and textbook writers know and use the new data now becoming accessible to them. This is the body of facts about American English coming from the great research projects collectively designated the Linguistic Atlas of the United States and Canada.

Of course, this is not the first mass of information about American usage available to teachers of English. During the past forty years an increasing number of studies have effectively demonstrated the unreliability of much that had been accepted as truth. The NCTE itself has led in the publication of the significant and familiar studies by Sterling Andrus Leonard, Albert H. Marckwardt and Fred Walcott, and Charles C. Fries. Dozens of articles on specific items of usage have appeared in our own Council publications as well as in *Language, American*

Speech, and a few other periodicals. Also there have been published the increasingly reliable commercial dictionaries and our first pronouncing lexicon, Kenyon and Knott's *Pronouncing Dictionary of American English.*

Now all this weight of evidence has had its clearly perceptible effects upon the handbooks and the school grammars. A comparison of those published in 1920 and those appearing since 1950 reveals a much higher proportion of sweet reasonableness, of honest recognition of the facts of linguistic life. But influential as this evidence has been, it generally has had one important limitation. On the whole, these studies and investigations of usage have assumed the validity of the criterion of national use, a criterion enunciated by the Scottish rhetorician Alexander Campbell in the late eighteenth century. Campbell insisted that national use must be one of the determinants of what is good usage. Following him, these studies assume that what is true in the determination of usage in a smaller country like England or France, with one cultural capital, is equally true for the vast United States with its cultural diversification and many cultural centers.

A second limitation of these studies is that generally they ignore the lexical and grammatical usage of the normal everyday, informal speech of cultivated people (though Leonard did record opinions classifying forms as "colloquial"). Part of this limitation, of course, is also the fact that these studies generally have not treated matters of pronunciation in informal speech. An exception, again, is Kenyon and Knott's dictionary, which did record conversational pronunciations reported by independent mail surveys.

These limitations are reflected naturally enough in the contents of the textbooks. The laudable improvement in the general treatment of usage is accompanied by conspicuous inadequacy in the treatment of any language matters having variations which correlate with geographical distribution. This improvement, furthermore, is offset also by the persistence of considerable misapprehension concerning various matters of pronunciation whether regional or not.

But any textbook or reference book with these inadequacies will soon be obsolete. Already valuable evidence about regional usage in words and grammar and pronunciation is beginning to emerge from the tremendous research activity within the framework of the Linguistic Atlas of the United States. Already enough evidence from this source is available so that textbook makers will shirk responsibility if they do not take these new facts into account.

Data on Pronunciation

What is the Linguistic Atlas of the United States? It is not a single project; it is a number of regional research projects using similar procedures and collecting the same kinds of evidence, hence producing results that can be added together and compared.

Essentially this evidence is gathered like this. Using a tested selective sampling technique, linguistically trained fieldworkers interview native residents representing three groups, older and uneducated speakers, middle-aged secondary school graduates, and younger college graduates. From each of these persons information is sought about more than 800 language items (in the first project there were 1200). Each response is recorded in a finely graded phonetic transcription, so that all responses have value as pronunciation evidence. Some items are included for that reason only; others are included for their lexical or grammatical or syntactic significance. The basic list of items in the questionnaire is usually modified slightly in each area through the dropping of some which are irrelevant there and the adding of others significant there. (It is pointless to ask a North Dakota farmer what he calls the Atlantic round clam, a /kwáhɑg/, /kwɔ́hɔg/, or /kwəhɔ́g/. He never heard of it by any name!) But this basic list is essentially the same countrywide, so that national comparative studies will be possible when the fieldwork is finished.

At present, organizations to gather this evidence have been effected in eight different areas: New England, Middle Atlantic States, South Atlantic States, North Central States, Upper Midwest, Rocky Mountain States, Pacific Coast, and Louisiana. The New England Atlas has been completed and published. From it and the unpublished materials of the other eastern surveys has come the evidence presented by Hans Kurath in 1949 in his *Word Geography of the Eastern United States* and by E. B. Atwood in 1953 in his *Verb Forms of the Eastern United States*. Derivative articles by Raven I. McDavid, Jr., Atwood, Alva Davis, Walter Avis, Thomas Pearce, David Reed, Marjorie Kimmerle, and others have made public additional usage evidence in *American Speech, College English* and *The English Journal, Orbis, Language,* and *Language Learning*. The volume by Kurath and McDavid on the pronunciation of the Eastern United States is shortly to appear, and Mrs. McDavid is about to complete her dissertation on the verb forms of the North Central and Upper Midwest regions. These publications, together with the Atlas files, constitute a vast accumulation of data for the use of teachers and textbook writers.

When we look at the information now available about regional usage we find that probably the most important single fact is the reconstruction of the picture of American language areas. It has been assumed for years that we have Eastern, Southern, and Northern (sometimes called General American) dialect divisions in this country. But evidence from the Atlantic field records presented by Kurath has led to the recognition of a quite different structure consisting of Eastern New England, Northern, Midland, and Southern, with various subdivisions in each region and, of course, with some overlapping of regions. Midland is the speech of the Pennsylvania-Delaware settlement area and of its derivative areas in central Ohio, northern Indiana, central Illinois, southern Iowa, and so on. It exists also in the variety called South Midland, which extends south along the Appalachians as "Mountain English" and into southern Illinois, Missouri, Arkansas, eastern Oklahoma, and eastern Texas.

For significant matters of pronunciation I would suggest reference to McDavid's excellent article, "Some Social Differences in Pronunciation," in *Language Learning* in 1953.[1] McDavid's thesis here is that, although certain pronunciations may lack recognition or distribution nationally, they can enjoy high prestige in a given region through the influence of such a focal center as Boston, New York, Philadelphia, Richmond, or Charleston. Differences in pronunciation, in other words, are not merely a matter of social and educational background; they may also be related to geographical differences.

For example, despite the tendency of the schools toward spelling-pronunciation, the unaspirated forms /wɪp/ "whip," /wilbæro/ "wheelbarrow," and /wɔrf/ "wharf" are in common cultured use in the Midland area and, as a matter of fact, occur sporadically elsewhere among cultured speakers. A few years ago a teacher in Utica, N.Y., yielding to the probably normal impulse to consider one's own speech or that of a textbook as the proper one, wrote to *College English* that she had never observed a person of true culture who lacked the /hw/ cluster in such words. Yet, as McDavid has observed, this teacher would have had to go only a few miles south to central Pennsylvania to observe thousands of cultivated speakers who say /wɪp/ and /wilbæro/; indeed, even in her own community the Atlas' cultivated informant is recorded as having /w/ and not /hw/ in these words. In the function words, of course, the customary lack of stress has resulted in the loss of aspiration everywhere, not just in certain areas; yet in my own state of Minnesota the new guide for instruction in the language arts enjoins the teacher to insist upon distinguishing /wɪč/ "witch" and /hwɪč/ "which" and /wɛðər/ "weather" and /hwɛðər/ "whether."

Similarly, the /hy/ consonant cluster in *humor* reveals primary geographical distribution. This cluster commonly occurs in Northern speech, but elsewhere in the nation the usual form among all speakers is simply /yumər/.

In Northern American English and in South Carolina, probably in some other sections, a restressing of the second vowel in *because* has led to the form /bɪkɔz/ as usual among cultivated speakers. Yet many teachers, likely influenced by spelling and lacking the information

---

[1] IV, 102–16.

forthcoming from the Atlas studies, insist punctiliously upon /bɪkɔz/. The sounds represented by the letter *o* in *orange, horrid,* and *forest* also vary according to region. In much of New York state and in eastern Pennsylvania, for example, an unround /ɑ/ appears instead of the more common /ɔ/. Not long ago a teacher came to Minnesota from New York state and promptly began insisting that her pupils say only /ɑrɪnǰ/ and /fɑrɪst/; and recently a textbook came out with the same injunction, that the only correct form is /ɑrɪnǰ/.

The dipthong /ɪu/, mistakenly called "long *u*," offers another case in point. In the South, as in British English, a strongly consonantal /y/ beginning is heard in this dipthong in post-alveolar contexts, as in *newspaper, tube,* and *due* or *dew.* But in the North this beginning is quite weak, often almost imperceptible, and it is gone completely in northeastern New England and in Midland. Yet many teachers in the Middle West diligently drill their pupils in the pronunciation /nyuz/ instead of their normal /nuz/. More than half my own students each year report that this was their high school experience, although on only a few of them did the attempted inoculation "take." (To prevent misunderstanding, it should be clear that there can of course be no objection to the form /nyuz/ where it is the normal prestige form. What is objectionable is well-meaning but unenlightened tampering with acceptable speech.)

The same kind of thing, but with a much more complicated geographical picture, occurs with the pronunciation of a group of words spelled with *oo.* I should be surprised if many of the readers of this article, or of the original audience hearing it read, would have for all of these words the same pronunciation which I, a native of southern Michigan, have: /ruf, rʊt, hʊf, hʊp, hʊpɪŋ kɔf, kup, rum, brum, fud, spuk/ (with /ʊ/ as in *put* and /u/ as in *moon*). But I should also be surprised if you have not sometime been in a situation—on either the giving or the receiving end—where someone was being instructed to pronounce *root* and *roof,* perhaps even *soot,* with /u/ rather than /ʊ/. The Atlas files reveal a complicated distribution of these forms, each word having its own distinctive regional pattern; and nothing in this information supports the familiar injunctions.

Another vowel dilemma with historical roots in Middle English is that offered by *creek.* Many Northern teachers, probably swayed by the double *ee* spelling, for years have insisted upon their pupils learning the Southern standard pronunciation /krik/ despite the fact, which should be obvious to an objective listener in a Northern community and which is fully attested by the Atlas records, that the basic Northern form is /krɪk/. Even in Battle Creek, Michigan, I am informed, there is this attempt to lift at least the school population to the cultural heaven, Southern division, where /krik/ is the shibboleth.

There are numerous other moot matters of pronunciation upon

which Atlas research now can provide information making possible an enlightened approach. I think, for instance, of such *loci critici* as /hɑg/ and /hɔg/, /rɑzbɛriz/ and /ræzbɛriz/, /grisi/ and /grizi/, /iðər/ and /aɪðər/, /kɑfi/ and /kɔfi/, /kɑnt/ and /kænt/ and /kent/ "can't," /ves/ and /vɑz/, /keč/ and /kæč/, /wɑter/ and /wɔtər/, /tord/ and /təwɔrd/, /sɝ·əp/ and /sɪrəp/, /təmetoz/ and /təmɑtoz/, /rædɪš/, and /rɜdɪš/, and /dɪfθɪryə/ and /dɪpθɪryə/—for information about which the Atlas sources are invaluable.

Data on Grammar and Idiom

Then the category of grammar and idiom is another in which Atlas materials contribute to our knowledge about usage. As with pronunciation we quite humanly yield to the notion that what is standard or customary for us either is, or ought to be, standard for others. A recent rhetoric textbook for the college freshman course was written by two authors of southern background. They say, "*Bucket* is more likely to be the ordinary word [;] *pail* . . . a little more old-fashioned and endowed with more 'poetic' suggestions." Any freshman speaking Northern English who finds this statement on page 372 must find it rather puzzling, for to him *bucket* refers to some unfamiliar wooden vessel in a well and is a word invariably preceded by *old oaken*. The Atlas files provide evidence for a much more objective statement about the relationship between *bucket* and *pail*.

Again, more than one textbook writer has condemned *sick to one's stomach* in favor of *sick at one's stomach*, but the Atlas findings reveal *sick to* as the usual Northern locution and *sick at* as a Midland variant, along with *sick from* and *sick with* and *sick in*.

Even those who have confidently relied upon the data in the 1932 Leonard report will now need to revise their statements in the light of what Atlas evidence tells them about *depot* (~ railroad station), *in back of* (~ behind), *mad* (~ angry), *off of* (~ from), and *like* (~ as if)—all of them rated as disputable usages by Leonard—as well as about the expressions *the dog wants in* and *all the further*, both of which actually are rated there as illiterate.

Now such matters of pronunciation and of vocabulary may readily be accepted by the teacher as likely to be clarified by research in regional language. We are accustomed to thinking of dialect as consisting of differences in sounds and words. Actually, regional linguistic studies may also considerably illumine certain other matters of high importance to the teacher, those in the field of grammar.

At least seven of the grammatical items that Leonard's monograph listed as disputable were included in the Atlas worksheets. These are *dived ~ dove, I'll ~ I shall, eat ~ et, aren't I? ~ ain't I? ~ am I not?*, it (*he*) *don't* ~ *doesn't, these kind* ~ *those kind,* and *sang* ~ *sung.* At least eight more Atlas items appeared in the group classified by Leonard as illiterate: *have drank* ~ *have drunk, began* ~ *begun, lay down* ~ *lie down, a orange* ~ *an orange, hadn't you ought* ~ *ought not you, run* ~ *ran, set down* ~ *sit down,* and *you was* ~ *you were.*

The Atlas records offer data, some of it surprising, about these items. For instance, the frequently found textbook admonition about the preterit *dove* implies that this is non-standard in contrast with the historical form *dived.* But the records show plainly that *dove* is the usual form among speakers of Northern English and *dived* is Midland and Southern. In other words, the present-day distinction is regional and not social.

But besides these items the Atlas files include comprehensive information about the social and regional distribution of many others that have been in controversy, such as the preterit forms *give* and *gave, did* and *done, dreamed* and *dremt, swam* and *swum, fitted* and *fit, shrank* and *shrunk, saw* and *seen, kneeled* and *knelt, taught* and *learned;* the participial forms *worn out* and *wore out, have taken* and *have took, I been thinking* and *I've been thinking, spoiled* and *spoilt, was bitten* and *was bit, have drove* and *have driven;* together with *you* and *you-all* and *it wasn't me* and *it wasn't I.*

Application of the Data

For teachers of English, clearly the immediate application of this new source of information about our language is in the revision of previous statements about usage. In the simple interest of accuracy this revision is demanded. Those of us who have anything to do with the training of future teachers have the responsibility of using such revision in attention paid to usage items in our language and methods classes. The classroom teacher has the special responsibility of using the new information in class drills, in class discussion, and in the evaluation of student oral and written language. As the experience of the South Carolina teacher with *hadn't ought* indicates, the teaching of standard forms must be done in full awareness of frequency and distribution of the contrasting non-standard forms.

But the teacher's application ordinarily must result from revision of usage statements in books of reference and in textbooks. Those who prepare texts, workbooks, drill exercises, and the like cannot in all conscience ignore the findings of the Atlases. Such revision is normal, of course, in the editing procedure of the main dictionaries, which constantly note the new evidence in published research. Full use of Atlas evidence is being made in the Council's own projected dictionary, the *Dictionary of Current American Usage*, under the direction of Professor James B. McMillan.

Here is an example. Preliminary treatments of various items are sent by McMillan to members of the advisory committee. In a recent batch of treatments appeared this tentative statement about the phrase *all the farther*: "In the sense of 'as far as,' this phrase is often heard, especially in the popular speech of the West. Cultivated speakers and writers, however, still avoid it. The preferred locution, therefore, is *as far as*."

After checking the Atlas record for the Upper Midwest, I was able to write McMillan that the imputation of western popularity to this expression, if not incorrect, needs clarification, for actually the incidence of its occurrence drops from about forty per cent in Iowa and twenty per cent in Minnesota to about four per cent in the area settled by the next wave of migration in the Dakotas and Nebraska. I could write him also that at least in the eastern half of the Upper Midwest area fifty per cent of the cultivated speakers use *all the farther*. When he receives additional data from the other regional atlases, he will be able to revise the treatment of this locution so as to represent much more accurately just where and by whom it is used.

But we may look forward to a second kind of application of Atlas materials in the classroom. It is high time to recognize the validity of some regional speech in the scope of standard American English. There *are* standard forms which are regional and not national. The label *dial.* in a dictionary does not necessarily consign a linguistic form to either the linguistic slums or the linguistic backwoods. If you want to refer to the strip of grass between the sidewalk and the street, you are driven to awkward circumlocution unless you use a dialect word; there simply is no national word for it. But the cultivated speakers who in various parts of the country call this strip of grass the *boulevard, berm, tree-lawn, curb, parking, terrace, curb strip, sidewalk plot,* or any of several other names would be surprised, if not disgruntled, to be told that they were not speaking standard English.

Recognizing the validity of our own regional speech as standard means also that we recognize the validity of the standard of speech of other regions. The time is surely long past when we need to take seriously such an unenlightened statement as this which appeared in a speech textbook several years ago: "There is perhaps no deviation from standard English that sounds as provincial and uncultivated as [the retroflex or inverted r-sound]. . . . Inverted sounds are not used in standard English pronunciation. They will do more to make one's speech sound uncultivated than any other one thing."

Students can be helped toward recognition of this regional validity through various kinds of inductive exercises, especially in the vocabulary. Through such an exercise students for the first time approach objectively the language of their family, their neighbors, the community leaders, and speakers of other areas whom they hear. This particular investigative activity, it may be observed, fits naturally also into a language arts program that seeks to draw upon community resources.

Then, finally, a further utilization of the Atlas data, possible in both college and secondary school, would be for the aim of developing awareness that language is a complex, changing, and always relative structure, not a set of absolutes. The use of regional language information can help our students attain a desirable degree of objectivity in their observation of language matters, can help them see that language is essentially a system of habits related at every point to non-language habits of behavior. And this kind of awareness, this kind of objectivity, is at the heart of a disciplined and informed ability to use language effectively for the communication of meaning.

STUDY QUESTIONS AND EXERCISES

1. Does Allen's story of students adopting "hadn't ought" recall any experience in your own schooling in which you were cautioned against "errors" which were not current in your community? What method would you suggest by which a teacher could determine which deviations from standard English are serious and frequent enough to require special attention?

2. Have you ever been drilled on any of the pronunciation "problems" cited? Did the person or persons "correcting" your pronunciation come from another region in which the "correct" pronunciation was used? If not, were you aware of personal attitudes, such as a desire to be "elegant," which resulted in overzealous purism? A Middle Western school teacher held up as an ideal a professor from the East. The teacher said to her students: "You would probably say *p'raps*, and I should probably say *per-haps*, but Miss Lowell says *pair-hops*." What would Allen say about that teacher's attitude?

3. Look up in *Webster's Third International* half a dozen of the expressions you have been taught to avoid but which you consider standard in your region to see whether they are listed as standard, regional standard, or regional substandard.

4. From common expressions or pronunciations which are sometimes questioned, choose one which you have verified as standard, one which is standard regional, and one which is substandard. Ask a dozen college students to classify them under the three categories. Do you find any consistent relation between a person's social, educational, and geographical background and his sense of what is regarded as

acceptable by authoritative lexicographers, according to recorded usage?

5. Check the entry for *all the farther* in Bryant's *Current American Usage* in light of Allen's discussion. What conclusions can you draw about the use of data from the *Linguistic Atlas*?

6. How do Allen's article and the other articles in this section demonstrate the fact that "language is a complex, changing, and always relative structure, not a set of absolutes"?

17

Regional and Local Words

Hans Kurath

The words discussed below are taken from A Word Geography of the Eastern United States (1949), *edited by Professor Kurath. The factual details are based on the field reports of investigators for the* Linguistic Atlas.

In the present chapter the regional and local vocabulary is arranged from the point of view of meaning. All synonyms for one and the same thing or situation are here treated together under one heading, so that the geographic variations in vocabulary can be seen at a glance. . . .

Whenever it seemed desirable to give a more precise indication of the area in which a word is current, the names of bays, rivers, watersheds, mountain ranges, and other topographical features have been employed to orient the reader. . . .

The social distribution of words is also carefully noted. Some are used only by the simple folk—especially the strictly local expressions; some are restricted to the cultured. Others are current among the simple folk and the large middle class, or among the cultured and the middle class. Others again can be heard from all the people in a given area. Whenever no comment is offered on social distribution it is to be assumed that the word has general currency within the stated geographic limits.

Care has been exercised to point out whether a given expression is in general use, common, infrequent, or rare; also, whether it is spreading or receding, an innovation or a relic. In some cases the apparent focus of dissemination has been identified—at least tentatively.

Striking trends from local to regional usage and from regional to national currency are duly noted. The general trend in the American vocabulary is unmistakably in these directions.

It will be observed that some words occur in two or more geographically separate areas, partly as the result of independent importation from the British Isles, partly as survivals in conservative areas.

Although pains have been taken to describe the geographic and the social spread of each word treated here as accurately as possible, many details—especially scattered occurrences—have not always been mentioned. The need for brevity and a desire to emphasize the more striking features of distribution have prompted this simplification. . . .

The wealth of detail recorded for the *Linguistic Atlas* is exhibited in the figures that are included in this chapter. The reader should bear in mind that more than 1,200 informants were interviewed in the Eastern States and that all statements made below concerning the currency of words rest upon this extensive record of usage.

quarter of eleven

Of, to, and *till* are all used over large areas in this phrase.

In the Northern area, on Delaware Bay, and on Chesapeake Bay *of* and *to* stand side by side in this expression. *Quarter of* predominates in the Boston area and in the Hudson Valley, elsewhere *of* and *to* seem to be in balance.

The greater part of the Southern area (Eastern Virginia, northeastern North Carolina, and the Low Country of South Carolina) has exclusively *quarter to,* the South Midland *quarter till.* The Midland *till* has been carried seaward along the Cape Fear and the Peedee rivers and even competes with the Southern *to* on the Neuse.

Pennsylvania presents a picture of great confusion. In the central part of the state the characteristic Midland *till* is still common, but it is yielding ground in the east to *of,* which now predominates in Philadelphia and the southeastern part of the state; and in the Pittsburgh area *of* and *to* are gradually superseding *till.*

(the wind is) rising

Along the Atlantic coast, from New Brunswick to Cape Fear in North Carolina, the wind is said to *breeze up, breeze on* (less commonly simply to *breeze*) when it gets stronger. This is one of a number of seafaring terms that are current the full length of the Atlantic coast but are known only to those who live within easy reach of the sea.

living room

In all the Eastern states *living room* and *sitting room* (*settin' room* among the common folk) are the usual names for the room in which the family gathers evenings, and receives and entertains friends. *Sitting room* is now rather a rural expression. *Living room* is fully established in the cities and among the younger generation in the country.

Only the larger houses have (or had) a "best" room for formal occasions such as weddings, funerals, and the reception of honored guests, which is known as the *parlor* from Maine to the Carolinas. The old-time *parlor* is now largely a thing of the past. Some now call it the *front room.*

All these terms are current nearly everywhere in the Eastern States, but with varying frequency.

In the simple homes of the piedmont and the mountains of North Carolina (also on the Peedee in South Carolina, rarely in West Virginia) the living room is called the *big-house* or the *great-house*, on the Eastern Shore of Virginia the *big-room*. . . .

andirons

The andirons in the fireplace are generally known as *fire dogs, dogs*, or *dog irons* in the greater part of the South, the South Midland, and in southwestern Pennsylvania. *Dog irons* predominates from the lower James River (the Norfolk area) to the lower Neuse in North Carolina and in the South Midland, *fire dogs* in South Carolina and the greater part of North Carolina.

Scattered instances of *fire dogs* occur also in Eastern Pennsylvania, and the term is not unknown in New England; but the usual expression in Pennsylvania and the North is *andirons*, which has also become well established on Chesapeake Bay and on the Potomac. As a literary term *andirons* is current also in Southern cities.

In the *andirons* area the common folk not infrequently say *hand irons*, especially (1) in an area extending from Delaware Bay to the Rappahannock in Virginia and (2) in the northern counties of Pennsylvania.

mantel shelf

The shelf over the opening of the fireplace is known as the *mantel* or *mantel piece* in most parts of the Eastern States. (These terms also denote the entire decorative frame of the opening, the uprights together with the shelf.) In eastern Virginia and adjoining parts of North Carolina, except for the central part of the Virginia Piedmont, *shelf* is widely used instead of, or by the side of, *mantel (piece)*.

The South Midland, including the drainage basin of the Kanawha, has the distinctive expression *fire board*, which has spread down to the Atlantic between the Cape Fear and the Peedee rivers.

In the vicinity of Raleigh, North Carolina, the strictly local term *frontis* is in use.

roller shades

Roller shades are a recent invention. The term *(roller) shades* has general currency in the Hudson Valley, the Virginia Piedmont, and the greater part of the Carolinas, and it is widely used in urban areas elsewhere. But in large parts of the Eastern States people still pull down the *curtains* or the *blinds*.

Curtain is widely used in this sense (1) in New England and the New England settlement area, (2) in the Philadelphia area, and (3) on Chesapeake Bay and in the coastal part of northeastern North Carolina. Scattered instances of it have also been noted in the Midland.

The Midland term is *blinds*. In the Philadelphia area and on Delamarvia *blinds* competes with *curtains;* in the remainder of Pennsylvania and in all of the South Midland *blinds* has complete sway. There this term is never used as a synonym of shutters; only the *curtains* area has *blinds* in this sense.

clothes closet

Throughout the New England settlement area and the North Midland, including the Shenandoah Valley and northern West Virginia, *clothes press* is still a common term for the clothes closet in rural areas. On Narragansett Bay, where *closet* is the usual designation for the pantry, and in Western Pennsylvania and the adjoining counties of Ohio and West Virginia, *clothes press* is current among all social classes in the country as well as in the cities. On the other hand, the urbanized areas around Boston, in the lower Connecticut Valley, in the lower Hudson Valley, and around Philadelphia now use *(clothes) closet* almost entirely. Since the Southern area has no trace of *clothes press,* the common occurrence of this expression on the Eastern Shore must be due to earlier Philadelphia influence, even though this term is now rare there.

store room

Many houses have a room in the attic or the cellar for storing old furniture and utensils. In the South Atlantic States we find a variety of terms to denote it: *lumber room, plunder room, trumpery room, junk room, catch-all.*

Lumber room is the Virginia Piedmont and Tidewater term, which is now current also on the Eastern Shore of Virginia (but not of Maryland) and in the Valley of Virginia. The greater part of North Carolina and adjoining parts of South Carolina have *plunder room,* and this term is not uncommon, by the side of *lumber room,* in Virginia south of the James. From Albemarle Sound to the lower Neuse *trumpery room* is current, on Delaware Bay, *catch-all.*

The expressions for this store room were not systematically recorded in the Middle Atlantic States and in New England, except for the eastern half of Pennsylvania. *Store room* appears to be the usual term in the Philadelphia area, *junk room* from the Susquehanna westward. *Junk room* is in use also in the Pennsylvania settlements of the piedmont of North Carolina and on the Cape Fear River by the side of *plunder room.*

porch

The screened porch and the sleeping porch are recent additions to man's comfort; they are known everywhere as *porches.* The unscreened porches of earlier days are also widely called *porches,* but other names are current, too: *piazza, stoop, veranda, gallery,* sometimes with different shades of meanings.

Piazza is found (1) in all of New England and, though less commonly, in the Hudson Valley and on Long Island; (2) in the Carolinas and south of the lower James in Virginia; (3) in southern Maryland west of Chesapeake Bay. The occurrence of *piazza* in southern Maryland permits the inference that this expression was once current all the way from Chesapeake Bay to the Georgia coast and that in the section of the Virginia Tidewater lying between the Potomac and the James, which is under Piedmont influence, the term has been given up.

The old-time *piazza* is usually long and narrow and sheltered by a roof supported by pillars.

Stoop is in general use in the Dutch settlement area—the Hudson Valley, northern New Jersey, and Long Island; it is common to Western New England and the New England settlements of New York State and northern Pennsylvania and has spread into Eastern New England to the very door of Boston. From Narragansett Bay to Cape Cod and on the coast of Maine *stoop* is known, but little used.

Stoop is one of the few Dutch words that have become established beyond the limits of the Dutch settlement area. The reason for the adoption of *stoop* in New England is that the Dutch type of entry to the house, the raised platform, became fashionable in New England. To this day *piazza* and *stoop* mean different things in the New England area.

gutters (on the roof)

Gutters is in regular use on all social levels (1) in the Southern area, (2) in the Hudson Valley, Long Island, and nearly all of New Jersey, and (3) in Eastern New England. In southwestern Connecticut and in Philadelphia and vicinity *gutters* is now very common, but older regional expressions are still used by many. Elsewhere *gutters* is strictly a trade name.

Most parts of the North and the Midland still possess vigorous regional terms.

Eaves troughs (sometimes *eaves troths*) is current in all of New England, except the coastal section from Cape Cod to Maine, and in the New England settlement area. Scattered instances of *eaves troughs*, *water troughs*, and simply *troughs* occur on Delaware Bay, Chesapeake Bay, the Carolina coast, and in western Virginia and North Carolina, mostly in the speech of older people who have not yet adopted *gutters*. Moreover, *eaves troughs* is rather common in west-central West Virginia, especially in the Ohio Valley section of it, where the *eaves troughs* of the New England settlements of Marietta and vicinity across the river supported this older Southern term.

The North Midland and all of West Virginia have the expressions *the spouting* and *the spouts*, the latter being most frequent in West Virginia.

A related *eaves spouts* is common in the Upper Connecticut Valley and to the east thereof, except for the coastal area; and relics of it are found in Rhode Island, on Cape Cod, and on Nantucket, all parts of Eastern New England.

Whether the *eaves spouts* of the northern counties of Pennsylvania and the Western Reserve of Ohio is a direct descendant of this New England expression or, at least in part, a blend of the New England *eaves troughs* and the Pennsylvania *spouting, spouts* is an open question. It is a very striking fact that the New England settlements in New York State have only *eaves troughs*, whose original home is in south-western New England. . . .

corn crib

Indian corn is often stored in sheds with flaring sides and a projecting roof. In the Midland and the entire New England settlement area this structure is called a *corn crib*, usually shortened to *crib* in Rhode Island. The simplex *crib* is characteristic of all of North Carolina and adjoining parts of Tidewater Virginia (south of the James), and of western-most Virginia and South Carolina.

The Virginia Piedmont, the Tidewater area north of the James, and the Western Shore of Maryland have the distinctive term *corn house* to the exclusion of *corn crib*.

In New England the two expressions stand side by side, but only scattered relics of *corn house* are found in the New England settlement area.

Two local expressions are worth noting, the *crib house* of southern New Jersey and the *corn stack* of southern Delamarvia (southern Delaware to Cape Charles).

hay cock

For the temporary small heaps of hay in the meadow two regional terms are widely current, *cock* in the New England area and the North Midland, *shock* in the Southern area and in the South Midland. The Midland *cock*, however, is still common in the Valley of Virginia, not uncommon in Western North Carolina, and relics of it have survived in central West Virginia. Moreover, this Midland term has spread all the way down to the mouth of Chesapeake Bay on Delamarvia and to the James River on the western shore of the Bay.

The Southern *shock*, on the other hand, has become established in the greater part of the South Midland and bids fair to replace *cock* altogether in that section. On the Eastern Shore *shock* is no longer common, and it is clearly losing ground in Maryland west of the Bay.

Other terms for the hay cock, more local in character, are: *heap* (1) in parts of New England and (2) in the Pennsylvania German area (cf. Pennsylvania German *Haufe*); *tumble*, scattered in northern New England; *doodle*, (1) in Western Pennsylvania and (2) on the lower

Kanawha in West Virginia; *hand stack*, scattered in Pennsylvania; *pile*, (1) on the Atlantic coast from Delaware to Georgia and (2) in Eastern Pennsylvania.

picket fence

Fences with pointed or blunt upright slats which commonly surround the dwelling and the garden are known as *picket fences* in the New England settlement area, and as *paling fences, paled fences*, or simply as *palings* in the Midland and the Southern area. The variant *paled fence* is characteristic of the Philadelphia area.

Picket fence appears as a modern term in large parts of the Midland and the South, especially in the Ohio Valley, on Chesapeake Bay, in northeastern North Carolina, and in the Charleston area in South Carolina.

rail fence

The old-fashioned rail fence built of overlapping rails laid zigzag fashion is simply called a *rail fence* in the Southern area, in New York State, and in the northern counties of Pennsylvania. This term is also widely current in West Virginia and is in regular use in the mountains farther south. In New England this type of fence is commonly known as a *Virginia rail fence* to distinguish it from the *post-and-rail fence* of New England.

The Midland term for the zigzag fence is *worm fence*, an expression that predominates in Pennsylvania, West Virginia, New Jersey, and Delamarvia and has made its way into northern Virginia.

Sporadic terms for this kind of fence are *zigzag fence* and *snake fence*.

Other types of fences are built of rails: the *post-and-rail* fence of New England, also known as the *Connecticut rail fence*, in which the rails are inserted in sturdy posts; the *herring-bone fence* = *stake-and-rider fence* = *buck fence* (Eastern Pennsylvania) = *rip-gut fence*, in which the rails are supported by crossed stakes. . . .

pail

The well-known metal container is called a *pail* in the entire New England settlement area and in the Hudson Valley, a *bucket* in all of the Midland and the South. However, on the New England coast north of Boston *bucket* is still used beside *pail* in this sense (sporadically also elsewhere in New England). On the other hand, *pail* has spread southward to central New Jersey and is now also current in Philadelphia beside *bucket*.

In parts of the Southern area *pail* has survived as the name of a wooden milk or water container which has one long stave serving as a handle.

Bucket, in turn, survives in New England in such compounds as *well bucket* and *fire bucket* (but cf. *cedar pail*).

Note also Northern *swill pail*, and Midland and Southern *slop bucket*.

frying pan (of cast iron)

The flat-bottomed cast-iron frying pan is now often called simply a *frying pan*, especially in urban areas. However, two older expressions, *skillet* and *spider*, are still extensively used for the cast-iron pan to distinguish it from the modern sheet-metal frying pan.

Skillet is current in all of the Midland from New Jersey to western South Carolina and westward. It is also the old term in the Virginia Piedmont, but it has here been largely supplanted by *frying pan*.

Spider occurs in two large separate areas: (1) in the New England settlement area (all the way to the Western Reserve of Ohio), and (2) in the tidewater area from the Potomac southward to the Peedee in South Carolina. It appears also on the Jersey coast from Sandy Hook to Cape May.

faucet

The water *faucet* is known by that name only in the Northern area. The entire Midland and the South have *spicket* (occasionally *spigot*). *Faucet*, to be sure, is not entirely unknown in this sense in the Midland and the South. . . .

paper bag

Paper bag and *paper sack* are both widely used in the Eastern States.

Poke is current, often by the side of *bag* or *sack*, in a large area extending from central Pennsylvania westward, and southward to the Carolinas. In Virginia the Blue Ridge forms the eastern boundary of the *poke* area, in North Carolina the Yadkin.

To the east of the *poke* area, in the bilingual Great Valley of Pennsylvania (from Reading to Frederick in Maryland), the Pennsylvania German term *toot*, riming with *foot*, is in common use in the English spoken there.

burlap bag

Burlap sack or *bag* is the most common term in the Eastern States for the rough loose-woven sack in which potatoes and other farm produce are shipped. It is regularly current throughout the North and the North Midland, and not uncommon in Tidewater Virginia and on the Kanawha. However, most of the Southern area and parts of the Midland have vigorous regional and local terms.

Sea-grass sack, grass sack is current on the coast from Delaware Bay to Albemarle Sound and also on the Western Shore of Chesapeake Bay north of the James River.

Croker sack, crocus sack is in common use (1) in the southern part of the Virginia Piedmont, (2) in South Carolina and Georgia (also in Wilmington at the mouth of the Cape Fear), and (3) on Martha's Vineyard off Cape Cod.

Tow sack is the North Carolina term. It is common throughout the state and rare outside of it, except around Norfolk, Virginia.

Guano sack is common in Maryland, both east and west of the Bay, and in the Shenandoah Valley—presumably as a Baltimore trade name. (Much guano was imported by way of Baltimore and distributed to the farm lands from there.)

Gunny sack is the regular term for the burlap bag in the Ohio Valley from Wheeling downstream. Scattered instances of it have been noted in Eastern Pennsylvania, in Metropolitan New York, and in New England.

STUDY QUESTIONS AND EXERCISES

1. Make your own list of terms by selecting the term in each of Kurath's groups that you would normally use or which sounds most familiar. After each term indicate where, to the best of your knowledge, you learned it: at home, school, through playmates, older friends, advertising, or fiction. Compare your lists with your classmates'.

2. Make a class list showing which terms in each group are used and by how many individuals.

3. Where there are decided individual variations—that is, only a few people use one term and the majority use another—investigate to discover where each of the nonconformists learned the term. Do facts in the person's previous environment or in the family history explain the deviations? Do several persons who use the same term have similar backgrounds?

4. List the terms Kurath uses that you recognize from reading but would never use, perhaps terms like *bucket,* in "old oaken bucket." For example, Southern stories use *croker sack, tote,* and *poke;* English stories use *lumber room* and *drawing room.*

5. List the terms you have heard but would not use.

6. List the terms that are completely new to you.

7. Do your findings confirm or contradict the generalization that regional differences are slight and do not cause misunderstanding?

8. From what sources do people learn most of the words with which *Linguistic Atlas* investigators are concerned?

9. In your findings, are any variations related to social distribution?

10. Do your findings show the trend from local to regional to national? One example of the trend would be the national currency of *blinds* due to the popularity of Venetian blinds.

18

American Regionalism
and the Harmless Drudge

Frederic G. Cassidy

An important aspect of language study, as Professor Cassidy of the University of Wisconsin suggests, is the study of regionalisms. In his speech which was given at the meeting of the Modern Language Association in December, 1966, and which appeared in PMLA *for June, 1967, he points out some of the procedures and details that will be incorporated in the* Dictionary of American Regional English.

Offspring, in the fullness of time, have to come of age; young nations have to come of age; so too with the language of young nations. And, as we are often slow to recognize, the experience of achieving maturity may be traumatic no less for the parent than the child. Yet time does its work, and has done it for our language; so that now not even the most jealous of the ancient nations can deny that the relatively young United States is old enough to vote—that our literature has earned the franchise, and that the language as we speak and write it today has established its individuality and identity.

Back in the 1920's when Mencken's *The American Language*,[1] raucously self-assertive, was flaunting its title, the words produced a certain shock. Mencken, of course, was fully aware of this—his chauvinism was nothing if not canny: the time was ripe for the nation to accept that flattering inaccuracy. For Mencken overdramatized our influence on British English, making it seem as if Americanisms, flooding down upon the older tongue, were quite submerging it. And he certainly underestimated the continuing influence of the language of England upon American intellectual life. Nevertheless, one thing he did establish clearly: that Americans had their own kind of English for which they saw no need to apologize; that they intended to go on using it without apology; and further, that they had the right to an ironic chortle when, amid cis-Atlantic strictures against horrid Americanisms, Englishmen began to claim as their own some transatlantic creations which they had unwittingly adopted.

---

[1] First edition 1919, 2nd, 1921 (New York: Alfred A. Knopf).

Mencken must have his due, then, for making us aware at last that American English had come of age. Others before him raised their voices in the wilderness with little effect; *he* gave a sideshow spiel, he razzed and Bronx-cheered the stuffier traditionalists, the Briticizing toadies, the pundits of elegance. He argued the realism, the salt, the honesty of our native product, coarse and earthy, but strong, free, and full of nimble wit. And, as the English were constrained in the end to admit, very much within the Anglo-Saxon spirit of the language. So at last we were moved to take it more seriously and to begin to document and study it. But this task, despite some notable achievements, is no more than well begun.

Long before Mencken's time, American English had attracted the lexicographers. At first they merely noted the new colonial words and senses. Later, and especially after the Revolution, American linguistic differences furnished in England a convenient object of distaste, extravagances to be inspected fastidiously through a quizzing-glass and, for the most part, rebuffed. In this post-Johnsonian period, when language in general was being subjected to the canons of Reason and Taste—not always the same reason or the same taste, be it said—when on both sides of the Atlantic elegance, euphony, and perspicuity were the idols of the literati, little patience could be expected for the popular ebullience or laconic abruptness of a practical nation. Dictionaries had become selective, guides to choice language for those bound upward in the social scale. And when Noah Webster attempted to break with English tradition in his *American Dictionary*,[2] he was forced to draw back by the competition of Joseph Worcester, a former editor of Johnson's dictionary. Meantime, of course, the language went its way, developing as needs arose and serving the nation's daily requirements quite apart from the designs of the language improvers.

With the advent in the nineteenth century of the science of language, however, the nature of the dictionary began to change. Emphasis shifted from selectiveness to inclusiveness. Good science must take account of *all* the data, not a limited part, however artfully chosen. The concept of the dictionary as a florilegium—a flower garden of words from which the weeds are strictly banished, or at least where they are warningly labeled: *poison* ivy, *deadly* nightshade—this concept fell into a slow decline, though it is not quite dead yet! Historical lexicography, the crowning product of which was the great *Oxford Dictionary*, showed that a word is not fully known until its origins, its congeners, its course of growth or decay, and many other facts about it are known. Thus the goal of the lexicographer today has become no less than to collect and document *all* words of *whatever* kind as fully as possible.

This does not mean that collecting must be indiscriminate or that

---

[2] *An American Dictionary of the English Language* (New York, 1828).

everything must go into a single dictionary. The lexicographer recognizes the advantages of classification and the role of special dictionaries. Before the *Oxford* was quite finished, one of its last editors, Sir William Craigie, proposed that the next task should be to prepare a series of special dictionaries for periods and areas—for OE, ME, EMnE; and for Scottish and American English. The latter two he set about himself. At the University of Chicago he began, and Professor James Hulbert finished, the *Dictionary of American English* (1940–44), which was followed a few years later by our other historical dictionary, Dr. Mitford Mathews' *Dictionary of Americanisms* (1951).

Another special field for which the scope of the *Oxford Dictionary* left insufficient room was that of dialect—the rich and historically valuable folk speech of Great Britain. When editing of the Oxford was just beginning, it was realized that this local vocabulary of the shires would call for separate, detailed treatment. The English Dialect Society accordingly appointed Joseph Wright to produce his great *English Dialect Dictionary* (1896–1905). And it was no accident that in the very year when Wright began editing, a group of American language scholars, meeting with the MLA, founded the American Dialect Society (1889), hoping to produce, for the United States, a study of our localisms parallel to what Wright was making for Great Britain.

Dialect Notes began the following year to publish word lists and other studies, and the work of the American Dialect Society has continued, with ups and downs, to the present time—a matter of seventy-seven years. But the task of producing an adequate dictionary is a huge and expensive one, and only recently have the two essentials been obtainable: adequate, full-time direction, and enough money to get the job done. Now at last, with the Federal Government funding large scholarly undertakings, the project for the *Dictionary of American Regional English* has become a reality. It began officially on 1 July 1965, to continue for five years, and is a cooperative project supported by the U.S. Office of Education (about two-thirds) and the University of Wisconsin (about one-third). We have contracted to collect and process, during this time, the materials from which, ultimately, a dictionary may be made.

The *Dictionary of American Regional English* hopes to profit by the mistakes and successes of the past and to satisfy a definite need in the broad area of American lexicography. By mistakes I mean—and this has been my theme for some twenty years—that before effective collecting can be done the collectors must think lexicographically—they must clearly understand what it takes to make a dictionary. What is collected has value only insofar as it furnishes the kinds of information upon which the editor can base full and accurate entries. Too many of the early contributions to *Dialect Notes* were extremely thin: terms were given out of context with a one-word gloss, and such far too general remarks as "found widely in the South," or "used by Yankees." Though not quite useless, this kind of imprecise stuff is nearly so. Much closer attention is necessary to the geographic and social range of a word or phrase, to the nature of its users, to its shades of meaning, to the kind of situation in which it is found.

Another requirement is that the *entire* region be studied. As Professor Raven McDavid has pointed out, a mere unsystematic amassing of items does not constitute a dictionary. The jesting remark has been made that by reading *Dialect Notes* one can discover where English professors spent their summer holidays—and there is a grain of truth in this. Certainly, coverage of the United States was extremely spotty and nothing was done in an organized way until the Linguistic Atlas of the United States and Canada[3] began its work in New England under Professors Hans Kurath and Miles Hanley, with support from the American Council of Learned Societies and many universities and colleges. Out of this have come the *Linguistic Atlas of New England* and at least half a dozen books and monographs; and the work, steadily pushing on, has now covered the greater part of the United States.

The Atlas did not and does not seek to produce a dictionary, but it does, in the field of dialectology, what a good dictionary would need to do: to abandon the random collecting of quaint or queer sayings—what have been called the two-headed calves of language—and, instead, to collect systematically, recording *all* the pertinent facts about the speaker of any item of idiolect, or dialect, or local or regional speech. The Atlas deserves the highest praise for rescuing American dialectology from the sentimental or patronizing word-hunters, who merely wanted to savor "Chaucerian" or "Shakespearean" survivals, or to chuckle over the malapropisms and solecisms of the natives.

The *Dictionary of American Regional English* hopes to be able to collect the greater part—nobody can hope to collect *all*—of the words and phrases, pronunciations, spellings, and meanings used by native speakers of American English in local and regional speech-communities throughout the United States up to the present time. In short, we plan this as a historical dictionary of American usages of less than national range. This might seem at first very likely to overlap with books already in existence, and some overlap there will be, but it should be minor. The *Dictionary of American English* and the *Dictionary of Americanisms*, though both are excellent and give us the best documentation obtainable in the field, were limited to written sources. D.A.E. came down only to the year 1900 and stopped entering anything considered dialectal from about 1880 on. D.A. excluded any item which could not be plausibly shown to have originated in the United States. The only *American Dialect Dictionary* ever to see the light of day, Dr. Harold

---

[3] On the inception of the Atlas see the *Handbook to the Linguistic Geography of New England* (Providence, R.I.: Brown Univ. Press, 1939), pp. xi–xii.

Wentworth's little volume,[4] had very limited coverage: it chiefly depended on what the Dialect Society had published, on Wentworth's knowledge of his home area (upstate New York), and on his reading of some 200-odd regional novels and other books. He made no reference whatever to the Atlas, though it would have been a valuable source. The *Dictionary of American Regional English* plans to have a much larger corpus, and we are making a fresh, broad-scaled collection from oral sources—the many, many expressions that people use but nobody ever writes down, or which, if they occasionally find their way into a novel or story, are still of unknown currency and geographic scope.

To get at these untapped or poorly understood sources *D.A.R.E.* has a program of field work in which we will collect by direct interview from 1,000 communities in fifty states. It should hardly be necessary to say that, profiting by Linguistic Atlas techniques, our communities and interviewees are chosen according to definite principles, taking into account *first* the settlement history of each state and region, emphasizing those where the population has been relatively stable, seeking out always as people to be interviewed those who clearly belong in each community, and whose families were there before them—thus people linguistically representative of each place. One thousand communities for fifty states averages twenty per state, but of course the actual number varies greatly. Vast areas of the west and north are thinly populated—Idaho, the Dakotas, New Mexico, and others. Florida and California, especially, have had such huge increments of population in this century that their present masses are hardly representative, and one has to seek out the older communities and go to fewer of them than present population figures would otherwise call for. This has all been worked out proportionally, balancing the statistics of fifty years ago against present ones. We find ourselves making only two interviews each in Alaska, Hawaii, Nevada, and Wyoming; only 19 in Florida and 56 in California; *but* 54 in Illinois, 73 in Pennsylvania, and 96 in New York.

Our Field Workers, five of them, go out in camper wagons equipped with stove, sink, refrigerator, and pullman seats which turn into a bed. Among ourselves we call these "Word Wagons," and one correspondent from Kansas referred to them recently as *logomobiles*. The field workers live in these, going south in winter and north in summer, generally stopping in state and national parks, and seeking out appropriate interviewees (whom we call 'informants') in designated communities, both urban and rural. The types of informants are also proportioned by age (about 50% old, 40% middle-aged, 10% young adults) and by social level. We want some cultivated local informants though the majority will be those with less or little education. We try to find people of many occupations, always including representatives of the

[4] New York: Crowell, 1944.

chief activities of the state or region, such as cotton planters, miners, fishermen, mill workers, lumbermen. Not only do we get tape recordings of these people describing how they go about their trade or occupation, but in our one thousand communities we are using a questionair made specifically for this job and tested in a pilot study.

This questionair contains upwards of 1,600 questions, each carefully phrased to indicate what we want without disposing the informant to any one of the alternative answers. Thus, for example, we ask the name of "an implement with X frame [gesture] to hold firewood for sawing." When the question was made we already knew fourteen names for this object, among them *sawbuck, sawhorse, sawframe, sawjack, woodrack,* and *trestle*; even so a new word turns up every once in a while. To put these variants down on maps is word-geography, of course, one of the things the Atlas does so well—and we have learned a great deal from them. The Atlas, however, concentrates on pronunciation and uses a limited lexical element: we necessarily put the lexicon first. Following Professor Harold Orton's practice in his English Dialect Survey, the phrasing of all questions is fixed; the field workers are expected to ask them as they stand. This should give us responses exactly comparable for the entire area.

Our questionair is relatively long—it requires the greater part of a week's interviewing to get through. Even so we consider it only a core around which we must spread out. Yet methodologically it is our most important tool: when we have asked the same question in the same words in one thousand communities demographically representative of the fifty states, and when we can deal statistically with such factors as the family background, the schooling, the age, the sex, and the occupation of our informants, it will be possible at last to make sound comparisons and pretty firm and detailed correlations between the words collected, their geographic and social distributions. Our questioning method should do away with the haphazardness of much past collecting.

These questionairs range, section by section, over the day-by-day concerns of most people. Everybody has to follow the clock around, day and night, and the four seasons. But the terms in which we speak of these common things may hide uncommon history. For example, the little difference between *to* and *till*. The man who says "quarter *to* eleven," though quite unaware of it, is somehow in the line of derivation from a south-English dialect; while the man who says "quarter *till* eleven" is historically tied to a northern one. It will be remembered that in Caedmon's seventh century Hymn of Creation, the Northumbrian version, God made "heben *til* hrofe," "as a roof to the world," whereas the West-Saxon version has "heofon *to* hrofe." This prepositional variation has been around for some thirteen centuries in the English language, and still patterns locally and regionally in the United States today.

Similarly we get variant responses for articles of clothing, houses, furniture and utensils, dishes and foods. If you call one of those sloping, outside cellar doors a *bulkhead* or *hatchway* your family probably had seafaring connections; if it is a *storm-door* you probably live in a region of heavy snow; if a *klop-door*, there is some association with speakers of German. Go around the nation from corner lunchroom to corner lunchroom and you will find on the list for breakfast *battercakes, griddlecakes, hotcakes, wheatcakes, flapjacks,* or *slapjacks.* And if you listen carefully, some of the local customers will ask for *flipjacks,* or just *flip, fritters, flitters,* or *pannycakes.* And what does one pour over them? In a lunchroom the flavor might be maple; in many homes one would find *corn seerup, serrup, surrup,* or *surp; dip, dope,* or *lick; molasses* or *lasses,* also known as *long sweetening.* The subject of foods is inexhaustible and universally interesting. By the time a field worker has reached this point, the informant should be thoroughly at ease, any suspicion of hidden motives removed. He has realized that this young person is obviously a harmless type, only interested in words.

Next we have an important section on farming—the buildings, crops, animals, implements, in which many terms are quite old. You will recall that when Sir Gawain went boar-hunting near Chester in the fourteenth century, the boar gnashed his *tushes.* This word survives widely, though *tusks* long ago became the standard form. And the plague that an Elizabethan might have invoked—as Thersites does in *Troilus and Cressida,* "A red *murrain* o' thy jade's tricks!" [5]—is still a disease of horses in the deep South. The farm questions give good occasion for reminiscence and comparison, since older informants have lived through successive states in the changeover from manual to mechanized and scientific farming, changes of method accompanied, of course, by changes in terminology.

Next come a series of questions on vehicles and transportation; boats, fishing, hunting; then birds, insects, wildflowers, and trees, in which, as always, we constantly seek the locally different name. Under transportation we provide for the newer terms of the automobile age. The "road that connects a big highway with stores and business places set back from it" is an *access road, frontage road,* or *service road,* depending on where you are. The "more expensive kind" of gasoline is *extra, super, high-test, premium, special,* or *ethyl*—the last sometimes, on homemade signs, personified with a feminine spelling: *No Ethel today.*

Our questions do not concern only concrete objects; many involve abstractions, which of course are far harder to deal with: buying and selling, honesty and dishonesty, crime and punishment; physical actions, mental actions, emotional states and attitudes. With these we cannot depend on a simple question, but furnish a typical conversation sen-

---

[5] Shakespeare, *Troilus and Cressida* ii.i.20.

tence with an empty "slot" to receive the appropriate word. For example: "Somebody who is *usually* mean and bad tempered: 'He's an awful——!'" The slot may be filled with *crab, crabapple, crank, crosspatch, grouch, grump, meanie, peeve,* or some other word—name your own!

Further on we come to family relationships, courtship, marriage, and childbearing—a rich field for euphemism of many tints, ranging from cute to sardonic. When a woman's pregnancy becomes obvious, one may say, "She swallowed a pumpkin seed" or "a watermelon seed"; she's "got a bun in the oven"; she's "wearing the hatching jacket"; or if the birth is very close, she'd "better start carrying a basket with her." For "a marriage that takes place because a baby is on the way" one gets, of course, the familiar "shotgun wedding," but also, "a case of have-to," a "rushed-up marriage," "they were married by the sheriff," and "she don't know what briar scratched her."

We have sections also on local entertainments and celebrations, and children's games—an extremely complex and variable subject, where ancient inheritances combine with modernization and fresh invention. The "one-a-leery-two-a-leery" game, as played in Irish neighborhoods, has naturally become "one-O'Leary-two-O'Leary." The hiding-game shout, "All-ee-all-ee-all in free," has become, in at least one Norwegian neighborhood, "Ole-Ole-Olson, all in free." School-going terms, despite great changes in education, hang on well among the children—terms especially for trying to "get in good" with the teacher, for cheating, and for staying away from school. As to the last you can *bag, bolt,* or *bum* school, *cut, dodge, hop,* or *jump* school, *cook Jack, lay out, skip class,* and several more.

Throughout the questionair, items in which pronunciation is known to vary markedly, as in *syrup* already mentioned, the field worker is required to make a phonetic transcription, using the International Phonetic Alphabet. Any other new or unusual pronunciation must also be transcribed. For each informant who answered all or a major part of the questionair we tape a half hour of running conversation, and our own version of the now famous story of Arthur the Rat. There are also the tapes of auxiliary informants describing various occupations and activities—"their gear and tackle and trim." So far we have good accounts of shrimp fishing, basket making, mining, moonshining, fox hunting, blacksmithing, peanut, rice, and tobacco growing, and many more. We shall have over two thousand tapes, from which we plan to combine the best on a long-playing record which will be included with the dictionary to give a living representation of American regional speech.

Finally, the questionair provides for morphological variants, especially in the irregular verbs. Here again we have found best the Atlas practice of distributing these among other questions, wherever they come in naturally, rather than keeping them together in one section. This we tried at first, but people soon caught on, became self-conscious, and resorted to schoolroom forms such as *swum, climbed,* and *saw* when, in conversation, they normally said *swam, clum,* and *seen.* Now we bring these questions in by ones or twos, and the responses are more natural.

Though the field work is probably the most important part of our collecting, it is by no means all: we have no intention of ignoring written sources, though they have to be treated with caution. With an informant you have a living speaker, who, unless he deliberately sets out to pull the field worker's leg and fake his answers—something that happens rarely and is not difficult for an experienced interviewer to recognize—what we get from local, native speakers is "firsthand" and can be taken as genuine. What one gets from regional literature—novels, stories, poetry, plays—is at best secondhand. Even very scrupulous authors tend to pretty-up or cosmetize actual speech—which is not the same thing as choosing what one needs without distorting it. The latter attitude, of course, is what we want—that the writer be true to the local speech of his characters. This kind of accuracy was rather rare until fifty years ago; the characters of Harold Bell Wright, for example, tend to be kitchy stereotypes, and their language too. Edward N. Westcott's *David Harum* is another matter; it is true to both character and language. Mark Twain can be trusted; he was meticulous in his own writing and critical of those who were not. Of Bret Harte he remarked, "Mr. Harte can write a delightful story; he can describe the miner and the gambler perfectly,—as to gait and look and garb; but no human being, living or dead, ever had experience of the dialect which he puts into his people's mouths." [6]

We hope to have read for us by volunteers at least a thousand of the best works of regional literature—best in truly presenting the language of their local characters. In addition we plan to read, if we can fit them in, local diaries, travel accounts, autobiographies, and the like. The number of these in existence is astronomical—Professor William Matthews once declared that every other soldier in the Civil War must have written a journal! [7] Again, we shall attempt, after due bibliographic investigation, to get the best from all over the country. We shall also choose and read representative newspapers, especially weeklies from small towns where the news is about the neighborhood people, and is written by and for them. Last summer this program was begun for us by Professor Audrey Duckert, who discovered, among other things, that the bigger newspapers ought not to be forgotten. The *San Francisco Chronicle* furnished some terms new to us, the most intriguing being the noun *wet bar,* which makes us wonder what other kind there can be.

---

[6] C. M. Babcock, "Mark Twain and the Dictionary," *Word Study,* XLII (Oct. 1966), 4.

[7] William Matthews, *American Diaries,* Univ. of California Pubs. in English, Vol. XVI (1945). (The remark was made in conversation.)

From another well-known local paper, *The New York Times*, came *mother-daughter*, the term for some sort of dwelling unit. Neither of these have we come upon elsewhere, and must presume them to be of limited range until the contrary is proved. Some other interesting terms found in newspapers are *Yankee steak* for a boneless chuck roast (*Salt Lake Tribune*); *Kokanee*, a fish—evidently an Indian name (*Denver Post*); *creep feeder*, which permits the smaller pigs to get their share of feed (Aurora, Nebraska, *News-Register* and Cynthiana, Kentucky, *Democrat*); *pitch-in supper*, where everybody pitches in—in other words a "potluck" (Rockport, Indiana, *Democrat*); *tureen supper*, apparently the same—and one good way to use the old fashioned chinaware (Dunkirk, New York, *Evening Observer*). Such terms, printed without explanation, are obviously in general use where each newspaper is read—it would be foolish to advertise a coming event, or something for sale, in terms that the customer would not understand. We will not know, of course, until all the evidence is in, just how widely known such terms are.

In addition to our fresh collections from oral and printed sources, there is the large backlog of materials collected by the Dialect Society these past seventy-seven years. Many terms now obsolete are recorded there and there alone, and since in principle directly collected material is the most trustworthy, we shall put this into our file. We have been lent, or are promised, the work sheets of the Linguistic Atlas from many areas, which contain lexical items not included on their maps. There are some 90,000 slips from fifty Wisconsin informants, collected from 1947 to 1951. In addition we have thousands of miscellaneous items sent in by collectors from many places, some gathered for student papers. And of course at the editorial stage, years hence, we shall utilize the many special studies that have been made by individual scholars. Our bibliography is "fat and sassy" to use a local phrase, and "growing like a house afire."

Now you may well wonder how such a large mass of material as we plan to collect can possibly be handled within the lifetime of man—and the answer is that by conventional methods using filing slips it would indeed be virtually impossible. Dr. Johnson worked for some eight years with the help of a handful of Scotsmen, harmless drudges all, to make a splendid, though not very large dictionary. The *Oxford Dictionary* had about three and a half million citation slips to handle. D.A.R.E. is planning to utilize the newest and fastest filing-clerk and amanuensis of them all—the computer. Professor Richard Venezky of our staff is in charge of this part of the project, and we have begun to test various methods. Painfully aware of the rapid obsolescence in computer hardware and methods, we shall not commit ourselves to a fixed program before we must. Nevertheless, at present we know that our file will not be on punch cards but will either be typed on sheets and read onto tapes with an optical scanner, or typed directly with a scope and key-board and stored on tapes. Either method will give us unlimited capac-ity, and we expect to store up to five million items. When the editing state comes, three or four years hence, we should be able to retrieve the stored materials, alphabetized, chronologized, and sorted in whatever other ways we feel desirable. The data should be projected on a screen very similar to a television screen, and the editor will be able to retain or reject items or add others with a light-pen and keyboard, and so produce the edited entry before his eyes. When he is satisfied with it, he pushes a button to store it. It can be recalled to the screen at any time for further editing, or can be printed out on paper. The original material is not lost; it too is retrievable in case of afterthoughts. This method of editing, in other words, will be an enormous advance on those used by dictionaries hitherto. It should completely eliminate the finger work of the past, and permit the editor to use his time fully for editing. Thus it becomes conceivable that a much larger amount of material than ever before can be winnowed rapidly, and that one or two editors could complete the dictionary in a few years.

Let me return to my original theme. The English language in America —*our* version of English—is in a way a historical record of the establish-ment, growth, and maturity of the nation. Nothing reflects better than language the people who use it—and let us not forget that this includes *all* the people. Since we must set limits and avoid unnecessary duplica-tion, we leave to others the standard part of the language, and special kinds such as scientific terminology, criminal argot, and the English of foreigners. We are aware of borderlines here, of course—the collector cannot always be certain whether some item is countrywide or regional, individual or local. The decision can only be made when all the evidence is in. In our collecting we therefore lean toward inclusiveness lest some-thing rejected too soon be irrecoverable.

Another borderline is with the technical language of trades and oc-cupations. We expect the distinction here to depend on the inclusive-ness or exclusiveness of the idiom: whether only the practitioners know and use it, or whether it involves whole communities. Whole communi-ties are involved, for example, in tobacco growing, coal mining, cattle raising, steel manufacture. The "trade talk" of such activities becomes common property; smaller trades remain more nearly private—their "trade talk" hardly gains currency beyond the workroom.

Another borderline concerns words of foreign origin, but decisions here should be less difficult since we insist that some form of English be the "first" or home language of every informant, even if he also knows a foreign language used by others in the community. A word of foreign origin can be considered naturalized when it is used normally by the native American speaker in an English context—especially if he does not know the foreign language. When such a word spreads be-

yónd the foreign-derived community or acquires the paradigmatic repertory of English words, that is further proof of its full naturalization.
Such words, of course, we must accept.

But despite the kinds of language we expect to exclude, what is
striking is the amount of material that remains to be included. Every
questionair that returns, every tape we make contains new and interesting items. I have mentioned several words that one might have thought
long dead, since they are gone from the literary or general standard language. Yet locally they may be very much alive—indeed, one thing we
have been impressed with is the remarkable tenacity of folk speech.

Yet it is not these preserved forms alone that deserve to be collected;
quite as interesting are the many creations, some new, some merely new
to us. One of my favorite folk-etymologies was reported by a friend from
a Wisconsin farm, where the language background had been German
but everyone had now gone over to English. The farmer was pouring
water from a spouted can for his poultry when my friend asked, "What's
that?" "A geese-can" replied the farmer. "Why do you call it that?"
"Because I use it to pour water for the geese." Of course the actual
source was German *Giesskanne*, though he did not know it. Here, the
English folk-etymology proved that this loanword was fully naturalized.
A similar instance occurred to me at the time when hybrid corn was
fairly new. The farmers universally pronounced the word "hybred" and
I wondered whether this was merely due to the substitution of the vowel
[ɛ] for [ɪ], or whether folk-etymology was involved. I had my answer in
a store one spring morning when a farmer, buying his seed corn, remarked, "You know, I tried that hybred last year, and it did so good
that I won't plant anymore of the low-bred!"

An example of a word escaping from its normal context came in a
tobacco-growing community in Wisconsin with the phrase *in case*.
When tobacco has been harvested, it is hung up in barns to cure. Late
in the year there usually comes a period of mild, moist weather—*case
weather*—which makes the tobacco leaves flexible. They are now said
to be *in case* and can be handled without damage. In this community
a housewife was sprinkling clothes to iron them. When they were moist
and limp she said, "They're ready to iron now—they're in good case."

An example of a term spreading geographically is *flash flood*, a word
originally of the southwest where rain that fell far away may suddenly
rush down a dry watercourse with devastating effect. In the past twenty-
five years this word has moved into the midwest and east, where it
means any sudden, destructive flood. Now, analogical extensions of it
are beginning to appear—from Chicago, recently, the term *flash storm*
was reported for an unexpected and destructive storm.

Finally let me say that in these unpoetic times we tend to forget that
there is such a thing as folk poetry. I except the ballad-collectors and
folklorists—they have kept better touch than the rest of us with the
springs of popular imagination and metaphor. Among the words and ex-

pressions we have collected, many are striking for keen observation, instant depiction, for pointed wit or earthy jocularity. Consider the ironic similes—"as busy as a one-armed paper-hanger"—or a farmer's description of muddy coffee as "too thick to drink and too wet to plow." I like the name *spoonholder* applied to a love seat, and a smoky lamp that is called a *slut*; a toothpick which unexpectedly becomes a *quittin'-stick*. If I had my *druthers* I'd choose to dine on *ten-toed squash, bull-nose peppers, slippery Jim pickles,* and *scuppernong wine.* I would not shoot deer out of season, but might bring down a *white-faced calf,* that is, if I was not afflicted with *deer fever* or *buckitis.* It is comforting to think that if I had to get out of here in a hurry, there are so many ways of doing it—I could *beat it, dig, high-tail it, hike it, hot-foot it, leave out, make tracks, pull stakes, scat, scoot, scram, slope, skidoo, skedaddle, skip town, twenty-three,* or *vamoose.* I would try to avoid the *droops,* not to *sull* about things that displease me, not to be *short-patient* or *ticky.* I'd steer clear of a man who had *beans up his nose.*

These are only a few examples out of the thousands in our files, but they are typical. Over the next four years our collection should increase rapidly. We feel that the large body of data amassed from the whole area and by systematic methods will add greatly to the resources of American lexicography. Further, because of computer processing, we shall fairly easily be able to make lists of special categories of words, to generalize about many features and treat some statistically, and even to print out maps showing the distribution of variant features, as we have done already in a trial run. We feel confident that the *Dictionary of American Regional English* will prove to be a valuable reference tool for scholarship in language and literature, and one which educators everywhere may use to advantage in the schools. We think that it will give us a greater respect for the rich and varied developments which the English language has undergone and is undergoing in the United States.

STUDY QUESTIONS AND EXERCISES

1. For an explanation of the title, see the definition of *lexicographer* in Dr. Johnson's dictionary. A convenient source is *Johnson's Dictionary: A Selection,* E. L. McAdam, Jr. and George Milne, eds. (New York: Pantheon Books, 1953).

2. Look up *flaunting* and *flout* in Evans and Evans, *Dictionary of Contemporary Usage,* and in the *American Heritage Dictionary.* Are these words likely to be used by uneducated people? What is the psychological association between the words? Does confusion between them blur or alter the intended meaning? Are educated people contributing to the loss of good, vigorous words for which there is no real substitute?

3. Does H. L. Mencken's selection in Part 2, "Hallmarks of American," fit Cassidy's description of *The American Language?* What did Mencken achieve for Americans and their language? What specific characteristics of American English, in vocabulary, syntax, and idiom are exhibited in the writing of Mencken? Of Cassidy?

4. The flower-weed analogy in language appears again here. How does Shakespeare's "lilies festered smell far worse than weeds" suggest a further analogy, illustrated by the controversy over *Webster's Third?*

5. What notable achievements and continuing projects in the study of dialects are cited here? What requirements must be met by the *Dictionary of American Regional English?*

6. What is the relation between the Linguistic Atlas and the *Dictionary of American Regional English?* How do they differ? How is the latter both historical and regional? How does it differ in its sources from the *Dictionary of American English* and the *Dictionary of Americanisms?*

7. What procedures do the field workers for *D.A.R.E.* follow?

8. "Their gear and tackle and trim" is quoted from "Glory be to God for dappled things" by Gerard Manley Hopkins. Look up the poem and examine the diction. What are the precise meanings of terms such as *tackle?* Are those meanings common to British and American usage? What compound words are original with Hopkins? Is his use of language conservative or innovative?

9. What does "kitchy stereotypes" mean, as used to describe Harold Bell Wright's characters? (Note Cassidy's confirmation of Mark Twain's accuracy in using dialect and his citation, like Babcock's, of Twain on Bret Harte.)

10. If you are familiar with a small-town newspaper, study a few issues and write a report on regional terms and idioms that appear in the paper. Letters from readers in small-town and city newspapers are a good source of such usages.

11. How has modern technology contributed to the gathering, handling, and editing of data on language?

19

Sense and Nonsense
About American Dialects

Raven I. McDavid, Jr.

Professor Raven I. McDavid, Jr. of the University of Chicago attempts to correct some of the misconceptions concerning American dialects, to suggest some of the influences that help to shape regional language patterns, and to enumerate some of the significant facts about them. His speech, given at the meeting of the Modern Language Association in December, 1965, was printed in PMLA *for May, 1966.*

In my boyhood—more years ago than I care to remember—we used to define an expert as "a damned fool a thousand miles from home." Since I am considerably less than a thousand miles from where I grew up, and stand but a few minutes from my residence in Hyde Park, it behooves me to avoid any claim to expertness about the problems faced in practical situations where the dialect of the school child is sharply divergent from what is expected of him in the classroom. For many of these situations, neither I nor any other working dialectologist knows what the local patterns actually are; for some, there has been no attempt, or at best a partial and belated one, to find out the patterns. Nevertheless, the implications of dialectology for the more rational teaching of English in the schools—and not only in the schools attended by those we currently euphemize as the culturally disadvantaged —are so tremendous that I am flattered to have John Fisher ask for my observations. The problems are not limited to Americans of any race or creed or color, nor indeed to Americans; they are being faced in England today, as immigrants from Pakistan and the West Indies compete in the Midlands for the same kinds of jobs that have drawn Negro Americans to Harlem and the South Side, and Appalachian whites to the airplane factories of Dayton. In fact, such problems are faced everywhere in the world as industrialization and urbanization take place, on every occasion when people, mostly but not exclusively the young, leave the farm and the village in search of the better pay and more glamorous life of the cities. In all parts of the world, educators and politicians are suddenly realizing that language differences can create major obstacles to the educational, economic, and social advancement of those whose true integration into the framework of society is necessary if that society is to be healthy; they are realizing that social dialects—that is, social differences in the way language is used in a given community—both reflect and perpetuate differences in the social order. In turn, the practicing linguist is being called on with increasing frequency to devise programs for the needs of specific groups—most often for the Negroes dwelling in the festering slums of our northern and western cities; and generous government and private subsidies have drawn into the act many teachers and administrators—most of them, I trust, well meaning—who not only have made no studies of dialect differences, but have ignored the studies and archives that are available, even those dealing with their own cities.

Perhaps a data-oriented dialectologist may here be pardoned an excursion into the metaphors of siegecraft, recalled from the time when under the tutelage of Allan Gilbert I learned something of the arts of war and gunnery, if not all their Byronic applications. In confronting our massive ignorance of social dialects, the professional students of the past generation have been a forlorn hope—burrowing into a problem here, clawing their way to a precarious foothold of understanding there, seizing an outwork yonder. Like many forlorn hopes, they have been inadequately supported, sometimes ignored, even decried—not only by their literary colleagues, with the usual patronizing attitude toward anything smacking of affiliation with the social sciences, but also by their fellow linguists who are interested in international programs for teaching English as a second language, in machine translation, in formulaic syntax, or in missionating to convert the National Council of Teachers of English. It is small wonder that some students of dialects have withdrawn from the assault to participate in these better-heeled campaigns; it is a tribute to the simple-minded stubbornness of the survivors that they have not only persisted but advanced. Today their work, their aims, are embarrassingly respectable, as legions spring from the earth in response to the golden trumpet sounding on the banks of the Pedernales. It is inevitable, perhaps even fitting, that the practical work in social dialects should be directed by others than the pioneers in research. But it is alarming that many of those now most vocally concerned with social dialect problems not only know nothing about the systematic work that has been done, about the massive evidence (even if all too little) that is available, but even have a complete misconception about the nature and significance of dialects. At the risk of drawing the fire of the House Un-American Activities Committee, I would agree with my sometime neighbor James H. Sledd that our missionaries should at least know what they are talking about before they set out to missionate.

I have a particular advantage when I talk on this subject: I am one of those who speak English without any perceptible accent. I learned to talk in an upper-middle-class neighborhood of Greenville, South

Carolina, among corporation lawyers, bankers, textile magnates, and college presidents, among families with a long tradition of education and general culture. Many of my playmates, like myself, represented the sixth generation of their families in the same county. It never occurred to any of us to tamper with our language; our only intimate acquaintance with non-standard grammatical forms in writing came from stories in literary dialect or from the quaint and curious exercises that infested our textbooks—though we knew that less privileged forms of speech than ours were found in our community, and were not above imitating them for rhetorical effect. Not a single English teacher of an excellent faculty—our superintendent had his doctorate, not from Peabody or from Teachers College, Columbia, but from the University of Berlin in 1910—made a gesture of tampering. Nor have I ever heard anything in the exotic dialects of the Northeast or the Middle West that would make me feel less content with a way of speaking that any educated person might want to emulate. And yet, a few years ago, my younger sister, who has remained in the South Carolina upland, told me over the telephone: "Brucker, you've been North so long that you talk just like a Yankee." Even though I doubt if I would fool many real Yankees, I know that something has rubbed off from my travels and teaching to make me talk a little different from the boys I grew up with. Still, whenever I go back and start talking with them again, I find myself slipping into the old ways; it is natural for us to shift our way of talking, according to the people we are talking with. In fact, it is the people we talk with habitually who give us our way of talking. Here, in essence, is the way dialects originate. And until everybody lives in a sterile, homogenized, dehumanized environment, as just a number on the books of an all-powerful state, we can expect differences in environment to be reflected in those differences in speech that we call dialects.

An appreciation of this fact would avoid a lot of nonsense expressed in categorical statements in educational literature. Two amusing if distressing examples are found in *Language Programs for the Disadvantaged: Report of the NCTE Task Force*, a booklet released at the 1965 convention of the NCTE. These statements, the more distressing because so much of the report is magnificently phrased, probably arose from the inevitable wastefulness of haste (the Task Force was in the field only last summer) and from the imbalance of the Task Force itself: there was only one linguist and not a single sociologist or anthropologist or historian in a group heavily loaded with supervisors and (to coin a term, which is probably already embalmed in educationese) curriculologists:

> Most disadvantaged children come from homes in which a non-standard English dialect is spoken. It may be pidgin, Cajun, Midland, or any one of a large number of regional or cultural dialects.

Many preschool teachers are concerned about the dialect of their children and take measures to encourage standard pronunciation and usage. (p. 70)

. . . the general feeling is that some work in standard English is necessary for greater social and job mobility by disadvantaged students with a strong regional or racial dialect. (p. 89)

Among the bits of nonsense to be found in these two statements we may notice:

1. A belief that there is some mystical "standard," devoid of all regional association. Yet the variety that we can find in cultivated American English, as used by identifiable informants with impeccable educational and social credentials, has been repeatedly shown in works based on the American Linguistic Atlas, most recently and in greatest detail in Kurath's and my *Pronunciation of English in the Atlantic States* (Ann Arbor: University of Michigan Press, 1961).

2. A belief that there are "racial" dialects, independent of social and cultural experiences.

3. A snobbishness toward "strong" dialect differences from one's own way of speaking. Would Bobby Kennedy, politically disadvantaged after the Atlantic City convention, have run a better race in New York had he learned to talk Bronx instead of his strong Bostonian?

4. A glib juggling of terms, without understanding, as in the parallelism of "pidgin, Cajun, Midland." *Pidgin* denotes a minimal contact language used for communication between groups whose native languages are mutually unintelligible and generally have markedly different linguistic structures; typical examples are the Neo-Melanesian of New Guinea and the Taki-taki of Surinam. However scholars may debate the existence of an American Negro pidgin in colonial days, speakers of pidgin constitute a problem in no Continental American classroom, though it would be encountered in Hawaii and the smaller Pacific islands. *Cajun* properly describes the colonial varieties of French spoken in southwestern Louisiana and in the parts of the Maritime Provinces of Canada from which the Louisiana Acadians were transported; even if by extension we use the term to describe the varieties of English developing in the French-speaking areas of Louisiana and the Maritimes, the problems of teaching English in these areas are really those of teaching English as a second language. *Midland* is a geographical designation for those dialects stemming from the settlement of Pennsylvania and embracing a broad spectrum of cultural levels. At one extreme, we may concede, are the impoverished submarginal farmers and displaced coal miners of Appalachia; at the other are some of the proudest dynasties of America—the Biddles of Philadelphia, the Mellons of Pittsburgh, the Tafts of Cincinnati, and their counterparts in Louisville and in St. Louis, in Memphis and in Dallas—people it were stupid as well as impractical to stigmatize in language like that of

the Task Force Report. So long as such glib generalities are used about social dialects, we must conclude that our educators, however well intentioned, are talking nonsense.

And regrettably, such nonsense is no new phenomenon in American culture; it has long been with us. Much of it, fortunately, runs off us like raindrops off a mallard's back. But enough lingers in the schoolroom to do positive harm. My friend Bob Thomas, the anthropologist —a Cherokee Indian and proud of it, though with his blond hair and blue eyes he looks far less like the traditional Cherokee than I do— tells of his traumata when he moved to Detroit from Oklahoma at the age of fourteen. Although Cherokee was his first language, he had picked up a native command of Oklahoma English. Since he had always lived in a good neighborhood, and his family had used standard English at home, he had no problems in grammar; through wide reading and a variety of experiences he had acquired a large and rich vocabulary. But his vowels were Oklahoma vowels; and some benevolent despot in Detroit soon pushed him into a class in "corrective speech." The first day the class met, he looked around the classroom and noticed everybody else doing the same. As eyes met eyes, it became apparent that the class in "corrective speech" contained no cleft palates, no stammerers, no lispers, no foreign accents, not even any speakers of substandard English—for again, the school was in a good neighborhood. The only thing wrong with the boys and girls in the class was that they had not learned English in Michigan, but in Oklahoma, Arkansas, Missouri, Kentucky, Tennessee, West Virginia, Mississippi, and Alabama. "We all realized immediately," Bob told me years afterward, "that they were planning to brainwash us out of our natural way of speaking; and it became a point of honor among us to sabotage the program." To this day, Bob flaunts his Oklahoma accent belligerently; if the teachers had let him alone, he might have adapted his pronunciation to that of the Detroit boys he played with, but once he felt that the school considered his home language inferior, nothing could make him change. The first principle of any language program is that, whatever the target, it must respect the language that the students bring with them to the classroom.

Another kind of nonsense was demonstrated by the head of the speech department at the University of Michigan during my first Linguistic Institute. Impelled by the kind of *force majeur* that only a four-star general can exert, I had compromised with my scientific interest in linguistics to the extent of enrolling in a course in "stage and radio diction," only to find myself bewildered, frustrated, and enraged from the outset. Typical of the petty irritations was the panjandrous insistence on the pronunciation /'pradjus/, though all my friends who raised fruits and vegetables for market, many of them gentlemen with impeccable academic credentials, said /'prodjus/. But far more distressing were the pronunciations advocated in the name of elegance. We were advised to reject the Middle Western and Southern /æ/, not only in *calf* and *dance* and *command,* but even in *hat* and *ham* and *sand,* for an imitation of the Boston /a/ in environments where Bostonians would never use it, so that we would say /hat/ and /ham/ and /sand/, pronunciations legitimate in no American dialect except that of the Gullah Negroes of the South Carolina and Georgia coast. A few departmental underlings even went all out for an equally phony British [ɑ], again in the wrong places, yielding [hɑt] and [hɑm] and [sɑnd], and all of them plumped for replacing the Midwestern [ɑ] of *cot* and *lot* with an exaggerated [ɔ]. Of course, Midwesterners ordering [hɔt hɑm 'sandwɪčɪz] are as suspect as counterfeit Confederate $3 bills. It is possible that some compulsive aspirants to social elegance docilely lapped up this pap; but those of us who were seriously concerned with English structure and usage laughed the program out of court and left the course, never to return. A second principle can be deduced from this experience: to imitate a dialect sharply different from one's own is a tricky and difficult assignment. A partial imitation is worse than none, since the change seems an affectation to one's neighbors, and the imperfect acquisition seems ridiculous to those whose speech is being imitated. Any attempts at teaching a standard dialect to those who speak a nonstandard one should be directed toward an attainable goal, toward one of the varieties of cultivated speech which the student might hear, day after day, in his own community.

At this point, perhaps, some of you may be muttering, "But what do these experiences have to do with dialects? I always thought that a dialect was something strange and old-fashioned." Many will share your opinion, especially in such countries as France and Italy, where an academy accepts one variety of the language as standard and casts the rest into outer darkness. In such countries the word *dialect* implies a variety of the language spoken by the rustic, the uneducated, the culturally isolated. To say that someone "speaks a dialect"—as one Italian professor patronizingly described one of the best soldiers working with me on our Italian military dictionary—is to exclude him forever from the company of educated men. For a dialect, to such intellectuals, is a form of the language they had rather be found dead than speaking.

True, there are other attitudes. Germans and Austrians make a distinction between the standard language—literary High German—and the dialects, local and predominantly rural forms of speech. But educated Germans do not always avoid dialect speech forms; in some areas, such as the Austrian Tyrol, an educated person will take particular pains to use some local forms in his speech, so as to identify himself with his home. The attitude may be a bit sentimental, but it does help to maintain one's individual dignity in a homogenizing world.

A more extreme attitude was prevalent in the Romantic Era. If the Augustans of the seventeenth and eighteenth centuries looked upon dialects as corruptions of an originally perfect language, the Romantics often alleged, in Wordsworth's terms, that people in humble and rustic life used "a purer and more emphatic language" than that to be met with in the cities. In this viewpoint, the dialects represent the pure, natural, unchanging language, unencumbered by the baggage of civilization. This attitude has long prevailed in Britain; even today the English Dialect Survey is heavily slanted toward archaic forms and relics and ignores modern innovations.

Nor are Americans wholly free from this attitude that a dialect is something archaic and strange. Time and again, a fieldworker for our Linguistic Atlas is told, "We don't speak no dialect around hyur; if you want *rale* dialect you gotta go down into Hellhole Swamp"—or up into Table Rock Cove, or at least across the nearest big river. To many of us, as my student Roger Shuy put it, a dialect is something spoken by little old people in queer out-of-the-way places.

When we become a little more sophisticated—as we must become on a cosmopolitan campus—we realize that cities as well as rural areas may differ in the ways in which their inhabitants talk. Thus we next conclude that a dialect is simply the way everybody talks but us and the people we grew up with; then, by force of circumstance, we realize that we speak a dialect ourselves. But at this point we still feel that a dialect is something regional or local. When we notice that people of our own community speak varieties of English markedly different from our own, we dismiss them as ignorant, or simply as making mistakes. After all, we live in a democratic society and are not supposed to have class markers in our speech. It is a very sophisticated stage that lets us recognize social dialects as well as regional ones—dialects just as natural, arising out of normal, everyday contacts.

By this time we have elaborated our definition of a dialect. It is simply a habitual variety of a language, regional or social. It is set off from all other such habitual varieties by a unique combination of language features: words and meanings, grammatical forms, phrase structures, pronunciations, patterns of stress and intonation. No dialect is simply good or bad in itself; its prestige comes from the prestige of those who use it. But every dialect is in itself a legitimate form of the language, a valid instrument of human communication, and something worthy of serious study.

But even as we define what a dialect is, we must say what it is not. It is different from slang, which is determined by vogue and largely distinguished by transient novelties in the vocabulary. Yet it is possible that slang may show regional or social differences, or that some regional and social varieties of a language may be particularly receptive to slang.

A dialect is also different from an argot, a variety of the language used by people who share a common interest, whether in work or in play. Everyone knows many groups of this kind, with their own peculiar ways of speaking and writing: Baptist preachers, biophysicists, stamp collectors, model railroad fans, Chicago critics, narcotic addicts, jazz musicians, safecrackers. But in the normal course of events a person adopts the language of such subcultures, for whatever part of his life it may function in, because he has adopted a particular way of life; he uses a dialect because he grows up in a situation where it is spoken. Again, some argots may show regional or social variations; the term *mugging*, to choose one example, is largely found on the Atlantic Seaboard; the sport has different designations in the Great Lakes region and on the Pacific Coast.

Nor are dialect differences confined to the older, pre-industrial segments of the vocabulary. Here European and American attitudes differ sharply. The late Eugen Dieth chided the editors of the *Linguistic Atlas of New England* for including such vocabulary items as window shades, the razor strop, and the automobile, such pronunciation items as *library* and *postoffice* and *hotel*, on the ground that these are not genuine dialect items. Yet if they have regional and social variants, as all of these have in North American English, they warrant inclusion. In my lifetime I have seen the *traffic circle* of the Middle Atlantic States become the *rotary* of Eastern New England; the *service plaza* of the Pennsylvania *Turnpike* become the *oasis* of the Illinois *Tollway*; the *poor boy* of New Orleans—a generous sandwich once confined to the Creole Gomorrah and its gastronautic satellites—appearing as a *grinder* in upstate New York, a *hoagy* in Philadelphia, a *hero* in New York City, a *submarine* in Boston. Nor will dialect terms be used only by the older and less sophisticated: a Middle Western academician transplanted to MIT quickly learns to order *tonic* for his children, not *soda pop*, and to send his clothes to a *cleanser*. And though some would consider dialect a matter of speech and not of writing, one can find regional and local commercial terms on billboards and television as well as in the advertising sections of local newspapers.

Finally, dialect terms are not restricted to sloppy, irresponsible usage —a matter of personality type rather than of specific vocabulary items. And though regional and local terms and usages are likely to appear most frequently in Joos's casual and intimate styles, the example of William Faulkner is sufficient evidence that they may be transmuted into the idiom of the greatest literature.

All of these comments are the fruit of centuries of observation, at first casual and anecdotal, later more serious and systematic. The grim test of the pronunciation *shibboleth*, applied by Jephthah's men to the Ephraimites seeking to ford the Jordan, the comic representations of Spartan and Theban speech by Aristophanes, the aspiration of the Roman cockney Arrius-Harrius, immortalized by Horace, the Northern English forms in the Reeves Tale—these typify early interest. With the Romantic search for the true language in the dialects came the growth of comparative linguistics, and the search for comparative dialect evidence in translations of the Lord's Prayer and the proverb of the prodigal son. The search for comparable evidence led, in the 1870's, to the monumental collections for Georg Wenker's *Deutscher Sprachatlas*, later edited by Ferdinand Wrede and Walther Mitzka—44,251 responses, by German village schoolmasters, to an official request for local dialect translations of forty-four sentences of Standard German. Designed to elicit fine phonetic data, the collections proved notably refractory for that purpose, but the sheer mass of evidence corrected the unevenness of individual transcriptions. More important, the discovery that questions designed for one purpose may yield a different but interesting kind of evidence—as *Pferd* proved useless for the /p:pf/ consonant alternation in dialects where the horse is *Roß* or *Gaul*—was reflected in greater sophistication in the design and use of later questionnaires. Less happy was the effect on German dialectology, with later investigations, such as Mitzka's *Wortatlas*, sticking to correspondence techniques, a short questionnaire, an immense number of communities, and an expensive cartographic presentation of the data. But the *Sprachatlas* and *Wortatlas*, and the Dutch investigations modeled upon them, provided us with the evidence on which to determine their own defects.

A valuable innovation was made at the turn of the century in the *Atlas linguistique de la France*, directed by Jules Gilliéron. Correspondence questionnaires gave way to field interviews on the spot, in a smaller number of selected communities (some six hundred in this instance) with a longer questionnaire; a trained investigator interviewed a native of the community in a conversational situation and recorded his responses in a finely graded phonetic alphabet. As with the German atlas, however, the communities chosen were villages; larger places were first investigated in the Atlas of Italy and Southern Switzerland, under the direction of the Swiss scholars Karl Jaberg and Jakob Jud, who also introduced the practice of interviewing more than one informant in the larger communities. With certain refinements, then, the basic principles of traditional dialect study were established by World War I. Some subsequent investigations have followed Wenker, others Gilliéron; some, like the current Czech investigations, have combined both methods, relying primarily on field interviews but using correspondence surveys in the early stages, so that the selection of communities can be made most effectively. Only the British Isles have lagged, perhaps because Joseph Wright's *English Dialect Dictionary*, with its claim to have recorded ALL the dialect words of English, has erected a Chinese Wall worthy of Mr. Eliot's scorn. Not till the 1950's did any kind of field work get under way in either England or Scotland; in both countries it was handicapped by a shortage of funds and field-workers, and in England by an antiquarian bias that overemphasized relics, shunned innovations, and neglected opportunities to provide data comparable to that obtained in the American surveys. Yet both Harold Orton in England and Angus McIntosh in Scotland have enriched our knowledge of English.

Perhaps because American linguists have kept in touch with European developments, the *Linguistic Atlas of New England,* launched in 1930, drew on the lessons of the French and Italian atlases. Although the transition from casual collecting to systematic study was not welcomed by all students, nevertheless—even with the Hoover Depression, World War II, the Korean intervention, and the tensions of the Cold War—a respectable amount of progress has been made toward a first survey of American English. *The Linguistic Atlas of New England* was published in 1939–43; scholars are now probing for the changes that a generation has brought. For four other regional surveys, field work has been completed and editing is under way: (1) the Middle and South Atlantic States, New York to central Georgia, with outposts in Ontario and northeastern Florida; (2) the North-Central States: Wisconsin, Michigan, southwestern Ontario, and the Ohio Valley; (3) the Upper Midwest: Minnesota, Iowa, Nebraska, and the Dakotas; (4) the Pacific Southwest: California and Nevada. Elsewhere, field work has been completed in Colorado, Oklahoma, Washington, and eastern Montana; respectable portions have been done in several other states, Newfoundland, Nova Scotia, and British Columbia; with a slightly different method the late E. Bagby Atwood produced his memorable *Regional Vocabulary of Texas.* In all of these surveys the principles of European dialect investigations have been adapted to the peculiarities of the American scene. Settlement history has been studied more carefully before field work, since English-speaking settlement in North America is recent, and its patterns are still changing. At least three levels of usage are investigated—partly because cultivated American speech has regional varieties, just like uneducated speech, and the cultivated speech of the future may be foreshadowed in the speech of the intermediate group; partly because until very recently general education has been a more important linguistic and cultural force in the United States than in most of the countries of Europe. Urban speech as well as rural has been investigated in each survey, and intensive local investigations have been encouraged. The questionnaires have included both relics and innovations. All of these modifications were suggested by Hans Kurath, first Director of the Atlas project, who is currently drawing on his experience in developing a new theory for the interpretation of dialect differences.

Just as warfare is still decided ultimately by infantrymen who can take and hold territory, so dialect study still depends on competent investigators who can elicit and record natural responses in the field. The tape recorder preserves free conversation for later transcription and analysis, and permits the investigator to listen repeatedly to a response about whose phonetic quality he is in doubt; but the investigator must still ask the right question to elicit pertinent data. He must re-member, for instance, that *chicken coop* is both a vocabulary and a pronunciation item—that the pronunciation in the American North and North Midland is /kup/, in the South and South Midland /kvp/, that *coop* in the North designates the permanent shelter for the whole flock, in the South a crate under which a mother hen can scratch with-out an opportunity to lead the little ones off and lose them in the brush. The full record for such an item may require three or four questions, which only a human interviewer can provide.

But if the fieldworker remains essential, the objects of his investiga-tion may change. Recent studies have turned increasingly to urban areas, urbanizing areas, and minority groups. To a long list of impres-sive early investigations one can now add such contributions as Lee Pederson's study of Chicago pronunciation and Gerald Udell's analysis of the changes in Akron speech resulting from the growth of the rubber industry and the consequent heavy migration from West Virginia. Among special groups investigated in detail are the Spanish-American bilinguals in San Antonio by Mrs. Janet Sawyer, the American Norwe-gians by Einar Haugen, the New York City Greeks by James Macris, the New England Portuguese by Leo Pap, the Chicago Slovaks by Mrs. Goldie Meyerstein, the Gullah Negroes by Lorenzo Turner, and the Memphis Negroes by Miss Juanita Williamson. In all of these studies the emphasis has been on the correlation between linguistic and social forces.

Another significant development has been the investigation of the way language attitudes are revealed by the choice among linguistic variants under different conditions. The most impressive work of this kind has been done by William Labov of Columbia University, in his study of the speech of the Lower East Side of New York. Limiting himself to a small number of items—the vowels of *bad* and *law,* the initial consonants of *think* and *then,* the /-r/ in *barn* and *beard*—phonological details that can be counted on to appear frequently and in a large number of contexts during a short interview, Labov gathers specimens of linguistic behavior under a wide range of conditions. At one end of the spectrum is the reading of such putatively minimal pairs as *bed* and *bad;* at the other is the description of children's games or the recounting an incident when the informant thought he was going to be killed. The difference between pronunciations in the relaxed situation and those when the informant is on what he considers his best linguistic behavior is an index of his social insecurity. Almost as reveal-ing is the work of Rufus Baehr with high-school students in the Negro slums of the Chicago West Side. It is no surprise that in formal situa-tions the students with greater drive to break out of their ghetto reveal striking shifts of their speech in the direction of the Chicago middle-class norm. This kind of discovery should give heart to all who believe that a directed program of second-dialect teaching can make at least a small dent in our problem of providing a wider range of economic and educational opportunities for the aspiring young Negro.

Out of all these investigations two patterns emerge: (1) a better understanding of the origin and nature of dialect differences; (2) a set of implications for those who are interested in providing every American child with a command of the standard language adequate for him to go as far as his ability and ambition impel him.

No dialect differences can, as yet, be attributed to physiology or to climate. Perhaps anatomists will discover that some minor speech-differences arise from differences in the vocal organs; but so far there is no evidence for any correlation between anatomy and dialect, and the burden of proof is on those who propose such a correlation. As for climate: it is unlikely that nasality could have arisen (as often asserted) both from the dusty climate of Australia and the dampness of the Tennessee Valley. And though it is a favorite sport among Northerners to attribute the so-called "Southern drawl" to laziness induced by a hot climate, many Southerners speak with a more rapid tempo than most Middle Westerners, and the Bengali, in one of the most enervating tropical climates, speak still more rapidly. For an explanation of dialect differences we are driven back, inevitably, to social and cultural forces.

The most obvious force is the speech of the original settlers. We should expect that a part of the United States settled by Ulster Scots would show differences in vocabulary, pronunciation, even in grammar from those parts settled by East Anglians. We should expect to find Algonkian loans most common in those regions where settlers met Algonkian Indians, French loans most frequent in Louisiana and in the counties adjacent to French Canada, Spanish loans most widespread in the Southwest, German loans clustering in cities and in the Great Valley of Pennsylvania, and indubitable Africanisms most striking in the Gullah country.

Speech forms are also spread along routes of migration and communication. The Rhine has carried High German forms northward; the Rhone has taken Parisian forms to the Mediterranean; in the United States, the same kind of dissemination has been found in the valleys of the Mississippi, the Ohio, and the Shenandoah.

If speech forms may spread along an avenue of communication, they may be restricted by a physical barrier. As Kurath has observed, there is no sharper linguistic boundary in the English-speaking world than the Virginia Blue Ridge between the Potomac and the James. The tidal rivers of the Carolinas, the swamps of the Georgia coastal plain, have contributed to making the Old South the most varied region, dialectally, in the English settlements of the New World.

The economic pattern of an area may be reflected in distinctive dialect features. *Fatwood*, for resin-rich kindling, is confined to the turpentine belt of the Southern tidewater; *lightwood*, with a similar referent, to the Southern coastal plain and lower Piedmont. *Case weather*, for a kind of cool dampness in which it is safe to cut tobacco, occurs over a wide area, but only where tobacco is a money crop. *To run afoul of*, a maritime phrase in the metaphorical sense of "to meet," seems to be restricted to the New England coast.

Political boundaries, when long established, may become dialect boundaries; in the Rhineland, pronunciation differences coincide strikingly with the boundaries of the petty states of pre-Napoleonic Germany. In the New World, on the other hand, political boundaries have seldom delimited culture areas. Yet *county site*, for the more usual *county seat*, is common in Georgia but unknown in South Carolina, and Ontario Canadians speak of the *reeve* as chief officer of a township, the *warden* as chief officer of a county, and a *serviette* instead of a table napkin—terms unfamiliar in the United States.

Each city of consequence may have its distinctive speech forms. The grass strip between the sidewalk and the curb, undesignated in South Carolina, is a *tree belt* locally in Springfield, Massachusetts (and hence unlabeled in *Webster's Third New International Dictionary*), a *tree lawn* in Cleveland, a *devil strip* in Akron, and a *boulevard* in Minneapolis and St. Paul. And only Chicagoans naturally refer to political influence as *clout*, or to a reliable dispenser of such influence as a *Chinaman*.

Nor are differences in the educational system without their effect. Where separate and unequal education is provided to particular social groups, we can be sure that a high-school diploma or even a college degree will be no indication by itself of proficiency in the standard language. That this problem is not confined to any single racial or cultural group has been shown by institutions such as West Virginia State College, which have undergone the process of reverse integration. This particular school, which once drew an elite Negro student body, is now eighty percent white, with the white students mostly from the disadvantaged mountain areas along the Kanawha. Since the teachers in the mountain schools are not only predominantly local in origin, but often have had little education beyond what the local schools offer, and then, since most of them habitually use many non-standard forms, it has been difficult for the college to maintain its academic standards in the face of increasing white enrollment, however desirable integration may be.

Most important, perhaps, is the traditional class structure of a community. In a Midwestern small town, it is still possible for one brother to stay home and run a filling station, and another to go off and become a judge—and nobody mind. But in parts of the South there is a social hierarchy of families and occupations, so that it is more respectable for a woman of good family to teach in an impoverished small college than to do professional work for the government at twice the salary. Here, too, an aristocratic ideal of language survives, and the most cultivated still look upon *ain't* as something less reprehensible than incest—but use it only in intimate conversation with those whom they consider their social equals. Here too we find the cultural self-assurance that leads an intelligent lawyer to ask the linguistically naive question: "Why is it that the educated Northerner talks so much like the uneducated Southerner?"

If social differences among the WASP population are reflected in linguistic differences, we should not be surprised if similar differences among later immigrants are reflected in the extent of linguistic borrowing from particular foreign-language groups, or even from the same foreign-language group at different times. Our longest continuous tradition of borrowing, with probably the largest and most varied kinds of words, is that from various kinds of German. Even the bitterness of two world wars cannot prevent us from seeing that of all foreign-language groups the Germans have been most widely distributed, geographically and socially, throughout the United States—as prosperous farmers, vaudeville comedians, skilled craftsmen, merchants, intellectuals. In contrast, the hundreds of thousands of Italian- and Slavic-speaking immigrants of the last two generations have left few marks on the American vocabulary; most of them were of peasant stock, often illiterate, and settled in centers of heavy industry as basic labor.

Even more striking is the change in the incidence of Texas borrowings from Mexican Spanish. In her study of the bilingual situation in San Antonio, Mrs. Sawyer has shown that although early Spanish loans were numerous, quickly assimilated, and widely spread—*canyon, burro, ranch, lariat, broncho, silo* are characteristic examples—there have been few such loans in the last seventy years. The explanation is the drastic change in the relationships between Anglos and Latins. When English-speaking settlers first moved into Texas, they found the hacienda culture already established, and eagerly took over culture and vocabulary from the Latins who constituted the local elite. Anglo and Latin, side by side, died in the Alamo 4 March 1836 and conquered at San Jacinto seven weeks later. But since 1890 the Texan has encountered Mexican Spanish most often in the speech of unskilled laborers, including imported braceros and illegally entered wetbacks; derogatory labels for Latins have increased in Texas English, and loans from Spanish have declined. We borrow few words from those we consider our inferiors.

We can now make a few clear statements about the facts of American dialects, and their significance:

1. Even though much work remains to be done, we can describe in some detail most of the principal regional varieties of American English and many of the important subvarieties; we can indicate, further, some of the kinds of social differences that are to be found in various dialect areas, and many of the kinds that are to be found in some of the most important cities.

2. We can be sure that in many situations there are tensions between external norms and the expectations of one's associates. These

tensions, most probably, are strongest in the lower middle class—a group anxious to forget humbler backgrounds but not sure of their command of the prestige patterns. Since the teaching profession, on all levels, is heavily drawn from the lower middle class, we can expect— as Marjorie Daunt found years ago—that anxiety is the characteristic attitude of the English teacher toward variations in usage. There is a strong urge to make changes, for the sake of making changes and demonstrating one's authority, without stopping to sort out the significance of differences in usage. This attitude is reflected in the two most widely known programs for teaching better English to the disadvantaged: a socially insignificant problem, such as the distinction between *Wales* and *whales*, is given the same value as the use of the marker for the third singular in the present indicative. Future programs should use the resources of the dialect archives, at least as a start, even though more detailed and more recent information may be necessary before one can develop teaching materials. The inevitable prescription in a pedagogical situation can be no better than the underlying description.

3. There is evidence that ambitious students in slum areas intuitively shift their speech patterns in the direction of the prestigious local pattern, in situations where they feel such a shift will be to their advantage. Some actually achieve, on their own, a high degree of functional bidialectalism, switching codes as the situation demands. In any teaching program it would seem intelligent to make use of this human facility.

4. The surest social markers in American English are grammatical forms, and any teaching program should aim, first of all, at developing a habitual productive command of the grammar of standard English—with due allowance for the possibility that the use of this grammar may be confined to formal situations in which the speaker comes in contact with the dominant culture.

5. Relatively few pronunciation features are clear social markers, though in many Northern cities there is a tendency to identify all Southern and South Midland pronunciations as those of uneducated rural Negroes. How much one should attempt to substitute local pronunciations for those which are standard in regions from which migrants come would probably depend on the extent to which variations in standard English are recognized and accepted in the community: Washington, for instance, may be more tolerant than New York City. In any event, programs to alter pronunciation patterns should concentrate on those pronunciations that are most widely recognized as substandard.

6. Few people can really identify the race of a speaker by pronunciation and voice quality. In experiments in Chicago, middle-class Middle Westerners consistently identified the voice of an educated urban white Southerner as that of an uneducated rural Negro, and

many identified as Negro the voice of an educated white Chicagoan. Similar experiments in New York have yielded similar results. And many white Southerners can testify to personal difficulties arising from this confusion in the minds of Northerners. In Ithaca, New York, I could not get to see any apartment advertised as vacant until I paid a personal visit; over the telephone I was always told that the apartments had just been rented; James Marchand, a Middle Tennessean now on the Cornell faculty, must carefully identify himself as "Professor Marchand," if he wants a garageman to come and pick up his car. And the telephone voice of my Mississippi-born chairman, Gwin Kolb, is racially misidentified with alarming regularity.

7. There can be no single standard in programs for the disadvantaged; the target dialect must vary according to the local situation. In Mississippi, the same program can be used for Negroes and whites, because they share most of the same grammatical deviations from the local standard, and share phonological patterns with that standard; in Cleveland, grammatical features in writing are sufficient to distinguish Negro college applicants from white better than ninety percent of the time, and deviations from local standard pronunciation are far more striking and numerous among Negroes than among locally-born disadvantaged whites.

8. To the suggestion that Southern Negroes should not be taught local standard pronunciation, but some external standard—the hypothetical variety some call "network English"—there is a simple answer in the form of a question: "Do you want integration in the South?" The Southern patterns of race relations have suffered too long from too many separate standards for Negro and white; it would be ironical if those speaking most loudly in behalf of the aspirations of the Southern Negro should create new obstacles to those aspirations. The language problems of the uneducated Southern Negro are the language problems, even to fine detail, of the uneducated Southern white in the same community; the South may well solve the language problems in its schools before Detroit does. Once the races are brought into the same classroom, a community will need only one intelligent program based on a solid body of dialect evidence.

9. While we are planning language programs for our disadvantaged, we must educate the dominant culture in the causes and significance of dialect differences; it is particularly urgent that we educate teachers on all levels, from kindergarten through graduate school. The disadvantaged will have enough to do in learning new patterns of language behavior; the dominant culture must meet them part way, with greater understanding, with a realization that dialect differences do not reflect intellectual or moral differences, but only differences in experience. Granted that this reeducation of the dominant culture is bound to be difficult, we should not be so cynical as to reject it, on the ground that it cannot take place. In an age when we are turning the heat off

under the melting pot and accepting the cultural contributions of Americans with ancestral languages other than English, in an age when we are learning the art of peaceful coexistence with a variety of economic and political and cultural systems, it should not be difficult to extend this acceptance to fellow Americans of different cultural backgrounds and linguistic habits, and especially to recognize that cultured American English may be found in many regional and local varieties. It is a poor cultural tolerance that would accept all cultivated speech except that in other parts of our own country.

With my deep-ingrained horror of patent-medicine salesmen, I would not leave you with the impression that we already have all the answers, or even all the evidence we need to arrive at those answers. We need many more kinds of investigation, and we should like to think that John Fisher, with his unlimited license to stalk money-bearing animals, might help us conduct some of them. We are still to do even the preliminary surveys in such parts of the country as Tennessee and Arkansas; we need many more studies of the actual patterns of social dialects in most American cities. We really have no serious evidence on regional and social differences in such prosodic features as stress and pitch and juncture. The recognition of paralanguage—the non-linguistic modulation of the stream of speech—is so recent that we have no idea as to the kinds of regional and social differences that may be found in tempo and rhythm, in range of pitch and stress, in drawl and clipping, in rasp and nasality and mellifluousness. We have not even begun to study regional and social variations in gesture and other kinds of body movement. But we do have a framework which we can fill in detail, continually building our teaching programs on solid research into the ways in which Americans communicate in various localities, and into the attitudes of specific speakers toward those whose usage differs from their own. In comparison with the immensity of our social problems, our linguistic knowledge is as a little candle in the forest darkness at midnight; let us not hide that candle under a basket, but put it in a lantern and use it to find our way.

BIBLIOGRAPHICAL NOTE

The significance of dialect differences has been often discussed, notably in Leonard Bloomfield, *Language* (New York, 1933), Ch. xix. The most detailed summary of dialect investigations to the mid-century is Sever Pop, *La Dialectologie*, 2 vols. (Louvain, 1950). Kurath's *Areal Linguistics: Problems, Methods, Results* (Bloomington, Ind., 1967), will be shorter but more up to date.

The most widely known summary of American dialects is to be found in Ch. ix of W. Nelson Francis, *The Structure of American English* (New York, 1958); the most accessible bibliographical summary is in the footnotes of Ch. vii of the one-volume 1963 edition of H. L. Mencken, *The American Language*. Annual summaries of research will be found in the reports of the Committee on Regional Speech and Dialectology, in *Publications of the American Dialect Society;* recent research is reported in the quarterly bibliographies in *American Speech,* less extensively in the supplement to *PMLA.* The method of the American atlases is discussed in detail in Kurath's *Handbook of the Linguistic Geography of New England* (Providence, R.I., 1939). For summaries of particular dialect features along the Atlantic seaboard, see Kurath, *A Word Geography of the Eastern United States* (Ann Arbor, Mich., 1949); Atwood, *A Survey of Verb Forms in the Eastern United States* (Ann Arbor, Mich., 1952); Kurath and McDavid, *The Pronunciation of English in the Atlantic States* (Ann Arbor, Mich., 1961). Atwood's *The Regional Vocabulary of Texas* was published by the University of Texas Press, Austin, in 1962. For particular regions see articles by A. H. Marckwardt for the Great Lakes, Harold B. Allen for the Upper Midwest, Marjorie M. Kimmerle and Clyde Hankey for Colorado, David W. Reed and David DeCamp for California. *A Dictionary of American Regional English,* directed by Frederic G. Cassidy, is currently under way at the University of Wisconsin.

The first direct attention to American social dialects is McDavid, "Dialect Geography and Social Science Problems," *Social Forces,* xxv, 168–172; basic for the problems of Negro speech is Raven I. and Virginia McDavid, "The Relationship of the Speech of American Negroes to the Speech of Whites," *American Speech,* xxvi, 3–17. A 1964 conference on social dialects, held at Bloomington, Indiana, is reported in *Social Dialects and Language Learning,* a publication of the NCTE, edited by A. L. Davis and Roger Shuy (Champaign, Ill., 1965); in 1965 the NCTE also published *Language Programs for the Disadvantaged: A Report of the NCTE Task Force,* and reprinted two of McDavid's articles as a monograph, *American Social Dialects.* A teachers' manual on the subject has been requested by the U.S. Office of Education; it is hoped that work can begin in the summer of 1966.

The most familiar American analysis of stress, pitch, and juncture was first sketched in G. L. Trager and H. L. Smith, Jr., *Outline of English Structure, Studies in Linguistics:* Occ. Paper 3 (Norman, Okla., 1951); a more detailed exposition is found in A. A. Hill, *Introduction to Linguistic Structures* (New York, 1958). A different analysis is that of Kenneth L. Pike, *The Intonation of American English* (Ann Arbor, Mich., 1945). The importance of paralanguage, previously discussed by Trager and Smith, is shown in Robert E. Pittenger, Charles F. Hockett, and John J. Danehy, *The First Five Minutes* (Ithaca, N.Y., 1960); the most detailed treatment of gesture is in Ray Birdwhistell, *Introduction to Kinesics* (Washington, 1952), later reprinted by the University of Louisville. A good popular treatment of communication in culture is Edward T. Hall, *The Silent Language* (New York, 1959), now available in paperback. Martin Joos's theories of style are summed up in *The Five Clocks* (Bloomington, Ind., 1962).

STUDY QUESTIONS AND EXERCISES

1. How is dialectology related to urgent social problems in the United States?

2. How does McDavid's account of his personal background illustrate the educated Southern attitude toward Southern speech?

3. What are the "bits of nonsense" in the quotation from a

1965 NCTE (National Council of Teachers of English) booklet? What are the meanings of: *pidgin, Cajun, Midland?*

4. "Bob flaunts his Oklahoma accent belligerently": is this the precise use of *flaunts?* How could *flouts* be used to describe Bob's attitude and motives? Write a sentence using both *flaunts* and *flouts* precisely to describe Bob.

5. In your experience, is "the first principle of any language program" adequately observed?

6. How was "the second principle" violated in the course McDavid took on stage and radio diction?

7. What attitudes toward dialects, common in Europe, have contributed to American unwillingness to admit speaking a dialect? What contrasting British attitude affects British dialectology?

8. Would McDavid accept the statement that standard English is a class dialect? What class does it represent? In light of the earlier statement that we "shift our way of talking to the people we are talking to," what has a student whose dialect is not standard English really chosen to do when he goes to college? Does he need to change the language he uses among his former noncollege associates?

9. Give further examples of regional and social variants of vocabulary such as McDavid cites.

10. What subdivisions of Southern dialect are found in William Faulkner's fiction? Which of these are *social* dialects within the regional dialects?

11. What progress has been made to date on the *Linguistic Atlas of the United States?* How is the overlapping of regional and historical aspects of the language illustrated in current work on the *Linguistic Atlas of New England?* What three levels of usage are investigated? Why? What historical aspects are included in the questionnaire?

12. If you live in a city, what minority dialect groups are included in the urban area of that city?

13. What can second-dialect teaching accomplish, socially and economically, for children in minority groups?

14. What is the explanation of dialect differences? (Refer to selection 8, "Language on the American Frontier" by Frederic G. Cassidy.) In what geographical patterns do speech forms spread? What geographical barriers limit spread?

15. Compare McDavid with Cassidy on dialect as reflecting economic features.

16. What influence does education have on dialect? Is language proficiency based on race or on educational opportunity and quality of education?

17. What is the most important factor in dialect? What is the attitude of socially superior Southerners toward their own speech? Why?

18. Which of the language groups mentioned by McDavid contributed significantly to the dialect of your own area?

19. Of the statements McDavid makes about dialects, which are most significant for teachers and students? Which are most significant for the individual: in his occupation; in his social life, as related to his occupation; in his intimate association with friends and family, apart from any social and economic changes resulting from his education?

20. What particularly convincing evidence does McDavid present as to whether race is revealed by pronunciation and voice quality?

21. Why will Southern communities need only one intelligent language program? Why may Northern communities need special programs for Negro students?

22. How is McDavid's principle that "cultured American English may be found in many regional and local varieties" relevant to the furor over *Webster's Third?* How many of the *American Heritage Dictionary* panel of 100 are Southerners? Why is this a pertinent question?

SUBJECTS FOR BRIEF PAPERS
OR WRITTEN REPORTS

1. Summarize briefly the English-speaking background of your community as revealed by such aspects of language as place-names, pronunciation, vocabulary, and idiom which you have recorded and classified and verified in historical sources.

2. Read one of the articles referred to by Baugh in "The American Dialects" (Albert Baugh, *A History of the English Language,* 2nd ed.) that deals with an area familiar to you and write a comparison or comparison-contrast of the author's findings and your own.

3. Collect data on vocabulary and pronunciation variants among college students and in a brief report present your observations and your explanatory comments.

4. Write a short paper on unfamiliar terms which you have collected in traveling or living outside your native area.

5. Select a foreign-language group in your town or city with whose speech you are familiar and write a brief account of their contributions to local vocabulary and idiom.

6. If you have lived in two notably different regions, write an analysis of either your observations, as a stranger, of regional dialect or of native reactions to your speech. Consider sound and vocabulary and idiom.

7. Report on your findings for the fourth question on Allen's

article, "The Linguistic Atlases," and give the relevant information about the individuals questioned, their answers, and your conclusions.

8. In paragraph three Allen refers to the studies of American usage by Leonard, Marckwardt and Walcott, and Fries. Examine one of these books, or Margaret M. Bryant's *Current American Usage*, and summarize the attitudes toward usage.

9. Have each member of the class make a list of terms used, from Kurath's list. Collect these lists and report on the results, comparing your data with Kurath's.

10. Study terms for common objects used in national advertising and report on the relation of your own vocabulary to the nationally adopted terms, with special attention to terms you adopted from such sources and terms you retain despite your awareness of the national norms.

11. From recordings or from published versions of American folk ballads, such as Alan Lomax, *The Folk Songs of North America*, collect and classify the data on regional language from ballads of one area, such as the Southern Appalachians, and write a report of your findings.

part 4

Literary and Colloquial Aspects

The articles in this section deal with some of the distinctions between spoken and written language. As Charles C. Fries observes in American English Grammar: "The language practices of conversation differ in many subtle ways from those used in formal writing," and should not be evaluated by a single standard: "Each set of language practices is best in its own special sphere of use; one will necessarily differ from the other."

Many students, intimidated by overzealous parents or teachers, have misinterpreted the label colloq. in the dictionary and have come to regard colloquial language as improper language. Nothing could be further from the truth. Colloquial in its literal sense means "pertaining to speaking together," and difficulty arises in trying to group all types of spoken expressions under one heading. Slang, jargon, trade talk, clichés, cultivated conversation, and a formal oration are all colloquial in the sense that they are spoken; but as Professor Kenyon points out in the following article, they differ widely in their cultural levels and functions. Too often colloquial is used as a term of disapproval, largely because many spoken words and phrases are culturally substandard and inappropriate for a higher social level. The student should observe the spoken and written expressions around him and adjust his vocabulary and mode of expression to fit the occasion. Other details of this problem will be treated in the section on the social and cultural aspects of language.

The question of appropriateness confronts every user of language. Some individuals, apparently more sensitive than others, can adapt themselves unerringly to each situation; but more frequently, through lack of skill or sensitivity, people are unable to adjust their speech or writing to the circumstances. The result can be confusion, embarrassment, or both. It is important for the linguistic fledgling to observe, analyze, and classify patterns and functions so that he can use his words effectively and appropriately.

In written communication appropriateness is also important. A note to a friend differs in tone and vocabulary from a closely reasoned formal argument. The more formal statements ordinarily use a larger proportion of learned words either because these are more appropriate to the circumstances *or because there are no colloquial words to express the idea. For most writing in college a combination of learned and popular words used flexibly and informally is the best solution. Again, however, it is necessary for the individual to determine what style and tone are most suitable for his purposes. Since absolute standards of appropriateness do not exist, one must choose one's pattern of expression on the basis of careful, sensitive evaluation of his purpose and the occasion.*

20

Cultural Levels and Functional Varieties of English

John S. Kenyon

In this article published in College English *for October, 1948, Professor Kenyon provides a simple workable pattern of classification of language into levels with social or cultural connotations and into functional varieties of words used in a formal or informal context.*

The word *level,* when used to indicate different styles of language, is a metaphor, suggesting higher or lower position and, like the terms *higher* and *lower,* figuratively implies "better" or "worse," "more desirable" or "less desirable," and similar comparative degrees of excellence or inferiority in language.

The application of the term *level* to those different styles of language that are not properly distinguished as better or worse, desirable or undesirable, creates a false impression. I confess myself guilty of this error along with some other writers. What are frequently grouped together in one class as different levels of language are often in reality false combinations of two distinct and incommensurable categories, namely, *cultural levels* and *functional varieties.*

Among *cultural levels* may be included, on the lower levels, illiterate speech, narrowly local dialect, ungrammatical speech and writing, excessive and unskillful slang, slovenly and careless vocabulary and construction, exceptional pronunciation, and, on the higher level, language used generally by the cultivated, clear, grammatical writing, and pronunciations used by the cultivated over wide areas. The different cultural levels may be summarized in the two general classes *substandard* and *standard.*

Among *functional varieties* not depending on cultural levels may be mentioned colloquial language, itself existing in different degrees of familiarity or formality, as, for example, familiar conversation, private correspondence, formal conversation, familiar public address; formal platform or pulpit speech, public reading, public worship; legal, scientific, and other expository writing; prose and poetic belles-lettres. The different functional varieties may roughly be grouped together in the two classes *familiar* and *formal* writing or speaking.

The term *level*, then, does not properly belong at all to functional varieties of speech—colloquial, familiar, formal, scientific, literary language. They are equally "good" for their respective functions, and as classifications do not depend on the cultural status of the users.

The two groupings *cultural levels* and *functional varieties* are not mutually exclusive categories. They are based on entirely separate principles of classification: *culture* and *function*. Although we are here principally concerned with the functional varieties of standard English (the highest cultural level), yet substandard English likewise has its functional varieties for its different occasions and purposes. Thus the functional variety colloquial English may occur on a substandard cultural level, but the term *colloquial* does not itself designate a cultural level. So the functional variety formal writing or speaking may occur on a lower or on a higher cultural level according to the social status of writer or speaker, and sometimes of reader or audience. It follows, for instance, that the colloquial language of cultivated people is on a higher cultural level than the formal speech of the semiliterate or than some inept literary writing.

Semiliterate formal speech is sometimes heard from radio speakers. I recently heard one such speaker solemnly announce, "Sun day will be Mother's Day." Because the speaker, in his ignorance of good English, thought he was making himself plainer by using the distorted pronunciation *sun day* instead of the standard pronunciation *sundy*, he was actually misunderstood by some listeners to be saying, "Some day will be Mother's Day." About forty years ago the great English phonetician Henry Sweet used this very example to show that "we cannot make words more distinct by disguising them." [1] He was referring to the use, as in this instance, of the full sound of vowels in unaccented syllables where standard English has obscure vowels. On the same page Sweet gives another example of the same blunder: "Thus in the sentence *I shall be at home from one to three* the substitution of tuw for tə [ə = the last sound in *sofa*] at once suggests a confusion between the preposition and the numeral." This was also verified on the radio. Not long ago I heard a radio speaker announce carefully, "This program will be heard again tomorrow from one two three." I have also recorded (among many others) the following such substandard forms from the radio: *presidEnt* for the standard form *presidənt*, the days of the week ending in the full word *day* instead of the standard English syllable *-dy*, *ay man* for the correct ə *man*, *cahnsider* for *cənsider*, *tooday* for *təday*, *too go* for *tə go*, *Coalumbia* for *Cəlumbia*, etc. This is merely one sort among many of substandard features in the formal speech of the semiliterate.[2]

---

[1] Henry Sweet, *The Sounds of English* (Oxford, 1910), p. 78.
[2] See further *American Speech*, VI, No. 5 (June, 1931), 368–72.

To begin my strictures at home, in *American Pronunciation* (9th ed., 4th printing, p. 17), I use the page heading "Levels of Speech." This should be "Functional Varieties of Standard Speech," for the reference is solely to the different uses of speech on the one cultivated level. Similarly, in the Kenyon-Knott *Pronouncing Dictionary of American English* (p. xvi, §2), I carelessly speak of "levels of the colloquial" where I mean "styles of the colloquial," as three lines above. For though there are different cultural levels of colloquial English, the reference here is only to standard colloquial.

S. A. Leonard and H. Y. Moffett, in their study, "Current Definition of Levels in English Usage," [3] say (p. 348): "The levels of English usage have been most clearly described in Dr. Murray's Preface ["General Explanations," p. xvii] to the *New English Dictionary*. I have varied his diagram a little in order to illustrate better the overlapping between the categories." It appears to me that Leonard and Moffett have so varied the diagram as to obscure Murray's intention. For he is not here primarily exhibiting levels of speech but is showing the "Anglicity," or limits of the English vocabulary for the purposes of his dictionary.[4] The only topical divisions of his diagram that imply a cultural level are "slang" and "dialectal," and the only statement in his explanation of the diagram that could imply it is, "Slang words ascend through colloquial use." This may imply that slang is on a lower cultural level than "colloquial, literary, technical, scientific, foreign." We may also safely infer that Murray would place "Dialectal" on a lower level than colloquial and literary if he were here concerned with cultural levels. Murray's diagram rests consistently on the same basis of classification throughout ("Anglicity"), and he emphasizes that "there is absolutely no defining line in any direction [from the central nucleus of colloquial and literary]." Moreover, Murray's exposition here concerns only vocabulary, with no consideration of the other features that enter so largely into "levels" of language—grammatical form and structure, pronunciation, spelling, and meaning—of styles, in short, only so far as they are affected by vocabulary. These he treats of elsewhere but without reference to levels.

It is not quite clear just how far Leonard and Moffett intend their grouping "literary English," "standard, cultivated, colloquial English," and "naïf, popular, or uncultivated English" to be identical with what they call Murray's "levels," his description of which they commend. But it is clear that they call their own grouping "three levels of usage" (p. 357) and classify them together as a single descending scale (cf. "the low end of the scale," p. 358). The inevitable impression that the

---

[3] *English Journal*, XVI, No. 5 (May, 1927), 345–59.
[4] The word *Anglicity* is a coinage of the *Oxford Dictionary*. They define it as "English quality, as of speech or style; English idiom."

average reader receives from such an arrangement of the scale is: Highest level, literary English; next lower level, colloquial English; lowest level, illiterate English; whereas, in fact, the first two "levels" are functional varieties of the one cultural level standard English, while the third ("illiterate or uncultivated," p. 358) is a cultural level.

Krapp has a chapter on "The Levels of English Speech," [5] in which he reveals some awareness of the confusion of cultural levels with functional varieties. He says:

> Among those who pay any heed at all to convention in social relationships, a difference of degree is implicit in all use of English. This difference of degree is usually thought of in terms of higher and lower, of upper levels of speech appropriate to certain occasions of more formal character, of lower levels existing, if not necessarily appropriate, among less elevated circumstances. These popular distinctions of level may be accepted without weighting them too heavily with significance in respect of good, better, and best in speech. A disputatious person might very well raise the question whether literary English, ordinarily regarded as being on a high level, is really any better than the spoken word, is really as good as the spoken word, warm with the breath of the living moment.

At the risk of having to own the hard impeachment of being disputatious, I must express the fear that the logical fallacy in treating of levels, which Krapp rather lightly waves aside, is having a serious effect on general ideas of speech levels, and especially of the significance of colloquial English in good usage. Krapp's grouping, frankly on a scale of "levels" throughout, constitutes a descending scale from the highest, "Literary English," through "Formal Colloquial," "General Colloquial," "Popular English," to the lowest, "Vulgar English." Here the fallacy is obvious: Literary English, Formal Colloquial, and General Colloquial are not cultural levels but only functional varieties of English all on the one cultural level of standard English. The last two, Popular English and Vulgar English, belong in a different order of classification, cultural levels, without regard to function.

So in his succeeding discussion *level* sometimes means the one, sometimes the other; now a functional variety of standard English, and now a cultural level of substandard or of standard English. It is functional on page 58 ("a choice between two levels") and on page 60 ("level of general colloquial"), cultural on page 62 ("popular level" and "cultivated level") and on pages 63–64 ("popular level," "level of popular speech"), functional on page 64 ("general colloquial level"), cultural

---

[5] George Philip Krapp, *The Knowledge of English* (New York, 1927), pp. 55–76.

again on the same page ("popular level," "still lower level"), cultural on page 67 ("vulgar . . . level of speech," "applying the term 'vulgar' to it at certain levels"), cultural on page 68 ("its own [popular] level"), cultural and functional in the same phrase on page 68 ("speakers from the popular and the general colloquial level meet and mix"), and so on most confusingly to page 75.

The same kind of mixture of cultural levels and functional varieties is thrown into one apparently continuous scale by Kennedy: "There is the formal and dignified language of the scholarly or scientific address or paper. . . . The precision and stateliness of this uppermost level . . . is a necessary accompaniment of thinking on a high plane." [6] Next in order he mentions colloquial speech, which he refers to as "the second level, . . . generally acceptable to people of education and refinement." Clearly this is not a cultural level but a functional variety of standard English, like the "uppermost level." The third level is, however, a cultural one: "the latest slang," workmen's "technical slang and colloquialisms which other persons cannot comprehend," "grammatical solecisms." "The speech of this third level can fairly be ranked as lower in the social scale." His fourth level is also cultural: "At the bottom of the scale is the lingo, or cant, of criminals, hobos, and others of the lowest social levels."

Finally, Kennedy fixes the false mental image of a continuous and logically consistent descent from "the cold and lonely heights of formal and highly specialized scientific and scholarly language" to "the stupid and slovenly level of grammatical abuses and inane slang." In reality there is no cultural descent until we reach his third "level," since "formal and dignified language" and "colloquial speech" are only functional varieties of English on the one cultural level of standard English.

In Perrin's excellent and useful *Index*,[7] under the heading "Levels of Usage," he names "three principal levels": "Formal English" (likened to formal dress), "Informal English" (described as "the typical language of an educated person going about his everyday affairs"), and "Vulgate English." From his descriptions it appears clearly that Formal and Informal English are functional varieties of standard English, while Vulgate is a substandard cultural level. A similar classification appears in his table on page 365.

On page 19 Perrin uses *level* apparently in the sense of functional variety, not of cultural level: "Fundamentally, good English is speaking or writing in the level of English that is appropriate to the particular situation that faces the speaker or writer. It means making a right

---

[6] Arthur G. Kennedy, *Current English* (Boston, 1935), pp. 15–17: "Speech Levels."

[7] Porter G. Perrin, *An Index to English* (Chicago, 1939), pp. 364–65.

choice among the levels of usage." His advice, however, involves two choices: (1) choice of a standard cultural level and (2) choice of the appropriate functional variety of that level.

A clear instance of the inconsistent use of the term *level* is found in Robert C. Pooley's *Teaching English Usage* (New York, 1946), chapter iii, "Levels in English Usage." He names five levels: (1) the illiterate level; (2) the homely level; (3) standard English, informal level; (4) standard English, formal level; and (5) the literary level. In (1) and (2) *level* has an altogether different meaning from that in (3), (4), and (5). In the first two *level* plainly means "cultural level"; in the last three it just as plainly means "functional variety of standard English," all three varieties being therefore on the one cultural level of standard English. So *level* in the two groups belongs to different orders of classification. All misunderstanding and wrong implication would be removed from this otherwise excellent treatment of levels if the last three groups were labeled "Standard English Level, Informal Variety"; "Standard English Level, Formal Variety"; and "Standard English Level, Literary Variety." Pooley's groups contain three cultural levels (illiterate, homely, standard) and three functional varieties of the standard cultural level (informal, formal, literary).

The misapplication to colloquial English of the term *level*, metaphorically appropriate only to cultural gradations, is especially misleading. We often read of English that is "on the colloquial level." For example, Krapp writes: "*Who do you mean?* . . . has passed into current spoken use and may be accepted on the colloquial level." [8] This implies that colloquial English is on a different cultural level from formal English (literary, scientific, etc.), and a too frequent assumption, owing to this and other misuses of the term *colloquial*, is that its cultural level is below that of formal English. This supposition, tacit or explicit, that colloquial style is inferior to formal or literary style, leads inescapably to the absurd conclusion that, whenever scientists or literary artists turn from their formal writing to familiar conversation with their friends, they thereby degrade themselves to a lower social status.

This misuse of *level* encourages the fallacy frequently met with of contrasting colloquial with standard English, logically as fallacious as contrasting white men with tall men. For instance, Mencken writes: " 'I have no doubt *but* that' . . . seems to be very firmly lodged in colloquial American, and even to have respectable standing in the standard speech." [9] This contrast, not always specifically stated, is often implied. For example, Kennedy writes: "Colloquial English is, properly defined, the language of conversation, and especially of familiar conversation. As such it may approximate the standard speech of the better

---

[8] *A Comprehensive Guide to Good English* (New York, 1927), p. 641.

[9] H. L. Mencken, *The American Language* (4th ed.; New York, 1936), p. 203.

class of English speakers, or it may drop to the level of the illiterate and careless speaker." [10] *May approximate* should be replaced by *may be on the level of.*

Similarly, on page 440: "Some measure words [are] still used colloquially without any ending in the plural . . . ; but most of these are given the *s* ending in standard English usage." Here *standard* is confused with *formal.*

Kennedy (pp. 534, 616) several times contrasts colloquial English with "standard literary English." This implies that colloquial English is not standard, while literary English is. If he means to contrast standard colloquial with standard literary, well and good; but I fear that most readers would understand the contrast to be of colloquial with standard.[11]

The term *colloquial* cannot properly designate a substandard cultural level of English. It designates a functional variety—that used chiefly in conversation—and in itself says nothing as to its cultural level, though this discussion, and the dictionary definitions, are chiefly concerned with cultivated colloquial, a functional variety of standard English. When writers of such standing as those I have mentioned slip into expressions that imply lower cultural status of colloquial English, it is not surprising that some teachers fall into the error. One teacher expressed the conviction that colloquialisms should not be represented as standard American speech. But the context of the statement indicated that its author was using *colloquialism* in the sense of "localism." I could hardly believe how frequent this gross error is, until I heard it from a well-known American broadcaster.[12]

The best dictionaries, at least in their definitions, give no warrant for the various misuses of *colloquial, colloquially, colloquialism, colloquiality.* I urge the reader to study carefully the definitions in the *Oxford English Dictionary*, with its many apt examples from standard writers, and in *Webster's New International Dictionary, Second Edition*, with its quotations from George Lyman Kittredge. Kittredge's views on the standing of colloquial English are well known. It is said that somebody once asked him about the meaning of the label "Colloq." in diction-

---

[10] *Op. cit.*, p. 26.

[11] Greenough and Kittredge in *Words and Their Ways in English Speech* (New York, 1909), chap. vii, only apparently treat literary English as the sole standard form: "What is the origin of standard or literary English?" (p. 80). They use *standard* in a special sense for their particular purpose, calling it "the common property of all but the absolutely illiterate," "The language which all educated users of English speak and write" (therefore including colloquial). For the usual current meaning, see the definitions of *standard* quoted in *American Pronunciation* (6th and subsequent eds.), pp. 14–15.

[12] Leonard and Moffett also mention the frequency of this blunder (*op. cit.*, p. 351, n. 5).

aries. He is reported to have replied, "I myself speak 'colloke' and often write it." I cannot verify the story, but it sounds authentic.

It seems to me inevitable that the frequent groupings of so-called "levels" such as "Literary, Colloquial, Illiterate," and the like, will lead the reader to suppose that just as Illiterate is culturally below Colloquial, so Colloquial is culturally below Literary. While I can scarcely hope that my humble remonstrance will reform all future writing on "levels of English," I believe that writers who confuse the meaning of the term *level* must accept some part of the responsibility for the popular misunderstanding of the true status of colloquial English; for I cannot avoid the belief that the popular idea of colloquial English as something to be looked down upon with disfavor is due in part to the failure of writers on the subject to distinguish between *cultural levels of English* and *functional varieties of standard English.*

STUDY QUESTIONS AND EXERCISES

1. Note the definition of *level,* as a noun, that Kenyon has in mind in the first sentence. Quote the definitions of *standard* and *substandard* that apply to the English language. How do these definitions confirm the evaluative implication of *levels* as used in reference to language?

2. Of the functional varieties listed in the fourth paragraph, which ones might be used on the substandard level by (1) an uneducated laborer, (2) a preacher in a poor church in a backward area, (3) a politician with a "plain-folks" approach to uneducated constituents? Which varieties would be used on the standard level by (1) a college-educated businessman, (2) an eminent clergyman, (3) a noted scientist, (4) a statesman, (5) a celebrated novelist?

3. In Robert Penn Warren's *All the King's Men,* study the public speeches of Willie Stark in Chapters 1 and 6 and his private conversations in Chapters 3 and 6. What varieties of style can you identify? Select sentences or passages to illustrate each. In each selection, identify deviations from standard English, their purpose and effect. When Willie uses standard English, do "borrowed" words of foreign derivation or native words from Anglo-Saxon predominate?

4. In G. B. Shaw's *Pygmalion,* Acts I and V, study the speeches of Alf Doolittle for varieties of style on the substandard level. Does he ever rise to and *maintain* standard English? What are the chief deviations from standard English in his more formal speech?

5. From radio, television, or other listening situations, collect examples of "substandard" features in "the formal speech of the semi-literate."

6. *Webster's Third New International Dictionary* omits *colloq.*

as a "Status Label." Consult the Preface to find out why. On the basis of Kenyon's article, do the reasons seem valid—that is, would the label *colloq.* be incorrectly interpreted by most dictionary users?

7. Drama and fiction have been the chief *recorded* sources of examples of colloquial language. Have modern recording devices greatly extended records of truly conversational English? In the quotations in *Webster's Third International*, what kinds of sources are likely to represent the colloquial variety of style?

8. Look up one of the following verbs in *Webster's Second International* and list the idiomatic phrases marked *colloq.: come, do, go, make, take.* In *Webster's Third* look up these idiomatic phrases. Are the examples sufficient, in suggesting context, to serve as a guide to appropriate use?

9. In a passage of dialogue from a modern American play or work of fiction, select the words and idiomatic phrases which you consider more suited to conversation than to formal situations. Compare the contexts with the examples in *Webster's Third International* illustrating those words or phrases. Do the examples suggest appropriate use in a context comparable to that in the literary source you used?

10. The analogy between language and dress is one of the most valid and helpful ways of showing that language is social and that it should suit the occasion. A snapshot of a person alone, with no background, gives no information about the suitability of his clothes, but a background and other persons will suggest the situation. A girl in a bathing suit on a dance floor would look as absurd as a girl in a formal gown on a beach. Do the "snapshots" of words in quotations in the dictionary give enough background? Collect ten or more examples of quotations and decide what variety of style each suggests. Do any fail to suggest variety?

21

Another Look at Kenyon's Levels

J. J. Lamberts

Professor Lamberts of Arizona State University suggests that perhaps John S. Kenyon's terminology should be changed or modified to reflect more adequately the sensitivities of some users of the language. His observations were published in College English *for November, 1962.*

Among the enduring preoccupations of language scholars has been the search for a formula by which it will be possible to reduce to order the vast and chaotic realm of English usage. Call it what you will, what we are after is a set of reasonably tidy rules or generalizations.

There are two ways of producing these. We may impose a prearranged order upon the language from the outside, or we may attempt to derive a pattern of regularity from the language itself. The first approach is familiar as the one that captured the imaginations of many eighteenth century grammarians and which was implemented in their efforts to reduce the language to rule. The same attitude continues to dominate much of our classroom instruction, to say nothing of popular folklore with respect to good and bad English.

The alternative to this has been formulated in several ways. Its advocates maintain that usage cannot be legislated, nevertheless it possesses a certain degree of regularity which we can discern if we look earnestly and intelligently. This idea received what was doubtless its most heartening encouragement during the 1920's when a number of investigators converged almost simultaneously upon the concept of "levels of usage." Here at last was an interpretation which could convincingly set at naught the assumption that some words are inherently good and others inherently bad. Language differences were simply to be correlated with social differences and these could presumably be studied as purely objective data.

In the brief, the levels of usage doctrine asserted that linguistic acceptability and social acceptability go hand in hand, and vice versa, to be sure. People had spoken about social classes for hundreds of years; now here was the same thing in language. One wonders, as a matter of fact, why it took so long for anyone to stumble on so obvious a relation.

We speak of social levels, and it follows clearly that there must be levels of usage. These levels were identified at once. "Standard" usage ranked at the top, "substandard" at the bottom and between these extremes a shadowy middleground that went by several names. The most elaborate specification of this view presently appeared in C. C. Fries *American English Grammar* in which the three levels of usage were derived from three social levels. "Standard" English was equated with the language of people engaged in the professions; "common" English with that of persons employed in the service occupations; "vulgar" English with the language of those doing unskilled labor. With minor modifications here and there the levels concept now went into the textbooks, having achieved the status of dogma.

The levels theory, however, incorporated two basic difficulties. The first was its assumption that American society is stratified like the society of a typical West European country into fairly clear class divisions. England has its aristocracy, and this aristocracy has its characteristic speech, as Nancy Mitford indicated several years ago (1956) in a little book called *Noblesse Oblige*. It has also a middle class and these people speak middle-class English. Finally, it has a laboring class with a typical manner of speaking. By contrast America has neither a hereditary aristocracy nor a hereditary peasantry. In a few generations the descendant of an immigrant laborer can be President of the United States and can speak with a Harvard accent. Rather than assume that America has a class society, we do better to think of it as a status society. The absence of any clear class structure in this country explains why no one has been able to isolate a characteristic middle-class speech, and why the investigators have been frustrated in trying to fit in designations like "common" or "colloquial" or "informal" or some such thing.

The other difficulty is closely related to this one and it was pointed out by John S. Kenyon a dozen or more years ago.[1] It is simply that language differences are not so much distinctions in level as in function. When we apply terms like "formal" or "informal" or "colloquial" or "technical" or any one of scores of others, we are actually dealing with functional varieties. These are quite independent of levels of usage.

Identifying functional varieties for what they were explained a good deal that had been obscure, but there remained some contrasting types of usage which did not fit any such category and Kenyon called them cultural levels. In these, it was apparent, some reference had to be made to social standing. To avoid being caught in the trap that had plagued his predecessors, Kenyon confined himself to two levels and these he identified as "standard" and "substandard." Some of the more

---

[1] "Levels of Speech and Colloquial English," *The English Journal*, 37 (January 1948), 25–31; "Cultural Levels and Functional Varieties of English," *College English*, 10 (October 1948), 31–36.

recent textbooks have also followed this shift in dogma and speak of only two levels.

What gives the entire usage problem significance, of course, is the tendency of users of the language to react unfavorably toward certain expressions. More specifically, we say that in one way or another speakers of standard English disapprove of the language of speakers of substandard English. In other words, an unguarded use of the latter will certainly bar a person from certain coveted employments, and will further exclude him from other social privileges. For this reason the schools are committed to teach standard English. Every boy and girl is to have an equal opportunity to make good.

Having said this much, I should like now to examine more closely the entire notion of levels as a device for explaining the vagaries of English usage. The concept of functional varieties has accounted for many of the differences and it has done so quite accurately; but to assume that everything else can be explained in reference to two social levels, one superior and the other inferior, seems to me an oversimplification.

Suppose we look briefly at three quite typical reactions toward certain usage situations. The first is described in an article by J. M. Steadman, Jr.[2] which appeared in *American Speech*. Apart from Steadman's comments, it consisted of a list of expressions which students at Emory University had regarded as affected and for that reason objectionable. First on the list was *limb* in the sense of "leg." This was followed in order by *It is I* and *retire* (go to bed). Then came *elegant, expectorate, cease, prevaricate, cinema, deceased, ablutions, conflagration, domicile, one* (as indefinite pronoun), *whom, anybody's else, arise, commence, dine, erudite, mortician,* and *piazza.*

The second appeared in an article by Norman Lewis in *Harpers*.[3] There is no need to summarize the article; let me simply quote a comment on the word *whom*, offered by Kyle Crichton, who was at the time associate editor of *Colliers*. Said Crichton: "The most loathsome word (to me, at least) in the English language is 'whom.' You can always tell a half-educated buffoon by the care he takes in working the word in. When he starts it I know I am faced with a pompous illiterate who is not going to have me long as company."

And now a personal experience. Some time ago I was visiting a friend, a man who had never gone beyond the eighth grade in school and who was employed as a welder in a factory. The generator in my Chevrolet was about to give out, so at my friend's suggestion I decided to call an auto wrecker to see what used parts he might have. I had

---

[2] "Affected and Effeminate Words" *American Speech*, 136 (February 1938), 13–18.

[3] "How Correct Must Correct English Be?" *Harpers*, 198 (March 1949), 68–79.

already dialed the telephone number when my friend reached over, took the phone out of my hand with these words: "Here, Doc; let me talk to him. The way you talk costs you money."

In each of these three situations we have one person consciously disapproving of the language habits of another person, not because they are too crude—as we commonly expect—but because they are too precious. Crichton and the college students objected to *whom*, which for many people is the very touchstone of refinement. My none-too-literate friend apparently found the whole package of my speech abominable.

Here we have more than a mere disapproval. Our reaction to most substandard usages is essentially passive. We may not like them, but it would never occur to us to make remarks about them. It is only the exceptional usage, the one that troubles us tremendously, that calls forth any kind of comment. The fact then that in each of these three cases the respondents were so articulate suggests what we seem to have overlooked, namely, that hearers and readers become greatly involved in these expressions. Evidently these precious usages are capable of generating more powerful rejections than we had supposed.

Over against standard English, Kenyon proposed simply a substandard level, in other words, a type of language we reject as being too crude, or as reflecting a general poverty of cultivated influences. Let me propose another level, this time not too crude, but too affected or too refined, that is to say, "hyperstandard." It does not indicate a lack of culture so much as the wrong kind of culture. A person can fall flat on his face, but he can also bend over too far backward.

All of this means that we have three levels again: hyperstandard, standard, and substandard. To lump the two extremes into a single category, nonstandard, ignores some significant attitudes toward usage.

Are we possibly begging the question when we call these "levels"? The only connection in which the term "level" makes any sense is when it has been tied to social differences, specifically social levels. Substandard usage we like to associate with substandard social conditions, and yet one can push the association too far. When we endeavor to determine social status by means of language, we are obviously arguing in a circle.

The real difficulty with these categories is their utter disregard for logic, plus their curious way of overlapping each other. One man's standard is another's substandard. Conversely, one man's standard is another's hyperstandard. This produces a very real problem in our schools. We have all heard tales of illiterate or semi-illiterate parents who belabored their children for refusing to say *ain't* and *it don't* and *can't hardly*. To such parents *isn't* and *it doesn't* and *can hardly* sound affected and therefore offensive. We may compare our own reactions to phrases like *I feel badly* or *None of the parents is here* or *It was a question of whom was to be in charge*. To make it even more pointed, what would we do if a teacher indicated that our preference for *I feel bad* or *None of the parents are here* or *It was a question of who was to be in charge* betrayed us as persons of dull sensibilities and limited taste. In other words, the reason many people refuse to adopt standard usages instead of substandard usages may not be cussedness or stupidity, but the uncomfortable feeling that some hyperstandard forms are being foisted on them.

Possibly instead of "level" we should speak of "quality" or "type." The distinctions are, after all, qualitative rather than geometrical.

When the linguists of the 1920's set up their three-part division of usage distinctions, they were playing a worthy hunch. They realized evidently that the differences were more complex than a mere contrast between acceptability and inacceptability. But they appear to have felt, and reasonably so, that their own language was best, and should therefore be standard.

I am not sure that the recognition of this organization of usage structure is going to make our problems any easier. But it should make our handling of them more realistic. These many years we have been busy trying to construct a ceiling over crudity as we belabored substandard usages. Possibly it is time to begin building a floor under preciosity too. As a matter of fact, maybe we should measure the house once more and determine the exact location of the ceiling and the floor.

STUDY QUESTIONS AND EXERCISES

1. The two methods of producing generalizations described by Lamberts are *deductive* and *inductive*. Look up these terms if you do not know them. Which method does the scientist use? Which method is responsible for "popular folklore" regarding good and bad English? Are the hypotheses derived from study of the language necessarily sound? For example, "levels of usage," a hypothesis based on study of the language, was generally accepted before Kenyon wrote his article. What hypothesis does Kenyon present? How does Lamberts modify it? What evidence does each present?

2. What are the basic assumptions of the "levels of usage doctrine"? What are the basic assumptions they reflect about American society? How may American society more accurately be described?

3. Look up Nancy Mitford's book, *Noblesse Oblige*. What are the general differences in speech between *U* or upper-class and non-*U*, or middle-class society in Britain. How do social assurance and social insecurity, respectively, affect language? How is Miss Mitford's evidence concerning British society relevant to Northern middle-class anxiety about correctness and Southern upper-class complacency?

4. Which of Kenyon's basic points does Lamberts accept? What level would Lamberts add to Kenyon's two?

5. Is the reason that "the schools are committed to teach standard English" based on linguistics or social/economic considerations?

6. What kind of unfavorable reaction to language did Kenyon omit and Lamberts consider?

7. Look up the articles by J. M. Steadman and Norman Lewis, cited by Lamberts. What does *precious* mean, as Lamberts uses it? What are some of your own pet peeves in "precious" language?

8. Which of Lamberts' levels are illustrated in the quotation from Mark Twain in Cassidy's article, "Language on the American Frontier" (pp. 98–99)? Does this example serve to confirm Lamberts' criticism that Kenyon's limitation to two social levels is oversimplified? From the point of view of Evans in "Editor's Choice," to which level might one assign the critics of *Webster's Third International*, among whom are a number of the 100 panelists of the *American Heritage Dictionary*?

9. Is "among whom are" in the previous sentence too "precious"? Would "among who are" be acceptable in speech or writing? Explain your answer. "A number of the panelists are among those whom Evans would say are examples of hyperstandard English." How does this *whom* differ from the previous one? (*This* one is a typical "pompous illiterate" use of *whom*.)

10. Do you agree that reaction to most substandard English is "essentially passive"? If hyperstandard is metaphorically bending over backward and substandard is falling on one's face, what is the metaphor for standard? How does the etymology of *standard* suggest the metaphor?

11. What objection does Lamberts make to *levels*, as categories? If a child's or young person's use of standard English sounds affected to his parents, as a kind of implicit criticism of their language, might he use their type of language at home and standard at school, just as he uses still another type of language with his own friends?

22

How Many Clocks?

Martin Joos

In his analysis of language usage Professor Martin Joos of the University of Toronto proposes scales of usage based on age, style, breadth, and responsibility, with each scale composed of five levels. His book The Five Clocks *(1962), from which this passage is taken, derives its title from these levels.*

Ballyhough railway station has two clocks which disagree by some six minutes. When one helpful Englishman pointed the fact out to a porter, his reply was 'Faith, sir, if they was to tell the same time, why would we be having two of them?'

*   *   *   *   *   *

Here are, in order of importance, four of the usage-scales of native central English:

Age	Style	Breadth	Responsibility
senile	frozen	genteel	best
mature	formal	puristic	better
teenage	consultative	standard	good
child	casual	provincial	fair
baby	intimate	popular	bad

These four scales are essentially independent; relations among them are not identities. (But isn't the best English genteel?—That must be Miss Fidditch talking.)

AGE: The frame within which all other scales develop. Though this is the most important of them all, we shall have very little to say about the age-scale of usage because nothing can be done about it directly, and that little will have to wait to near the end.

STYLE: Here are the five clocks to which we shall principally devote our attention. They may be called 'higher' and 'lower' for convenience in referring to the tabulation; but that doesn't mean anything like relative superiority. More later.

BREADTH: This scale measures breadth of experience and of self-limitation. From popular English up to standard English, your experiences broaden your usages; and from there up to genteel you narrow them again to suit your personality. Nothing further.

RESPONSIBILITY: Here at last is the actual usage-scale nearest to Miss Fidditch's mythical scale of excellence, and we borrow her scale-labels but not her meanings for them, eliminating her favorite synonym 'correct' for the top. More immediately.

Much as linguists hate to admit it, the responsibility scale does exist. It even has considerable though minor importance. Its importance is minor because we use it only in forming social clusters, momentary or lasting. If we have done a good job, the cluster is homogeneous on the responsibility scale, which holds it together as a social group. Then we can forget the responsibility-ratings of the group's members, because we are done using them: they are used only in first forming the group or in adding or dropping members. This responsibility scale needs to be cleared out of the way, to prevent confusion, before we consider the five clocks of style.

The reason why linguists dislike acknowledging the responsibility scale is that any acknowledgment of its existence is customarily taken as an endorsement of the 'quality' theory of usage which they of course reject. That quality theory holds that usages are intrinsically good or bad—that each usage is by itself absolutely good or absolutely bad, under a taboo-rule, without inquiring into what good or evil it performs in real life. For example, 'ain't' and 'hisself' are rated as bad English (or 'not English' to make the condemnation stronger by including a self-contradiction in it); and every essay at discussing their badness counts as an attempt to introduce poison into the water-supply. (What does Webster say? Well, that settles it, doesn't it? I don't see what good it would do to discuss the matter any further.)

Now those linguists are right to a certain extent. 'Ain't I?' has just as respectable an origin as 'Aren't we?'—and, ultimately, a more respectable origin than 'Aren't I?' as it is pronounced by most of those Americans who use it. Again, in view of everybody's 'myself, ourselves, yourself, yourselves' the bad minority's 'hisself, theirselves' would be more grammatical if logic governed grammar. Yet the origin and the logic don't matter; here the master rule has been known for centuries: Treason doth never prosper; what's the reason? Why, if it prosper, none dare call it treason. In short, the community's choice of what shall count as the norm and what shall be rated as 'bad' (in general, even by those who use it) apparently is an arbitrary choice, so that usage is never good or bad but thinking makes it so.

What, never? There is more to it than that. There is something about social living that creates a responsibility-scale of usage; and when we have examined the natural basis of that scale, we shall see why the folklore calls it a quality scale.

The community's survival depends on cooperation; and adequate cooperation depends on recognizing the more and the less responsible types of persons around us. We need to identify the natural burden-bearers of the community so that we can give them the responsibility which is heaviest of all: we make them responsible for cooperation itself. Then the majority of us can function carefree in our square and round niches, free of the burden of maintaining the cooperation-net which joins us all. Some few of us have a strong interest in cooperation-nets without much competence in them; we are placed as letter-carriers and writers and legislators and teachers and so on; and for those jobs we are selected by tests which discriminate between interest and talent in the maintenance of cooperation.

In any case, the community places us principally by language-use tests which measure us on the various usage scales. Conversely, each of us selects others. For the present, we are interested in just one scale, namely responsibility—a personality scale and a usage scale running quite accurately parallel to each other.

We start very early learning to use this scale. It would be an exceptionally foolish ten-year-old who trusted a well-groomed sharper in preference to a judge in a bathing-suit. And he selects the more responsible person principally by listening, for the same reason that an employer wants an interview with each job-seeker—an interview for which no handbook is needed, for the oral code is public property.

The oral code for responsible personalities is indeed in part arbitrary, conventional: 'himself,' not 'hisself.' But the convention has a natural base, and in a very simple way. Responsible language does not palter. It is explicit. It commits the speaker. The responsible speaker is under a sort of almost morbid compulsion to leave himself no way out of his commitment. The responsibility-dialect does not mumble; its grammar does not contradict itself; its semantics doesn't weasel. That is its basis; 'himself' and the rest are conventional, but they borrow their strength from the natural basis; they are overlays, but the basis is strong enough to overpower the illogicality of 'himself.'

Miss Fiddinch's shibboleths are about half conventional overlays. Did she create them? No; the community did, on the theory that birds of a feather flock together. Through some historical accident—some random fluctuation in the distribution of 'himself' and 'hisself' among members of the community—it happened that 'himself' came to be regarded as relatively more common in the responsibility-dialect. It may not have been actually more common there, but the community at large at least thought it was, and that was enough. Flocking did the rest. Those young people who aspired to responsibilities (perhaps only subconsciously aspired) selected 'himself' (normally without awareness of what they were doing or why), while those who aspired to irresponsible lives selected 'hisself' if it was conventionally available to them.

If it was not, they instead selected effete usages. Vulgarity and effeteness use equivalent signals in our culture. Each supplies its fellowship with passwords. For the community at large, the passwords are signals saying 'No responsibilities wanted!' And we take them at their word—for this part of our communication-system—the more certainly because the whole code works subconsciously.

Miss Fidditch's mistake is in trying to work out the code consciously and logically, instead of simply listening to what clearly responsible people actually say. Sometimes, however, she does listen; and then if she tries to teach what she has learned, and if her more responsible pupils learn to speak that way, Miss Fidditch is apt to imagine that her teaching is what taught them. That is an illusion. Responsibility earns respect; therefore most people (not all!) try for a step higher on the responsibility scale of English usage: simply to earn the respect of others, even irresponsible persons will try this if they don't feel the danger in it. In any case, that is why usages once labeled 'bad' always dwindle and ultimately vanish. Not because Miss Fidditch banned them! The kids aren't listening to her; they listen to Uncle David who is an aviator and to Dr. Henderson, perhaps also to historical and fictional characters if the school is doing its proper job. Miss Fidditch is convinced that bad English is gaining ground; she is only looking for burglars under the bed; statistics says the opposite, item by item. (Don't cry, Miss Fidditch! Homeostasis will keep up your supply of bad English, never fear!)

Finally, the community prefers the center of the scale: 'good' usage, not 'best.' It routinely rejects morbidly honest candidates for office, and the best English counts as the disqualification that makes a teacher.

STUDY QUESTIONS AND EXERCISES

1. Miss Fidditch, with whom Joos carries on a dialogue throughout *The Five Clocks*, is borrowed from Henry Lee Smith, Jr. and Robert A. Hall, Jr. Hall introduces her in *Linguistics and Your Language* as a "very puristic lady" who teaches her class always to say "It is I" and answers "Who's there?" with "It's me—Miss Fidditch." What mistake does Miss Fidditch make concerning Joos's four usage scales?

2. With which one of the four scales is Joos chiefly concerned? Which scale is the one about which least can be done? How has Miss Fidditch's personality caused her to narrow her usage? What is the implication of *narrow* in this context? Would the top two usages in the breadth scale seem "precious" to those for whom standard English seems the maxium achievement? The subtitle of *The Five Clocks* might be "Miss Fidditch's Conversion." Read it (108 pages) and see why.

3. How do style and breadth differ essentially? Does position on the scale indicate higher and lower degrees of superiority?

4. How does Joos differ from Miss Fidditch in his attitude toward responsibility in usage? What is the importance of the responsibility scale? Why do linguists dislike acknowledging this scale? What light does this discussion throw on the charges of permissiveness and a policy of "anything goes" that were directed at *Webster's Third*? (See selections 5, 10, and 11 by Bergen Evans, Walter Ong, and Philip B. Gove.) The parenthetical remarks, beginning "What does Webster say?" are by Miss Fidditch. Would she defend or censure *Webster's Third*?

5. What generally determines which of several forms is preferred, logic or arbitrary choice by respected members of a community? How does a community select its respected members?

6. Joos advises listening to historical and fictional characters. Try listening to young Charles Mallison and V. K. Ratliff, at the end of Chapter 16 in William Faulkner's *The Town*. Ratliff is trying to talk like the lawyer, Gavin Stevens, and keeps changing *hisself* to *himself*, *drug* to *dragged*. Gavin's young nephew, Charles, thinks that *drug* is more effective, and Gavin has been borrowing such substandard terms from Ratliff. How is Ratliff, a self-made man, showing *responsibility*? Is Gavin abdicating *responsibility* in using folk speech or is he bridging the gap between himself and the common man? In which variety of *style* might he use Ratliff's kind of language without descending to *bad* or *fair* in *responsibility*? Examine the chapters narrated by Gavin in *The Town*, when he is speaking to the reader and when he is quoting what he said to others, to determine both his *style* and his *responsibility* scales. What does Ratliff's speech in the dialogue with Charles show about his place in the *breadth* and the *responsibility* scales? What does Gavin's friendship with Ratliff and Ratliff's terms of easy familiarity with people in the town and county indicate about community respect for Ratliff? How does Ratliff illustrate specifically the point in the fourth paragraph from the end of the selection from Joos? If you have read *The Town*, how do the facts about Ratliff's earlier life explain why he was late in selecting standard forms?

7. What signals does the community receive if a college graduate uses substandard English? How will prospective employers act?

8. How is the statement that the community prefers "'good' usage, not 'best'" related to the point made by Lamberts? How do the political careers of Al Smith and Adlai Stevenson substantiate Joos's conclusion?

23

Functional Variety in English

W. Nelson Francis

A speaker of language adapts his speech to the circumstances in which he finds himself. In classifying the resulting styles Professor Francis of Brown University uses the categories suggested by Martin Joos in The Five Clocks: *the intimate, the casual, the consultative, the formal, and the frozen. This selection comes from Professor Francis'* The English Language *(1965).*

Whether his natural speech be educated, vernacular, or uneducated, no person uses the same kind of language for every occasion. Within the regional and educational variety of language which he speaks, he has different **functional varieties**, sometimes called **styles** or **registers**, appropriate to the occasion, the size of the group spoken to, the degree of familiarity within the group, and even the subject discussed. Selecting the proper style for a given occasion and shifting from one to another as the circumstances change are not primarily linguistic decisions, but social ones. Learning to make such decisions quickly and accurately is part of the process of socialization that we all must go through. Some people become more skillful at it than others; no doubt a large element in the complex of personal traits known as "getting along with people" is the ability to size up a situation or a person and select the appropriate style on the basis of a few clues.

Preschool children usually have only one style, especially if their experience of the world has been confined chiefly to family and playmates of the same social level. When they go out into the larger world, they learn that not all adults are to be addressed in the same way as parents and other relatives. Much of this they learn for themselves; some of it is taught them by parents and teachers. Although people often find the direct and familiar sayings of children amusing, these sayings are often the result of inappropriate style, which parents and teachers correct with such admonitions as "You mustn't speak to the principal like that." By the early teens the lesson is usually well learned and the child has at least three working styles—one for his peers, one for parents and other adults he knows well, and one for strangers—the minimal stylistic repertory needed for normal social life.

For educated adult speakers, Martin Joos has identified and named five styles, each suited to a particular kind of occasion and characterized by certain features which identify it to the listener.[1] The central and, in a sense, unmarked style Joos calls **consultative.** In this style we open a conversation with a stranger; it is safe for that purpose because it will neither offend him by unsolicited intimacy nor throw him off by undue formality. It is also the appropriate style for a discussion of more or less serious matters by a relatively small group; it pays listeners the compliment of assuming that they are interested and serious and hence do not need to have their interest aroused by either the elaborate figurative language of the formal style or the slang and occasional profanity of the casual style. As Joos says,

> The diction is kept in accurate balance with the requirements: the pronunciation is clear but does not clatter, the grammar is complete but for an occasional anacoluthon [mixed construction], the semantics is adequate without fussiness.[2]

It is obviously a style whose major purpose is communication, with a minimum of the social, esthetic, and emotional overtones that characterize other styles.

The **casual** style is that appropriate to easy conversation among acquaintances and friends, except when the seriousness of the occasion or the subject calls for the consultative. In pronunciation it makes much use of elided and slurred forms like /gɔnə/ for *going to* and /wáčə dú:in/ for *what are you doing.* Its sentences are often elliptical, even telegraphic, dropping redundant grammatical and semantic features in the interest of directness and brevity, as in *Coming tonight?* for *Are you coming tonight?* and *Joe here?* for *Is Joe here?* Depending on the speaker, it may include slang and occasional profanity. In America, at least, it makes use of first names more often than titles and surnames. Since it is not used to convey very serious or complex information (even close friends shift to consultative for that), it makes considerable use of general-purpose, semantically nearly empty words and phrases like *gimmick, thingumajig,* and *nice.* Its deficiencies in communicative power are often acknowledged by frequent interpolation of phrases like *you know, I mean, as a matter of fact,* and *actually.* When written, as in informal friendly letters, it uses contractions like *won't* and *can't,* abbreviations and clippings like *Dr.* or *doc* for *doctor* and the dash as a general-purpose punctuation mark. It is the style most commonly used by high school and college students except in class, where they usually shift to consultative.

---

[1] Martin Joos, *The Five Clocks* (Bloomington: Indiana University Research Center in Anthropology, Folklore, and Linguistics, 1962).

[2] *The Five Clocks*, p. 24.

People who habitually use casual style where the situation normally calls for consultative are considered "refreshing" or "fresh" depending on the attitude of the person making the appraisal. On the other hand an occasional shift to casual style, either in writing or in speech, may produce a desirable special effect. A teacher who habitually uses it in class usually loses the respect of his students, who feel they are being patronized. But if in a particular emergency he can switch from the consultative *I'd like you students to be quiet* to the casual *Shut up, you guys*, he may get the quiet he wants. Some writers, particularly humorists, are adept at exploiting the surprise value of a casual sentence in a consultative or formal context:

> One reason the Ford anatomy was never reduced to an exact science was that, having "fixed" it, the owner couldn't honestly claim that the treatment had brought about the cure. There were too many authenticated cases of Fords fixing themselves—restored naturally to health after a short rest. Farmers soon discovered this, and it fitted nicely with their draft-horse philosophy: "Let 'er cool off and she'll snap into it again." [3]

Here the basically formal literary style is enlivened by the lapse into the casual in the last sentence. Such mixing of styles demands great skill if its effect is to be surprise and pleasure rather than mere inappropriateness.

The **intimate style** is used by people who know each other so well and whose relationship is so close that each can predict the other's reactions to a given situation with accuracy a large part of the time. It thus serves chiefly to maintain contact and corroborate the accuracy of each speaker's judgment of the other's reactions. Much of this communication is carried on by other than linguistic means—between intimates a raised eyebrow, a shrug of the shoulders, or a groan can serve as well as or better than verbal expression. Grammar is reduced to a minimum; utterances are typically very short; there may be long periods of silence that in any of the other styles would be interpreted either as rudeness or as a desire to end the conversation. Vocabulary, too, is much reduced, and the words that are used often have special meanings deriving from some shared experience which the world outside the intimate group (usually but not always a pair) does not know about. Pronunciation, too, may be altered; an intimate pair may use a broad form of regional dialectal pronunciation, even though one or both of them are not native speakers of that dialect. Words are slurred and clipped, accidental mispronunciations may be purposely preserved. Sometimes

---

[3] E. B. White and Richard L. Strout, "Farewell, My Lovely!" in *The Second Tree from the Corner* (New York: Harper & Brothers, n.d.), p. 38.

the intimate message may be carried by intonation alone, and the segmental phonology filled out with nonsense sounds or syllables. Everything about the intimate style serves to emphasize the close familiarity of the speakers and the resulting ability to reduce redundancy to a minimum. In terms of the discussion with which this chapter began, the conservative forces of society are virtually absent, which allows free play to arbitrariness.

As has already been observed, the parties to an intimate conversation are usually a pair: husband and wife, siblings (especially identical twins), lovers. But any small group who are thrown into close and frequent contact and who do not have to maintain social distance because of differences of status may develop an intimate style to be used at least in the area of their greatest common interest and application. The small crew of a boat on a long ocean voyage, an athletic team, a string quartet, a high-wire balancing act—any group where there must be complete cooperation, mutual trust, and a high degree of specialized skill—any of these, however separate their private lives may otherwise be, almost inevitably develops a laconic, stripped-down style, augmented by minute gesture and aided by empathetic understanding, that to the outsider seems almost telepathic. But unless the group is small—not more than four or five—various kinds of social complexity enter in to make the intimate style inappropriate.

When intimates wish to communicate information about something outside the very restricted range to which intimate style is appropriate, they shift to casual or even consultative style. For this reason, intimate style does not often get written down. The act of writing, relatively laborious as it is, usually is the result of the desire to convey some kind of new information to whoever is going to read the product. A love letter is, of course, an exception; its primary purpose is usually simply to communicate the fact that the writer's feelings about the reader have not changed since the last time he was able to communicate this information in person. For this reason, people outside the intimate pair usually find love letters either unintelligible or comic. Letters such as those of Abelard and Héloise or of Keats to Fanny Brawne convey much more than this basic information, and therefore range far beyond the intimate style, often to the level of formal literary style.

One famous example of intimate style in writing is the "little language" that Jonathan Swift occasionally lapsed into in his *Journal to Stella*. This journal was in the form of a series of letters, with almost daily entries, written to two women, Esther Johnson (Stella), who was an intimate correspondent and often a companion of Swift's for thirty years, and her companion, Rebecca Dingley. Although most of the *Journal* consists of an account of Swift's busy life as an important though unofficial member of the Tory administration, he occasionally interpolates an intimate passage like this:

> Poor Stella, won't Dingley leave her a little day-light to write to
> Presto? Well, well, we'll have day-light shortly, spight of her teeth;
> and zoo must cly Lele and Hele, and Hele aden. Must loo minitate
> pdfr, pay? Iss, and so la shall. And so leles fol ee rettle. Dood mol-
> low.[4]

A good deal of this becomes clear when we see that it represents a kind
of phonemic substitution similar to "baby-talk," with *l* used in place of
r, and *d* in place of *g*. Also characteristic of intimate style is the use of
pet-names—*Stella* for Miss Johnson and *Presto* for himself—and of
cryptic abbreviations like *pdfr* (according to Swift's editor, this last was
pronounced "Podefar" and stood for either *Poor Dear Foolish Rogue*
or *Poor Dear Fellow*).

The three styles so far discussed have in common the fact that they
are primarily conversational; they imply the presence and participation
of another beside the speaker. The participation, especially in consultative style, may be no more than signaling at brief intervals that one is
paying attention, which may be done by brief oral attention-signals
(*yes, unh-hunh*) or, when the two parties can see each other, by unob-
trusive gestures. But the listener is usually expected to become a speaker
in his turn, and he knows the signals that mark the places where he can
begin speaking without causing a rude interruption. When written, the
consultative, casual, and intimate styles suppose a specific reader or
small group of readers who would respond in this way if present, and
are more or less expected to answer letters addressed to them.

In contrast, the other two styles, the **formal** of expository discourse
and the **frozen** of literature, are not conversational but informative and
discursive. The hearer or reader is not given the opportunity to intervene, to ask questions, to make comments, or to indicate his lack of
comprehension. Instead of the give and take of the conversational situation, the user of formal style—the lecturer, preacher, newscaster, com-
mencement speaker, judge, or legislator speaking on the floor (not in
committee)—is alone before an audience. Without benefit of the "feed-
back" that is available to the conversationalist, he is obliged to hold his
audience's attention on the one hand by making sure that he is understood and on the other by avoiding boresome explicitness or repetition.

The grammar of formal style is more closely organized and less tolerant of loose or mixed constructions. The vocabulary is more ample than
that of the conversational styles, with a wider range of nearly synonymous words and phrases, though large areas of vocabulary—slang, for
example—are ruled out except for special effects which actually constitute lapses into the conversational mode. Pronunciation is meticulous;

---

[4] Jonathan Swift, *Journal to Stella*, edited by Harold Williams (Oxford: Claren-
don Press, 1948), vol. I, p. 210.

254 Functional Variety in English

slurring and contractions are avoided, and tactical features like disjunc-
ture, stress, and intonation are carefully observed. The general pattern
of organization avoids backtracking, second-thought interpolation, and
repetition in varied terms, all of which are characteristic of conversation.
The result is to place a much heavier burden of thought and planning
upon the formal speaker or writer. As Joos puts it:

> Formal text therefore demands advance planning. Consultative
> speakers never plan more than the current phrase, and are allowed
> only a limited number of attempts to return to their muttons be-
> fore abandoning them; the formal speaker has a captive audience,
> and is under obligation to provide a plan for the whole sentence be-
> fore he begins uttering it, an outline of the paragraph before in-
> troducing it, and a delimitation of field for his whole discourse
> before he embarks on it. One who does all this currently, keeping
> the three levels of his planning under continuous control, is cor-
> rectly said to think on his feet; for clearly it calls for something
> other than brains, and intelligent persons do not attempt it but
> instead have the text all composed and written out at leisure.[5]

The formal style is thus the typical style of responsible public writing.
By native speakers it is learned relatively late, if at all—usually not until
the beginning of schooling and in most cases not until long after that.
It has for many, perhaps most, people the qualities of a mode of language that has been learned consciously, as one learns a foreign language, rather than largely unconsciously, as one learns one's mother
tongue. The range of competence of its users is greater than that of
users of the conversational styles, from the virtuosity of a Churchill to
the inept and platitudinous fumblings of a poor after-dinner speaker.
Most of the effort in a typical college composition class is concerned
with increasing the students' skill in formal style. And rightly so: the
central mode of written language for the educated man in our society
is formal educated standard English. Ninety-nine people out of a hundred must learn this in school.

What Joos calls **frozen** style is primarily the style of literature, at
least in the broad sense of the word. In this sense, literature can be defined as those samples of language which the whole community or a
segment of it values to the point of wishing to preserve its exact expression as well as its content. Once the words have been arranged, they are
set or frozen into an unchangeable pattern (though the author himself
may exercise the privilege of changing them). This definition would not
satisfy the literary critic, who usually would like to include an esthetic
criterion in his definition. Nor is it a value judgment. Not all literature

---

[5] *The Five Clocks*, p. 26.

is good, by any standard of measurement including its use of language. But all literature does have the quality of rigidity of language.

A piece of literature is a **text**. A good deal of literary scholarship is exerted in the task of making sure that the texts of literary works, especially those that are highly valued, are made available to readers in a form that most accurately represents the author's wishes. The story of Hamlet, Prince of Denmark, can be told in many ways, even that of the comic book. But these are not Shakespeare's play, which must be presented in the language he wrote, as nearly as a modern editor can discover it. In this case the editor's problem is compounded by the fact that the text was frozen in several forms, the most important of which are the first two quartos and the first folio. The text the editor produces will not be identical with any of these, but it will represent his best judgment of what Shakespeare intended the play to be, word by word.

Not all literature is frozen in printed form. Societies that have no writing system may have a large body of oral literature, which is memorized in its frozen form and passed down from generation to generation by oral transmission. This method of transmission allows changes and variations to creep into the text, especially as the language itself changes; but, for all that, oral texts remain remarkably constant for generations, even centuries. Members of preliterate societies usually have better trained memories than literate people, and they insist that a text be repeated in the exact words in which they first heard it. The same is true of children before they learn to read, as anyone knows who has read a familiar story to a child and been corrected for the smallest departure from the text. Even in highly literate cultures like our own, at least a small body of literature is passed on by oral transmission—folk songs and nursery rhymes particularly. But we normally expect a frozen text to be available in print, and we customarily read it privately and silently. The literary experience thus becomes a detached and individual one, the solitary reader and the solitary writer do not know each other and never meet except through the medium of the printed page. At least until the modern vogue for recorded readings of their own works by writers, especially poets, such features of the spoken language as intonation have had to be supplied by the reader solely on the evidence of the printed text before him. The burden of communication is carried almost wholly by grammar and vocabulary, with some help from graphic convention or originality.

The great advantage of the frozen style, especially in written form, is that it is freed from the pressures of time which exert very powerful influence on the conversational styles. A writer may spend a lifetime perfecting one poem or novel, if he chooses. A reader, likewise, may reread and study a frozen text as often as he wants to, finding new meanings each time.

Not all the texts that society wants to preserve in their exact language come under the more usual definitions of literature. Some of them, such as scriptures and liturgies, are important to the maintenance of religion. Political documents like treaties and laws must be treated as texts alterable only through elaborate procedures resulting in an acceptable new text: witness the Constitution of the United States and its amendments. Contracts, agreements, bonds, deeds, and other such legal documents follow set formulas which must not be changed lest their binding force be lost. Ceremonies such as weddings, initiations, and the awarding of academic degrees are accompanied by frozen texts, so familiar that people seldom stop to analyze their meaning but simply take them as customary parts of accepted rituals. These are all special types of frozen style, in which the basic meaning of the language is heavily overlaid with interpretation and customary understanding. It is naïve to assume that even the most intelligent and gifted reader of English can extract "the real meaning" from such documents as the Constitution or the New Testament simply by reading the text alone. What these documents mean in our society can only be discovered by prolonged study of other documents devoted to their interpretation.

Joos has succinctly summarized the primary functions of the five styles:

> Good intimate style fuses two personalities. Good casual style integrates disparate personalities into a social group which is greater than the sum of its parts, for now the personalities complement each other instead of clashing. Good consultative style produces cooperation without the integration, profiting from the lack of it. Good formal style informs the individual separately, so that his future planning may be the more discriminate. Good frozen style, finally, lures him into educating himself, so that he may the more confidently act what rôle he chooses.[6]

STUDY QUESTIONS AND EXERCISES

1. Which of the previous writers in this section provided the term "functional varieties" and established the point with which Francis begins? Is ignorance or wilful disregard of appropriate style a significant cause of social friction?

2. Trace the stages in your acquirement of appropriate styles.

3. In a child's "three working styles," is it practical and, in some instances, desirable, for a child's style with his peers and with his family and their friends to remain substandard while he uses standard English in school and among those who customarily use standard English? Should he be encouraged to vary his language in this way: would his self-respect and his self-development benefit? Explain your answer.

---

[6] The Five Clocks, p. 27.

4. Is it advisable in consultative style between, say, a customer and a salesman, or an employer and a workman, for the better educated person to imitate the other? Is it advisable for the better educated person to avoid preciosity that flaunts his superiority? (See selection 21, by Lamberts.)

5. Why is the casual style limited in range of vocabulary and lacking in precision and completeness of expression? How does intimate differ from casual style both in the relationship between speakers and in the ways of conveying meaning? With a tape-recorder, record conversation between two casual acquaintances and between two intimate friends or members of one family. What similarities and differences do you observe between the two dialogues?

6. If possible, compare tape-recorded conversations with letters by the same speakers. How do speech and writing differ?

7. How do *formal* expository discourse and the *frozen* style of literature differ from the other three styles? Does the frozen style of literature exclude the consultative, casual, and intimate styles? If not, how may a frozen style include the others and why do they become frozen?

8. What are the characteristics of formal written style exhibited by Francis in this selection, by McDavid in selection 19, and by Evans in selection 5? Do you find characteristics of conversational style in any of these? If so, specify.

9. What justification does Francis give for teaching college students to write formal English? Would the same reasons justify teaching formal writing to all high school students? Explain your answer. How is Joos's scale of responsible usage relevant to this problem?

10. Why does Joos call literature *frozen* style? How does a child insist on this "rigidity of language" in listening to poems and stories?

11. Can you cite specific examples of literature frozen in oral tradition before it could be preserved in writing and literature transmitted by oral tradition after writing was common? How and why do present texts of the latter kinds of works differ significantly?

12. How do readings of works by the authors enhance the work? Follow the text as you listen to recordings or "live" readings.

13. Why are nonliterary documents *frozen*?

14. What role do all five styles play in the development of the educated, responsible person?

24

Slang and its Relatives

Paul Roberts

Professor Roberts discusses the role and relevance of slang in human communication in Understanding English *(1958), from which this selection is taken.*

Slang is one of those things that everybody can recognize and nobody can define. Not only is it hard to wrap slang in a definition; it is also hard to distinguish it from such similar things as colloquialisms, provincialisms, jargon, trade talk. As we shall see, these areas blend into one another, and it is often a waste of time to look for the boundary.

One characteristic of a slang term is that it exists side by side with another, more general term for the same thing. Take for example the word *chick*, which has been used by some speakers in the meaning *girl* or *young woman*. The difference between *chick* and *girl* can be stated only in reference to the people who use the words: some say, "This chick is my sister"; others "This girl is my sister." *Chick* is slang and *girl* is not, because *chick* is used by a limited part of the population, mostly young people, whereas *girl* is used by everybody, including those who use *chick*.

It is often said that a slang term ceases to be slang when it is "accepted by the dictionary." This is not really the test. You will find many slang terms duly registered in dictionaries and still slang terms. The term ceases to be slang when it drives out of use its respectable synonym, or when it acquires a meaning that cannot be expressed otherwise. If, for instance, people ceased to use the word *girl* and all used *chick* instead, then *chick* could no longer be called a slang term.

Such things have happened. The term *hot dog* was once a slang term, but it couldn't be considered so now. No one in America would go up to a counter and order a "sausage sandwich." Similarly *varsity*, originally a slang contraction of *university*, has acquired special meanings which only it expresses and is no longer slang. *Jazz*, when it means a particular kind of music, is scarcely a slang term, since there is no more respectable word meaning that kind of music.

Certainly respectability must enter into any discussion of slang. Slang is essentially not respectable. There is always a more elegant way of saying the thing but one chooses the slang term for reasons. The reason may be a desire to be thought witty or clever or up to date. More often it is a desire to show, by a particular use of language, that one is a member in good standing of a particular group of people.

Criminals have always been prolific producers of slang because they are so obviously marked off from respectable society. They deliberately widen the gulf by multiplying lanuage differences, and they often use the differences for practical purposes: to recognize one another, to shield their conversation from hostile ears. Criminal groups of the seventeenth and eighteenth centuries in England developed large vocabularies of slang—or *cant*, as it was then called—which rendered their talk almost meaningless to an outsider.

Much of the slang in common use today comes ultimately from characters on the other side of the law. This will be recognizable, for example, in words relating to American money. For "money" in general we have such terms as *dough*, *lettuce*, the *green* or the *big green*, *folding stuff*, and various others. The different denominations all have their slang terms: *singles* or *fish* for one dollar bills; *fin* for a five; *sawbuck* for a ten and *double sawbuck* for a twenty; *C-note* or *century* for a hundred; *grand* for a thousand. All of these are old, well-weathered terms and are familiar to many people who wouldn't dream of holding up a drugstore. But it is clear that they have their highest frequency in those districts where policemen would prefer to go in pairs.

In games slang is common everywhere, but it is most prolific in those games which are more or less disreputable. Bridge and golf have their slang terms, but gambling games have more, and roulette, for which the participants may wear evening clothes, has fewer than craps or poker, for which they usually do not. Poker has a wide variety of slang terms —or at least had when the writer had the game explained to him by an obliging friend. Thus in addition to the general names for the cards— *ace*, *deuce*, *king*—another set of slang terms are, or were, in use: *bull* or *bullet* for "ace," *cowboy* for "king," a *pair of ducks* for "a pair of deuces." Two aces and two eights are a *dead man's hand*, three tens are *thirty miles* or *thirty miles of railroad*, a flush of any sort is *all blue*.

Dice, even more disreputable than poker, has a correspondingly higher incidence of slang terms.

The connection between slang and the criminal element is seen again in the dope racket, the terms of which have been made more or less generally familiar by the movies and television. The word *dope* itself is originally slang, but it is now in more general use than *narcotics*. Within the racket, terms abound. The words *marijuana* and *heroin* seem scarcely to occur among users or peddlers of the drugs, as is suggested by the fact that addicts speaking of heroin on a television program pronounced it to rhyme with *groin*. Usually, apparently, they say *H* or *big H* or *horse* or *caballito* (a Spanish word meaning "little horse" or "horsey"). Marijuana is referred to by several slang terms, of which *hay* seems to be most enduring. An injection of a narcotic is a *fix*. To inject it in the vein is to *mainline*. A salesman or peddler is a *pusher*. An addict is a *junkie*. To rid oneself of an addiction is to *kick the habit*. It will be seen that a narcotics addict can discuss his troubles at some length without being understood by anyone outside the circle.

Musicians are another fertile source of slang terms. Again the element of more or less respectability enters: symphony orchestras are less prolific of slang terms than are purveyors of more popular music—jazz, swing, bebop, rock 'n' roll bands. Many of the slang terms in this area, as in others, have only the briefest existence, but others linger. Even the youngest readers will be acquainted with *dig* (understand or appreciate), *cool* (excellent or moving), *crazy* (inspired), *cat* (talented musician or knowledgeable music lover), *real* (exceptionally moving).

High school and college slang probably derives as much from music language as from any other source. More than one college professor in the 1950's had to learn that the expression "dig that crazy course," coming from one of his earnest young disciples, was not a criticism but a high tribute. But colleges fill out their slang with terms that apply particularly to college activities. Many of these terms are simple abbreviations: *math, prof, exam, poly sci, econ, phys ed*. Others are names, varying from year to year and from campus to campus, for hard or easy courses, hard or easy teachers, passing and failing, studying, cheating, flattering the teacher (*apple-polishing* is an old term that persists). There are slang terms for those who raise class averages and for those who don't, for campus politicians, for campus reporters, for deans and college presidents, for football players, for serious students, for frivolous students, for fraternity and sorority men and women, for nonfraternity and nonsorority men and women, for pretty girls, for other girls, and for girls in general. Everyone and everything connected with college life can be referred to by a slang term as well as by a more general one.

Slang words are mostly nouns and verbs, but the adjective class has its slang too. Any college group at any given time uses one adjective to express general approval. This can be anything at all, even a newly coined noise. It is just something that slips into the pattern "That's very ———," and means that the speaker likes whatever is referred to. When the writer was in college the word was *gruesome*. If, in those days, you said "She's a real gruesome girl," you meant that she attracted you strongly and compelled your admiration.

Since then scores of words have successively taken the place of *gruesome*. The life expectancy of slang in this particular slot is not great. Middle-aged readers will perhaps remember *zorch* and *George*, both illustrations of the truth that all a word has to do to become an adjective is to occur in an adjective pattern. *George*, which until 1952 or so had been an unassuming proper noun, became an adjective as soon as people started saying "That's very George," or more likely, "That's real

George." This started the practice, short-lived, to be sure, of pushing other proper nouns into this position: "That's real Robert" (good), "That's real Tom" (bad), "That's strictly Alexander" (genuine).

Slang connects with grammatical structure at more points than one. For example, it could be stated almost as a law of language that an irregular word which picks up a slang meaning will be regularized. Thus the irregular verb *slay* at one time acquired, in addition to its older meaning of "kill," the slang meaning "interest, amuse": "You really slay me, kid." In this meaning it never occurs with the old past form *slew*. One would say not "He slew me" but always "He slayed me." Similarly *louse* has the plural *lice* when it refers to insects but *louses* when it refers to people.

It is sometimes said that the trouble with slang is that it is constantly changing, that a term becomes old-fashioned almost at birth. It is certainly true that some terms, particularly those that get quick and heavy use, wither faster than the rose. One has only to consider how obsolete terms like *zorch, George, hot* (hot music), *skirt* (girl), *flame* (girl or boy friend), *squire* (escort) sound today.

However, a short but merry life is by no means the rule for slang terms. Some linger on decade after decade, century after century indeed, never becoming quite respectable and never dying out either. The word *dough* for money is just as hardy as it ever was, though no more reputable. Others which seem likely to outlive the century are *cop* (policeman), *nuts* (insane), *plastered* (drunk), *wino* (drunkard), *limey* (Englishman), *jalopy* (automobile), *cram* (study hard). There are thousands of such—well below the salt but also well established at the table.

Teachers of English are often libeled to the effect that they are dedicated to a relentless pursuit of slang and are never so happy as when they are stamping out a slang term. This is part of the larger charge that teachers of English aren't people. Everybody uses slang as a natural result of speaking a language, though it is presumably true that the young and effervescent like to play with language more than their elders do. It is also true that what sounds gay and cute and clever to the young may sound merely banal to older ears.

The effect of slang is closely bound with the personality of the user. It is not simply a question of whether the slang is new or not or clever or not or incisive or not. It is a question of the total effect of the speaker. The writer can remember a friend who used a rather small selection of slang, none of it particularly witty, and used it rather constantly with no infusion of new terms; yet his conversation always seemed to have a pleasant sparkle to it, presumably because he himself sparkled pleasantly. On the other hand, there was another character who always—*always*—greeted one with the salutation, "Dig that crazy cat." He usually prefaced this with the expression "Hey, hey!" This grew tiresome.

Slang spreads fast sometimes, but it doesn't transfer very easily. A person who moves into a new group and brings with him an old group's slang *may* find his language admired and imitated. More likely people will consider him boring or affected or unpleasantly foreign. If he persists with his old talk and doesn't adopt that of the new group, he will find that people begin saying, "Here comes that type; let's get out of here."

The language that we call slang merges imperceptibly with other varieties. Every trade or profession, vocation or avocation has a set of terms more or less peculiar to it and often differing little or not at all from what we think of as slang. Trade talk often serves much the same purpose that slang does—to give coherence to the group and to exclude outsiders. If you think of peddling dope as a profession, then such terms as *fix, mainline, horse, junkie* are not slang but technical terms of the business.

A familiar example of terms of a trade are those employed on ships. Since sailors have for centuries led a life apart, a whole vocabulary has grown up, not only for those activities peculiar to the sea but also for many that go on under other names ashore. Thus a sailor speaks of a *ladder*, not a *staircase*; a *deck*, not a *floor*; a *bulkhead*, not a *wall*; a *head*, not a *toilet*; a *companionway*, not a *corridor*; a *galley*, not a *kitchen*; *fore* and *aft* and *port* and *starboard*, not *front* and *back* and *left* and *right*.

These terms, as in many other trades, are often jealously guarded. The landlubber inspecting the ship, the apprentice making his first trip are likely to evoke the seaman's cheerful scorn as they use land words for sea things. On the other hand, the landsman isn't any better off if he comes aboard with the proper vocabulary. During the Second World War, when young men were trained ashore in their duties before being assigned to ships, they would often come onto the ships with the right words and lisp assuredly of going below and going aloft, of galley and messroom and fo'c'sle. This also would irritate the oldtimers, who sometimes revenged themselves by talking of going downstairs instead of below and out on the front porch instead of to the bow.

Ship talk is but an obvious example of the kind of special language that any trade or profession or occupation, indeed any coherent human activity cultivates. In printing, in wrestling, in dentistry, in the automobile trade, the participants tend to develop terms which they use and the outside world does not. One difference between this trade talk and slang is that the trade term has a respectability that the slang term lacks. Thus one can say that *dope addict* is more dignified than *junkie*, *policeman* more dignified than *cop*. But one could hardly say that ship's *wall* is more dignified than ship's *bulkhead*.

Slang and much trade talk too merge imperceptibly with that broad area of language that we call *colloquialism*. "Colloquial" is a rather vague word with different meanings for different people, but it would seem most generally to mean words and constructions that occur more commonly in speech than in writing. As such it would include slang but would not be limited to slang. It would include all the forms that people—educated as well as uneducated—use in conversation but tend to avoid in writing. A further distinction is that *slang* usually denotes words rather than phrases, whereas *colloquialism* can mean a word, a phrase, a sentence—indeed can apply to the whole tone of the utterance.

Compare the sentences "He better take it easy" and "He should proceed carefully." Both might be uttered by people of impeccable breeding and both might occur in writing as well as in speech. The difference is simply one of frequency and likelihood. "He better take it easy" is what you are likely to say if you are chatting casually with someone about the activity of a mutual friend. "He should proceed carefully" is what you are likely to write in a letter to the newspaper.

Colloquialisms are not hard to find, since they make up the bulk of our daily conversation. At random we can compare such colloquial and literary expressions as "do your darndest" (strive), "put something over on someone" (fool), "lend a hand" (assist), "kept his mouth shut" (refused to divulge something), "hit the books pretty hard" (studied diligently), "an awfully cute kid" (a strikingly handsome young man), "who you trying to fool" (whom are you seeking to mislead).

At some periods of history people have had the idea that writing is better the farther it is from speech and that colloquialisms should therefore regularly be avoided. But this is scarcely the mood of the present day. Naturally, if you want to sound dignified—and one *does* want to sound dignified sometimes—you choose dignified language and eschew terms that smack of shirtsleeves and ginger ale. If you're seeking a position with a corporation, you might damage your chances by writing, "I sure hope you'll let me take a crack at the job. I got a notion I'd do real well at it. Sure would try anyhow." It would normally be better sense to say, "I am hoping that you will find it possible to try me in the position. I feel that I would be able to do the work successfully. Certainly I would try very hard."

However, it is undeniable that the trend of much modern writing is toward a more colloquial tone. Not only in advertising, which is ever pally, but also in more or less serious books, magazine articles, newspaper accounts, the tendency is to reflect more and more the words and rhythms of ordinary speech. One finds, for example, a greater use than formerly of contracted forms: *don't, shouldn't, he'll,* in place of *do not, should not, he will.* Plain or folksy or even slang words are often preferred to elegant ones, and writers pay less attention than their predecessors did to the niceties of schoolbook grammar.

The explanation of this trend is no doubt to be sought in sociological developments. The educated class, formerly a pretty exclusive group, is now the great mass of the population. Reading and writing, even a hundred years ago, was the accomplishment of relatively few; now everybody does it. Today's writer is talking not to the country club set but to everybody in town, and he tries to talk everybody's language.

But he shouldn't try too hard. Writing should above all be consistent and natural and honest, and the writer who labors the "jus' us plain folks" approach is spotted as a phoney by the plain folks as well as the fancy ones. Here, from a cereal box, is an example of nobody's language:

> Often, when I'm out ridin' the range, I find myself thinkin' about all the daredevil deeds the Indian Chiefs did in days gone by, and of the unforgettable adventures of the gallant scouts and frontiersmen who met them in battle. I reckon all you young pardners of mine would like to hear all about them, too!

Even the youngest pardners may have an inkling that this cowboy rides the range on his portable typewriter.

One of the troubles of colorful language, slang or other, is that its color rubs off. The first time you hear and understand an expression like "Dig that crazy cat" you may find it exceptionally expressive, piquant, and moving. The second time you hear it, it isn't quite so exciting. The tenth time it has no effect at all. The fiftieth time it grates a little. The five hundredth time it may make you want to brain the speaker with a trombone.

If language isn't colorful to begin with, it doesn't pale. You can hear the sentence "Listen to that musician" five hundred times with no more pain the last time than the first. Clichés, or trite expressions, are simply dried up metaphors, figures of speech. They are racy ways of saying things but they have slowed down.

The first person who said "It was like walking on eggs" thought up a pretty clever comparison. When you read this for the first time, you get not only the information that the situation was delicate but a picture that reinforces and impresses the message. But this happens the first time only. After that you get only the information that the situation was delicate plus the fact that the writer is not very inventive. So also with "He fought like a tiger," "He behaved like a lamb," "He ran like a deer," "He ate like a pig," "He took a powder," "He pulled the wool over my eyes," "He's all wool and a yard wide," "She's pretty as a picture," "He spelled out the government's policy," "We'd better shake a leg," "An ocean of faces looked up at him," "A forest of masts filled the harbor," "She led him a merry chase," "It slid off him like water off a duck's back," "You can't fly on one wing," "He was as drunk as a lord, but his brother was as sober as a judge." All of these were more or less effective once.

Some groups of people seem to run more to clichés than others. Politicians are notorious, and some of their clichés, like "point with pride" and "view with alarm," have been laughed out of use. Sports writers and announcers also have difficulty avoiding trite phrases. One thinks of such expressions as "the fourth and final quarter" (one knows that the fourth quarter of a football game is the final one, but announcers seldom fail to point it out), "the bags are bulging," "circus catch," "smart little field general." All quarterbacks are smart little field generals, though some of them are also magicians. Line drives, proceeding toward the outfield, always scream, unless they go past something, like first, in which case they whistle. Pitchers are mostly big right-handers or little southpaws. Successful players come through in the clutch.

In fairness we should realize that sports writers and sports announcers deserve sympathy as much as criticism. They have to report, day after day and year after year, activities in which the same features are endlessly repeated. Moreover, they must always report these activities feverishly. The announcer is scarcely at liberty to say that today's football game is a pretty routine affair and the performers of no more than average competence. He must, every Saturday, bubble about how this is the most exciting grid spectacle that he and his colleagues have been privileged to see in a long time and how he wishes all us fans could be out there in the stadium with him to see these two great teams fighting their hearts out.

The cliché is every writer's enemy. Good writers fight clichés all the time, but few, even among the very best, win all the time. The triter the phrase, the more readily it comes to the mind, the more likely it is to slip into the sentence. You want to describe a mob, and you don't want to just say it was a big mob. You want to impress the reader with its size. "Sea of faces," you think, and you write it down. The trouble is that so many other writers have also written it down that it's lost all its blood. It no longer means anything more than "big mob," so you might as well have written "big mob" and been done with it.

The cliché is a difficulty for the young writer particularly, because he may not recognize the cliché when he sees it. "Sea of faces" may strike him as a bright new figure, not only expressive but original. One solution to this problem is experience. As we mature as readers, we become better equipped to recognize the stock phrases of the language as stock phrases. But the principal solution is to learn to distrust the pleasing phrase that comes too readily. It is only reasonable to suppose that the metaphor that jumps at you will have jumped at thousands of others before you.

It is very easy to write, to speak, to think in clichés. That's what most people do. They don't think for themselves but let the popular mind think for them. Their language is not personal but general, composed of public sentences with a few names changed to fit private conditions. There is nothing sinful about talking in clichés, and nobody can avoid it altogether. But those who don't avoid it at all betray laziness and mediocrity.

STUDY QUESTIONS AND EXERCISES

1. If you read crime stores or watch crime programs on television, list as many slang variants as you can think of or collect for such terms as *dope, gun, money, policeman, robbery*. Which of these slang terms would you avoid using among strangers as likely to suggest your association with criminals?

2. List as many slang terms current among college students as you can. What classifications are represented, such as abbreviations or initials for standard terms, terms for activities characteristic of college, local or temporary allusions, and so forth? Which slang terms would be familiar to most college-age young people? Which would be familiar to college students in general? Which would be familiar only to students on your own campus?

3. What are the current slang adjectives and nouns signifying approval? Signifying disapproval? Do you find the slang meanings in a general dictionary? In a slang dictionary?

4. Collect slang terms used by children and those used by your parents' generation. Do you use the same terms? Which terms can you find labeled as slang in a general dictionary? In a slang dictionary?

5. Conformity to current fads in dress is usually most noticeable among teen-agers. What fads in dress and slang are now current? Are they intended to identify the individual with the group and to dissociate him from other groups? What comparison can you make between teen-agers and trade groups? Is adult disapproval of certain styles of dress and haircuts analogous to disapproval of some speech habits as suggesting undesirable associations and fostering undesirable attitudes?

6. In view of Roberts' remarks about the present trend toward colloquialism, is the omission of *colloq.* in *Webster's Third International* in harmony with current trends in language?

7. Compare style in dress of the 1860's, the gay '90's, pre–First World War, the roaring '20's, and present styles: how may the trends in fashions be related to the trends in language? For what occasions in your life do you "dress up"? What people do you call by titles rather than by first names? Are you more likely to risk being too informal in speech and dress or being too formal? How can you apply your attitudes in matters of dress to your use of language? Some modern ministers are disturbed by members of their congregation coming to church in sports clothes. Ask your parents and grandparents if this is a new problem or, like many complaints about modern times, one characteristic of every older generation deploring the ways of youth.

8. Look up the literal meaning of *cliché* and *steretoype*. How does the origin of the terms emphasize the lack of individuality they stand for in language?

9. Frank Sullivan has written a number of "cliché expert" interviews. Look up one of them, in a subject you are fairly familiar with, and analyze the characteristics of the clichés used.

10. Supply the missing term in these pairs or triplets of clichés: "nip and ———," "hale and ———," "bright and ———," "kith and ———," "sink or ———," "live or ———," "survive or ———," "hammer and ———," "free, white, and ———," "wine, woman, and ———," "without regard to race, creed, or ———."

11. Turn to the appendix of Wentworth and Flexner's *Dictionary of American Slang* and study the slang expressions relating to *boy, eater, fiend, head, jockey, man,* and *pusher*. Analyze the slang patterns into which these words fall in combined forms.

12. In a collegiate dictionary, select an alphabetical section, such as "dod-dol," either two consecutive columns or two separate ones, and compare with the same alphabetical area in Wentworth and Flexner's *Dictionary of American Slang*. Which words appear in both dictionaries? Which *definitions* of those words in Wentworth and Flexner do not appear in the collegiate dictionary? Which *words* in Wentworth and Flexner do not appear in the collegiate dictionary? What seems to be the relation between slang and nonslang vocabulary?

13. Browse through a collegiate dictionary and collect a dozen entries marked *Slang*. Look up the same terms in an older unabridged dictionary and in *Webster's Third International*. Have you found examples of slang which became acceptable, of slang that died out, of slang that survives as slang? What conclusions can you draw from your small list of terms as to what kind of slang survives and why?

14. In the Preface to Wentworth and Flexner, *Dictionary of American Slang*, pp. ix–x, read the two linguistic "case histories." Using them as models, do a case history of yourself or a close friend, showing contacts with subgroups and a few examples of slang acquired from each. How does this case history illustrate Flexner's "three cultural conditions" (p. x)?

15. List as many slang terms as you can which are used among your own subgroup to describe people and actions. Do these terms show subgroup criteria? Do they illustrate Flexner's statement, in the Preface to the *Dictionary of American Slang* (p. xi), that slang "tends toward degradation rather than elevation"?

16. If you belong to an occupational subgroup, list a dozen or so terms found in the cant or jargon of that group. Are any of these terms offensive or vulgar? Would any of these terms be unintelligible outside the group?

17. Test the awareness of slang as an entity by collecting from students who are not in your English class definitions and examples of

slang. How do their definitions of slang compare with those in the discussion by Roberts and in Flexner's Preface to the *Dictionary of American Slang*? Are the students' examples classed as slang in the dictionary? Would the general public be more aware or less aware of slang as an entity than college students are?

25

Now Everyone Is Hip About Slang

Bergen Evans

Although slang is generally regarded as improper for standard usage, many words which begin as slang later become acceptable. In this article in the New York Times *Magazine for March 22, 1964, Professor Bergen Evans of Northwestern University discusses the background of some words once considered slang.*

One of the most interesting changes taking place in our language today is the acceptance of an enormous amount of slang into standard English. Formerly it often took centuries for a piece of slang to gain such acceptance, if it ever gained it. Dr. Johnson, in 1755, insisted that words such as **frisky, gambler** and **conundrum** "ought not to be admitted to the language." But times have changed. So rapid, indeed, has the process of absorption become that there is a possibility that slang, as a clearly delimitable form of language in America, may be on the way out.

Square, for instance, in its slang meaning, has lost almost all of its original sting of irreverence (a characteristic of slang). It is no longer "secret" talk and its use certainly doesn't mark the user as one who is "in." It seems highly likely that it will soon be regarded as standard.

Hip, to choose another example from the beatnik talk which only yesterday seemed so wild and strange, is listed in Merriam-Webster's Third International merely as a variation of **hep,** and **hep** (though I would disagree) is not labeled slang. (That Merriam-Webster chose to define **hep** as the dominant form, illustrates the unavoidable lag of dictionaries; **hep** has been "out," decidedly un-hip, for years!) Also not marked as slang is **gig**—a job, especially a jazzman's job. **Dig, cool, chick, bug, bag** and **hung up** are labeled slang but it is not unreasonable to assume that these will either have disappeared from use, or will have been accepted as standard, within a decade or two. (A good deal of British slang has apparently already been accepted. A new edition of The Concise Oxford Dictionary, published last month, contains a number of "slang" expressions without indication in the text that they differ from standard English.)

Those who get disturbed about slang as something "modern" that is "corrupting" the language ought to know that it is as old as language itself. Indeed, it *is* language, and one of the minor pleasures of reading is to come across it in the literature of the past. Chaucer, for instance, uses **gab** exactly as we use it today. A desirable woman was a **piece** in the 14th century, and a **broad** or a **frail** in the 16th. Bishop Latimer, in a sermon before Edward VI (1547), said that those who had defrauded the King of money ought to "make restitution . . . cough up." John Adams, in a morning-after letter (1774) said, "We drank sentiments until 11 o'clock. Lee and Harrison were very high." Charlotte Brontë referred to a foolish person as a sap—as others had been doing for 200 years before her.

From the difference between certain standard words in Latin and in the Romance languages, we know that even the Romans used slang. Thus, although the formal Latin word for head was *caput*, the French is *la tête* and the Italian *la testa*—which obviously derive from the Latin *testa*, an earthen pot. And where the formal Latin word for leg was *crus*, the French is *la jambe* and the Italian *la gamba* (whence "gams" and "gamboling"), derived from the Latin *gamba*, hoof. The Romans wrote formally about the head and the leg, but they apparently spoke of "the pot" and "the hoof."

One of the purposes of using slang, as with thieves' cant, from which much of it has sprung, is to make it possible for certain groups *not* to be understood by the uninitiated. Its use marks the user as one of the knowing, a member of a prestigious in-group. (And when the word is no longer good slang, its user is no longer "in.") It is also used to shock and, if possible, irritate. Thus **neat** is a term of approval with the younger set even though a labored defiance of neatness is obligatory among them. Even more useful, or more used, are expressions of contempt—**drip, clod, creep, dope, jerk** and **fink**—which reinforce status by rejecting the unworthy.

A large element in the creation of slang is sheer playfulness, an extension of the impulse that leads to such duplications of sound as **hotsy-totsy, heebie-jeebies** and **okeydoke.** The word **slang** is itself slang and embodies much of what it designates: it is breezy, catchy, eminently suitable, yet intriguing; we feel that we know its meaning but we find it hard to define and difficult to trace. It is probably language that is being slung about instead of being handled with stately consideration. In an early-15th-century poem we are told of one who "bold words did sling" and there *is* a boldness and a sling in slang. It risks daring metaphors and audacious allusions; it impudently defies propriety and dissolves with triumphant laughter into meaninglessness when solemnity indignantly demands that it explain itself.

Pomposity is slang's natural enemy, which may account for the fact that there are probably more slang words that describe drunkenness—the antithesis of dignity—than any other state or activity. Solemnity meets the condition with the plain **drunk**, the disapproving **drunken**, the scientific **intoxicated** and the highfalutin **inebriated**. The Quakers, with gentle evasion, called it **tired**. But slang riots in every degree of its indignity, from the mild **lit**, through the hilarious **plastered** to the terminal **stiff**.

Benjamin Franklin once compiled a "Drinker's Dictionary" containing 228 terms, but "The American Thesaurus of Slang" found it necessary 200 years later to list four times that number. And it is interesting, and perhaps significant, that modern slang seems to represent drunkenness less as a disruptable escapade, a breaking away from dull routine (as in **spree, toot, jag, bender, binge**) than as a sodden stasis (**loaded, pie-eyed, stewed, blotto**).

Much slang is humorously euphemistic. There are some situations so ghastly that one must ignore them or laugh at them. Airsickness, for example, is so outrageous an assault on our dignity (coupled, as it usually is, with humiliating fear) that it has come to be "one of those things we just don't talk about." The airlines—who can't ignore it—refer with ludicrous delicacy to the equipment provided in the seat backs as "discomfort containers." But college students—who, at least in retrospect, seem to find the business amusing—call them "barff bags."

At one end of the gamut of slang's humor is the inane—what Oliver Wendell Holmes called "the blank checks of a bankrupt mind" —such fatuities as "Sez you!", "Banana oil!" and "So's your old man!" But at the other are such concepts as "to join the majority" (to die), which goes back to ancient Rome, or the 18th century's "scandal broth," for tea, or the British lower classes' late-19th-century "nobby" (also "with knobs on") for smart, elegant or fashionable—a shrewder appraisal of Victorian design and decor than the upper classes were capable of making.

Grose, in his "Classical Dictionary of the Vulgar Tongue" (1796), tells us that "a forward girl, ready to oblige every man that shall ask her" was called an "Athanasian wench"—and is so flattering to his reader as not even to explain why. The explanation is that the first two words of the Athanasian creed are: "Whosoever desires. . . ."

If such allusiveness seems too recondite for anyone but dwellers in the groves of Academe, one must consider rhyming slang, which originated in the underworld, was developed by London Cockneys in the 19th century, enjoyed a vogue for several generations and is now disappearing.

Here the meaning lies in a word which is not spoken at all but which rhymes with the last of two or more words in a phrase. At first, similarity of sound was the sole connection—as **cherry ripe** for pipe or **apples and pears** for stairs. But Cockney wit and humor and linguistic imaginativeness (what ignorant nonsense in Shaw to assume that Professor Higgins's English was better, as speech, than was Eliza Doolittle's —Eliza's class danced linguistic circles around the gentry!) soon wove an implication of meaning into the allusion of sound. So a liar became a **holy friar**, a church, a **chicken perch**, a lodger, an **artful dodger**, a gal, **rob my pal**, kids, **God forbids**, and so on—in one of the giddiest whirls language has ever been swept into.

And then, as though this were not involved and clever enough, the rhyming word itself was sometimes merely implied as a part of a well-known phrase. Thus **china** came to mean mate because "plate" rhymes with "mate"; and **Oliver** to mean fist because the unspoken "Twist" rhymes with "fist."

Now all of this surely marks slang, not as a degeneration of language, but rather as a sort of spume or spindrift of language riding its forward-surging wave; but, even so, language, as much a part of it as law or liturgy and shaped and controlled by the same forces that shape and control standard speech.

This is illustrated by the thousands of instances in which slang repeats the etymology of a standard word. Thus **to impose** is, literally, "to put something over on," **to excoriate** "to take the hide off," **to apprehend** "to catch on," **to converse** "to go round with" and **to exaggerate** "to pile it on." He who is **ecstatic** is "beside himself"; he has been driven out of himself, or "sent." He who is **replete** is "fed up," and that which is **superlative** has been "laid on thick." **Handsome** originally meant "pleasant to handle" or, as the young now say, "smooth." To be **recalcitrant** is to "kick" backwards (from Latin *calx, calcis*, heel).

To be **dependent** is to be a "hanger-on" and to be **enraptured** is to be "carried away"—gone, man, gone! Where the meticulous speaker of standard English might ask "What's fretting you?", a slangy speaker might ask, "What's eating you?" And where the standard speaker might stiffly aver that he was "not prone to accept" a certain imposition, the other might more vividly insist that he "would not take it lying down." Yet both have said the same thing; for **fretting** means voracious or gnawing eating and **prone** means lying face downwards.

Many slang words pass into standard use and once they do, of course, they don't sound slangy at all. Among such now-sturdy-respectables are **club** (social), **dwindle, flout, foppish, freshman, fretful, glib, hubbub, nice, ribaldry, scoundrel, simper, swagger, tidy, tantrums, tarpaulin** and **trip** (journey).

Even more interesting is that many slang words stay in the language for centuries, but remain slang. **Booze**, once standard, became dialectal and then slang and has remained slang for centuries, spawning recently, in British slang, **boozer** (a pub). **Brass** (impudence) is also centuries old. So is to **chisel** (to use trickery), and so are **frisk** (to search a person for weapons), **corporation** (large belly), **leery, pad** (bed), **mum, blab, gag** (joke), **pigeon** (dupe), **hick** (rustic), **grub** (food) and hundreds of others.

A word can remain slang and undergo a semantic change just as if it were standard. Forty years ago a **nut** was a ludicrous eccentric; today he is one who is dangerously deranged. Like so many other things in the world, the word has acquired a menace.

Still other words pass from slang to standard within a few years of their creation. **Cello,** a 19th-century clipping of **violoncello,** and printed as 'cello up until a few years ago, is now standard. **Bleachers** was slang in 1904, but fully standard within two decades. **Sweater** was slang in 1880, but standard by 1914. These last two words, by the way, illustrate the way in which a slang word can lose its metaphorical vitality in the process of becoming a standard verbal symbol. We have to stop to think of the idea of bleaching in the **bleachers** and, offhand, would see nothing contradictory in a reference to a woman's wearing a dainty cashmere **sweater.**

Except through the caprice of usage, there's no accounting for the status of words. **Bored** (wearied by dullness), for instance, was listed as slang in 1722, but is now standard. But **flabbergast,** which was included in the same list, remains slang. The modern slang use of **dizzy** to mean foolish in a featherheaded way ("dizzy dame") recaptures the word's original standard meaning: a 9th-century West Saxon version of Matthew XXV, 1–3, says of the 10 virgins who went forth to meet the bridegroom, "Five of them were dizzy . . . and took lamps but they didn't take no oil with them."

It is, in fact, becoming increasingly difficult to draw a hard and fast line between slang and colloquial, and colloquial and standard, and thus to establish that this or that word is definitely not acceptable in dignified speech or writing. **Blues,** for instance, is still slang for it means low spirits. But if it means a genre of songs expressing low spirits, it is standard.

Jazz in its meaning of sexual intercourse is still low slang, very close to the underworld cant it originally was. As a description of a kind of music, however, it is standard. But in its recently acquired vogue meaning of fussy routine or nonsense ("and all that jazz") it is slang again.

Kid meaning a child was cant in the late 16th century, but had become slang by the mid-18th century, and is now colloquial. The verb **to kid** (to tease by jesting, as with a child), remains slang. But **kidnap** has been standard for almost 300 years. **Gal** is slang only when a deliberate mispronunciation of girl; if it is the speaker's natural pronunciation, it is simply a social or regional variant. In 1748 Swift singled out **mob** (a clipping of *mobile vulgus,* the moving or fickle populace) for particular detestation as a corruption of the language. But despite the Dean's disapproval the word stuck and is now standard when it means a riotous assemblage.

A striking illustration of the extent to which even experts disagree in this matter of labeling is furnished by comparison of Wentworth and Flexner's "Dictionary of American Slang" (1960) with the Merriam-Webster Third International (1961). Of 2,355 words which Wentworth and Flexner list as slang, and with the meanings of which the Third International agrees, the Third International lists only 549 as slang.

In the face of such a divergence one must wonder if slang is not losing its identity. The increasing frankness of all expression has weakened its euphemistic value. The disappearance of fixed social classes has removed one of the chief motivations for its impertinence. And its universal use has destroyed its secrecy and reduced its value as an expression of in-group superiority.

There is also just too much of it around for it to be in any way esoteric. "The American Thesaurus of Slang" lists over 100,000 terms and the "Dictionary of American Slang" estimates that slang makes up perhaps one-fifth of the words we use. A single issue of Time—that of Jan. 10, 1964—contains 266 words and phrases that in the days of The Literary Digest would have been considered substandard and unfit for serious writing. The Washington Post of the same date contains 152.

Very little contemporary slang has enough shock value left to tickle our fancy. The beatnik and teen-age jargon, of which so much has been made, is pretty unimaginative stuff when compared with, say, rhyming slang or the 18th-century slang in Grose's "Classical Dictionary of the Vulgar Tongue." Impudence, impiety and indecency are now in the public domain and rarely startle. Greed, brutality and what passes for religion can still shock, but the mark of the in-group today is more the capacity to *be* shocked than the ability to shock.

American slang had a period of vigor and we were proud of it. "When Americans are through with the English language," Mr. Dooley boasted, "it will look as if it had been run over by a musical comedy." Perhaps our delight in slang was part of our traditional defiance of the British; after all, it was the *King's* English that we were tying in knots. But now that we are the senior partner, and it is the *President's* English, some of the fun may have gone out of twisting its tale. And perhaps there will be a renaissance of slang in British English—to mock and startle *us*.

STUDY QUESTIONS AND EXERCISES

1. Look up some slang meanings of common terms, such as *broad* and *frail*, in both Wentworth and Flexner's *Dictionary of American Slang* and the *Concise Oxford Dictionary* (1964): does the latter give the slang meanings? Are they labeled as slang?

2. In Hemingway's novel *The Sun Also Rises, piece* is used in speaking of Brett. What other slang terms do you find? What relation might there be between "a frail" and Hamlet's "Frailty, thy name is woman"? Can you cite other uses in literature of any of the slang terms Evans uses for examples? (By an amusing coincidence, *broadcloth* was once called *ladycloth*.)

3. Have you observed changes in in-group language that serve to exclude those who do not keep up with the group?

4. What are the impulses behind slang, according to Evans? What is "slang's natural enemy"? Look up in the Appendix of Wentworth and Flexner, *Dictionary of American Slang*, the terms for drunkenness and a list of Cockney rhyming slang.

5. Can you further illustrate Evans' point that standard speech often began with a slanglike concept? Look up *supercilious:* what facial expression does the literal meaning suggest?

6. Compare Roberts and Evans on the passing of slang words into respectable English and the continuation of slang status of words for centuries. What principles are stated or can be derived from the examples?

7. To appreciate fully the point about *sweater*, consider the "proper" distinctions that used to be made by genteel females: "Horses sweat, men perspire, ladies glow." Men should wear perspirers and ladies, glowers!

8. For what reasons is slang losing its identity? Do you find it difficult to recognize slang as such? Why?

26

The Tainted *Ain't* Once More

Archibald A. Hill

Professor Hill of the University of Texas, writing in College English *for June, 1965, reviews the controversy surrounding the usage status of* ain't *as well as the phonological development of the word.*

A recent issue of *College English* devotes twenty pages to *Webster's III* and *ain't*.[1] Professor Sheridan Baker leads off with a denunciation of the sinful union of linguists and lexicographers which he holds responsible for the illegitimate monosyllable. Some of the more personal of his charges are well answered by the lady he attacks. Father Ong closes the discussion with a calm and urbane defense of the *Third*. It may be unnecessary to defend the *Third* further, since it has been holding its own quite well against all the claymores of Clan Macdonald, but it is still worth while to discuss *ain't* in an endeavor to add to the facts and minimize the moralizing.

First of all, *ain't* has a history, long enough to show that it is not the product of merely recent linguistic carelessness and decay. Its phonological development has been touched on in a number of the standard histories, and has been the subject of one brief article.[2] *Ain't* must be assigned to a blending of several developments. One is the form *air* /ehr/ for *are*, with an immediately following *-nt*, reduced by loss of juncture and stress from an independent *not*.[3] In position before /-nt/, the post-vocalic /r/ was subject to loss not only in the areas of

---

[1] *College English*, Nov. 1964: "The Error of *Ain't*," p. 91; Virginia McDavid, "More on *Ain't*," p. 104; and "Hostility, Literacy, and *Webster III*," p. 106.

[2] Raven McDavid, "*Ain't I* and *Aren't I*," *Language*, 17 (1941), 7–59.

[3] The pronunciation /ehr/ for *are* is attested by rhymes in Donne. See H. C. Wyld, *A History of Modern Colloquial English*, p. 248. Gustav Kirchner, *Die Zehn Hauptverben Des Englischen* (Halle, 1952), p. 58, erroneously derives *ain't* directly from a form spelled *airn't*. The *air* sequence did not, and does not, represent * /eyr/, but /ehr/.

The notation used in this article is that of Trager and Smith, and statements about juncture indicate a physical event.

general loss of post-vocalic /r/ as in Received Standard in Britain, and in Eastern New England, but in most other dialects as well. Examples of this earlier loss of /r/ are forms such as *passel* for *parcel*, or *gal* for *girl*.[4] The immediate product of /r/-loss in this word would be /ehnt/ with a centering off-glide, a vocalic nucleus which also arose, but from different sources, in /kehnt/ for *can't*. The vowel nucleus then underwent further development, replacing the centering off-glide by a glide to high front, giving /eynt/ for *ain't*, and /keynt/ *cain't* for *can't*.[5] This particular line of development gave the form which replaces *we aren't, they aren't,* and so forth.

A second source, belonging properly to the first person singular, is the form *amn't* pronounced as [ǽmnt], phonemically /ǽmənt/. This form with the enclitic /-nt/ added directly to *am*, is said by Jespersen to be common in Ireland.[6] The form was often unstressed and rapidly pronounced, so that assimilation and loss of the /m/ is a natural process. This gives the form spelled in the eighteenth and nineteenth centuries as *an't*, one of whose pronunciations was probably /æhnt/, with off-glide.[7] This nucleus was leveled, I believe, with the /eh/ of the plural /ehnt/, and shared in its later development. The process here described seems preferable to assuming that the result of loss of /m/ in *amn't* gave a long *a*, phonemically /ah/, at a date early enough to share in the development of long *a* to /ey/ as in *name*. The chronology is uncertain at best, but a long *a* in *an't* would have to have arisen before 1400, in the usual view, to share in this development.[8]

A third source for *ain't* is *haven't*, again with the enclitic /-nt/. This form shows exactly the same loss of /v/ and development of the vowel nucleus to /ey/ as has occurred in *lady* from Middle English *lauedie*.[9] There are two possible sources for the vowel nucleus /ey/ in (*h*)*ain't* from *haven't*. The less probable one is that *have* in this form preserves the vowel lengthened in an open syllable which is the source for /ey/ in *behave*. It is true that there are occasional rhymes like that in *have-grave* found in "On Top of Old Smokey," but in general /ey/ forms are not found in the paradigm of *have*, and would be somewhat specially unlikely in the rapid and unstressed form which gives the enclitic /-nt/. The second source is lengthening after the loss of /v/, though assigning the vowel to this source involves some revision of the chronology. Jordan, on grounds that seem quite secure, places the loss of /v/

---

[4] See my "Early Loss of *r* Before Dentals," *PMLA*, 55 (1940), 308–59.

[5] Cf. McDavid for examples of /keynt/, and /eynt/ for *aunt*.

[6] Otto Jespersen, *A Modern English Grammar on Historical Principles*, vol. V, pp. 432–33.

[7] Jespersen, pp. 430–34.

[8] Wyld, p. 247.

[9] Richard Jordan, *Handbuch der Mittelenglischen Grammatik* (1925), p. 190.

with lengthening of the vowel in the fourteenth century, yet the forms spelled -'*nt* do not appear until the mid-seventeenth century.[10] It is not necessary, however, to suppose that the fully enclitic form /-nt/ developed three centuries earlier than the spelling evidence for it. It is only necessary to suppose that the juncture which marked off the completely independent *not* was lost early enough to produce the conditions for loss of /v/. If so, then, this carries back the first step in the complex development of *ain't* well into the middle ages.

The phonological development throws some light on the disapproval of *ain't*. McDavid remarks, quite rightly, that *ain't* lost favor because of the spread of the socially privileged form /ahnt/, but this is not the whole story. There are reasons for believing that the "broad a" words are the result of restoration of an /r/, or in some instances an /l/, in words where these consonants had been subject to early loss. Thereafter, a restored sequence /ar/ would be subject to the general loss of post-vocalic /r/ which gave /ah/ as in British /kahv/ and /stahv/ for *carve* and *starve*. The restoration of a popularly lost /r/ would explain the preference for /arnt/ and its derivative /ahnt/, and would also explain the preference for the etymologically unjustified /kahnt/ for *can't*. These forms are, in this view, all examples of regressions, some of them false. Furthermore, the /r/-less forms were rejected by the same process which rejected *passel* for *parcel*. A fact of distribution suggests something further about this development. It is striking that it is just in the regions where post-vocalic /r/ is preserved as a retroflex consonant that forms like *aren't I* and /káhnt+ay/ are rejected. That is, the so-called "loss of *r*" was actually a loss of retroflexion, giving a centering off-glide, strictly an /h/ in Trager-Smith phonemics, but identified with /r/ in popular analysis. I take it that it was just this non-retroflex *r* which was restored, and this is the final explanation of rejection of /árnt+ay/ beside acceptance of /áhnt+ty/.

If the phonological history of *ain't* explains some things about it, its syntactic distribution explains some others. Almost all writers since Fowler, including McDavid and Atwood, have commented that *ain't I* is more needed than *I ain't* or *ain't he* and thus presumably more common. These comments are often misunderstood or ignored, so that it seems worth while to give a complete statement, even at the risk of repetition.

The construction in which *ain't* is particularly likely is the tag-question sentence, that form of it in which the first half is positive and the second negative, as in

They're American, aren't they?

The reverse form, as given below, is not involved—

---

[10] Jordan, p. 190, and Jespersen, p. 430.

They aren't American, are they?

In all but the first person singular, two forms of the negative tag are possible

They are American, aren't they?

You			you
We			we
He	is	isn't	he
She			she
It			it

OR

They are American, are they not?

You			you
We			we
He	is	is	he
She			she
It			it

In the first person singular we have only one of these forms

I am American, am I not?

The form with enclitic /-nt/ leads to *ain't, aren't* or *am'nt* and so to trouble. The depth of the trouble can be measured without disputes by contrasting the distribution of *is he not* with *isn't he* since both these forms are undisputed. If the positive half of the tag-question sentence is one which is formal, elevated, or bookish, then *is he not* is the more likely, as in

He is dressed with meticulous attention to detail, is he not?

If the positive half is informal, then *isn't he* is the more likely, as in

He's all dolled up, isn't he?

It is, of course, in sentences of this latter type that the pull to *ain't I* is most strongly felt, and for testing, sentences of both types should be used. I do not believe that the Linguistic Atlas type-question, "I'm right," with tag, was sufficiently clearly marked to give a clear picture of the distinction.

When we pass on to describe the status and use-habits of *ain't* we discover that there is some evidence that *ain't* has gone down in status, rather than risen as the Clan Macdonald fears. Here is Jespersen on the subject—

> Dean Alford says: "It ain't certain. I ain't going . . . very frequently used, even by highly educated persons." And in Anthony Hope people of the best society are represented as saying it ain't and ain't it. Dr. Furnivall is the only educated man I personally have heard using this form habitually.[11]

Whether these uses are to be explained on the principle that only a duchess can afford to wear rags, I leave to the reader.

In what follows, I base my description on my own usage, with a statement as accurate as I know how to make it. Results of questioning of informants, with percentages, are not readily available to me, and I also think that if we had a dozen or more full descriptions like that here given, the status of *ain't* would be better clarified than by more samples, which are usually lamentably thin.

To give a brief statement of background, necessary before usage is described, I am educated, experienced in formal speaking and writing, and in upper middle age. My dialect type is that of Southern California, with a parental background from Northern Kentucky.

In the styles appropriate to formal speaking and to all forms of writing, I avoid *ain't* completely in all syntactic situations, except for the exceptions named below.

I. Formal Speaking and Writing

1. *Ain't* occurs in quotations, as in the song-line, "Ain't we got fun." Also in proverbial sayings and tags like "that ain't hay."
2. *Ain't* occurs in word-plays and other jokes, as "What's the worst word in the language? *T'ain't ain't.*"
3. *Ain't* occurs in deliberate contrast with an otherwise elevated style. An example of this occurs in Professor Baker's article—

> The old pervading desire to show the schoolmarm that the cultured ain't so cultured . . . . (p. 94)

The contrastive use is often for the purpose of shocking the reader or hearer, something I try to avoid.

4. *Ain't* occurs in narrative, as a means of characterizing the speaker. This use occurs in my speech only in anecdotes, and does not occur in my writing, since I do not write fiction. I should add that

---

[11] Jespersen, p. 434.

anecdotes are usually informal, but may occur in speech or lecture which is otherwise formal enough.

II. Informal Speaking and Writing

1. When I pass to my use of *ain't* in informal speech, two sets of limitations appear. The first of these depends on the social status of the person or persons addressed. I may use *ain't* only to persons of approximately my own age group. That is I would not use it to children or young adults not past college age. I may use *ain't* only to persons of approximately the same social status as myself. Thus I would not use *ain't* to the president of my university, but would use it to colleagues. I would not use *ain't* to a servant, but do use it freely to my family.

2. A second set of limitations concerns my own relationship to the person or persons addressed, and my own emotional and social re-action to the addressee. I must have established a personal relation with the addressee, he must be a person I like, and I must believe that he is not the sort of person likely to be shocked by informal speech. Thus I do not ordinarily use *ain't* unless I am on a first-name basis with the person addressed. Even were I on a first-name basis with Professor Baker, my speech with him would be impeccable, not to say stilted. Within these social and personal limitations, use of *ain't* is always possible and meaningful for me. It is a way of establishing friendly relations, and as with the use of first names, I should retreat from all informality if the person addressed did not respond.

In the negative tag-question, my use of *ain't* does not quite parallel other types. First of all, the only alternative open to me is *am I not*. *Amn't I*, and the form quoted by Fowler, *am not I*, are both unknown to me. As to *aren't I*, which I should certainly pronounce with a retro-flex /r/, I agree with Fowler's statement that the construction is un-grammatical. It is perhaps ironical that I know that such a reaction is emotionally rather than logically based, since *aren't I* would be a step towards removing an anomaly in the paradigm of *be*. Reactions of acceptance and rejection are no more free of emotional components for me than for any speaker. In situations where the style makes me reject *am I not*, the social and personal situation can also make me reject *ain't I*. When this happens, I avoid the construction altogether, and fall back on such a circumlocution as

I'm all dolled up, isn't that so?

Professor Baker and others object to the *Third's* treatment of *ain't* because of an inadequate labelling of types of usage. I do not believe that labels applied to *ain't* in the *Second* are really adequate either. A set of labels something like those given below would be required for the types I have described, and the other common ones we all know.

I. In Formal Speaking and Writing

1. Low prestige—The habitual use of *ain't* without respect to social and personal limitations. But remember Jespersen's description of Dr. Furnivall!
2. Quotative—Use in quotations, as "that ain't hay."
3. Jocular—In word plays and jokes. It should be added that a form can not be safely labelled jocular unless there is some evidence of witticism, however weak.
4. Contrastive—See the example quoted from Baker. As with 3 above, it is not safe to assume contrastive use without evidence, since to label all occurrences of *ain't* as either jocular or contrastive gives an all too convenient way of rejecting exceptions.
5. Characterizing—Placed in dialogue to characterize the speaker.

II. In Informal Speech

1. Friendly—Used by a speaker to establish friendly relations under the social and personal limitations described, or variants thereof.
2. Congruently informal—Used in a style which shows by characteristics of grammar, syntax and vocabulary, that it is informal. The congruently informal style can occur, of course, in either writing or speaking.

Such a proliferation of divisions and subdivisions in labelling would hardly be practical for any dictionary, yet had it been adopted even for this most important of shibboleths alone, it might have saved much ink, paper, and ill-will.

I do not wish to say more about *ain't* specifically. However, Professor Baker shares many confusions, and these may be the reason that he seems to fear bogeymen. Most of his confusions have been often refuted, and would be easy to point out again, but there is one of them which is worth attention. Professor Baker is sure that it is linguistics and linguists who have captured the *Third*, and have deliberately falsified facts and destroyed standards in order to produce the entry on *ain't*. It is worth comparing this entry with a much earlier one, from a book which can not have been unknown to, and without influence on, the editors of the *Third*. Here is Dr. Gove's entry

> though disapproved by many and more common in less educated speech, used orally in most parts of the U.S. by many cultivated speakers esp. in the phrase *ain't I*.

Here is the crucial part of the earlier article on *ain't*

> Though *I'm not* serves well enough in statements, there is no ab-
> breviation but *a(i)n't I* for *am I not?* or *am not I?* and the shame-
> faced reluctance with which these full forms are often brought out
> betrays the speaker's sneaking affection for the *ain't I* that he (or
> still more she) fears will convict him of low breeding.

If we strip away the Olympian superiority, the diffuseness of style, and
the possible mistake in *am not I* (in speech known to me this form
does not occur without something following), the information in this
passage is exactly the same as that in Dr. Gove's entry. Dr. Gove has
said that he and his staff never relied on books about language except
as corroborative evidence, yet the parallel is striking. Indeed it is so
striking that I believe this passage is the ultimate source of the Gove
entry, though Dr. Gove may well not have realized it. This passage
seems to me also to underlie the choice of test sentences in the Atlas,
and consequently the chain of descriptions based on the Atlas; that is,
those of Atwood, Mrs. McDavid, and Mrs. Malmstrom. Is this passage
then from a linguist, carrying on "the linguistic crusade"? Not at all.
The passage is from Fowler.[12]

STUDY QUESTIONS AND EXERCISES

1. Father Ong is the author of selection 11 in Part 2. Virginia
McDavid is the wife of Raven McDavid, author of selection 19 in Part
3. The opponents of *Webster's Third*, Sheridan Baker and Dwight Macdonald, are on the panel of 100 of the *American Heritage Dictionary*.
Why does Hill continue the discussion of *ain't* in which the above
persons were involved?

2. What, according to Hill, are the three sources of *ain't*?

3. When and why did *ain't* lose favor? Which use of *ain't* fills
a need in the language and should therefore logically be the most
common? There is a parallel need in English for a question appealing
for confirmation, less formal than "Isn't that so?" (German "*Nicht
wahr?*" French "*N'est-ce pas?*" and Spanish "*No es verdad?*" have an
idiomatic frequency lacking in any equivalent phrase in English.) English spoken in Milwaukee supplies the lack with "enna?" or "aina?"
This may be a version of "Ain't it?" by analogy with "Ain't I?" In
Milwaukee speech, Hill's sentence, "I'm all dolled up, isn't that so?"
would be "I'm all dolled up, aina?"

---

[12] *A Dictionary of Modern English Usage* (1926), p. 45.

4. Describe your own use of *ain't*, and, after careful observation, that of someone else: (a) of your age and social status; (b) an older, well-educated person; (c) an older person of less than high school education. Using Hill's classifications of uses, what range of uses do you discover?

5. Why does Hill withhold until the last word the source of the quoted entry on *ain't*? Compare *ain't* in Wilson Follett, *Modern American Usage*, and Evans and Evans, *Dictionary of Contemporary American Usage*, with the discussion by Hill and the quotation from Fowler. What do you conclude about the use of *ain't* syntactically and socially?

27

Big Daddy's Dramatic Word Strings

Dan Isaac

*Professor Isaac of Queens College analyzes Tennessee Williams' manipula-
tion of language in the speeches of Big Daddy in* Cat on a Hot Tin Roof,
*giving special attention to Williams' use of poetic rhythm and repetition as
vehicles of dramatic intensity. Professor Isaac's article appeared in* American
Speech *for December, 1965.*

Sometimes you can be too successful. Tennessee Williams was
just that when he created the character of Big Daddy, who so dominates the second act of *Cat on a Hot Tin Roof* that Elia Kazan would
not direct the play unless the third act were rewritten.[1] The original
version sent Big Daddy offstage at the end of the second act and allowed him only to groan in pain from the wings during the third. Kazan
simply did not want to lose a character who generated so much dramatic excitement from the climactic moments of the play. His request
had little to do with plot. The second act was almost overwhelming because of Big Daddy; the third act, without his reappearance, would be
a letdown beyond any director's ability to trick things together.

What is the excitement about Big Daddy? How does he succeed in
arousing the emotion of the audience to such a high pitch of admiration and active concern? To a certain extent it is by his dramatic function, but that does not fully explain it. After all, the plot is simply that
old hack theme of who is going to be included in the family will—the
how and the why of the hungry heirs. A dying patriarch who has yet to
dispose of his property need not necessarily be sympathetic or even dra-
matically exciting. But the way Tennessee Williams does him, he is
both.

The explanation is in his use of language. Big Daddy is a rough, crude
poet who can command and strategically employ both bombast and
lyricism. He delights us with the poetic power of his speech, while care-

---

[1] Tennessee Williams, *Cat on a Hot Tin Roof* (Copyright 1955 by Tennessee
Williams. All rights reserved. Reprinted by permission of the publisher, New Directions Publishing Corporation), pp. 151–52.

fully maintaining the pose of a man who contemns culture. To do this successfully, he must stay within the circumscribed word choice of slang. Anything fancy would be peculiar or precious, and he is, therefore, forced to fall back upon the natural rhythms of local speech for his effect. This is his starting place. Just how he maneuvers into more complex patterns is the interesting secret of his dramatic success.

Big Daddy's most forceful rhythmic device is the obvious and almost primitive one of simple repetition:

> Everywhere she went on this whirlwind tour, she bought, bought, bought.[2]
>
> All that stuff is bull, bull, bull! [3]
>
> Shut up, shut up, shut up! [4]

There is nothing very original about this triple repetition of a word or phrase, but it certainly makes effective bombast. On one occasion when using this simple rhythmic formula, he substitutes synonyms:

> All my life I been like a doubled up fist . . .
> —Poundin', smashin', drivin'!—[5]

But more frequently he merely lengthens the repetition:

> And old Straw died and I was Ochello's partner and the place got bigger and bigger and bigger and bigger.[6]
>
> The human machine is not so different from the animal machine or the fish machine or the bird machine or the reptile machine or the insect machine.[7]

Such obsessive word repetition is merely the monotone of a stubborn child, and it succeeds insofar as it is emphatic and irritating.

But when the repetition is of phrases, and when the repeated phrase is embedded in successive word strings that seem to grow and lengthen and continue to grow and lengthen because of an unusual energy released by the increasing excitement of the rhetorical device in progress—then we have a complicated instrument of speech worth praising:

> I put up with a whole lot of crap around here
> because I thought I was dying.

---

[2] *Ibid.*, p. 70.
[3] *Ibid.*, p. 77.
[4] *Ibid.*, p. 66.
[5] *Ibid.*, p. 76.
[6] *Ibid.*, p. 61.
[7] *Ibid.*, p. 85.

And you thought I was dying and you started taking over,
well, you can stop taking over now, Ida,
because I'm not gonna die,
you can just stop now this business of taking over
because you're not taking over because I'm not dying,
I went through the laboratory and the goddam exploratory operation
and there's nothing wrong with me but a spastic colon.
And I'm not dying of cancer which you thought I was dying of.
Ain't that so?
Didn't you think
that I was dying
of cancer, Ida? [8]

The phrases *thought I was dying* and *started taking over* are like two nuclei around which words cluster and grow into word strings by fits and starts. The fascination is in witnessing the progress of their growth as they set about to establish their own special rhythms of expansion and contraction.

This speech is printed as prose in the text of the play, but I have arranged it in verse—and have done this with all subsequent speeches—hoping to highlight some of the essential rhythmic qualities that might otherwise go unnoticed. But even this rearrangement has some disadvantages. Unfortunately, the printed page is not wide enough to show the longest climax string on one continuous line:

. . . you can just stop now this business of taking over
because you're not taking over because I'm not dying . . .

Notice that it is only after the line has grown to its optimum length (a length that seems to be determined by how much you can get into one breath's worth)—and only then—that a new string is begun:

I went through the laboratory and the goddam exploratory operation
and there's nothing wrong with me but a spastic colon.

This proves to be but a brief respite before picking up the old string again. The completion was only an apparent one, and what is missing must be added before putting to rest for good the nuclear phrases and the strings they engender. True completion does not take place until *of cancer* is added to the nuclear word *dying*. And notice the little movements of contraction that result after the true completion, as though the phrase-making machine were breaking down and the words were having difficulty coming forth, almost stumbling into a helpless silence.

[8] *Ibid.*, p. 60.

There are several other good examples in the speeches of Big Daddy in which the repetitive phrase becomes a growing word string:

> Well I got a few left in me, a few,
> and I'm going to pick me a good one to spend 'em on!
> I'm going to pick me a choice one,
> I don't care how much she costs,
> I'll smother her in—minks! Ha. Ha.
> I'll strip her naked and smother her in minks
> and choke her with diamonds. Ha. Ha.
> I'll strip her naked and choke her with diamonds
> and smother her with minks and hump her from hell
>   to breakfast. Ha aha ha ha ha! [9]

When we examine this set of word strings carefully, we come to see how much variety and freedom a seemingly limited device permits. Actually, there are only two constants involved:

1. The phrase that becomes a nucleus is always repeated.
2. Each repetition must add at least one new sound element or word. We have several false starts with the phrases *a few* and *I'm going to pick me*, but we finally begin to unwind on *I'll smother her in—minks*. And once it does get started, it is not the simple logical progression that could be represented as:

$(x), (x \& a), (x \& a \& b), (x \& a \& b \& c),$ and so on.

This formulation may be analyzed as follows:

1. x is the nuclear word or phrase.
2. Any other letter represents an arbitrary word or phrase attracted to the nuclear one.
3. Anything within a given parenthesis is a word string uttered in one breath.
4. The entire equation is a string set or string series. When the possibility of ambiguity is at a minimum, it is simply referred to as a growing or unwinding string.

The speech quoted directly above is a considerable variation from this most obvious and formulaic way of building a string series. It might well be represented as follows:

$(x), (a \& x \& b), (a \& b \& x \& c).$

The continuous repositioning of the nuclear phrase, plus an uneven progression of added elements, presents limitless possibilities for enrichment of this device.

Having found a formula for powerful expression, Tennessee Williams uses it again and again in the speeches of Big Daddy:

---

[9] *Ibid.*, p. 80.

What do you know about this mendacity thing?
Hell! I could write a book on it!
Don't you know that?
I could write a book on it
and still not cover the subject?
Well, I could,
I could write a goddam book on it
and still not cover the subject anywhere near enough.[10]

If we represented this speech with the symbol system given above, we would get an equation that would look something like a logical progression. But even a superficial glance would indicate that there is much more going on than that. We have the rhyming interjections of *hell, well,* and *still*. Even more interesting is the expanding of a second nuclear phrase, *I could write a book,* by the repetition of *I could* and the introduction of *goddam*. Besides suggesting that one nuclear phrase might begin to orbit around another, it clearly demonstrates how the nuclear phrase can be powerfully altered internally by the mere insertion of a particular word. What we are beginning to get now is something considerably more than a simple rhetorical device: not simply the growing string that builds by adding and repeating phrases, but rather the immeasurable heightening of the power of an utterance by adding words that create subtle internal rhyme schemes and regulate the rhythm. What we are witnessing is the transformation of rhetoric into poetry.

This movement from hard-driving, repetitive rhetoric to a more varied and broken rhythmic pattern that approximates poetry can be observed in one speech:

All that stuff is bull, bull, bull!—
It took the shadow of death
to make me see it.
Now that shadow's lifted,
I'm going to cut loose and have,
What is it they call it,
have me a—ball! . . .

That's right, a ball, a ball! Hell!
—I slept with Big Mama till,
let's see, five years ago, till
I was sixty and she was fifty-eight,
and never even liked her,
never did.[11]

---

[10] *Ibid.,* p. 92.
[11] *Ibid.,* p. 77.

This speech does not completely forsake the rhetoric of repetition. The repetitiveness serves as an introduction and, after relaxing into some interesting iambics, reoccurs. It is almost as if Williams were consciously using it to begin a second stanza of a poem, as my arrangement demonstrates. Not only does the return to rhetoric in the middle of the speech provide an obvious formal structure but it serves an important dramatic function. Big Daddy's psychological equation of motivation is underlined for the benefit of the audience. His recent death-scare has caused him to throw off all regard for social and religious propriety and has increased his sexual appetite for a woman he might enjoy more than his wife. The rhetoric emphasizes his determined rejection of one set of standards and his heated affirmation of another. The iambic remainder of each stanza supplies us with the reasons.

In two notable instances Big Daddy has this tendency toward repetition under such perfect control that he is able to integrate key statements into an even more lyrical framework:

> Life is important.
> There's nothing else to hold onto.
> A man that drinks is throwing his life away.
> Don't do it, hold onto your life.
> There's nothing else to hold onto . . .[12]

The expanding phrase that endlessly unwinds like a fisherman's reel is absent, sacrificed for the sake of focus. In its place is a simple statement with an early terminus. It is an effective way of suggesting certainty and finality. The repetition is there, but now it is simply a restatement that sets its seal on the little speech, after allowing two powerful though greatly differing iambic lines to intervene. That haunting, choral effect is achieved in one other speech, also dealing with the subject of death:

> —the human animal is a beast that dies
> and if he's got money
> he buys and buys and buys
> and I think the reason he buys
> everything he can buy is
> that in the back of his mind he has
> the crazy hope that one of his purchases
> will be life everlasting!—
> Which it never can be . . .
> The human animal is a beast that—[13]

---

[12] *Ibid.*, p. 68.
[13] *Ibid.*, p. 73.

Here the final word of the choral line is never uttered because Big Daddy is interrupted by Brick. This, incidentally, shows us how quick Tennessee Williams is to give up a poetic effect for a dramatic one. Even though the last word of the choral line is left unspoken, our mind supplies it for us. This is the third time Big Daddy has spoken the phrase.[14] Had the choral phrase not been interrupted, it would have served here as it did before, to set the speech off as a significant utterance. It is also interesting to note that although the last speech cited contains all the previously catalogued tendencies—triple repetition, phrase building, alliteration, assonance—none of them dominate; all are made subordinate to the more lyrical mood that should accompany a carefully considered lament about life and death.

Big Daddy's poetic ability cannot be said to consist of his unique word choice. Indeed, his language is filled with clichés, colorful and explosive, but clichés nevertheless. Unlike Blanche Dubois, who uses bizarre and complicated personal images that turn out to be signs of her inner confusion, Big Daddy displays little versatility or originality with imagery. It is as though he were afraid of being found out, afraid someone will discover that he is a poet.

He will allow himself some lyricism and a little alliteration when considering his world under the aspect of eternity; his disgust and anger will occasionally yield some rich sarcasm. With reference to Europe, he says:

> Those gooks over there,
> They gouge your eyeballs out
> In their grand hotels.[15]

Notice how careful he is to remain "non-poetic" with his use of the slangy *gooks*. Significantly, his most powerful speech is reserved for a subject much approved of by male society: sex as an aggressive display of masculine power.

If Kenneth Burke could talk of Coleridge "dancing an attitude" [16]— that is, the writing of something that is accompanied by, or stands in place of, a particular action—what might we say about Big Daddy's speeches that build with such insistent power? What physical action do they suggest? We need only turn to Big Daddy himself for a clue to the answer:

> I haven't been able to stand
> the sight, sound, or smell

---

[14] It occurs once just before this speech begins (*ibid.*, p. 72).

[15] *Cat on a Hot Tin Roof*, p. 70.

[16] Kenneth Burke, *The Philosophy of Literary Form* (New York, 1957), pp. 9–11.

of that woman for forty years now!
—even when I *laid* her!
—regular as a piston . . .[17]

The piston image is perfect, describing not only his style of sexual performance but the relentless pace of his verbal assaults as well. The obsessive driving force of the phrases that build and build and build until they reach a climax of breathless exhaustion and then taper off is the rhythm and orgasm of sexual intercourse—but not the sex that is an act of love. For Big Daddy sex is a distasteful duty that produces anger and aggressiveness.

During much of Big Daddy's life, he wedded his strong impulses of disgust and desire into one physical act. His dramatic power resides in his ability to represent this act and its accompanying emotion, not half so much through narrative exposition as through the very rhythm of his language.

Happy birthday, Big Daddy! You have shown us how rhetoric can evolve into poetic speech and poetry into dramatic representation. Your speeches imitate the very mood and rhythm of your sexual intercourse, and they become for you the dance of death.

STUDY QUESTIONS AND EXERCISES

1. Note the contrast between *slang* and *precious* in the third paragraph. Which terms in the quotations are labeled as slang in a recent dictionary or are included in Wentworth and Flexner? Does Isaac mean "circumscribed word choice" strictly or loosely?

2. What are the specific structural and rhythmic devices Isaac identifies in Big Daddy's speech? What poetic devices does Big Daddy use?

3. Read *Cat on a Hot Tin Roof* and study the language of Ida and Brick, using Isaac's article for a model. Does the study of rhythm prove equally fruitful for these characters? Is the effectiveness of Big Daddy's speech increased by the contrast with the speech patterns of other characters?

4. What is the relationship between the first three and the last two paragraphs in Isaac's essay? How does Isaac's *general* method lend itself to analysis of almost any character in a play? Would it be equally useful for the dialogue of a character in a short story? Would the device of printing passages as poetry be useful for most characters?

---

[17] *Cat on a Hot Tin Roof*, p. 92.

28

A "Bitch" by Any Other Name Is Less Poetic

Edward Hanford Kelly

Today many people regard the word bitch *as vulgar. Professor Kelly of State University College, Oneonta, New York, studies the historical changes in the word, revealing many technical and precise meanings. His article first appeared in* Word Study *for October, 1969.*

" 'I'll light a piece of fat pine,' shouted the boy. . . . 'Where's your bitch?' asked Dillon"; and, a modern reader of Elizabeth E. Robins' *Magnetic North* (1904) might very well ask, what a *bitch* has to do with lighting a fire. But this bitch was essential to the frontiersman of the northwest on long winter nights when, without the luxury of an oil lamp or candle, he had to depend on it alone for a source of light. The bitch, a tin cup filled with bacon grease and with a twisted rag wick,[1] was only used when circumstances prohibited a more civilized means of obtaining fire. Similarly when the need arises today, one often resorts to the term "bitch" for lack of a more civilized means of expression; however, this newer usage exemplifies a shift in meaning by metaphoric association as the word emerges etymologically in English. Yet it would be incorrect to think that the many modifications evident in the history of "bitch" point toward linguistic degeneration ending in mere vulgarism.

A native English word, "bitch" derives from the OE *bicce* (akin to ON *bikkja*)[2] and has a long literary history as a substantive, an adjective (attributive in combination forms), and as a transitive and intransitive verb. Its original Anglo-Saxon meaning, the female of the dog, wolf, fox,[3] or others of the genus *Canis*, is still the first listed in diction-

---

[1] Mitford M. Mathews, "Bitch," *A Dictionary of Americanisms on Historical Principles* (Chicago, 1951).

[2] The *OED* lists other older English forms: *bicge, bicche, bycche, bytch,* etc.; and cites Aelfric's use of the word (1000). OE *bicce* ME *bicche* Mod. E. *bitch.*

[3] In OE *bicce* might occasionally refer to the female of other animals too, as *dēor* meant "animal" before denoting specifically "deer." See also *An Anglo-Saxon Dictionary,* J. Bosworth and T. N. Toller (London, 1964).

aries today; but because words mean what particular cultures make them mean the first listed is not always the popular choice. Few twentieth-century American city dwellers would think it polite to refer to a female dog as a bitch, although they might use the word on other occasions. Yet a person raised in a rural area would probably think the word appropriate. Because the English-speaking population is largely urban, the second and third entries would be in more general usage today. The second entry defines bitch as a "bad, lewd, sensual woman," and warns of the slang term's indecency; the third reference cites the word as a slang verb "to complain," and some dictionaries do not bother to list its adjectival usages. Even the *OED* fails to discuss the word in full despite its lengthy native pedigree, but the concrete definition must have developed into the figurative in the Anglo-Saxon period. Although female animals of the canine variety behave similarly when in heat, man's early companionship with the dog allowed him to observe at first hand the male's reaction to the female in estrus. *The Maistre of Game* (c. 1410), a treatise on hunting, describes this propensity in simile, "As houndes folowyn after a bicche or a brach" (l. 14) and "As houndes do after a byches, when she is Joly" (l. 31). It was a simple analogy to compare two-legged promiscuity with that which went on four.

From the ME period to the present, English-literature records both the denotative and connotative meaning of bitch side-by-side. Chaucer's Pardoner laments the fruit that comes from the "bicched bones two" (l. 656), or from shooting dice. Bones, for dice, has fallen into the category of slang too. In the Renaissance period all-embracing Shakespeare used both the original sense of the word and its metaphoric associations in four plays. For example, in *The Merry Wives of Windsor* Falstaff complains of being tossed in the river "as they would have drowned a blind bitch's puppies" (III, v, 15); and in *Lear* Kent curses Oswald as "the son and heir of a mongrel bitch" (II, ii, 24); later in the play, when Regan and Goneril are "in heat," Shakespeare depends on the audience to fulfill the metaphor of the two sisters as bitches. Milton, partial to aureate poetic diction, never uses bitch; he puts the words "execrable son" into Adam's mouth (PL, XII, 64), and once uses "son of despite," which terms may be appropriate and accurate but less emotionally satisfying to the caller. In Thomas Hobbes' translation of the *Odyssey* (1675) Odysseus calls the unfaithful maids "bitches" (XVIII, 310); but of the modern translators only T. E. Lawrence uses the same term on the same occasion. E. V. Rieu leans toward euphemism, calling them "brazen hussies," while Robert Fitzgerald renders the fairly effective "sluts," another term for female dogs. In *Tom Jones* (1749) Squire Western's technical metaphor on seizing Tom at the inn, "we have got the dog fox, I warrant the bitch is not far off" (X, vii), contrasts with his later inexact but purposefully opprobrious description of the male landlord as a "vast, comical bitch" (XV, iii). The term "bitch" applied to a man becomes humorous, even ironical, and casts doubts on the landlord's masculinity, for a man cannot logically be a bitch; and in the modern homosexual's parlance the appellation "bitch" is a testy compliment.

About the same time *Tom Jones* was published another noun form of the word was coming into being. Miners used what they called a "bitch" for boring and drawing up sunken rods. To hold this iron bitch while unscrewing it, they used two other instruments called "dogs," capable of recovering broken rods from a borehole. The lewd connotation is obvious, and in today's shop jargon machinists employ bitches to clamp work to a lathe. In these instances the term reinforces the function of the tool so named; and, as in the case of the frontiersmen, it is interesting to note that the word is applied to devices expected to perform necessary duties for rough men living in isolation or working outside the immediate association of women.

As a verb, "to bitch" originally meant to frequent the company of "bad" women. In his burlesque of the *Aeneid* (1675), Charles Cotton writes "Jove, thou now art going a-bitching." The more exact "to whore" seems to have replaced "to bitch" in our society, the infinitive form having shifted again in connotation to complaining. But "to bitch" in the sense of "to complain" was in use both early and late in the eighteenth century. Edmund Burke's correspondence (1777) shows "bitch" in still another shade of meaning, "to hang back or hedge": "Norton bitched a little at last; but though he would recede, Fox stuck to his motion." [4] And to "bitch up," meaning to spoil or bungle, some etymologists find thinning in polite usage to "botch" or "botch up"; but botch, according to Skeat, might have always been a separate word.[5]

Victorian writers avoided the slang use of bitch and stuck to its denotative meaning if they used it at all. They had to fulfill the demands of editors who catered to family readers with impressionable daughters, so "bitch" was unquestionably taboo to the Grundian guardians of moral, social, and literary conventions of the period. Mencken saw similar conventions prevailing in America. He points out that from 1820–1880 in England and America sow, stallion, buck, bitch, and even mare were thought of as "racy" in refined circles. Nice swearers in those days often reached for a blend like "bastrich," a combination of bastard and bitch, but considered to be more respectable.[6] Imagine having to consider an oath before spontaneously uttering it! But twentieth-century vernacular has moved to a pole opposite to any antipathy toward the use of "bitch" and other stronger words.

Eric Partridge lists many common expressions using bitch in various contexts. At Cambridge and Oxford hostesses "stand bitch," or preside

---

[4] *OED*, for examples from Cotton, Burke.

[5] Skeat, *Principles of English Etymology*.

[6] H. L. Mencken, *The American Language*.

at tea. They even "bitch the pot" (pour) at their "bitch gatherings," a more pointed label than our nice "hen parties." He notes that since 1840 the queen in playing cards has been called a bitch[7]—and what poker player has not taken the stakes at one time or another with three bitches? And like Barney's bull, men too become "bitched, b***red, and bewildered"—a catch phrase not far removed from the recurrently popular song of *Pal Joey* (1940), "Bewitched" (bothered, and bewildered), which certainly recalls the older rural alliterative expression.

Perhaps the sense of opprobriousness attached to the word early in its history accounts for the current lexicographical stigma still associated with it, but the fact remains that one gets a perverse satisfaction from merely uttering "bitch," especially in its combination and attributive forms. Robert Burns says "I've been bitchfou 'mang godly priests" (1786), or literally "drunk as a bitch." One might be sick as a dog, but he generally has a bitch of a cold or hangover, as the case may be. One might be plastered or bitchified; he might "sound off" or "bitch-off," and whether one is using slang or being vulgar would depend on the tone and context of such utterances. A laborer working on a hot summer day could sincerely complain of a "bitch of a sun," while simple chiasmus of sound in this expression gives the English language one of its most offensive and provoking appellations, while at the same time, paradoxically, one of the most satisfying to say.

The glorious release of emotion one experiences in mouthing "son of a bitch" [8] is almost poetical in the light of Pope's statement that "the sound must seem an echo to the sense." And if Korzybski, Stuart Chase, Carnap, *et al.* had ruled that overuse had wrung dry the meaning of the term, its effect on human emotion would still be therapeutic. Son of a bitch! To say it meaningfully one must set his teeth firmly, bare them to the gums, and let the air hiss lingua-dentally through taut lips as he vehemently stresses the first word. The unaccented "of a" is uttered with no unclenching of teeth, and the speaker is then ready to explode BITCH! with all the residual air he can muster: teeth, gums, lips, facial expression keeping the same ferocious attitude held at beginning the sibilant as the air exhausts itself in [tʃ]. Even in isolation, bitch, if uttered with sincerity, remains a word of great force in releasing pent-up feelings. The voiced stop-plosive [b] can be uttered at any volume, the vowel continuant [i] can be held at length, while the unvoiced affricate [tʃ] moves away from the plosive in a whisper—and all without ever thinking of a lewd woman or even directing the expression at an animate object. Although our society generally thinks a sow dirtier than a female dog, and a rat or snake certainly more odious than man's

---

[7] Eric Partridge, "Bitch," *A Dictionary of Slang and Unconventional English* (London, 1963).

[8] First reference to "son of a bitch" *per se* seems to occur in *Arthur and Merlin* (1330): "Bice sone! thou drawest amiss," (8487), OED.

best friend, the balanced assonance of "son of a sow" does not offer the cathartic benefits of the older term. Although all meaning has been wrung from the word in its present poetic usage, the biological gestures, coupled with sound and movement, provide it with a satisfying sublinguistic, almost symbolical meaning.

STUDY QUESTIONS AND EXERCISES

1. This selection and the two that follow are included as models for short studies of single words, prefixes or combining forms, and suffixes, respectively, in literary and colloquial usage. The mechanics of such studies demand special attention to the use of italics and quotation marks; to parenthetical source identification; and to footnotes, as exemplified in the selection by Edward Kelly. What other details of the mechanics of documentation do you observe?

2. What is the basic principle of organization in this selection? How is continuity provided between examples? Identify the topic sentences and analyze their structural function.

3. What previous selection concludes with an anecdote which would serve to illustrate Kelly's conclusion?

4. How do the term *bitch* and the central image it suggests function in Hemingway's *The Sun Also Rises*?

5. Look up *chiasmus* and explain Kelly's point about "bitch of a sun."

6. Kelly's point in the second paragraph is confirmed by an academic anecdote. An eminent and dignified scholar startled a lady guest by addressing his dog as *bitch*. To his query, "What's the matter? Have you never heard that word before?" she replied, "Oh, yes, but not applied to a dog."

29

Mini-

F. Stuart Crawford

Words, like ladies' fashions, have periods of popularity. Dr. Crawford, assistant editor of the Merriam-Webster dictionaries, discusses the flood of words in recent years that incorporate the combining form mini-. *His article appeared in* Word Study *for December, 1967.*

The remarkable proliferation in the last two or three years of words coined with the initial combining form *mini-*, used to denote something unusually small of its kind, has suggested that it might be interesting to review the history of this currently extremely popular element in English word formation. In the past thirty years the vocabulary files of the Merriam-Webster dictionaries have accumulated examples of over 120 new words formed by prefixing *mini-* to already existing words, and in all but three or four of these the sense reveals plainly that the source of the combining form was the adjective *miniature*. One cannot, to be sure, always comfortably substitute *miniature* for the *mini-*, because the full adjective tends to suggest a more or less exact scale model, while the combining form may mean more loosely "of smaller than normal dimensions," the diminution in some cases being in only one dimension, as in length (*miniskirt*) or width (a *minigroove* phonograph record). In the few exceptions mentioned above *mini-* is clearly a shortening of *minimum*, as in *minivalence*, a technical term of chemistry. But this sense for *mini-* has never been a popular one and now seems unlikely to be productive in the future. I shall confine my survey to words where the sense is "miniature." I shall leave out of consideration also a large number of trademarked names beginning with *Mini-*, whose proprietors are prepared to maintain in the lawcourts that they have no etymology whatever.

What looks like an early forerunner turns up surprisingly in 1849. This is *minibus*, a name for a kind of cab with seats for four passengers. It resembled a horse-drawn omnibus in that its door was in the rear and the passengers sat with their backs to the windows. But various clues lead us to conclude that this word was not formed by prefixing part of *miniature* to an already existing *bus* but rather as a "blend" of *miniature* and *omnibus*, the *-ni-* being derived from both the constituent words, and hence was pronounced, like *omnibus*, with only one stress, unlike the modern auto *minibus*, which has a secondary stress on the -*bus*. So the nineteenth century *minibus* can hardly be regarded as the ancestor of the large twentieth century family.

It is, in fact, not until 1935, when the old minibus was long obsolete, that we find another new word beginning with *mini-*. This is *minicam*, used for a small camera. In the same year we find a well-known naturalist referring to the life at the bottom of a pond as "the multiplex and *miniform*." But this latter coinage did not, so far as is known, survive its first appearance, whereas *minicam* had a considerable currency for some time and may, I believe, be credited with being the ancestral prototype of the long line. There was no great rush at first; until 1965 the rate of neologisms beginning with this element of which we have record is just about one a year. Not surprisingly a considerable number are, like *minicam*, names of mechanical devices, including vehicles. *Minipiano* in 1939 is the first, followed by *minijet* (a model jet plane), *minicycle*, *minicar*, *minicorder* (a small tape recorder), *miniradio*, *minicab*, among others, and in 1964 the modern *minibus*, which is, as we have said, a new formation, not just a revival of the horse-drawn *minibus* of 1849. Outside of the machine world notable coinages are *miniburger* (1957; hamburger in 1½ oz. "two-bite patties") and *minimagazine* (1964).

It is perhaps desirable to state at this point that a great many of the new coinages mentioned in this article will not be found in any dictionary either now or in the future; they have not achieved and never will achieve sufficient currency to be regarded as permanent parts of our language. Many of them may never be used by anyone except their inventors. But the very fact that they have been coined not only illustrates the popularity of the type but contributes to its further proliferation.

For some unknown reason 1954 seems to have been an unusually fruitful year. Here we find for the first time *minifilm*, the *minigroove* phonograph record, *minicube*, an extra small ice cube, and *minipig*, a miniature pig of less than a quarter the weight of an ordinary pig and bred especially for medical research. It may come as a surprise, in view of recent trends, that the earliest uses of *mini-* in the clothing fashion world which are recorded this year are in the field of men's, not women's, wear. We find advertised a *ministripe* in suiting fabrics and a *minipleated* dress shirt.

It was not, however, until 1965 that coinages of *mini-* terms began to increase so rapidly as to inspire comment in the press. The craze was reported as particularly virulent in England. Among the thirteen new creations of this year are *mini-cabbage*, *mini-chips* (french fries), *mini-plant*, *mini-play*, and *mini-moke* (a pet donkey only three feet high). The hyphen appearing here for the first time will be found frequently in subsequent coinages, but without any significant pattern. The only American contributions of this year of which we have record are *mini-*

weather (strictly local climate) and *miniphoria* (with its derivative *miniphoriac*), suggested by a writer in the *New York Times* to designate "the odd euphoria that comes over people hunched in miniature machines." He describes it as very satisfying, when catching up with a Volkswagen driver at a red light, to lean out the window and roar, "You stupid Miniphoriac!"

It can hardly be doubted that the one coinage most directly responsible for the extraordinary volume of new *mini-* words now being coined was *miniskirt*. We have not been able to find this in print earlier than April 15, 1966, though it seems highly probable that the word originated in England in the preceding year, when we do have evidence for *mini-dress*. The total number of new *mini-* combinations recorded in 1966 is twelve, actually one fewer than in 1965, but the popularity of the miniskirt brought its name to the attention of the public every day and inspired imitation which was to show such impressive results in 1967. In 1966 a number of the coinages are, like their immediate model, in the women's fashion world, such as *mini-bag* (a handbag), *mini-sarong*, and adjectives such as *miniskirted, minisleeved,* and *mini-print*. The older category of vehicle names is represented by the sightseeing *minitrain* plying the streets of Washington. A significant extension of the meaning of the prefix to the realm of the intangible is found in a description of present-day London as a place "where the minimorals match the miniskirts and life is one mad giggle."

In 1967 the dam burst. We have already recorded during this still unfinished year over 65 new *mini-* coinages—more than in all previous years put together. The sphere of clothing is still well represented with *mini-gown, mini-jupe, minishift, mini-Shetland* (sweater), and the adjectives *mini-length* and *mini-pant*. Mechanical devices and means of transportaton are not quite so conspicuous as in previous years, but we do have the *mini-combo* (combination radio, TV, and hi-fi), Expo 67's *minirail*, and in the naval department *minisub* and *minicarrier*. The category of animals is expanded by the addition of *minipenguin* and *minimutt*, and the prefix is even applied to human beings of small dimensions, as when a certain very popular *mini-bosomed* model is described by her manager as "sort of the mini-queen of the mod scene." In the realm of food we find a *mini-loaf* of bread, a *mini-meal*, and specifically a *mini-luncheon*. In the world of sports and entertainment there is *minigolf, mini-Olympics,* and *minitheater*. The academic community has created the *mini-semester* and not only the *minimultiversity* but the *miniversity* as opposed to the multiversity. In economics we find the *mini-bank*, and even in some ordinary-sized banks you may be required to maintain only a *mini-balance*. A well-known supermarket chain advertises its *miniprices*, and a financial analyst reports the good news that 1967 has experienced only a *mini-recession*. Finally, as a companion to 1966's *minimorals*, 1967 has added *minimind* and its adjective *miniminded*.

It was almost inevitable that so popular a combining form should in time break away and become a free form. As early as 1963 *mini* alone was being used as short for *minicar*, and soon after its introduction in 1966 *miniskirt* was frequently reduced to *mini*, which in turn has undergone further compounding in the formation *micromini* denoting an exceptionally short miniskirt. A free-form adjective is attested in "There's nothing *mini* about their wages," and this may even be compared, as in "the *miniest* of miniskirts." An inflected verb appears in a dress advertisement in which the model announces, "I *mini-ed* almost a year ago."

A curious recent development has been the attempt to create an antonym for *mini*. In contrast to the miniskirt a skirt whose hemline comes as low as midcalf has been called a *midiskirt*, but this new prefix obviously has a pretty limited usefulness. Another term for this same comparatively long garment is *maxi-skirt*, formed, by a process familiar to etymologists, as if *mini-* were derived from *minimum* rather than from *miniature*. Note that the maxi-skirt is certainly not a maximum skirt, which would reach at least to the ankles; it is merely vaguely felt that as *maximum* is the antithesis of *minimum*, so the contrast to *mini-* should be *maxi-*. In somewhat the same way about three years ago there was coined the name *monokini* for a topless bikini. And now, in contrast to Twiggy, "the mini-queen of the mod world," a newspaper story about the recent coronation of the 350-pound King George Tupou III refers to him as "Tonga's maxi-monarch."

The history of *mini-* is certainly by no means finished. As I write, new words with this beginning continue to turn up at the rate of about two a week. This has been the average for the present calendar year, so we may suspect that the peak has been reached and that the pace of new coinages will soon begin to decline. One thing sure is that only a few of the over 125 *mini-* words of which we now have record will have a very long life.

STUDY QUESTIONS AND EXERCISES

1. How does Crawford's method resemble Kelly's?

2. How does his subject differ from Kelly's, both in the categories to which the term belongs and its uses? What are his sources? How does he have access to these sources?

3. What is the current status of *mini-* —have miniskirts and the term gone out of fashion, do both continue in favor, or have fashions in skirts changed and not those in words? Do *mini-*, *midi-*, and *maxi-* remain established in the language?

4. Make a study of *midi-*, or *maxi-*, paralleling Crawford's study of *mini-*.

5. Make a study similar to Crawford's on *auto-*.

30

Humor As A Factor In Language Change

D. E. Houghton

Like the prefix, the suffix may be used excessively in popular discourse. In an article in the English Journal *for November, 1968, Professor Houghton of Sacramento State College illustrates how the humorous use of* -wise *has caused a change in language patterns.*

A common practice among teachers, writers, and other educated literate people is the satiric or humorous use in their own discourse of words or expressions they do not approve of in the speech and writing of others. Henry James, for instance, wrote in a letter, "Again I must say I feel 'real badly,' as D.[aisy] M.[iller] would have said. . . ." An article by John Fischer in *Harper's* is titled "Why Nobody Can't Write Good." *Ain't* is often used humorously by the educated. Archibald MacLeish in the *New York Times Magazine* writes: "What is wrong with all this, of course, is that it just ain't so." James Laughlin, Director of New Directions Press, is quoted in *Newsweek*: "Some of these kids who come around to see me seem to think that all you have to do is take a pill and sit back and whatever comes out is literature. Well, it ain't."

The reasons for this practice are no doubt many and complex. Certainly one ostensible reason is that since satire and humor are generally thought to be critical and corrective, educated people probably consciously or unconsciously feel that a humorous-critical use of certain expressions by people with education and prestige is one way of discouraging the use of these expressions by those less sensitive to language. This assumption overlooks so many other factors involved in the context in which language is used that it may be quite false, and the results may be quite opposite to those desired by those who engage in this practice. I suggest that *any* use of any word or expression may well have the effect of establishing that word or expression more firmly in the language. In language matters, familiarity breeds not contempt but acceptance, and new words or expressions thrive on publicity, even bad publicity.

Most educated people, however, do not want to appear ignorant of standard English and so they choose to use sub-standard English humorously only in certain ways and under special circumstances so that, hopefully, their audiences understand fully that the speaker or writer knows better. But it is difficult to prevent misunderstanding all of the time because rarely will everyone in every audience get the joke. When this happens, the educated speaker or writer lends his prestige as an educated person to the very word or expression he would hope to eliminate from the language. In addition, the language habits of the speaker or writer may have been subtly changed so that it will be just a little easier for him to use this expression again in the future, and still again, until he no longer uses it humorously and critically.

Ain't is probably not a good example to use here. School teachers have been so successful in convincing us that ain't, above all other words, is to be avoided that it is probably not true that the critical-humorous use of it by educated people contributes to its acceptance. The matter becomes much more complicated, however, if the expression is one such as the current and widespread suffix -wise, as used in "taxwise" or "advertisingwise."

Wise has long been accepted as standard English in words such as likewise and otherwise. It has also been long accepted in the adverbial sense in words like crabwise, meaning like a crab, as in "The man sidled crabwise across the beach." But in the last decade or so, wise has been used as a suffix to coin new adverbs meaning "with regard to" or "in reference to," as in "This is a nice day, weatherwise" or "The fishermen have had a good year, crabwise." While this use of wise seems well on its way to becoming accepted as standard English, many educated people still object to it and often do so by using wise in their own speech and writing to poke fun of it. This practice is encouraged by Follett, who finds this current use of wise offensive, an "instrument of havoc." He writes in Modern American Usage: "What was handy as a device has thus been made hideous as a mannerism, and it deserves to be outlawed from decent use. Until the rage abates, a sensible writer will resort to such coinages in -wise only to make fun of them, as S. J. Perelman does when he speaks of what was going on, prosewise, from 1930 to 1958." Morris Freedman, in his Compact English Handbook, follows Follett's advice. He advises against the use of wise, but at the same time uses it himself to poke fun of it: "Speechwise, the suffix -wise started on Madison Avenue, in New York advertising agencies, and has infiltrated the whole country. Dictionwise, it is classified as JARGON. It is likewise barbaric." But if wise has already "infiltrated the whole country," surely a great many people will not recognize a humorous use of wise when they encounter one. To the extent this occurs, the speaker or writer who uses wise humorously is merely contributing to a wider acceptance of it.

To alert his audience to his humorous intent, the speaker may use stress, pause, raised eyebrows, a smile, a brief aside, or a combination of these. In the course of a recent lecture at Sacramento State College, a history professor began a sentence as follows: "Time-wise and geographicwise. . . ." At this point the speaker paused, gave a little laugh, and added, "If there is such a word." The speaker obviously found "geographicwise" at least mildly amusing. One wonders, however, why she used an "amusing" word in a scholarly lecture. Perhaps because she had already committed herself to "time-wise," a word she apparently did *not* find amusing or unusual, and then coined "geographicwise" to go with "time-wise."

Mass media offer special problems to those who wish to use humor critically. A larger, less homogeneous audience makes risky the use of subtle humor. The movie *The Apartment* made clear through frequent repetition that *wise* was being used humorously. The audience was quite prepared to laugh when late in the picture Jack Lemmon said, "That's the way it crumbles, cookiewise." But when comedian Stan Freberg on TV drops one use of *wise* into a rapid-fire exchange between himself and his puppet Oswald, how many of the possibly several million listener-viewers know that Freberg has subtly criticized the use of *wise,* or can anyone be certain that he has?

Removal of the visual image may make for even more confusion. Between acts of a Metropolitan Opera Broadcast on a national radio network, one of the participants in the discussion of the opera asked: "How about something Wagnerian-wise?" The remark was followed by laughter of the other participant. Even if we take into consideration that opera lovers may be fairly well educated and relatively sensitive to language, surely many of the vast radio audience did not associate the laughter they heard with "Wagnerian-wise."

Writers, like speakers, are often caught between wanting to be subtle and not wanting to be misunderstood. The writer who wishes to use *wise* humorously can protect himself by repetition, unusual typography, or some other means of exaggeration to make clear he is not serious. William Zinsser in the *New York Times Magazine* writes of a restaurant "that is congested every noon with men and women talking agency-wise, retail-wise, resort-wear-wise, residual-rights-wise, and every wise but social-wise." Mort Gaines, in a column in the *Sacramento Union,* lists the wonders of California:

THE GREATEST STATE IN THE UNION:
POPULATION WISE
PRODUCTION WISE
SCENIC WISE
BUSINESS WISE
RESOURCE WISE
CLIMATE WISE

Granville Hicks, in an interview with himself in the *Saturday Review,* uses an aside to alert the reader to his nonserious use of *wise.* Hicks has the interviewer ask, "Do you think that this has been a good year fictionwise?" Hicks then adds these stage directions in parentheses: "(Mr. H. winces and staggers slightly but recovers.)." In a nationally syndicated column, John Crosby writes, "Managementwise—ah, there's a nugget for you—NBC is a mess of colossal proportions."

An obviously humorous framework or context will also alert the reader to a critical-humorous use of *wise*. The next to last frame of a "Peanuts" comic strip shows Charlie Brown saying to his sister, "I refuse to argue with you because you are becoming very obnoxious. . . ." In the last frame Charlie turns to her and shouts in big black letters, "BIG-SISTERWISE, THAT IS." A *New Yorker* cartoon shows a sophisticated, well-dressed couple having a cocktail in their New England home. They are looking out the window at the snow and at a tree with a pail attached to it, and the man says, "I can tell you this—it's very comforting to be self-sufficient syrupwise." On the wall of a Sacramento pizza parlor, among many humorous signs, one reads: "Pizza-wise, pledge allegiance to Shakey's."

Fiction writers also have attacked the use of *wise*, but since their humorous use of *wise* is so often part of a broad satiric context, the reader often cannot be certain that the intention of the writer *is* satiric. To the extent that *wise* registers only vaguely in the reader's consciousness, the writer is reenforcing in the reader any tendency he may have to make *wise* a part of his everyday language. In *Set This House on Fire*, William Styron presents an exchange between a hostess at a cocktail party and a departing minister. Dr. Bell is an up-to-date, swinging minister, possessed of a "rakish sanctity," and we know from much evidence Styron gives us that he is a fool:

> "Oh, Dr. Bell, are you going so soon?" Rosemarie exclaimed.
> "I told you to call me Irving, my dear," he said with a smile, seizing her hand and patting it. "Yes, I've got to be up and away to Paestum early in the morning. Please tell young Mason how much I enjoyed his hospitality. I've got Sol Kirshorn to thank for so many things but nothing, pleasurewise, so much as being put in touch with"—and here I thought I saw him wink up at her through his bifocals—"with such beauty."

The general satiric intent is clear, and Styron probably deliberately chose *pleasurewise* to contribute to the satiric effect, but one can not be certain he did, and probably many readers find nothing particularly amusing in *pleasurewise*.

Bernard Malamud's use of *wise* in *A New Life* is even more difficult for the reader to interpret. Gerald Gilley's fatuousness is revealed in part by his trite language, but only in part. At one point early in the book, Gilley says, "[The University] is afraid if we keep on gaining at the rate we have since the end of the war, they'll lose out percentagewise on funds for buildings and faculty salaries. . . ." Nearly three hundred pages later, Gilley says: "Never mind who told me. . . . If the University gets ahead of us student-wise, they'll collect most of the budget and we'll get beans." Malamud throughout the novel is obviously critical of Gilley, but can any reader be certain that Gilley's use of *wise* is part of the criticism, especially since he uses *wise* only twice and one use, *percentagewise*, is perhaps the most common example of the current use of *wise*. Indeed, some readers may be unconsciously encouraged to use *wise* in their own speech; Gilley, after all, is an English professor.

Near the end of John Fowles' novel, *The Magus*, a psychiatrist reads to other psychiatrists a scholarly report which analyzes the main character of the novel. At one point the report reads, "He has careerwise continually placed himself in situations of isolation." Since the report as a whole contains much of the jargon of psychology and psychiatry, it would appear that Fowles is mildly critical, at least mildly amused, by the language of the profession and that his criticism, if it is criticism, is meant to include *careerwise*, but we have no way of knowing this, and so must only conclude once again that many readers would not attach any particular significance to *careerwise* in this context.

How difficult it is for a reader to determine how a writer means for him to respond to the presence of a neologism such as *wise* is illustrated in a passage from a Mary Dikeman story in the *Atlantic*. In this story a woman at a suburban cocktail party looks across the street and makes this comment on the woman who lives there: "Housekeeping-wise, she is in mighty bad shape." A few minutes later the same woman says, in response to something another guest at the party said about the woman across the street, "Psychologywise, she should take herself in hand." Although one can not be certain, what *seems* to be happening here, and which makes this example different from the others cited from fiction, is that the woman in the story is herself using *housekeepingwise* and *psychologywise* deliberately in order to poke fun of *wise*. She does so, presumably confident that her sophisticated friends at the party share her distaste for *wise* and will understand she is having fun with it. Or, to refine this further, the woman in the story possibly used *wise* the first time only *half*-humorously, perhaps even unconsciously, and, feeling a little uncomfortable with it, then used it a second time consciously and humorously to cover her first use of it.

Like so many educated people, the woman in the story has seen and heard *wise* used so often without humorous intent in the speech and writing of even educated people, has seen so many TV shows and movies in which *wise* was used humorously, has read so many stories and novels in which *wise* was used satirically, has heard *wise* used more or less humorously by her educated friends, and, finally, has so often used *wise* herself humorously in the presence of her friends, that she is now very close to using *wise* as a part of her regular discourse. And aren't we all?

STUDY QUESTIONS AND EXERCISES

1. Compare the point and the examples in the first paragraph with Hill's account of his own use of *ain't*. Does he use *ain't* in the article in the way that Archibald MacLeish and James Laughlin do in the quotations given here?

2. How is Houghton's main point, the last sentence in the second paragraph, related to the controversy over *Webster's Third*? Is it sufficient to know who used the word and the sentence in which it was used? Are the larger context and the user's general practice significant?

3. *Hopefully* is given only as the adverbial form of *hopeful* in *Webster's Third*. In the sense in which Houghton uses it (sentence 1, paragraph 3), it is defined without label in the *Random House Dictionary*. This definition has a usage note in the *American Heritage Dictionary*; only 44 of the 100 panelists consider this use acceptable. Does Houghton's use of *hopefully* illustrate the point made in that sentence? If not, is he unconsciously proving the point of his previous sentence? Why is the word not defined in that sense in *Webster's Third*? (Consider the dates of publication of the three dictionaries.)

4. Does Archibald Hill try to prevent his use of *ain't* from lending the word prestige and contributing to its acceptance among those striving for correctness?

5. Collect as many uses of -*wise* as you can, with specific examples.

6. Of the panel of 100 for the *American Heritage Dictionary*, 84 considered -*wise* unacceptable in general usage. Why does the humorous use of -*wise*, poking fun at it as a barbarism, usually defeat the purpose, according to Houghton? How may the practice of *Webster's Third* of omitting usage notes for expressions used with such intent further defeat the purpose?

7. What is the logical parallel for *timewise*? Why does the speaker use instead the awkward and less logical *geographicwise*?

8. How does speech, especially if the speaker is seen as well as heard, serve better than print to convey humorous intent? By what devices can such intent be conveyed in print?

9. One way to check Styron's intent would be to compare the language of satirized characters, such as Dr. Bell, with that of self-portrayed and sympathetic main characters, Peter Leverett and Cass Kin-

solving. Can the author of a long and stylistically extravagant work of fiction expect readers to make such subtle distinctions between speech of characters?

10. Note Houghton's use of the construction "what seems . . . and which." See Fowler, *Modern English Usage*, "Elegant Variation": *that, which*. How do *what* and *which* differ from *that* and *which*, as grammatically interchangeable? What does one expect after *and* instead of *which*?

11. Look up *-wise* in Fowler's *Modern English Usage*. Can you explain how Fowler's tolerant view of *-wise* may be implicit evidence for the soundness of Houghton's case?

SUBJECTS FOR BRIEF PAPERS OR WRITTEN REPORTS

1. Write a paper on President Eisenhower's style as represented in "The West Point Address" and as parodied in "The Gettysburg Address in Eisenhowese," in *Parodies*, compiled and edited by Dwight Macdonald (1960). Pay particular attention to literary and colloquial vocabulary and syntax.

2. Analyze Lincoln's "Gettysburg Address." Which words are popular? Which are learned? Write a short paper on the diction and the effect, with particular attention to popular words used for dignified effect, such as *forefathers* and *brought forth*.

3. Although *Pygmalion* is British, the theme of the social and economic importance of language applies—somewhat less stringently— to the United States. Write a brief paper on the speech of *one* of the characters in *Pygmalion*. Discuss how the character's speech reveals his social class and note expressions that are British rather than American.

4. Discuss the varieties of style which you consciously employ, with examples of how you would orally express the same idea in different situations. You may find it amusing and helpful to indicate how you would be dressed on each occasion.

5. Select from *Writers at Work* (New York: The Viking Press, Compass Books, 1959) a recorded interview with an American author with whose works you are familiar: good possibilities are James Thurber, Thornton Wilder, William Faulkner, and Robert Penn Warren. On the basis of the interview, write a brief analysis of colloquial aspects of the writer's speech, with special attention to any regional characteristics. Would it be justifiable to regard the author's mode of expression in the interview as "below" his literary style?

6. Report on the use of *levels* in reference to language and style in the freshman composition text used in your institution; compare the

patterns of classification with Kenyon's, using Kenyon's technique of analyzing and illustrating.

7. Present as a factual report the survey of college slang on your campus suggested in the second question on Roberts' "Slang and Its Relatives." See William White, "Wayne University Slang," * for suggestions as to sources and method.

8. Write a brief paper on changes in slang as represented by three generations, yourself and your friends, your parents, and your subteen or early-teen acquaintances. Refer to both a general dictionary and a slang dictionary for status and meanings.

9. Analyze the slang used in a long passage in *The Catcher in the Rye* by J. D. Salinger or in one of his short stories or some other modern short story. As a model see Donald P. Costello, "The Language of *The Catcher in the Rye*," *American Speech* (October, 1959).

10. In Robert Penn Warren's *All the King's Men*, compare a passage from Cass Mastern's journal in Chapter Four with a passage comparable in seriousness and emotional quality by Jack Burden, the narrator. In a short paper discuss the chief differences in tone, idiom, diction, and sentence structure which may be ascribed to the difference in historical period.

11. Look up one or several of Frank Sullivan's "cliché expert" pieces: football (1938), politics (1940), war (1940), radio (1941), the atom (1945), campaign oratory (1948), baseball (1949), drama satire (1951), the campaign (1952). Write a "cliché expert" sketch of your own on a different subject, one which you read about and hear about frequently.

12. In a chosen portion of Wentworth and Flexner's *Dictionary of American Slang*, classify and discuss the words and meanings of words which do not appear in a collegiate dictionary. Evaluate the contribution of a slang dictionary to knowledge of spoken and written American English. (Note sources given in Wentworth and Flexner.)

13. Compile a glossary of space-age slang; list your sources and add analytical comments.

14. Write your autobiography in terms of the slang vocabulary associated with each phase of your life and the subgroups from which you acquired it.

15. Report on the cant or jargon of an occupational subgroup with which you are familiar: give a classified list of characteristic terms used, with comments on social and economic status of the users and the general tone of their language. Consult the Preface, Wentworth and Flexner, *Dictionary of American Slang*, for a discussion of cant and jargon, and examples.

---

* *American Speech* (December, 1955), pp. 301–05.

16. Compile a glossary of teen-age slang or of the slang of a sport or activity. Comment on the relation of the slang terms to non-slang—different meanings for regular words, clipped forms, and so forth —and the characteristics of the words which occur only as slang. What proportion of the terms are monosyllables? Do your findings support Flexner's observation that monosyllables are prominent in slang?

17. Study one of George Ade's *Fables in Slang* or one of Ring Lardner's "You know me, Al" stories and report on differences between past and present slang. Which terms are still used? Which have ceased to be used but have a modern equivalent? Which are obsolete with no substitute? Is there any difference between the life of general slang and of slang which belongs to an activity or sport, such as baseball?

18. Using selection 29 by Edward Kelly on *bitch* as a model, write an article on the etymology, meanings, and varying status of ac-ceptability of an analogous term, such as *hen, chicken, cock, bull, dog, vixen, donkey,* or *ass.*

part 5

Social or Class Aspects

The following selections consider various facets of the problem of using language appropriate for different groups in a mobile society. "Just as the general social habits of such separated social groups naturally show marked differences, so their language practices inevitably vary," Charles C. Fries says, in American English Grammar. *"We must, therefore, recognize the fact that there are separate social or class groups even in American communities and that these groups differ from one another in many social practices including their language habits."*

These groups, which can be classified into categories, such as educational, occupational, or social, act as status symbols for those who feel inferior or insecure. By imitating the language of those they admire, the insecure hope to gain assurance, advancement, prestige, and status. In order to preserve certain social or class distinctions, some grammarians and lexicographers have tried to set themselves up as dogmatic guardians of linguistic stability, issuing rules and pronouncements while they mistakenly assume that they can arrest the changes of a living language. Although their prescriptions provide a comfortable crutch for the socially insecure to lean upon, they do not stop the changes or provide a permanent solution to the problem of appropriateness. As most of the writers in this section indicate, the prescriptions are of necessity relative, and any generalizations may be qualified by the four aspects of language considered in this collection of readings.

31

Standard English

Charles C. Fries

In this passage from American English Grammar (1940) *Professor Fries defines standard English as the particular language habits that have become socially acceptable in most communities throughout the United States.*

In order to grasp the significance of . . . social differences in language practice for the obligation of the schools one must understand clearly what is meant by "standard" English, and that can perhaps best be accomplished by tracing the course by which a particular kind of English became "standard." As one examines the material written in England during the twelfth and thirteenth centuries—a period from one hundred to two hundred years after the Norman Conquest—he finds a situation in which three things are of especial note:

1. Most of the legal documents, the instruments which controlled the carrying on of the political and the business affairs of the English people, were not written in the English language but in French or in Latin. This fact was also true of much of the literature and books of learning familiar to the upper classes.

2. Although some books, especially historical records and religious and moral stories and tracts, were written in English, there was no single type of the English language common to all English writings. The greatest number used what is called the Southern dialect. This particular kind of English had been centered in Winchester, which was the chief city of King Alfred and his successors until the time of the Norman Conquest.

3. There was, therefore, no "standard" English in twelfth and thirteenth century England, for no single type of the English language furnished the medium by which the major affairs of English people were carried on. Instead, English people used for these purposes French, Latin, and at least four distinct varieties of English. The particular kind of English spoken in southern England came nearest to fulfilling the function of a "standard" English because more writings and more

significant writings were produced in this type of English than in any other.

In the fourteenth and early fifteenth centuries, however, this situation changed. London had become the political and in some respects the social head of English life in a much more unified England. Many of the major affairs of the realm had to be handled in London. More and more the English language, the English of London, was used in the legal documents of politics and business. Solely because of the fact that more of the important affairs of English life were conducted in this London English rather than in Winchester English, London English became "standard" English. Naturally, then, the growing use of this particular type of English for the important affairs of English life gathered such momentum that even writers to whom other types of English were more natural felt constrained to learn and to use the fashionable London English. Gower, for example, a Kentishman, did not write his native kind of English but practically the same forms, constructions, and spellings as Chaucer, a Londoner born. Naturally, too, this London English gained a social prestige because of the fact that its use connoted or suggested relations with the center of affairs in English life, whereas the inability to use London English suggested that one did not have such social contacts. "Standard" English, therefore, is, historically, a local dialect, which was used to carry on the major affairs of English life and which gained thereby a social prestige.[1]

Many changes occurred in this dialect of English and these changes especially affected the usage of the younger rather than of the older generations in the centers of fashionable social life. Thus the continued use of the older forms rather than the newer changes always suggested a lack of direct contacts with those who were active in the conduct of important matters. In this connotation lay the power of "standard" English to compel the ambitious to conform to its practices.

In America, however, we have had no one recognized center for our political, business, social, and intellectual affairs. More than that, the great distances between various parts of the United States made very difficult frequent actual social contacts in the earlier days. Our coast cities, Boston and New York, maintained direct relations with London long after the earlier settlers had moved west, but the middle western settlements had practically no relations with Boston and New York. This fact can probably explain the differences between our middle-western speech and that of nineteenth century Boston and New York. Because of the fact that New England so long dominated our intellectual life there has been a good deal of feeling in many parts of

---

[1] "Standard" French, "Standard" Italian, "Standard" Dutch, etc., have similar histories.

the United State that the language usages of New England connoted a connection with a higher culture than did the language of the Middle West. Hence the rather widespread attempt to imitate certain New England speech characteristics. On the whole, however, if we ignore the special differences that separate the speech of New England, the South, and the Middle West, we do have in the United States a set of language habits, broadly conceived, in which the major matters of the political, social, economic, educational, religious life of this country are carried on. To these language habits is attached a certain social prestige, for the use of them suggests that one has constant relations with those who are responsible for the important affairs of our communities. It is this set of language habits, derived originally from an older London English, but differentiated from it somewhat by its independent development in this country, which is the "standard" English of the United States. Enough has been said to enforce the point that it is "standard" not because it is any more correct or more beautiful or more capable than other varieties of English; it is "standard" solely because it is the particular type of English which is used in the conduct of the important affairs of our people. It is also the type of English used by the *socially acceptable* of most of our communities and insofar as that is true it has become a social or class dialect in the United States.

STUDY QUESTIONS AND EXERCISES

1. The prestige of Harvard University reflects the past prestige of New England. Does Harvard set the standard in pronunciation to a degree comparable with the influence of Oxford and Cambridge universities on British pronunciation? What historical, geographical, and social facts about the United States have both contributed to uniformity and prevented a too restrictive standard of uniformity?

2. Standard English may be called a class dialect. If a person does not come from an environment where he has learned standard English, where can he acquire it? If he does acquire it thoroughly, is he at any real disadvantage in competition with those born to it?

3. Standard English establishes what is considered correct on the social and economic level where it is required. What may be the penalty for "incorrect" language?

4. If a person does not aspire to the social and economic level which demands standard English, does he personally need to acquire it? How does the flexibility of social classes in the United States result in different generations of one family having different speech habits?

5. Will most high school graduates have an absolute need for standard English? Will all college graduates have an absolute need for

standard English if they remain among college-educated people? What are the implications of these facts about language for high school students preparing for college and for college students?

6. Like slovenly dress, slovenly speech is likely to suggest either ignorance of or indifference to what is acceptable. Which type of person can *least afford* to risk being considered ignorant or indifferent: the person content with a low social and economic status, the person established in high social and economic status, or the person seeking to establish himself in the status to which he aspires?

32

Speech Communities

Paul Roberts

This chapter from Understanding English *(1958) considers various speech groups and their effects upon the language patterns of speakers who come into contact with them.*

Imagine a village of a thousand people all speaking the same language and never hearing any language other than their own. As the decades pass and generation succeeds generation, it will not be very apparent to the speakers of the language that any considerable language change is going on. Oldsters may occasionally be conscious of and annoyed by the speech forms of youngsters. They will notice new words, new expressions, "bad" pronunciations, but will ordinarily put these down to the irresponsibility of youth, and decide piously that the language of the younger generation will revert to decency when the generation grows up.

It doesn't revert, though. The new expressions and the new pronunciations persist, and presently there is another younger generation with its own new expressions and its own pronunciations. And thus the language changes. If members of the village could speak to one another across five hundred years, they would probably find themselves unable to communicate.

Now suppose that the village divides itself and half the people move away. They move across the river or over a mountain and form a new village. Suppose the separation is so complete that the people of New Village have no contact with the people of Old Village. The language of both villages will change, drifting away from the language of their common ancestors. But the drift will not be in the same direction. In both villages there will be new expressions and new pronunciations, but not the same ones. In the course of time the language of Old Village and New Village will be mutually unintelligible with the language they both started with. They will also be mutually unintelligible with one another.

An interesting thing—and one for which there is no perfectly clear explanation—is that the rate of change will not ordinarily be the same for both villages. The language of Old Village changes faster than the language of New Village. One might expect that the opposite would be true—that the emigrants, placed in new surroundings and new conditions, would undergo more rapid language changes. But history reports otherwise. American English, for example, despite the violence and agony and confusion to which the demands of a new continent have subjected it, is probably essentially closer to the language of Shakespeare than London English is.

Suppose one thing more. Suppose Old Village is divided sharply into an upper class and a lower class. The sons and daughters of the upper class go to preparatory school and then to the university; the children of the lower class go to work. The upper-class people learn to read and write and develop a flowering literature; the lower-class people remain illiterate. Dialects develop, and the speech of the two classes steadily diverges. One might suppose that most of the change would go on among the illiterate, that the upper-class people, conscious of their heritage, would tend to preserve the forms and pronunciations of their ancestors. Not so. The opposite is true. In speech, the educated tend to be radical and the uneducated conservative. In England one finds Elizabethan forms and sounds not among Oxford and Cambridge graduates but among the people of backward villages.

A village is a fairly simple kind of speech community—a group of people steadily in communication with one another, steadily hearing one another's speech. But the village is by no means the basic unit. Within the simplest village there are many smaller units—groupings based on age, class, occupation. All these groups play intricately on one another and against one another, and a language that seems at first a coherent whole will turn out on inspection to be composed of many differing parts. Some forces tend to make these parts diverge; other forces hold them together. Thus the language continues in tension.

The child's first speech community is ordinarily his family. The child learns whatever kind of language the family speaks—or, more precisely, whatever kind of language it speaks to him. The child's language learning, now and later, is governed by two obvious motives: the desire to communicate and the desire to be admired. He imitates what he hears. More or less successful imitations usually bring action and reward and tend to be repeated. Unsuccessful ones usually don't bring action and reward and tend to be discarded.

But since language is a complicated business it is sometimes the unsuccessful imitations that bring the reward. The child, making a stab at the word *mother*, comes out with *muzzer*. The family decides that this is just too cute for anything and beams and repeats *muzzer*, and the child, feeling that he's scored a bull's eye, goes on saying *muzzer* long after he has mastered *other* and *brother*. Baby talk is not so much invented by the child as sponsored by the parent.

Eventually the child moves out of the family and into another speech community—other children of his neighborhood. He goes to kindergarten and immediately encounters speech habits that conflict with those he has learned. If he goes to school and talks about his *muzzer*, it will be borne in on him by his colleagues that the word is not well chosen. Even *mother* may not pass muster, and he may discover that he gets better results and is altogether happier if he refers to his female parent as his ma or even his old lady.

Children coming together in a kindergarten class bring with them language that is different because it is learned in different homes. It is all to some degree unsuccessfully learned, consisting of not quite perfect imitations of the original. In school all this speech coalesces, differences tend to be ironed out, and the result differs from the original parental speech and differs in pretty much the same way.

The pressures on the child to conform to the speech of his age group, his speech community, are enormous. He may admire his teacher and love his mother; he may even—and even consciously—wish to speak as they do. But he *has* to speak like the rest of the class. If he does not, life becomes intolerable.

The speech changes that go on when the child goes to school are often most distressing to parents. Your little Bertram, at home, has never heard anything but the most elegant English. You send him to school, and what happens? He comes home saying things like "I done real good in school today, Mom." But Bertram really has no choice in the matter. If Clarence and Elbert and the rest of the fellows customarily say "I done real good," then Bertram might as well go around with three noses as say things like "I did very nicely."

Individuals differ, of course, and not all children react to the speech community in the same way. Some tend to imitate and others tend to force imitation. But all to some degree have their speech modified by forces over which neither they nor their parents nor their teachers have any real control.

Individuals differ too in their sensitivity to language. For some, language is always a rather embarrassing problem. They steadily make boners, saying the right thing in the wrong place or the wrong way. They have a hard time fitting in. Others tend to change their language slowly, sticking stoutly to their way of saying things, even though their way differs from that of the majority. Still others adopt new language habits almost automatically, responding quickly to whatever speech environment they encounter.

Indeed some children of five or six have been observed to speak two or more different dialects without much awareness that they are doing so. Most commonly, they will speak in one way at home and in another on the playground. At home they say, "I did very nicely" and "I haven't any"; these become, at school, "I done real good" and "I ain't got none."

Throughout the school years, or at least through the American secondary school, the individual's most important speech community is his age group, his class. Here is where the real power lies. The rule is conformity above all things, and the group uses its power ruthlessly on those who do not conform. Language is one of the chief means by which the school group seeks to establish its entity, and in the high school this is done more or less consciously. The obvious feature is high school slang, picked up from the radio, from other schools, sometimes invented, changing with bewildering speed. Nothing is more satisfactory than to speak today's slang; nothing more futile than to use yesterday's.

There can be few tasks more frustrating than that of the secondary school teacher charged with the responsibility of brushing off and polishing up the speech habits of the younger generation. Efforts to make *real* into *really, ain't* into *am not, I seen him* into *I saw him, he don't* into *he doesn't* meet at best with polite indifference, at worst with mischievous counterattack.

The writer can remember from his own high school days when the class, a crashingly witty bunch, took to pronouncing the word *sure* as *sewer*. "Have you prepared your lesson, Arnold?" Miss Driscoll would ask. "Sewer, Miss Driscoll," Arnold would reply. "I think," said Miss Driscoll, who was pretty quick on her feet too, "that you must mean 'sewerly,' since the construction calls for the adverb not the adjective." We were delighted with the suggestion and went about saying "sewerly" until the very blackboards were nauseated. Miss Driscoll must have wished often that she had left it lay.

When the high school class graduates, the speech community disintegrates as the students fit themselves into new ones. For the first time in the experience of most of the students the speech ways of adult communities begin to exercise real force. For some people the adjustment is a relatively simple one. A boy going to work in a garage may have a good deal of new lingo to pick up, and he may find that the speech that seemed so racy and won such approval in the corridors of Springfield High leaves his more adult associates merely bored. But a normal person will adapt himself without trouble.

For others in other situations settling into new speech communities may be more difficult. The person going into college, into the business world, into scrubbed society may find that he has to think about and work on his speech habits in order not to make a fool of himself too often.

College is a particularly complicated problem. Not only does the freshman confront upperclassmen not particularly disposed to find the speech of Springfield High particularly cute, but the adult world, as represented chiefly by the faculty, becomes increasingly more immediate. The problems of success, of earning a living, of marriage, of attaining a satisfactory adult life loom larger, and they all bring language problems with them. Adaptation is necessary, and the student adapts. The student adapts, but the adult world adapts too. The thousands of boys and girls coming out of the high schools each spring are affected by the speech of the adult communities into which they move, but they also affect that speech. The new pronunciation habits, developing grammatical features, different vocabulary do by no means all give way before the disapproval of elders. Some of them stay. Elders, sometimes to their dismay, find themselves changing their speech habits under the bombardment of those of their juniors. And then of course the juniors eventually become the elders, and there is no one left to disapprove.

Speech communities are formed by many features besides that of age. Most obvious is geography. Our country was originally settled by people coming from different parts of England. They spoke different dialects to begin with and as a result regional speech differences existed from the start in the different parts of the country. As speakers of other languages came to America and learned English, they left their mark on the speech of the sections in which they settled. With the westward movement, new pioneers streamed out through the mountain passes and down river valleys, taking the different dialects west and modifying them by new mixtures in new environments.

Today we are all more or less conscious of certain dialect differences in our country. We speak of the "southern accent," "the Brooklyn accent," the "New England accent." Until a few years ago it was often said that American English was divided into three dialects: Southern American (south of the Mason-Dixon line); Eastern American (east of the Connecticut River); and Western American. This description suggests certain gross differences all right, but recent research shows that it is a gross oversimplification.

The starting point of American dialects is the original group of colonies. We had a New England settlement, centering in Massachusetts; a Middle Atlantic settlement, centering in Pennsylvania; a southern settlement, centering in Virginia and the Carolinas. These colonies were different in speech to begin with, since the settlers came from different parts of England. Their differences were increased as the colonies lived for a century and a half or so with only thin communication with either Mother England or each other. By the time of the Revolution the dialects were well established. Within each group there were of course subgroups. Richmond speech differed markedly from that of Savannah. But Savannah and Richmond were more like each other than they were like Philadelphia or Boston.

The Western movement began shortly after the Revolution, and dialects followed geography. The New Englanders moved mostly into upper New York State and the Great Lakes region. The Middle Atlantic colonists went down the Shenandoah Valley and eventually into the heart of the Midwest. The southerners opened up Kentucky and

Tennessee, later the lower Mississippi Valley, later still Texas and much of the Southwest. Thus new speech communities were formed, related to the old ones of the seaboard, but each developing new characteristics as lines of settlement crossed.

New complications were added before and after the Revolution by the great waves of immigration of people from countries other than England: Swedes in Delaware, Dutch in New York, Germans and Scots-Irish in Pennsylvania, Irish in New England, Poles and Greeks and Italians and Portuguese. The bringing in of Negro slaves had an important effect on the speech of the South and later on the whole country. The Spanish in California and the Southwest added their mark. In this century movement of peoples goes on: the trek of southern Negroes to northern and western cities, the migration of people from Arkansas, Oklahoma, and Texas to California. All these have shaped and are shaping American speech.

We speak of America as the melting pot, but the speech communities of this continent are very far from having melted into one. Linguists today can trace very clearly the movements of the early settlers in the still living speech of their descendants. They can follow an eighteenth century speech community West, showing how it crossed this pass and followed that river, threw out an offshoot here, left a pocket there, merged with another group, halted, split, moved on once more. If all other historical evidence were destroyed, the history of the country could still be reconstructed from the speech of modern America.

The third great shaper of speech communities is the social class. This has been, and is, more important in England than in America. In England, class differences have often been more prominent than those of age or place. If you were the blacksmith's boy, you might know the son of the local baronet, but you didn't speak his language. You spoke the language of your social group, and he that of his, and over the centuries these social dialects remained widely separated.

England in the twentieth century has been much democratized, but the language differences are far from having disappeared. One can still tell much about a person's family, his school background, his general position in life by the way he speaks. Social lines are hard to cross, and language is perhaps the greatest barrier. You may make a million pounds and own several cars and a place in the country, but your vowels and consonants and nouns and verbs and sentence patterns will still proclaim to the world that you're not a part of the upper crust.

In America, of course, social distinctions have never been so sharp as they are in England. We find it somewhat easier to rise in the world, to move into social environments unknown to our parents. This is possible, partly, because speech differences are slighter; conversely, speech differences are slighter because this is possible. But speech differences do exist. If you've spent all your life driving a cab in Philly and, having inherited a fortune, move to San Francisco's Nob Hill, you will find that your language is different, perhaps embarrassingly so, from that of your new acquaintances.

Language differences on the social plane in America are likely to correlate with education or occupation rather than with birth—simply because education and occupation in America do not depend so much on birth as they do in other countries. A child without family connection can get himself educated at Harvard, Yale, Princeton. In doing so, he acquires the speech habits of the Ivy League and gives up those of his parents.

Exceptions abound. But in general there is a clear difference between the speech habits of the college graduate and those of the high school graduate. The cab driver does not talk like the Standard Oil executive, the college professor like the carnival pitch man, or an Illinois merchant like a sailor shipping out of New Orleans. New York's Madison Avenue and Third Avenue are only a few blocks apart, but they are widely separated in language. And both are different from Broadway.

It should be added that the whole trend of modern life is to reduce rather than to accentuate these differences. In a country where college education becomes increasingly everybody's chance, where executives and refrigerator salesmen and farmers play golf together, where a college professor may drive a cab in the summertime to keep his family alive, it becomes harder and harder to guess a person's education, income, and social status by the way he talks. But it would be absurd to say that language gives no clue at all.

Speech communities, then, are formed by many features: age, geography, education, occupation, social position. Young people speak differently from old people, Kansans differently from Virginians, Yale graduates differently from Dannemora graduates. Now let us pose a delicate question: aren't some of these speech communities better than others? That is, isn't better language heard in some than in others?

Well, yes, of course. One speech community is always better than all the rest. This is the group in which one happens to find oneself. The writer would answer unhesitatingly that the noblest, loveliest, purest English is that heard in the Men's Faculty Club of San Jose State College, San Jose, California. He would admit, of course, that the speech of some of the younger members leaves something to be desired; that certain recent immigrants from Harvard, Michigan, and other foreign parts need to work on the laughable oddities lingering in their speech; and that members of certain departments tend to introduce a lot of queer terms that can only be described as jargon. But in general the English of the Faculty Club is ennobling and sweet.

As a practical matter, good English is whatever English is spoken by the group in which one moves contentedly and at ease. To the bum on Main Street in Los Angeles, good English is the language of other L.A. bums. Should he wander onto the campus of UCLA, he would find the talk there unpleasant, confusing, and comical. He might agree, if pressed, that the college man speaks "correctly" and he doesn't. But in his heart he knows better. He wouldn't talk like them college jerks if you paid him.

If you admire the language of other speech communities more than you do your own, the reasonable hypothesis is that you are dissatisfied with the community itself. It is not precisely other speech that attracts you but the people who use the speech. Conversely, if some language strikes you as unpleasant or foolish or rough, it is presumably because the speakers themselves seem so.

To many people, the sentence "Where is he at?" sounds bad. It is bad, they would say, in and of itself. The sounds are bad. But this is very hard to prove. If "Where is he at?" is bad because it has bad sound combinations, then presumably "Where is the cat?" or "Where is my hat?" are just as bad, yet no one thinks them so. Well, then, "Where is he at?" is bad because it uses too many words. One gets the same meaning from "Where is he?" so why add the *at*? True. Then "He going with us?" is a better sentence than "Is he going with us?" You don't really need the *is*, so why put it in?

Certainly there are some features of language to which we can apply the terms *good* and *bad*, *better* and *worse*. Clarity is usually better than obscurity; precision is better than vagueness. But these are not often what we have in mind when we speak of good and bad English. If we like the speech of upper-class Englishmen, the presumption is that we admire upper-class Englishmen—their characters, culture, habits of mind. Their sounds and words simply come to connote the people themselves and become admirable therefore. If we knew the same sounds and words from people who were distasteful to us, we would find the speech ugly.

This is not to say that correctness and incorrectness do not exist in speech. They obviously do, but they are relative to the speech community—or communities—in which one operates. As a practical matter, correct speech is that which sounds normal or natural to one's comrades. Incorrect speech is that which evokes in them discomfort or hostility or disdain.

STUDY QUESTIONS AND EXERCISES

1. What examples of the language conservatism of the lower class have appeared in previous selections?

2. How do the articles on slang by Roberts and Evans supplement Roberts' account of speech communities?

3. From your own experience or observation, can you cite examples of radical changes in speech communities from home to school and from school to college?

4. Do younger generations influence older generations in dress as well as in speech? How would Whistler's mother be dressed today? How significant is the present American emphasis on youthfulness in speech, dress, and conduct?

5. What kinds of place-names—see Mencken—serve as clues to the migration patterns and dialects Roberts discusses? Do names in your own state agree with Roberts' generalizations? Can you find in your own community speech habits that reveal the history of the area?

6. What examples can you find, in your own experience or observation, of individuals whose language reflects their similar education and occupation, but who were born into widely separated social classes?

7. If "good" English is that spoken by a group in which one is at ease, what are the implications for the college graduate who enters, let us say, a profession and whose parents speak substandard English? Need the parents speak as their son does if they are content to remain with their own age and occupation group? If they wish to enter his group, can they be at ease if their speech is different? Is the essential point "good English" or "correctness," or is it, like good manners, a question of an arbitrary standard? Can natural dignity, poise, and good sense enable a person to be at ease even though his speech and manners differ from those of the group?

33

Social And Educational Varieties In English

W. Nelson Francis

Professor Francis of Brown University explains the distinctive characteristics of educated, vernacular, and uneducated English, classifications based upon the social positions or educational levels of the particular users of language. This discussion is a section of The English Language (1963).

We have already noted that there are social varieties of English, differing in pronunciation, grammar, and vocabulary. These are the natural modes of speech of people who differ in education and in the positions they occupy in the social system. It is here, even more than in regional variation, that value judgments are most likely to be made. Specifically, the dialect of educated people who occupy positions of influence and responsibility is commonly called "good English" and that of people lower on the educational and social scale "bad English." Let us briefly investigate the implications of these terms.

Applied to language, the adjective *good* can have two meanings: (1) "effective, adequate for the purpose to which it is put" and (2) "acceptable, conforming to approved usage." The first of these is truly a value judgment of the language itself. In this sense the language of Shakespeare, for example, is "good English" because it serves as a highly effective vehicle for his material. On the other hand, the language of a poorer writer, which does not meet adequately the demands put upon it, might be called "bad English." The second meaning of *good* is not really a judgment of the language itself but a social appraisal of the persons who use it. An expression like *I ain't got no time for youse* may be most effective in the situation in which it is used, and hence "good English" in the first sense. But most people, including those who naturally speak this way, will call it "bad English" because grammatical features like *ain't, youse,* and the double negative construction belong to a variety of English commonly used by people with little education and low social and economic status.

This second meaning of the terms *good English* and *bad English* is much more common than the first. It is easier, no doubt, to identify a dialect by certain overt items of grammar and vocabulary than it is to estimate the effectiveness of a specific sample of language. Furthermore, the notion that the language of social and educational inferiors is "bad" has been extensively taught in schools, so that even those who speak it naturally often get the idea that there is something intrinsically wrong with their language, usually without clearly understanding why. Others, of course, alter their language to make it conform more nearly to what they have been taught to consider "good." In effect, they adopt a social dialect appropriate to a higher position on the educational and social scale.

It is unfortunate that these two notions—effectiveness and social prestige—have both come to be expressed in the same terms, as value judgments of the language itself. They are not necessarily connected. What is called "bad English" in the usual sense may be highly effective in the appropriate context. Conversely, language which is socially and educationally impeccable may be most ineffective, as anyone who has listened to a dull speech can testify. It is true that on the whole the language of the more educated is likely to be more effective, since it has a larger vocabulary and somewhat more complex grammar and hence is capable of finer and more subtle shades of meaning as well as finer effects of rhythm and tone. But unless these resources are used skillfully they do not necessarily produce better language from the point of view of effectiveness. On the other hand, writers like Mark Twain, Ring Lardner, and William Faulkner have shown that vernacular or uneducated English can be used with great effectiveness in literature.

As with other kinds of variation, social levels of English shade gradually into one another. But we can recognize three main levels. At the top is **educated** or **standard English;** at the bottom is **uneducated English,** and between them comes what H. L. Mencken called the **vernacular.**[1] These have in common the larger part of their grammar, pronunciation, and basic vocabulary but are marked by significant differences in all three areas.

Educated or **Standard English** is that naturally used by most college-educated people who fill positions of social, financial, and professional influence in the community. Some people learn it as their native speech, if they come from families that already belong to this social class. Others acquire it in the course of their schooling and later by conscious or unconscious imitation of their associates. Control of standard English does not, of course, guarantee professional, social, or financial success. But it is an almost indispensable attribute of those who attain such success.

In addition to its social importance, educated English is on the whole

---

[1] H. L. Mencken, *The American Language*, 4th ed. (New York: Alfred A. Knopf, 1937), p. 417.

a more flexible and versatile instrument than the other social varieties. As the language of the professions and the learned disciplines, it is called on to express more complex ideas, for which it has developed an extensive vocabulary. Its grammar, too, is more complex, and it uses longer sentences with more levels of subordination. This does not mean that it presents greater difficulties to the listener or reader, provided he is familiar with its vocabulary and grammar. But the fact that it is often used to express complicated and difficult material means that, unskillfully used, it can be vague or obscure. When its resources of vocabulary and grammar are overexploited in the expression of simple ideas, it may become the inflated jargon sometimes called "gobbledygook."

> With regard to personnel utilizing the premises after normal working hours, it is requested that precautions be observed to insure that all windows and doors are firmly secured and all illumination extinguished before vacating the building.

This is obviously only a much elaborated expression of the request that can be more simply and effectively stated:

> If you work late, be sure to lock the doors and windows and turn off the lights when you leave.

In the first sense of the phrase "good English," this translation is good and the gobbledygook which it translates, though it contains no errors of grammar or usage, is incredibly bad.

The British version of standard English, RP, is the same for all speakers regardless of their place of origin. In America, however, there is no such thing as a single standard form of American English, especially in pronunciation. The nearest thing to it is the speech of anonymous radio and television announcers, which one linguist has aptly called "network English." [2] In contrast to the well known individual commentators, who are allowed to use their native regional pronunciation, the network announcers all use a common version of English which is in most features that of the Inland Northern area. The contrast between a routine sports announcer and Dizzy Dean is the contrast between "network English," faultless but rather dull, and a picturesque use of South Midland vernacular.

Because of its nationwide use, network English is an acceptable standard form everywhere. But it is not a prestige dialect. Educated speakers in Boston, New York, Philadelphia, Richmond, Charleston, Atlanta, or New Orleans use the dialects of their own regions in educated form. The last five Presidents of the United States are a good

---

[2] William A. Stewart, in a discussion of the problem of teaching standard English to nonstandard speakers, Bloomington, Indiana, August 1964.

example of the diversity of pronunciation to be found in standard English. President Johnson speaks the educated South Midland speech of Texas. President Kennedy's Boston speech, with its lack of postvocalic /r/ and its intrusive /r/ at the end of words like *Cuba,* was very distinctive. President Eisenhower's speech was a good illustration of the Middle Western variety sometimes called General American. It betrayed his Kansas origin in spite of a military career that took him to many parts of the English-speaking world. President Truman retained many of the South Midland features of his native Missouri, and President Roosevelt spoke the educated version of New York City speech, somewhat modified by his Harvard education and New England connections. Although most of these men had long careers in politics and frequently addressed nationwide audiences, each of them used the educated version of his native regional dialect.

Vernacular English is the variety naturally used by the middle group of the population, who constitute the vast majority. Their schooling extends into or through high school, with perhaps a year of college or technical school. They occupy the lesser white-collar jobs, staff the service trades, and fill the ranks of skilled labor. Many of these jobs require considerable verbal skill and have extensive occupational vocabularies. Vernacular speakers, when "talking shop," characteristically show considerable control of technical vocabulary and relatively complex grammar.

Just as jargon and gobbledygook are the result of overpretentious style in standard English, so the **hyperurbanism** or **hyperform** is in the vernacular. A hyperurbanism is a usage which results from the overcorrection of one of the supposedly "bad" (*i.e.* nonstandard) features of the vernacular. For example, the usage of pronoun case in the vernacular differs from that of standard English in several respects, one being that a pronoun subject when coordinated with another pronoun or with a noun may be in the objective case:

vernacular:	Him and Joe went.
standard:	Joe and he went.
vernacular:	You and me can do it.
standard:	You and I can do it.

The native speaker of the vernacular who aspires to speak standard learns to change this use of the objective case to the standard subjective. But this change often leads to uncertainty about pronoun case in coordination constructions elsewhere than as subject. The vernacular speaker who has learned that *you and me* is incorrect as subject is likely to be suspicious of it anywhere, so he says *between you and I,* which is just as much a violation of standard grammar as *you and me can do it.*

This is not the place for an extended discussion of the features which distinguish the vernacular from standard educated English. Many of them are identified and discussed in the standard handbooks and dictionaries of usage, a few of which are listed at the end of this chapter. Since the vernacular shades gradually into educated standard, many of these items characterize only the varieties of vernacular nearest to uneducated English. Many points of usage which are condemned as nonstandard by handbooks actually represent **divided usage;** that is, they are accepted and used by some standard English speakers but rejected by others. Sometimes the division is regional: a form or construction which is vernacular or uneducated in one region may be standard in another. An example is the use of *like* in such sentences as *It looks like it might rain* and *He acts like he's hungry.* This usage, condemned as nonstandard by most handbooks, is certainly standard in England and in the American South in all but the most formal style. In the American North and Midland it is probably to be classed as vernacular. At least, a recent advertising slogan that used *like* in this way stirred up considerable discussion and condemnation among those who feel responsible for protecting standard English from vernacular encroachments. In fact, some aspirants to standard "correctness" avoid the use of *like* as a subordinator entirely, replacing it with *as* in sentences like *He drove as a crazy man.* This hyperurbanism throws away the nice semantic distinction between the prepositions *like* and *as,* as in the following:

> He is acting *like* a lawyer in this affair.
> He is acting *as* a lawyer in this affair.

The implication of the first is either that he is not a lawyer at all or that his lawyerlike behavior is inappropriate or unwelcome. In the second, no such judgment is implied; the sentence merely states that in the affair in question his participation is limited to the role of lawyer. It is frequently the effect of a hyperurbanism to gain a supposed (but spurious) "correctness" at the expense of precision. It thus becomes an example of "bad English" in the first sense discussed above. If preciseness in communication is an important quality of language, which certainly few will deny, the hyperurbanism that blurs preciseness in the interest of a fancied correctness is a greater linguistic offense than the nonstandard vernacular usage which is accurate and clear.

The vernacular is very much with us and presumably always will be. It is the stratum of English where there develop many new features of grammar, pronunciation, and vocabulary which are ultimately accepted into standard usage. In a democratic society like that of America, it is an essential medium of communication even for the educated, who must at least understand and accept its usage, though they do not necessarily have to speak it. In fact, if they can speak it only with conscious and obvious effort, educated speakers should avoid it, for people are quick to take offense at what they consider patronizing. But those native speakers of the vernacular who have also acquired a command of educated standard English should not lose control of the vernacular, since a native command of it can be of great value on many occasions.

A practical illustration is the case of the college professor of English, a native speaker of educated English, who needed a rare part for his car. He consulted a colleague who had at one time been a garage mechanic and spoke the appropriate form of the vernacular. The colleague told him where to telephone to inquire for the part, but added, "You'd better let me do the phoning; it'll cost you twice as much if you do it." [3]

Uneducated English is that naturally used by people whose schooling is limited and who perform the unskilled labor in country and city. Certain grammatical features, such as the double or multiple negative (which was standard in Chaucer's English) and the use of *them* as a plural demonstrative, are common to most regional varieties. But in other respects uneducated English shows much regional variety in all its features. An uneducated speaker may find that he has difficulty making himself understood outside his home region. Such features as past-tense *holp* for *helped* and *drug* for *dragged* have clear-cut regional distribution. [4] Likewise regional differences of pronunciation, which, as we have seen, exist on all levels, are much greater in uneducated speech. The same is true of vocabulary; the local words and expressions which more educated speakers avoid (though they may consider them picturesque and use them occasionally for special effect) persistently survive in uneducated speech. For this reason dialectological investigations like the Linguistic Survey of England often confine themselves almost wholly to uneducated, preferably illiterate, informants. [5]

Uneducated English doesn't often get into writing, since its users have little occasion to write and may be semiliterate or even wholly illiterate. [6] In literary writing, uneducated speakers are often marked as such by attempts to represent their pronunciation by distorted spelling, including a liberal use of eye dialect. But a truly skillful use of unedu-

---

[3] This anecdote is told of himself by Professor J. J. Lamberts of Arizona State University.

[4] E. Bagby Atwood, *A Survey of Verb Forms in the Eastern United States* (Ann Arbor: University of Michigan Press, 1958), pp. 9f., 16f.

[5] Harold Orton and Eugen Dieth, *Survey of English Dialects* (Leeds: E. J. Arnold & Son, Ltd., 1962), pp. 14–17, 44. In the Linguistic Atlas of the United States and Canada, however, three types of informants—representing roughly what we have called uneducated, vernacular, and educated English—are used. See Hans Kurath, *Handbook of the Linguistic Geography of New England* (Washington: American Council of Learned Societies, 1939), pp. 41–44.

[6] C. C. Fries, in preparing his *American English Grammar* (New York: Appleton-Century-Crofts, 1940), found a plentiful source of uneducated written English in letters written to a government bureau whose constituents included many uneducated speakers.

cated English in literature suggests the level of the speaker without resorting to the rather cheap device of eye dialect. Notice in the following passage from William Faulkner's great novel *As I Lay Dying* how the nature of the speaker—an uneducated Mississippi farmer—is indicated by grammar and vocabulary, without any attempt to illustrate pronunciation at all.

> It was nigh toward daybreak when we drove the last nail and toted it into the house, where she was laying on the bed with the window open and the rain blowing on her again. Twice he did it, and him so dead for sleep that Cora says his face looked like one of these here Christmas masts that had done been buried a while and then dug up, until at last they put her into it and nailed it down so he couldn't open the window on her no more. And the next morning they found him in his shirt tail, laying asleep on the floor like a felled steer, and the top of the box bored clean full of holes and Cash's new auger broke off in the last one. When they taken the lid off they found that two of them had bored on into her face.
>
> If it's a judgment, it aint right. Because the Lord's got more to do than that. He's bound to have. Because the only burden Anse Bundren's ever had is himself. And when folks talks him low, I think to myself he aint that less of a man or he couldn't a bore himself this long.[7]

Here the markers of uneducated regional dialect are such grammatical items as the verb phrase *had done been buried* and the double negative in *couldn't open the window on her no more*, the lexical item *toted*, and idioms like *talks him low* and *he aint that less of a man*.

The uneducated English of this sample contrasts with the following passage from the same novel, representing the English of a country doctor from the same region:

> When Anse finally sent for me of his own accord, I said "He has wore her out at last." And I said a damn good thing, and at first I would not go because there might be something I could do and I would have to haul her back, by God. I thought maybe they have the same sort of fool ethics in heaven they have in the Medical College and that it was maybe Vernon Tull sending for me again, getting me there in the nick of time, as Vernon always does things, getting the most for Anse's money like he does for his own. But when it got far enough into the day for me to read weather sign I knew it couldn't have been anybody but Anse that sent. I knew that nobody but a luckless man could ever need a doctor in the face of a cyclone. And I knew that if it had finally occurred to Anse himself that he needed one, it was already too late.[8]

---

[7] From *As I Lay Dying*, by William Faulkner, p. 68. Copyright 1930 and renewed 1957 by William Faulkner. Reprinted by permission of Random House, Inc.
[8] *As I Lay Dying*, p. 37.

There are items here which are not educated standard—*wore* as past participle, for example. But the general level of the English is educated colloquial, quite different from that of the previous passage. Note especially the grammatical complexity of the last sentence.

The speaker who is confined to uneducated English finds himself under a great handicap if he wishes to improve his position in society. This is true even in his own region; it is doubly so when he moves to another dialect area, where he may find not only that his speech is a liability when it comes to getting a good job, but even that he can't make himself understood at all. Furthermore, in an age when more and more of the unskilled tasks are being done by machines, the number of jobs available to persons unable to use any but uneducated English gets smaller every year. The geographical and social mobility of our people presents a great problem to the schools, one of whose tasks is to help students acquire a kind of language which will be an asset to them rather than a handicap. The problem is especially acute in the Northern cities which have had a large influx of uneducated people from the South. It is encouraging to observe that linguists, especially dialectologists, are being called on to help with this problem. The idea is getting about that the speaker of uneducated English is better served if an attempt is made not to "correct" his language and eradicate his "bad language habits," but to extend his linguistic range and versatility by helping him acquire a new dialect that is socially more acceptable. Some educators are even experimenting with the techniques developed for teaching foreign languages, in order to emphasize that the task is the positive one of learning something new rather than the negative one of eliminating something bad. Already the results of tentative efforts of this sort are showing promise.

Helping speakers of uneducated English to a command of the vernacular or of standard English is only part of the problem, of course. There must be other kinds of training, and above all there must be tangible evidence that the effort will be worth while; otherwise motivation will be lacking, and without motivation learning is impossible. But in this area the informed student and teacher of language can certainly be of great social usefulness.

STUDY QUESTIONS AND EXERCISES

1. Compare Francis' discussion of "good" and "bad" English with Joos's style scale of *Responsibility* and discussion of it.

2. Why is the language of well-educated people likely to be more effective than that of the common man? How can wit and intelligence compensate in language for lack of education? How, according

to Lamberts, can education lessen effectiveness of language? In William Faulkner's *The Town*, compare the language of Ratliff, an uneducated man, with that of Gavin Stevens, a Harvard-educated lawyer with a Ph.D. degree from Heidelberg. Is Ratliff able to express himself forcefully? What evidences do you note of self-education? (See Joos, selection 23, question 6.)

3. How do Francis' three social levels of English compare with Kenyon's two levels and Lamberts' three? What elements do the three classifications have in common?

4. How does "gobbledygook" differ from what Lamberts calls hyperstandard? Which is more likely to be the expression of the user's own personality?

5. How does British RP (Received Pronunciation) differ from American standard English? What are some of the reasons for this difference, as presented in other articles in this text? Do Americans of all regions recognize the acceptability of language of regions other than their own? (See the preceding article, by Roberts.)

6. Francis refers to the dialect of recent Presidents. In the United States, is a person's rise from humble beginnings to eminence regarded as creditable or something to be concealed? Does the phrase "from log cabin to White House" suggest approval or condemnation of such a rise? How does social mobility, in contrast with fixed social classes, affect both the language used by self-made leaders and the attitudes of the public toward the language of their leaders? How would you describe the speech of Richard Nixon? Does it fit the concluding sentence of Francis' paragraph on the speech of Presidents? Describe the original social and economic status of each of the Presidents mentioned by Francis in this paragraph.

7. What social group uses the vernacular? What characterizes the vernacular equivalent of pretentious standard English? How do the disputes on acceptable usage referred to in previous selections illustrate Francis' point about divided usage and regional variations? By what author or authors in this text was *like* discussed? What is the advertising slogan referred to by Francis?

8. How does Francis' statement about preciseness as an important quality in language apply to confusion of terms like *flaunt* and *flout* or to the use of *alibi* (look it up) to mean excuse? Does this confusion reflect the influence of the vernacular? Should responsible style avoid imprecision which deprives the language of useful words?

9. How does the vernacular contribute to the development of standard English? Which of the specific usages that are in dispute in this selection represent the influence of the vernacular? How important is slang in this influence?

10. Why is it unnecessary and often undesirable for the educated to try to use the vernacular? Why should those who acquire standard English retain the vernacular? What is the particular signifi-

cance of this principle for those who speak a minority dialect of the vernacular?

11. Who is the college professor referred to as an example of loss or lack of control of the vernacular? How does his own version of the incident differ from Francis' version?

12. What are the characteristics of uneducated English? Which terms in the first quotation of William Faulkner belong to regional dialect rather than to social level? In the next quotation, note *like* as a conjunction. Is this suitable in the speech of an educated Southerner?

13. How can the responsible person overcome the social and economic limitations imposed by uneducated dialect? What obstacles may prevent him from succeeding in his efforts? How does selection 20, by McDavid, illustrate what Francis says about dialectologists and the principle of acquiring the new without eliminating the old?

14. From your own observation or experience, provide examples of the three social varieties of English, including the *hyper-* variations, and identify in each the characteristics Francis specifies. Do you find any other characteristics that are purely idiosyncratic?

34

The Non-Standard Vernacular of The Negro Community: Some Practical Suggestions

William Labov

The verbal patterns of a particular group often reflect the cultural attitudes and values of that group. Professor William Labov of Columbia University suggests that even though Negro speakers of English can communicate their ideas to their peers in a nonstandard dialect, they should learn the standard patterns for their usefulness in influencing and controlling other people. This study was published in 1967 by the Education Resources Information Center (ERIC).

Before we approach any of the theoretical or practical problems connected with the language of the urban ghettos, it is necessary to arrive at some kind of *modus vivendi* with the term "Negro dialect." A great many people, including educators, speak of "Negro dialect," and a great many others object and even deny the existence of such a form. Furthermore, there is considerable resistance within the school systems to any mention of the particular characteristics of Negro students or Negro speech.

First, it is obvious to anyone that there is no one speech form, and no linguistic markers, that are common to all Negro people. There is no racial, genetic or physiological feature involved here. There is a culturally inherited pattern which has been transmitted to the centers of most Northern cities by migrants from the South, the great majority of whom happen to be Negroes. Most of the forms heard in the Northern ghettos are also used by some white Southerners. However, it is also a fact that the Negro residents of Northern cities are the chief representatives of these Southern regional traits for white Northerners. These traits have lost their geographical significance for most Northerners, and taken on the social significance of identification with the Negro ethnic group.

Not all Southern features survive in the Northern ghettos. A selected set of them are common, while others tend to disappear; the most extraordinary fact is that in city after city the end result is quite similar. The speech of Negro children in Philadelphia, New York, Chicago, or Los Angeles is cast in much the same mold: the differences that do appear can be traced to differences in the surrounding dialect of the white community.

We are currently engaged in a study of the structural and functional differences between the non-standard English of the urban vernacular and the standard English of the schoolroom.[1] In several publications, we have provided some preliminary information on the principal structural conflicts involved here, and some of the immediate consequences for the teaching of reading.[2] Though I will not attempt to summarize this data here, it will be useful to think of these alternations under four general headings:

[1] There are a number of systematic differences in the sound pattern which have little grammatical significance. There is an asymmetrical neutralization of /θ/ and /f/ in final position, for example,[3] so that *Ruth* is merged with *roof*.

[2] A much more important set of phonological differences intersect grammatical features: along this phonological-grammatical intersection lie the most important problems for teachers of speech and reading. The simplification of consonant clusters operates so that *muss* and *must* are homonyms, but also *miss* and *missed*. The phonological process which eliminates final and preconsonantal *r* and *l* is deeply involved with the grammatical problems of the copula and the future respectively. We have dealt with this topic more than any other in our previous publications.

[3] A fairly obvious set of morphological differences might be singled out: plurals such as *mens*, *teeths* or metathesized forms such as *aks* for 'ask.' Although these forms are quite resistant to alternation with the standard forms, they do not belong to a highly organized system in equilibrium which challenges linguistic analysis.

---

[1] This research is supported by the U.S. Office of Education as Cooperative Research Project 3288.

[2] Labov, William, Paul Cohen and Clarence Robins. A *Preliminary Study of the Structure of English Used by Negro and Puerto Rican Speakers in New York City.* Final Report—Cooperative Research Project No. 3091, Office of Education, 1965.

Labov, William. "Some Sources of Reading Problems for Negro Speakers of Non-Standard English." In Frazier, Alexander (ed.) *New Directions in Elementary English.* Champaign, Illinois: National Council of Teachers of English, 1967.

Labov, William and Paul Cohen. "Some Suggestions for Teaching Standard English to Speakers of Non-Standard Urban Dialects." For Chapter V of *Oral Language for Speakers of Non-Standard English.* Submitted to the Bureau of Curriculum Research of the Board of Education of the City of New York, 1967.

[3] This feature, like many such purely phonological differences, is of little pedagogical significance. By "asymmetrical" I mean that *Ruth* is heard as *roof*, but not vice-versa. Negro speakers seldom confuse the two classes of words, since they do not give hypercorrect *roof* as *rooth*. The distinction is quite hard to hear consistently, even for white speakers.

[4] There are many syntactic rules by which non-standard Negro English differs from standard English. Some, like the optional deletion of the copula in *He with us*, are commonplace and are easily converted to the standard form by speakers. But many other syntactic differences are governed by deep-seated and abstract rules. Embedded yes-no questions such as *I asked Alvin if he knew* appear as *I asked Alvin did he know*. In this case we are dealing with two alternate realizations of an underlying "Question" element: the use of *if* with declarative order, as opposed to no *if* with the inverted order of auxiliary and subject. This non-standard form is surprisingly regular and resistant to conversion to the standard form. The comparative produces a wealth of complex forms very different from standard English: *He runs the same fast as Jim can run*. But, as interesting and complex as such syntactic rules may be, they cannot be considered as important as the items described under [2], which will undoubtedly draw the major share of pedagogical attention for some time to come.

At this point it may be proper to ask just how deep-seated and extensive are the differences between the non-standard and standard forms we are considering. There are various viewpoints on this subject: some scholars believe that the underlying phrase structures and semantics of non-standard Negro English are quite different, and reflect the influence of an hypothesized earlier Creole grammar. Others believe that this English dialect, like all other dialects of English, is fundamentally identical with standard English, and differs only in relatively superficial respects. One way to look at this argument is to ask whether differences in surface structure (the order of words and the forms they assume) are greater or less than the differences in the most abstract generative rules.

It is not important that we attempt to resolve this issue here. Our own research is concerned more with discriminating the relative depth or abstractness of the rules which govern various forms, and it may be useful to indicate the results of one investigation we have recently conducted into the ability of Negro boys, 10 to 14 years old, to imitate sentences. These trials are conducted as "memory tests," in which groups of Negro boys that we know well are given very strong motivation to try to repeat back sentences exactly. Such tests have been carried out before with young children 3 to 6 years old, but no one has studied imitation or "shadowing" of older children across a dialect boundary. We find that some boys are relatively good at repeating standard sentences, even very long ones, while a good many others find great difficulty with standard sentences and do better in reproducing the non-standard sentences. The greatest interest for us lies in the differential ability of children with different rules. If we consider the copula, for example, in sentences like *Larry is older than George and George is a friend of mine*, we observe very little difficulty in the preservation of the *is*. In our first trials, 21 out of 22 such copulas were given back to us in the standard form. But if we consider the problem of negative concord, which produces such sentences as *Nobody never know nothing about no game today*, we find a different situation. In about half of the cases, the sentences were repeated back with non-standard negative concord. *Nobody ever said that* becomes *Nobody never said that*; and one can re-emphasize the standard form insistently with little change in the repetitions produced by the boys. Similarly, sentences such as *He asked if I could go to the game today* are repeated instantly without hesitation as *He asked could I go to the game today*. Such results indicate that the deletion of the copula is a relatively superficial rule which occurs relatively late in the grammar and alternates easily with the undeleted form, while the other cases are more fundamental differences in the compulsory rules of the transformational component of the grammar.

We can draw a further set of conclusions from the results of this work. Consider for a moment what is implied about the competence of the speaker who repeats instantly *He asked could I go . . .* when we say *He asked if I could go. . . .* His sentence may be considered a mistake, for which he is penalized in the testing procedure. But what kind of a mistake? It is the correct vernacular form corresponding to the standard form: it means the same thing as the standard form. To produce this non-standard sentence the listener must first *understand* the standard form, automatically convert this into an abstract representation, then produce his own form by a complex series of rules ultimately appearing as *He asked could I go. . . .* We cannot explain this response by imagining that the listener is trying to remember individual words, or failing to match one word to another in the right sequence. This phenomenon is a convincing demonstration of the abstract character of the language mechanism involved, and it also indicates that the structure of Negro non-standard English is quite complex. For many rules, there are *two* perceptual routes but only one production route. The teacher's task here will be to supply the practice in producing sentences by rules which are already well established in the perceptive apparatus.

We may wish to turn our attention now to the important and complex question of the relative *evaluation* of the two forms of English being considered here. Our studies of language within the speech community indicate that the evolution of language is strongly influenced by sets of social values consciously or unconsciously attributed to linguistic forms by the adult members of the community. So far, each of the studies that we have carried out indicate that there is greater agreement on the normative side than in speech performance, and the Negro community is no exception. Our subjective reaction tests show extraordinary uniformity in the unconscious evaluation of the non-standard forms by all sections of the Negro community, middle class and working class, of Northern or Southern origin.

With the rise of strong nationalist feelings in the Negro community, some observers have thought that separate linguistic norms would appear, and that the non-standard vernacular of the urban ghettos would be treated more positively by the leaders of the Negro community. In actual fact, this has not been so, and there is little reason to think that it will be the case in the future. The norms of correct speech are the same for the Negro community as for the white community; although various groups may move in different directions in their informal, spontaneous and intimate styles, they converge in their attitude on the appropriate forms for school, and public language. Suggestions have been received that reading primers be prepared in the vernacular, to accelerate the process of learning to read in the early grades. The results of our investigations throw considerable doubt on the acceptability of such a program. The Negro adults we have interviewed would agree almost unanimously that their children should be taught standard English in school, and any other policy would probably meet with strong opposition.

This unanimity is a characteristic of the *adult* community; we obtain no such uniform pattern from teen-agers. When we consider that a child learns his basic syntax from 18 to 36 months, and by eight years old has settled most of the fine points of phonology and morphology, it is surprising to discover how late in life he acquires the adult pattern in the evaluation of language. Children learn early, of course, that there is careful and casual style, and they are perfectly able to recognize the teacher's special style—but the wider social significance of dialect differences seems to be hidden from them to a surprising extent. Clearly one approach to facilitating the learning of standard English is to accelerate the acquisition of evaluative norms. At the age of 25, almost everyone comes to realize the import of language stratification, but by then, of course, it is difficult to change patterns of language production.

Our subjective reaction tests determine the unconscious evaluation of individual variables within the dialect pattern. The first evaluation scales that were devised allowed the listener to place the speaker along a scale of job suitability: what was the highest job that a person could hold speaking as he did? In our work in Harlem, we have added to this scale others which register converse attitudes: If the speaker was in a street fight, how likely would he be to win? or How likely is it that the speaker become a friend of yours? As we expected, complementary sets of values are attributed to most non-standard forms. To the extent that the use of a certain form, such as fricative *th* in *this thing*, raises a speaker on the job scale, it lowers him on the scale of toughness or masculinity. These opposing values are equally strong in all social groups: we find that the middle-class adults are most consistent in attributing both sets to a given group of speakers.

We have long been aware of the fact that the non-standard forms are supported by the values of group identity and opposition to middle-class norms which are strong among working-class people. The recent results of our subjective reaction tests suggest that the school system may actually be supporting this opposition or even inculcating it. The adolescent boy knows that there is no correlation in fact between toughness and the use of non-standard English: he knows a great many bad fighters who have perfect command of the vernacular, and many good fighters who do fairly well with school language. But the teacher is not as keenly aware of the limitations of her stereotypes; I think it quite possible that while she attempts to teach the middle-class values of good English, she is simultaneously conveying the notion that good English is inconsistent with toughness and masculinity which is highly valued by adolescent boys. Teaching programs should be carefully examined by men raised in the community who can help detect and eliminate the association of standard English with effeminacy, gentility, and overcultivation. It seems to be true that a perfect command of standard English weakens one's grasp of the vernacular: I have met no one who excelled in both forms. But I think it is important to minimize the loss, and particularly to minimize the opposition of middle-class and working-class values which has come to cluster about the language issue in such a stereotyped manner.

A great deal of our current research is concentrated upon the *functional* conflict between standard and non-standard English. It is too early to make any strong statements in this direction, although we believe that the most important educational applications will stem from an understanding of differences in the use of language. It is worth pointing out that most language testing which takes place within the schools gives a very poor indication of the over-all verbal skills of the children being tested. In an adult-dominated environment—the school, the home, or the recreation center—many children have learned elaborate defensive techniques which involve a minimum of verbal response. Monosyllabic answers, repressed speech, special intonation contours are all characteristic of such face-to-face testing situations. As a result, a great deal of public funds are being spent on programs designed to supply verbal stimulus to "non-verbal" children. The notion of cultural deprivation here is surely faulty: it is based on a mythology that has arisen about children who receive very little verbal stimulus, seldom hear complete sentences—children who are in fact supposed to be culturally empty vehicles.

In our research, we frequently encounter children who behave in a face-to-face encounter with adults as if they were "non-verbal." But when we utilize our knowledge of the social forces which control language behavior, and stimulate speech with more sophisticated techniques, the non-verbal child disappears.

These children have an extremely rich verbal culture; they are proficient at a wide range of verbal skills, even though many of these skills are unacceptable within the school program. The problem, of course, is to teach a different set of verbal skills, used for different purposes; but the teacher should be absolutely clear on the fact that she is opposing one verbal culture with another. If the task were only to fill a cultural vacuum, it would be much easier than it actually turns out to be.

In conclusion, I might suggest one implication of our studies of language use which might have value within the school system. Intelligence and verbal skill within the culture of the street is prized just as highly as it is within the school: but the use of such skills is more often to manipulate and control other people than to convey information to them. Of course it is the school's task to emphasize the value of language in cognitive purposes. But in order to motivate adolescent and pre-adolescent children to learn standard English, it would be wise to emphasize its value for handling social situations, avoiding conflict (or provoking conflict when desired), for influencing and controlling other people. This is the use for which verbal skills are already prized in the vernacular culture, and it seems to be good strategy to take advantage of the values that are already present, even while one is modifying them and teaching new ones. Long before the child has learned the full range of middle-class educational values, he must make a good start in mastering the fundamental rules of standard English. Any strategy which gives him strong motivation for reading and writing in standard English should be followed; we are all familiar with the fact that success or failure in these fundamental skills is an important determinant of success or failure in the school program as a whole.

STUDY QUESTIONS AND EXERCISES

1. What social facts explain the failure of Northerners to recognize "Negro dialect" as geographical rather than social? How does Labov define "Negro dialect": what is it not, and what is it?

2. In what broad study of nonstandard English are Labov and fellow linguists engaged? (See the item by Labov in the Bibliography in this text for a detailed treatment of nonstandard English as part of the sociolinguistic structure of the English language.) In light of previous selections in Part 5 of this text, why is such a study necessary?

3. What four kinds of differences does Labov specify between the variety of nonstandard dialect in question and standard English? Which of these differences have you noticed, in speech or in written representation of dialect?

4. What is metathesis? Look up *spoonerism* in a dictionary: how is this common phenomenon of language, often humorous, related to metathesis?

5. Can you provide other examples than the "embedded yes-no questions" of a combination of two alternative forms instead of a choice between them? In a dictionary of usage, look up the origins of

"cannot help but" and "can't hardly" or "hardly": what conclusion might be drawn as to ultimate acceptability into informal standard English of expressions originating in this fashion?

6. In imitation of standard sentences by children, what contrast was observed between superficial and fundamental nonstandard forms? What does Labov mean by referring to "He asked could I go" as "the correct vernacular form"? How is this structure more complex than that which appears in the story of the schoolboy who finished a remedial task and left a note for the teacher: "I wrote 'I have gone' 500 times and I have went home"? How are the two examples comparable?

7. How are the norms of correct speech of the Negro community related to those of the white? Where do they differ and where do they converge?

8. What variety of English did Negro adults who were interviewed wish their children to be taught in school? Would white parents have had the same wish?

9. Why is the teenage period so crucial in the learning of standard English? Can you explain how the general problems of teenagers in reaching maturity are exemplified in this specific example?

10. What opposition between socio-economic success and status among one's peers is reflected in standard versus nonstandard speech? Is this opposition peculiar to minority groups? Which previous selections in this text deal with unfavorable reactions to what seems to the hearer "hyperstandard" English? How does the basic principle of suiting one's language to the hearers and the occasion minimize the problem if one has command of both nonstandard and standard English?

11. For what groups does standard English often become associated with effeminacy? Can you suggest ways to minimize the creation of such linguistic stereotypes?

12. In your experience and observation, what situations and approaches in language testing stimulate a nonverbal response? How might this unfavorable reaction be lessened: would tape-recording, for example, allow more spontaneity than writing? How could the value of written expression still be gained?

13. What suggestions have been made in previous selections in this text for dealing with the problem of "opposing one verbal culture with another"?

14. Which values of verbal skills does Labov advise stressing in order to motivate children and adolescents in language study?

15. Why are the fundamental skills of reading and writing standard English becoming increasingly necessary in our society? What social and economic trends and developments are rapidly altering employment opportunities and changing the situations an individual faces during his working years, in both trades and professions?

35

Folk Speech

John Nist

Folk speech is a vigorous mode of communication on a popular or unso-phisticated level. Professor Nist of Auburn University discusses this phe-nomenon in A Structural History of English (1966).

Whereas regionalisms generally indicate the geographical distri-bution of various forms of American English, *levels of usage* indicate the status of the speaker of the language. The four major levels of usage in American English are standard formal (literary), standard informal (well-bred colloquial), trade or technical (commercial, scientific, dip-lomatic, etc.), and popular or illiterate (uncultivated folk speech). Be-cause "ungrammatical" statements are usually more forceful and clear than their refined equivalents, vulgar American English—commonly called *folk speech*—is a fascinating linguistic phenomenon. Strong verbs, for example, find refuge in this level of usage, where the final *t* in forms like *slept* is often dropped and where the preterit morphology frequently substitutes for that of the perfect participle. The subjunctive in vulgar American English is virtually nonexistent. The contraction *ain't* runs rampant in folk speech; so also does the archaic past participle *gotten*. Other features of this level of usage are the replacement of *have* with *gotta*, of *must* with *hafta*; the preference for *useta* to indicate the past tense; the slurring of *n't* to *n* and of *can't you* to *cancha*; the use of *don't* for *doesn't* in direct analogy with *won't*; a reliance upon the vulgar historical present, as in verbs like *gives* and *says*; and the con-stant employment of double or even multiple negation.

The pronoun system of American folk speech is characterized by the replacement of *s* with *n* in the absolute possessive (*theirn* for *theirs*); by the use of *they, them,* and *their* as forms of the common indefinite; by adding either *-s, -uns,* or *-all* to *you* to indicate plurality; by affixing *-all* to *who* and *what* to form an intensive interrogative; by using *them* as a demonstrative and adding *here* and *there* to strengthen the demon-stratives themselves: *this-here, these-here, that-there, those-there,* and *them-there;* by the substitution of *who* for *whom* and of *em* for *them;* and by the scarcity of *whose.* The American vulgate merges the nominative and the objective forms of the personal pronouns into those of the conjoint and the absolute so that the following expressions prevail: "*Us* girls was there" and "*Him* and Mary got hitched." American folk speech prefers the objective case in all post-verb constructions (*that's him*), except when the pronoun is separated from its governing word by either a noun, a noun word group, or another pronoun (*between you and I*). In this vulgar level of usage, *self* operates as a reflexive noun to form compounds such as *hisself* and *theirselves*. In the inflectional treatment of nouns American folk speech is notorious for indicating plurality and possession at the end of a compound noun or noun phrase (*two mother-in-laws, the girl around the corner's glove*); for creating false singulars (*Chinee, Portugee*), double plurals (*oxens, sheeps, womens*), and an objective-case disregard of plurality (*give me forty bushel*).

As for the adjective, American folk speech chooses *-y* as the distinctive suffix, often omits *-ed* from the converted past participle, generally prefers *-er* for the comparative and *-est* for the superlative, and almost always slurs *than* to *'n*. The so-called flat adverb in the American vulgate, by which the adjectival form predominates, is admission of the importance of stress and syntactical positioning in determining grammatical function. As a matter of fact, use of the "flat" adverb indicates the native wisdom inherent in this level of usage, which has given Modern American English such standard constructions as the split infinitive; the use of *between, either,* and *neither* when more than two items are involved; the comparative formula of *different than;* the use of *like* as a conjunction; the terminal positioning of the idiomatic preposition; the preference for *loan* over *lend* as a verb; the choice of *their* as the reference to an indefinite singular; and the prevalence of such accepted idioms as *good and, try and,* and *it's me.*

So vigorous is American folk speech that it proves that communication and communion in language need not be either elegant or universally socially acceptable to be effective and eloquent. Literary art is most tolerant of the American vulgate—in fact, cannot do without it. Since what is frowned on today may be praised tomorrow, American folk speech is indispensable for the future development of the language. People yield usage; usage yields language; language yields literature. Without the impact of the vulgate upon its authors, twentieth-century American literature would not occupy the position it does.

STUDY QUESTIONS AND EXERCISES

1. Compare Nist's "levels of usage" with the levels and varieties discussed by Kenyon, Lamberts, Joos, and Francis. What point, made by Kenyon and accepted by the others, does Nist not consider?

2. Does Evans, in "Editor's Choice" (selection 5), agree with

Nist about the subjunctive? Which author provides evidence? Look up *get, gotten,* in Bryant, *Current American Usage,* Evans and Evans, *Dictionary of Contemporary American Usage,* and the recent dictionaries. Is *gotten* either archaic or illiterate? Is *don't* for *doesn't* illiterate? (See the above references.)

3. Examine the verbs, pronouns, and adjectives in the folk speech of uneducated characters in a work of fiction by Faulkner, Erskine Caldwell, or some other writer whose characters use modern substandard dialects. Do you find evidence that Nist's statements about these forms are correct? Is this folk speech "effective and eloquent" as represented in fiction?

4. Which partially or fully accepted forms and constructions come into standard English from substandard folk speech? See the list at the end of the next to the last paragraph of this selection. Which of these are really survivals of older forms? (Look them up in an unabridged dictionary.)

36

The Language of Soul

Claude Brown

The black American writer, Claude Brown, examines some of the distinctive elements of one pattern of Afro-American speech. Mr. Brown's observations were published in Esquire *for April, 1968.*

Perhaps the most soulful word in the world is "nigger." Despite its very definite fundamental meaning (the Negro man), and disregarding the deprecatory connotation of the term, "nigger" has a multiplicity of nuances when used by soul people. Dictionaries define the term as being synonymous with Negro, and they generally point out that it is regarded as a vulgar expression. Nevertheless, to those of chitlins-and-neck-bones background the word nigger is neither a synonym for Negro nor an obscene expression.

"Nigger" has virtually as many shades of meaning in Colored English as the demonstrative pronoun "that," prior to application to a noun. To some Americans of African ancestry (I avoid using the term Negro whenever feasible, for fear of offending the Brothers X, a pressure group to be reckoned with), nigger seems preferable to Negro and has a unique kind of sentiment attached to it. This is exemplified in the frequent —and perhaps even excessive—usage of the term to denote either fondness or hostility.

It is probable that numerous transitional niggers and even established ex-soul brothers can—with pangs of nostalgia—reflect upon a day in the lollipop epoch of lives when an adorable lady named Mama bemoaned her spouse's fastidiousness with the strictly secular utterance: "Lord, how can one nigger be so hard to please?" Others are likely to recall a time when that drastically lovable colored woman, who was forever wiping our noses and darning our clothing, bellowed in a moment of exasperation: "Nigger, you gonna be the death o' me." And some of the brethren who have had the precarious fortune to be raised up, wised up, thrown up or simply left alone to get up as best they could, on one of the nation's South Streets or Lenox Avenues, might remember having affectionately referred to a best friend as "My nigger."

The vast majority of "back-door Americans" are apt to agree with

Webster—a nigger is simply a Negro or black man. But the really profound contemporary thinkers of this distinguished ethnic group—Dick Gregory, Redd Foxx, Moms Mabley, Slappy White, etc.—are likely to differ with Mr. Webster and define nigger as "something else"—a soulful "something else." The major difference between the nigger and the Negro, who have many traits in common, is that the nigger is the more soulful.

Certain foods, customs and artistic expressions are associated almost solely with the nigger: collard greens, neck bones, hog maws, black-eyed peas, pigs' feet, etc. A nigger has no desire to conceal or disavow any of these favorite dishes or restrain other behavioral practices such as bobbing his head, patting his feet to funky jazz, and shouting and jumping in church. This is not to be construed that all niggers eat chitlins and shout in church, nor that only niggers eat the aforementioned dishes and exhibit this type of behavior. It is to say, however, that the soulful usage of the term nigger implies all of the foregoing and considerably more.

The Language of Soul—or, as it might also be called, Spoken Soul or Colored English—is simply an honest vocal portrayal of black America. The roots of it are more than three hundred years old.

Before the Civil War there were numerous restrictions placed on the speech of slaves. The newly arrived Africans had the problem of learning to speak a new language, but also there were inhibitions placed on the topics of the slaves' conversation by slave masters and overseers. The slaves made up songs to inform one another of, say, the underground railroads' activity. When they sang *Steal Away* they were planning to steal away to the North, not to heaven. Slaves who dared to speak of rebellion or even freedom usually were severely punished. Consequently, Negro slaves were compelled to create a semi-clandestine vernacular in the way that the criminal underworld has historically created words to confound law-enforcement agents. It is said that numerous Negro spirituals were inspired by the hardships of slavery, and that what later became songs were initially moanings and coded cotton-field lyrics. To hear these songs sung today by a talented soul brother or sister or by a group is to be reminded of an historical spiritual bond that cannot be satisfactorily described by the mere spoken word.

The American Negro, for virtually all of his history, has constituted a vastly disproportionate number of the country's illiterates. Illiteracy has a way of showing itself in all attempts at vocal expression by the uneducated. With the aid of colloquialisms, malapropisms, battered and fractured grammar, and a considerable amount of creativity, Colored English, the sound of soul, evolved.

The progress has been cyclical. Often terms that have been discarded from the soul people's vocabulary for one reason or another are reaccepted years later, but usually with completely different meaning. In the Thirties and Forties "stuff" was used to mean vagina. In the middle

Fifties it was revived and used to refer to heroin. Why certain expressions are thus reactivated is practically an indeterminable question. But it is not difficult to see why certain terms are dropped from the soul language. Whenever a soul term becomes popular with whites it is common practice for the soul folks to relinquish it. The reasoning is that "if white people can use it, it isn't hip enough for me." To many soul brothers there is just no such creature as a genuinely hip white person. And there is nothing more detrimental to anything hip than to have it fall into the square hands of the hopelessly unhip.

White Americans wrecked the expression "something else." It was bad enough that they couldn't say "sump'n else," but they weren't even able to get out "somethin' else." They had to go around saying *something else* with perfect or nearly perfect enunciation. The white folks invariably fail to perceive the soul sound in soulful terms. They get hung up in diction and grammar, and when they vocalize the expression it's no longer a soulful thing. In fact, it can be asserted that spoken soul is more of a sound than a language. It generally possesses a pronounced lyrical quality which is frequently incompatible to any music other than that ceaseless and relentlessly driving rhythm that flows from poignantly spent lives. Spoken soul has a way of coming out metered without the intention of the speaker to invoke it. There are specific phonetic traits. To the soulless ear the vast majority of these sounds are dismissed as incorrect usage of the English language and, not infrequently, as speech impediments. To those so blessed as to have had bestowed upon them at birth the lifetime gift of soul, these are the most communicative and meaningful sounds ever to fall upon human ears: the familiar "mah" instead of "my," "gonna" for "going to," "yo" for "your." "Ain't" is pronounced "ain'"; "bread" and "bed," "bray-ud" and "bay-ud"; "baby" is never "bay-bee" but "bay-buh"; Sammy Davis Jr. is not "Sammee" but a kind of "Sam-eh"; the same goes for "Eddeh" Jefferson. No matter how many "man's" you put into your talk, it isn't soulful unless the word has the proper plaintive, nasal "maee-yun."

Spoken soul is distinguished from slang primarily by the fact that the former lends itself easily to conventional English, and the latter is diametrically opposed to adaptations within the realm of conventional English. Police (pronounced pō′ lice) is a soul term, whereas "The Man" is merely slang for the same thing. Negroes seldom adopt slang terms from the white world and when they do the terms are usually given a different meaning. Such was the case with the term "bag." White racketeers used it in the Thirties to refer to the graft that was paid to the police. For the past five years soul people have used it when referring to a person's vocation, hobby, fancy, etc. And once the appropriate term is given the treatment (soul vocalization) it becomes soulful.

However, borrowings from spoken soul by white men's slang—particularly teen-age slang—are plentiful. Perhaps because soul is probably the most graphic language of modern times, everybody who is excluded from Soulville wants to usurp it, ignoring the formidable fettering to the soul folks that has brought the language about. Consider "uptight," "strung-out," "cop," "boss," "kill 'em," all now widely used outside Soulville. Soul people never question the origin of a slang term; they either dig it and make it a part of their vocabulary or don't and forget it. The expression "uptight," which meant being in financial straits, appeared on the soul scene in the general vicinity of 1953. Junkies were very fond of the word and used it literally to describe what was a perpetual condition with them. The word was pictorial and pointed; therefore it caught on quickly in Soulville across the country. In the early Sixties when "uptight" was on the move, a younger generation of soul people in the black urban communities along the Eastern Seaboard regenerated it with a new meaning: "everything is cool, under control, going my way." At present the term has the former meaning for the older generation and the latter construction for those under thirty years of age.

It is difficult to ascertain if the term "strung-out" was coined by junkies or just applied to them and accepted without protest. Like the term "uptight" in its initial interpretation, "strung-out" aptly described the constant plight of the junkie. "Strung-out" had a connotation of hopeless finality about it. "Uptight" implied a temporary situation and lacked the overwhelming despair of "strung-out."

The term "cop" (meaning "to get") is an abbreviation of the word "copulation." "Cop," as originally used by soulful teen-agers in the early Fifties, was deciphered to mean sexual coition, nothing more. By 1955 "cop" was being uttered throughout national Soulville as a synonym for the verb "to get," especially in reference to illegal purchases, drugs, pot, hot goods, pistols, etc. ("Man, where can I cop now?") But by 1955 the meaning was all-encompassing. Anything that could be obtained could be "copped."

The word "boss," denoting something extraordinarily good or great, was a redefined term that had been popular in Soulville during the Forties and Fifties as a complimentary remark from one soul brother to another. Later it was replaced by several terms such as "groovy," "tough," "beautiful" and, most recently, "out of sight." This last expression is an outgrowth of the former term "way out," the meaning of which was equivocal. "Way out" had an ad hoc hickish ring to it which made it intolerably unsoulful and consequently it was soon replaced by "out of sight," which is also likely to experience a relatively brief period of popular usage. "Out of sight" is better than "way out," but it has some of the same negative, childish taint of its predecessor.

The expression, "kill 'em," has neither a violent nor a malicious interpretation. It means "good luck," "give 'em hell," or "I'm pulling for you," and originated in Harlem from six to nine years ago.

There are certain classic soul terms which, no matter how often borrowed, remain in the canon and are reactivated every so often, just as standard jazz tunes are continuously experiencing renaissances. Among the classical expressions are: "solid," "cool," "jive" (generally as a noun), "stuff," "thing," "swing" (or "swinging"), "pimp," "dirt," "freak," "heat," "larceny," "busted," "okee doke," "piece," "sheet" (a jail record), "squat," "square," "stash," "lay," "sting," "mire," "gone," "smooth," "joint," "blow," "play," "shot," and there are many more.

Soul language can be heard in practically all communities throughout the country, but for pure, undiluted spoken soul one must go to Soul Street. There are several. Soul is located at Seventh and "T" in Washington, D.C., on One Two Five Street in New York City; on Springfield Avenue in Newark; on South Street in Philadelphia; on Tremont Street in Boston; on Forty-seventh Street in Chicago, on Fillmore in San Francisco, and dozens of similar locations in dozens of other cities.

As increasingly more Negroes desert Soulville for honorary membership in the Establishment clique, they experience a metamorphosis, the repercussions of which have a marked influence on the young and impressionable citizens of Soulville. The expatriates of Soulville are often greatly admired by the youth of Soulville, who emulate the behavior of such expatriates as Nancy Wilson, Ella Fitzgerald, Eartha Kitt, Lena Horne, Diahann Carroll, Billy Daniels, or Leslie Uggams. The result— more often than not—is a trend away from spoken soul among the young soul folks. This abandonment of the soul language is facilitated by the fact that more Negro youngsters than ever are acquiring college educations (which, incidentally, is not the best treatment for the continued good health and growth of soul); integration and television, too, are contributing significantly to the gradual demise of spoken soul.

Perhaps colleges in America should commence to teach a course in spoken soul. It could be entitled the Vocal History of Black America, or simply Spoken Soul. Undoubtedly there would be no difficulty finding teachers. There are literally thousands of these experts throughout the country whose talents lie idle while they await the call to duty.

Meanwhile the picture looks dark for soul. The two extremities in the Negro spectrum—the conservative and the militant—are both trying diligently to relinquish and repudiate whatever vestige they may still possess of soul. The semi-Negro—the soul brother intent on gaining admission to the Establishment even on an honorary basis—is anxiously embracing and assuming conventional English. The other extremity, the Ultra-Blacks, are frantically adopting everything from a Western version of Islam that would shock the Caliph right out of his snugly fitting shintiyan to anything that vaguely hints of that big, beautiful, bountiful black bitch lying in the arms of the Indian and Atlantic Oceans and crowned by the majestic Mediterranean Sea. Whatever the Ultra-Black is after, it's anything but soulful.

STUDY QUESTIONS AND EXERCISES

1. How do the contexts Brown provides for the use of *nigger* by black people serve to emphasize the complexities of connotation, intonation, and irony that isolated quotations cannot convey?

2. Dick Gregory called his autobiography *Nigger*, perhaps in ironic self-abasement but also, as the dedication to his "Momma" says, so that: "Wherever you are, if you hear the word 'nigger' again, remember they are advertising my book." How does his attitude suggest that pride may replace humility? Is there evidence that this is happening to a significant degree among black people? Is it true of Brown, in this article?

3. How else than in language is soulful usage expressed?

4. How does Brown define the "Language of Soul"? When and where did it originate? What analogy is there between the "Language of Soul" and the slang of any subgroup, such as the hippies? How does the "Language of Soul" differ from such slang? (Refer to Joos's *age* scale in "How Many Clocks?" selection 23.)

5. Do Brown's remarks on white men's attempts to use soul language confirm or disprove Francis' advice, in selection 33, to educated people about using nonstandard language?

6. Would a Southerner be able to use soul language better than a Northerner does? Why? (Refer to McDavid's article, "Sense and Nonsense About American Dialects," selection 20.)

7. What is the difference between slang and soul language?

8. What terms borrowed from white slang have different meanings in soul language? Consult Wentworth and Flexner, *Dictionary of American Slang*: are the latter meanings given?

9. What soul terms have been taken over into white slang? Note the "generation gap" in the meaning of *uptight*. Is this characteristic of soul language in general?

10. How does *cop* illustrate the process of generalization? (See Pyles's "Words and Meanings," selection 14.)

11. What soul terms are classic? What does *classic* mean?

12. What causes a trend away from soul language among black people? How can the advice of Francis in "Social and Educational Varieties of English" (selection 34), and of McDavid and other dialectologists be of value in preserving the language of soul without losing the advantages—to extend the metaphor—of physical well-being gained by mastery of standard English and consequent opportunity for economic rise?

37

There's Nothing Wrong with Your Language

Robert A. Hall, Jr.

The concluding chapter of Professor Hall's Linguistics and Your Language *(1960) brings into focus many of the aspects of language discussed in the preceding essays. His call for an objective, scientific approach to language is one that the editors of this collection support enthusiastically. Professor Hall teaches at Cornell University.*

In 1945, the distinguished Ralph Linton published a book named "The Science of Man in the World Crisis," a collection of essays by 22 anthropologists and sociologists on what their particular branch of the science of man could contribute to solving the world's problems. Although linguistics is basically a branch of anthropology, no discussion of its contribution, such as we have been trying to give in this book, was included in Linton's volume; as a reason for this omission, Linton said in his preface: ". . . linguistics is still unable to make any great contribution toward the solution of our current problems. For that reason it has been ignored in the present volume."

How justified this statement was, the reader may be able to judge for himself from our discussion in the last few chapters. We have seen how linguistics can help us reach a conclusion on a number of points which are concerned in whatever crisis exists in our culture at present: on the questions of education and international understanding, as reflected in the problems of teaching our own language, of spelling (items which waste at least two years of every school child's life!), of foreign language learning, and of an international language. These are matters which concern, not only the specialist's technique of resolving particular problems (such as methods of teaching and writing textbooks), but the general public's attitudes towards the problems. The teachings of linguistics can help us all to save energy, time, and money by seeing the situation in better perspective and applying our efforts more effectively.

But that is not all; for, even though linguistics has definitely a practical application to these problems of language learning, literacy, and international languages, those are still simply specific problems. If that were all the contribution linguistics had to make, it would still be on the level of technology and "applied science" without any more general implications. Linguistics and its results, however, have very broad implications for all of our daily living, and for our attitudes towards many of the problems that beset us even when we don't realize, perhaps, that they exist. All of our thinking, as such, involves the use of language, and if we have no clear notion of the nature of language and our use of it, we are bound to get confused on the nature of our thinking itself. What we say and how we say it is dependent, to a certain extent, on what we know about our language; and, even more so, our attitude towards what other people say and how they say it.

On this score, linguistics has a message which is largely in direct opposition to what we get taught in schools and in other sources of opinion (newspapers, magazines, and the like). Many people uphold, and (perhaps) most people accept, the notion that it is just "common sense" to insist on "correct" speech, and to hold it against people if they do not speak "correctly." Untutored and natural speech is very often made an object of reproach and condemnation; the general attitude towards talking naturally, the way we learn to from family and playmates without benefit of schoolmastering, is usually that it shows ignorance, neglect, carelessness, or stupidity. . . .

The amount of snobbery and social discrimination which goes on in the name of "correctness" is enormous; each one of us can think of many instances in his own experience. The case I remember most clearly is the one in which two ladies condemned a girl thoroughly, and held her in quite low esteem, simply because she said *Armitice* for *Armistice*, *buffet* (rhyming with *Miss Muffet*) *dress* for *bouffé dress*, and made similar substitutions. She was not a very bright girl, and the two ladies justified themselves by claiming that "her speech reflected her personality traits." In fact, there is no correlation, and many other more intelligent and likeable persons might make the same "mistakes." The point is that the determination of her intelligence and merits ought to have been made on some more rational and analytical basis than by the mere catchword of "correct" speech. Plenty of people have been turned down for jobs just because they said *ain't* or *it's me*, and others of inferior worth accepted because they said *is not* or *it is I* instead. If we make decisions on such a basis as this, we are cutting off our noses to spite our faces, and we are setting up an artificial, superficial, meaningless basis for separating some of the sheep and goats from others, rather than using our intelligence to get to the bottom of the matter and find out what people's true worth is, and really learning how to tell sheep and goats apart. This misdirection of our energies is probably due to at least two factors: 1) desire for some easy criterion on which we can base a judgment instantly, the minute somebody opens their mouth—which is essentially a lazy man's criterion; and 2) desire to satisfy our own egos by setting up our own ways as superior to others', and looking down on others because they do not conform to our standards.

Linguistics, on the other hand, points out that such standards, although they have a perfectly real existence in many people's behavior, have nothing to do with language itself. They are criteria imposed from the outside, for motives of laziness and snobbery, as we have just suggested. The real reason behind condemning somebody for saying *Armitice* or saying *buffet dress* is the desire to put that person in his or her place. The further conclusion is twofold: first, as we suggested in Chapter 11, that if we find it necessary to change our speech from nonstandard to standard, we should do so by objective and rational means rather than by making a stab at it in the dark, and we should have a clear-eyed recognition of the fact that we are thereby trying to change our social status, rather than with a false humility and needless self-depreciation; and second, that it is up to users of standard speech to be less snobbish, less overbearing, and less rigorous in their insistence on a false "correctness." What does it matter if someone says *Armitice, it's me*, or *the minute somebody opens their mouth*, or splits an infinitive, or does one of the hundred other things the grammarians object to but everyone does? The merit of what a person says or does is not in any way affected by the way in which they say or do it, provided it is the most efficient way of saying or doing it; and to accept or reject someone just because of "correct" or "incorrect" speech is to show oneself superficial, lazy, and snobbish.

The damage done by this kind of attitude on the part of standard speakers is incalculable, and extends much farther than we may think at first glance. The non-standard speaker, when he meets up with this kind of snobbery, is at first perplexed and then badly thrown off the track. He is usually at a disadvantage for economic reasons, and finds that he has to change his natural speech-patterns to conform to those of the people that have more social and economic prestige and who hence have power over him. But when he tries to conform, he finds that it is by no means easy. Very few people can tell him what to do in order to conform, and those who do try to tell him, do it rather by invective ("your English is bad," "your language isn't English") and by preaching ("Saying *it ain't me* shows that you are neglectful and careless and sloppy in your speech; you should say *it is not I*"), than by objectively telling him what is not acceptable in his speech and in what way it needs to be changed.

The psychological harm thus done is very great. The non-standard speaker is made insecure, and this insecurity shows up in many ways. It is evident in all the over-corrections to which such speakers are prone, as when they say *between you and I*; they have been preached at for saying things like *you and me done it*, and they carry the substitution of *you and I* too far. The use of *whom* is gradually dying out in English, and would probably be completely lost by now (and no harm done) if it had not been for the over-zealous exertions of purists; as it is, many speakers to whom the use of *who* comes natural in all positions, have been confused on the distinction between *who* and *whom;* such a speaker will tend to use *whom* by over-correction, even where it does not belong, uttering such sentences as *Senator Blank, whom it is well known is opposed to the proposal . . .* and the like. (Edward Sapir has a very discerning and penetrating discussion of the *who–whom* question in Chapter VII of his book *Language,* which ought to be read by everybody interested in the question of "correctness.") This insecurity shows up especially at crucial moments, as when a speaker is in front of a microphone, or orating at a banquet, when he is more likely to pull a "boner" than on any other occasion—a thing that would not happen if he had not been made needlessly insecure about his speech by browbeating and excessive insistence on "correctness."

It shows up, too, in the extreme vulnerability of the ordinary person to those who offer to sell him instruction on "correct" speech. Our newspapers and magazines are full of advertisements of individuals and institutes offering to teach "good English," and of syndicated columns in which supposed "authorities" put forth their views on what is right and what is wrong. Dictionaries, grammar-books and "guides to good usage" are sold in bookstores, with claims on the jackets and in the books to an authoritative basis for their pronouncements. But, as we have seen, any claim to being "right" or knowing what's "correct" is, by the very fact of its being such a claim, a pure fake and an imposture. Anybody who tries to sell you his own dictum about "good English" as being authoritative or correct, is cheating and defrauding you, fully as much as the unscrupulous physician or drug manufacturer who tries to sell you a patent medicine guaranteed to cure this, that, or the other disease. It has not come yet, but we may look forward to the time (probably some centuries hence!) when a claim to dispensing "correct" speech will be treated as being equal in fraudulence to a claim to dispensing a cure-all in medicine; when anybody who sets himself up as an "authority" on language without any scientific training and competence will be prosecutable under law in exactly the same way as a person who tries to practice medicine without proper training; and when newspapers and magazines will, simply as a matter of common ethics, refuse advertisements for correctness-mongers and vendors of "authoritative" pronouncements in the same way they now refuse advertisements for quack physicians and fraudulent patent medicines.

But such frauds are able to live by battening on ordinary people's insecurity; if I do not know whether I should say *it's me* or *it is I,* and am insecure about my present behavior in that respect, I am an easy victim for somebody who comes along and offers to set me right—for a consideration, of course, whether it be a fee paid directly or a fraction of the price I pay for my evening paper. Of course, the way to get rid of such victimization is to get rid of the insecurity, and to reassure the person being victimized that he doesn't need to be. This means that we must realize, all around, that—as I put it in the title of this chapter—

there's nothing wrong with our language, and that we had better find other and more serious things to worry about. It means that those of us who start out our lives speaking non-standard English have nothing inherently wrong about our speech, and that any change we make in our speech-patterns later on need be only such as we feel necessary. It means that those of us who are brought up on standard English have no right to lord it over non-standard speakers just because of our language, and that we would do better to take an attitude of humility towards our own speech and tolerance towards others', with a willingness to accept deviations from our own practice.

"Well"—it may be objected at this point—"by destroying standards in this way, you're simply removing all barriers to people's talking any way they want to, and if we don't try to preserve the language from corruption, within fifty years everybody'll be talking his own language and nobody will understand each other at all." I have heard this objection made numerous times; but such an argument fails to take into account the cohesive, centripetal forces of society, as well as the disintegrative, centrifugal forces at work. That is, abandonment of absolute standards does not necessarily mean abandonment of all standards (as we have already pointed out), and just because we tolerate deviations from our own practice, we do not have to expect everything to fly apart immediately. As a matter of fact, the pressure of human need for communication will always insure people's keeping their speech reasonably uniform; the difficulty arises mainly over certain moot points (like *he did it* vs. *he done it, it's me* vs. *it is I*) which normally do not make any difference in communication and which simply serve as criteria to determine social and intellectual standing. Relaxation of over-rigid and absolute standards would bring no harm at all to mutual communication and understanding, in fact would rather improve it by removing sources of needless disagreement and friction.

Once we have cleared the ground by ridding ourselves of prejudices of "correctness" and the like, and by substituting a relativistic for an absolutistic point of view, we begin to see some further considerations with regard to human speech as a whole. We begin to realize that our own language is nothing special in comparison to other languages, nothing particularly God-given or superior or peculiarly fitted for higher intellectual activity, any more than our own dialect of our language is better than any other dialect. Our own language—English—and all the other so-called "civilized" languages are civilized only in that they happen to have been spoken by particular groups of people who achieved enough technological progress along certain lines to build "civilizations," that is, more complicated cultures. There is nothing about English or French or German or Italian that makes them more especially fitted to be the vehicles of civilization than any other languages; if we think so, it is just because we are committing the logical error of reasoning backward from the events.

In fact, our West European languages are almost all (except for Hungarian, Finnish, and Basque) of only one language family, the Indo-European, and represent only one basic type of language structure. There are many other types, all of them equally fit to be used for "high" civilizations if the need should ever arise. In many languages, there are distinctions of form and meaning that we do not have in our familiar languages, and that it would actually be very useful to have. The Hupa language of northern California has tenses for its nouns; and Hopi, a language of Arizona, has in its verbs a special form to indicate that the action takes place in repeated segments.

Thus, the speaker of Hupa can make such a distinction, in speaking of a house, as that indicated by the following forms:

xonta "house now existing"
xontaneen "house formerly existing, i.e. in ruins"
xontate "house that will exist, i.e. not yet built"

The following pairs are examples of Hopi verbs, in each of which the left-hand form refers to action taking place at a single point of time, and the right-hand form refers to action taking place in repeated segments:

hó'ci "it forms a sharp acute angle"

hocícita "it is zigzag"

wála "it (e.g. a liquid) makes one wave, gives a slosh"

walálata "it is tossing in waves, it is kicking up a sea"

ríya "it makes a quick spin"

riyáyata "it is spinning, whirling"

héro "he (or it) gives out a sudden hollow gurgle from within"

herórota "he is snoring"

yóko "he gives one nod of the head"

yokókota "he is nodding"

rípi "it gives a flash"

rípípita "it is sparkling"

Benjamin Lee Whorf, the linguistic analyst who first observed this distinction in Hopi verbs, said of it:

All this . . . is an illustration of how language produces an organization of experience. We are inclined to think of language simply as a technique of expression, and not to realize that language first of all is classification and arrangement of the stream of sensory experience which results in a certain world-order, a certain segment of the world that is easily expressible by the type of symbolic means that language employs. [In other words, a grammatical process of one kind or another serves as a symbol for—in this instance—vibratory phenomena.] In other words, language does in a cruder but also in a broader and more versatile way the same thing that science does. We have just seen how the Hopi language maps out a certain terrain of what might be termed primitive physics. We have observed how, with very thorough consistency and not a little true scientific precision, all sorts of vibratile phenomena in nature are classified by being referred to various elementary types of deformation process. The analysis of a certain field of nature which results is freely extensible, and all-in-all so harmonious with actual physics that such extension could be made with great appropriateness to a multiplicity of phenomena belonging entirely to the modern scientific and technical world—movements of machinery and mechanism, wave process and vibrations, electrical and chemical phenomena—things that the Hopi have never known or imagined, and for which we ourselves lack definite names. *The Hopi actually have a language better equipped to deal with such vibratile phenomena than is our latest scientific terminology.* [Italics mine— RAHjr.] This is simply because their language establishes a general contrast between two types of experience, which contrast corresponds to a contrast that, as our science has discovered, is all-pervading and fundamental in nature. According to the conception of modern physics, the contrast of particle and field of vibrations is more fundamental in the world of nature than such contrasts as space and time, or past, present, and future, which are the sort of contrasts that our own language imposes upon us. The Hopi aspect-contrast which we have observed, being obligatory upon their verb forms, practically forces the Hopi to notice and observe vibratory phenomena, and furthermore encourages them to find names for and to classify such phenomena. As a matter of fact the language is extraordinarily rich in terms for vibratory phenomena and for the punctual events to which they are related.

This is news indeed—a "primitive" language, spoken by a tribe of supposedly ignorant, backward Indians that live in pueblos on top of mesas in Arizona, without any of the benefits of civilized education, commerce, science, religion, or plumbing, and yet which is better equipped to deal with vibratile phenomena than the very languages of the peoples whose scientists have (so they thought) "discovered" these phenomena after long and laborious analysis! What has happened to these supposedly "superior" and "civilized" languages, that they have been outstripped by a "primitive" language in this way? For a short while, we might be tempted to reverse the scales, and in our new realization that our own languages aren't all we think they are, exaggerate in the other direction, proclaiming the superior merits of "primitive" languages. That would be just as bad an exaggeration, however, since it would be simply a continuation of our previous technique of applying value-judgments to languages, only turning things upside down. That will hardly do either. But, as soon as we stop applying value-judgments to languages as wholes, we see something important: that no one language symbolizes, either in its grammatical forms, or in its meanings, all the different ways in which our universe might be analyzed. That would be impossible, just because of the sheer number of different possible items to be symbolized, if we took into account all the various possible analyses. Each language picks out only certain ones of the possible contrasts that are to be found in the universe around us, and symbolizes them, leaving the others out of consideration or expressing them with relative difficulty. Hopi is better than our West European languages for symbolizing vibratory phenomena; but our languages are better for symbolizing some other things, like time relationships. (Don't be misled into saying "But time relationships are more important than other relationships, aren't they?"—because our notion that they are more important is just a conclusion that we have reached because they are emphasized by the structure of our languages and by certain aspects of our mechanized culture.) In the last analysis, one language turns out to be just as good as another in the long run, and here again we need to adopt a purely relativistic point of view.

We see, moreover, that there is no reason at all for assuming that a language reflects in any way—even, as we can see from the Hopi example, in its vocabulary—the degree of complexity of its speakers' civilization. If this were true, we might expect the Hopi to have been far out in front of us, in investigation and analysis of the vibratory phenomena of physics. Actually, we know that they are far behind us; but the grammatical inadequacy of English, French, German, etc., has not kept our scientists from working on these phenomena and arriving in the end at a recognition and classification of wave-like motion, oscillation, vibration, etc. The point is that the differences between West European and other "higher," i.e. in some respects (e.g. mechanically) more complex, cultures on the one hand, and so-called "primitive," i.e. less complex cultures on the other, have been brought about by differences in technology, not by differences in linguistic structure.

Once we realize that all languages are equal in merit, we are in a position to stop treating language differences as something to worry about, something to condemn, and something to eradicate on nationalistic grounds. It is a common habit of mankind to think that difference in speech must necessarily imply difference in nationality, and that hence the first thing to be done to assure national unity is to enforce linguistic unity. Central Europe, as we all know, has been a stamping-ground for this kind of linguistic nationalism. One of the worst offenders was the old Austro-Hungarian Empire, whose two parts—Austria and Hungary —conducted a ruthless campaign, before 1914, to Germanize and Hungarianize their respective parts of the empire. Languages of subject groups were given a less favorable standing in the political and educational system, and the government did all it could to force its subjects to talk German or Hungarian, instead of their native Slavic or Roumanian tongues. The pre-1914 German Empire was even more savage in its attempt to eradicate minority languages, like Danish and Polish. There was no justification for these campaigns, which served no useful purpose, were an expression of nothing but the brutal domineering of the ruling nations, and in the end caused immense damage.

What naturally happened was that the subject peoples—Czechs, Croats, Serbs, Roumanians, Poles, etc.—developed, as a result of this un-called-for oppression, a fierce and utterly unreasoning love for their own languages, as opposed to all others, an emotion equally unjustified on an objective basis, but quite comprehensible in terms of psychological reaction. And after the First World War ended in 1918, the successor states like Czechoslovakia, Yugoslavia, Roumania, and Poland tried to turn the tables on their former oppressors by stamping out German and Hungarian with equal ruthlessness. This, of course, only aggravated the trouble, since Germans and Hungarians resented the stigmas and disadvantages placed on their languages, and the evil thus returned for evil contributed greatly to the German and Hungarian desire for revenge and renewed dominance which led to the Second World War.

We have already mentioned Switzerland as a good example of a country whose citizens are fully as devoted to their native land as those of any other, yet who speak four different languages. This example in itself is enough to prove that there is no necessary connection between language and nationality or patriotism. The popular notion that there is such a connection is quite mistaken; to win and hold the affection of its citizens, a government does not need to ram the majority language down the throats of all its minorities. Actions, here as elsewhere, speak louder than words, and decent, fair treatment is essential rather than enforced linguistic unity. Following this principle, there is no harm in the majority language being treated as a foreign language—though a favored one, due to its special position—in schools wherever necessary. Some Spanish-speaking regions under United States rule, such as Puerto Rico and New Mexico, have suffered from politicians' misconceptions on this point. Nationalistic politicians in Washington have insisted on English being taught in Puerto Rico in just the same way it is taught in schools on the continent to children who are native speakers of English, despite the fact that the language situation is wholly different in Puerto Rico and that over 99 per cent of the island's population are native speakers of Spanish. Puerto Rican education has suffered badly from this wrong emphasis, the children's learning of English being very much reduced by inappropriate teaching and their knowledge of what they learn in Spanish being also reduced by much-needed time being wasted on poorly taught English. Why not teach English as a foreign language, which it certainly is in Puerto Rico? That would indeed be the most sensible thing to do; but can you persuade a United States politician of such a self-evident truth? No; because he is sure to come back with the argument—which seems to him unanswerable—"Puerto Rico is American territory, isn't it? Then they have to speak English there; and if we let them learn Spanish in the schools and treat English as a foreign language, they won't be good American citizens." An argument which is based, as you can see, on the fallacious assumption we have just been demolishing, that good citizenship depends on linguistic unity.

The contribution that linguistics can make to the world's affairs is roughly parallel to that which any other branch of the science of man, such as cultural anthropology, can make. This can be in the fields of analysis and of practical application, and in the latter, both within our own society and in the relations of our own with other societies or nations. Just as cultural anthropology and sociology analyze the structure of social groups, linguistics analyzes the structure of language systems, giving us a technique to make exact statements about languages as they exist and as they change in time. Of course this analysis will never be absolute; linguistics is like other sciences, in that it is cumulative, each generation builds on the work of preceding generations and goes farther, and the frontiers of knowledge are always being pushed ahead more and more. That is the way it should be, if linguistics is to remain truly scientific; otherwise, it would petrify into a theology, like traditional grammar has become in the last two thousand years. Present-day linguistics will undoubtedly be obsolete a hundred years from now, just as the linguistics (or chemistry or physics) of a hundred years ago is obsolete now. But the principles that linguistics seeks to follow are the only ones that can help us to get a real understanding of what language is, what rôle it plays in our lives, and how we can use our knowledge of it in improving our living.

But most linguistic analysts have been so concerned, until now, with working out their technique that they have not had much time to devote to practical considerations. To date, they have not made it known, as they should, that linguistics can tell us what notions about language that are prevalent in our society—such as "correctness" and our misconceptions about writing—are wrong, what harm they do in our society, and how the situation could be improved. Our society should know that linguistics can also tell us what part language does and does not play in inter-society and international relations, showing us for example how the "international language" problem can best be resolved, and how false ideas of linguistic superiority have misled nations into needlessly imposing their languages on other nations or groups. Here, too, there is a parallel with applied anthropology, which shows us how we can use the findings of anthropological and sociological analysis in dealing with such problems as race relations and with cultural minorities like immigrant groups; and, on the international level, in determining the proper understanding of how colonial peoples and tribes live, and in interpreting the cultural and psychological backgrounds of national "character" and behavior, as Geoffrey Gorer did in his study of American psychology.

But to return to our basic point: the message that linguistics has for our society at present is primarily this: Don't Meddle Ignorantly With Your Language! Any meddling with our language, by ourselves or others, in the name of "correctness," of spelling, or of nationalism, is harmful. As we mentioned before, this message is both negative and positive. It is negative, in that it warns us to give up, to abandon entirely the old dogmatic, normative, theological approach of traditional grammar and of social snobbery; and to substitute the relativistic, objective approach of scientific study and analysis. It is positive, in that it tells us, once we've cleared the ground in this way, to go ahead and find out for ourselves what the facts really are, to analyze and describe them as accurately as we can, and then to apply the knowledge we have obtained in that way. In both these respects, the contribution of linguistics is simply a part of the effort of all science in modern democratic society, to find out the truth and to act upon it; in this sense, the linguistic analyst, like other scientists, may take as his motto that noblest of all slogans: "Ye shall know the truth; and the truth shall make you free."

STUDY QUESTIONS AND EXERCISES

1. What seems to be the conflict between the message of linguistics and other sources of opinion about language? How does Claude Brown's article above reflect attitudes toward himself and his people engendered by belonging to a minority with a nonstandard dialect?

2. Are judgments based solely on "errors" in speech valid? Which of these character or personality traits might such errors indicate: indifference, irresponsibility, lack of ability to learn, lack of opportunity to learn, defensive pride? Which of these qualities, if confirmed, would be valid bases for unfavorable judgment in regard to employing a person for a responsible position? What harsh facts of social and economic life, in relation to "correct" English, do college students need to realize? What do teachers need to realize about usage and their responsibility for teaching both what is true about language and what is true about society?

3. Why is "correct" language used as a criterion? What do those who use this criterion reveal about themselves? (Spelling is an even handier criterion. Why?)

4. What psychological harm, done to those who try to acquire standard English, is reflected in the kind of hyperform discussed by Francis?

5. Which of the dictionaries and books on usage referred to throughout this book aim to be authoritative on usage? Which disclaim this function and present what can be objectively established as facts of present usage, leaving the reader to make his own choice? Which attitude would Hall say was fraudulent?

6. Why may it be necessary for a person to change speech patterns? What analogy is there between changing social levels and going to live in a foreign country? Does this necessity mean abandoning the native dialect under all circumstances? Should one, on getting home from work, feel free figuratively to slip into comfortable language as into comfortable clothes?

7. What facts about human society will prevent disintegration of language, even if regard for "correctness" as an arbitrary standard is abandoned?

8. What facts about primitive languages are stated and illustrated by Whorf? Where else in this text have primitive languages been used to illustrate "how language produces an organization of experience"?

9. How does the intolerance of standard-English-speaking citizens toward other dialects resemble eradication of the language of a conquered people by the conquerors? What example of political unity with full linguistic diversity proves that "peaceful coexistence" may result from tolerance of other languages? Which of the possible courses in a bilingual or bidialectal situation is the most practical and rewarding: separation into different societies? elimination of the minority language? universal bilingualism or bidialectalism? bilingualism or bidialectalism for those who seek to improve their status?

10. What, according to Hall, is the message of linguistics for our society, in both negative and positive senses?

11. Does the title of this selection apply equally to everyone or chiefly to those who wish to remain in their present status, social and economic? What does Hall assume about the status and education of his readers that limits the application of his advice?

SUBJECTS FOR BRIEF PAPERS OR WRITTEN REPORTS

1. Prepare, from your own experience, a comparative analysis of two distinctly different speech communities, for example, a small private school and a large university, and discuss how you adapted to them.

2. Using the biography or autobiography of a self-made man who has risen from one social level to another, with or without formal education, prepare a brief account of his attitude toward language and the relation of language skill to his success. *George*, by Emlyn Williams, is an example of such an autobiography. Abraham Lincoln is an obvious subject.

3. In *The Rise of Silas Lapham* William Dean Howells contrasts the speech patterns of the Laphams and the Coreys as a means

of showing their social differences. Analyze and classify the types of speech contrasts. Comment also upon Howells' use of contrasts in clothing to show the difference in social status between the upper class and the *nouveaux riches*.

4. Examine a copy of William Strunk's *The Elements of Style*, with E. B. White's introduction and concluding essay on style. Analyze one or several other examples of White's writing. Report on White's style as following or deviating from Strunk's precepts. What are the merits of Strunk's approach? What are the limitations?

5. Listen to several television or radio programs with British announcers and report on the chief differences from American speech that you observe in pronunciation and usage, arriving at a general conclusion as to typical differences.

6. In the *Oxford English Dictionary*, *Webster's Second International Dictionary*, and Wentworth and Flexner, *Dictionary of American Slang*, look up *brawl*, *loon*, and *cuckoo*. In what senses did Shakespeare use each term? Report briefly on the relation between the Shakespearean and the modern slang meanings.

7. Write an analytical report on an article by an eminent current writer in your chosen field: consider variety of style, diction, and usage, particularly usage that represents such problems as *who* and *whom*, *like* and *as*.

8. Study the dialogue in a contemporary American short story and, in a short paper, show how levels of usage and colloquialisms reflect time, place, and social class and how the dialogue differs from the nondialogue passages.

9. In Faulkner's *The Town*, study the speech of Gavin Stevens, Ratliff, and the various Snopeses and write a paper on the social levels represented and on colloquial standard and colloquial substandard deviations from formal usage.

10. Discuss Professor Higgins in Shaw's *Pygmalion* as representing self-confident freedom in speech and manners. What is Higgins' social status? His professional status?

11. Choose a nonfiction selection in *The New Yorker* written in the first person, with some dialogue, and analyze it as standard colloquial, with special attention to usage problems which have been called to your attention.

12. Read all of Joos, *The Five Clocks* (New York: Harcourt Brace Jovanovich, 1967) and write a paper on the conversion of Miss Fidditch: consider her original attitudes and the reasons for them, the stages in her conversion, the changes in her attitudes toward language and the reasons for them, and her final attitude and its effect on her personality.

13. Report on the status, in *Webster's Third International*, of a short list of expressions often taught as incorrect in standard English.

Compare evidence in *Webster's* with that in Bryant, *Current American Usage*, or Evans and Evans, *Dictionary of Contemporary American Usage*.

14. Analyze your chief problems in learning and using standard English: the nature of your problems; the chief causes of them; the ways in which the scientific approach to language may aid you in solving them; the professional and social importance to you of ability to use standard English with facility.

15. Write a paper on the terms of soul language used by Brown in selection 36, "The Language of Soul": give the etymology, meanings, and uses of the terms as given in regular and special dictionaries. Arrive at some conclusions as to the accuracy and adequacy of such information to an understanding of denotations and connotations of spoken soul language.

Suggestions for Longer Papers
Contributors
Selected Bibliography

Suggestions for Longer Papers

A number of subjects suggested for short papers may be extended in scope for long papers. The subjects given below, however, generally cover material from more than one part. Parenthetical numbers indicate parts most relevant to the topic. Part 1 is not specifically indicated because the general principles it covers should be referred to whenever pertinent to any subject.

1. From an issue of *American Speech* that is at least five years old, select ten or fifteen new words and look them up in the most recent dictionary available. Compare the *American Speech* and the dictionary entries and arrive at some conclusion as to what kinds of words achieve a place in the language and what kind of evolution they may go through. (1)

2. Compare selected sections of different editions of the same dictionary to show changes in vocabulary and meanings of words and to identify the language processes represented. (2)

3. Study the dialogue in a pair of comparable British and American plays or short stories to determine differences in British and American vocabulary and idiom, with special attention to cultural levels. (4)

4. Compare a few selections in this text as representing current usage, applying Evans and Evans, A *Dictionary of Contemporary American Usage.* (5)

5. Study the place-names in a limited area of your own state to ascertain how they illustrate principles of naming and characteristics of American English and how they reflect social and historical background. (2 and 3)

6. Examine the discussions of colloquial English and slang in this text to determine whether the confusion between cultural levels and functional varieties is evident. If it is, analyze the selections involved, following Kenyon's method. Or make a similar study of half a dozen composition texts for college courses. (4)

7. From the materials in this text select passages that represent

formal style, informal style, and colloquial style. By comparative analysis determine the characteristic features of each. Make intensive use of dictionary usage classifications for vocabulary and idiom. (4)

8. Study definitions of *colloquial* in both collegiate and unabridged dictionaries. Study the vocabulary and idiom of at least two selections in this text for the use of colloquial language, selecting one which seems relatively formal and one which seems relatively informal. Note that *Webster's Third New International Dictionary* does not use *colloq.* (4)

9. Study the regional variations in the dialogue in a play, a short story, or a novel in which locality is important and discuss how they represent special aspects of American English. (3)

10. Analyze the slang vocabulary of a special group, such as Hippies, to show language processes and principles at work. (4)

11. From Kurath, *A Word Geography of the Eastern United States*, make a list of common regional variants and test a number of individuals on terms and pronunciations used to determine what factors have influenced usage. (3)

12. Study the vocabulary and idiom of a specific group—such as a group in a dormitory—that represents varied backgrounds, and report on the effects of family, class, and region on speech habits. (3 and 5)

13. Make a collection of slang used by members of a family, including different ages and distinct subgroups, to determine sources of slang vocabulary, the "lifetime" of slang, and the effect of the age group on frequency and kind of slang used. (4)

14. Classify and analyze current slang among college students to demonstrate which of the psychological motives for the use of slang seem to be most prevalent and what emotional and intellectual attitudes are revealed. (4)

15. From sources in Part 3 of the text, identify the speech area in which you live and, with the additional aid of dictionaries, write a short documented account of the characteristics of the speech in your region, providing examples from your own observation. (3)

16. "Words are more easily transferred than regional types of pronunciation." Test the truth of this statement by comparing the speech of students from distinctly different regions, noting vocabulary and pronunciation. (3 and 5)

17. "Within a small area a number of interesting variants for the same thing can often be found in the half-hidden recesses of popular speech." Test this by observing variants for names of common objects in everyday life. Clerking in a store is likely to offer opportunities for observation. (3)

18. If you have lived in different areas, write a paper on the chief differences in pronunciation, vocabulary, and idiom that you have observed, classifying and analyzing the speech habits of both areas according to regional dialects. (3)

19. "Words of course spread with people, following routes of migration." Test this by observing routes of migration indicated by place-names from another section of the country and investigating vocabulary and idiom in a community known to be settled by a group from another area, such as New England groups in the Middle West. (2 and 3)

20. If you know someone who retains vocabulary and speech habits acquired in another dialect area or derived from a foreign-language background, assemble and classify deviations from local speech and apply principles of word migration and dialect variations to see if the deviations can be fully explained by such principles. (3 and 5)

21. "Literacy always blunts the edge of dialects." If you know a group or community with marked difference in "book-learning" between generations, see what evidence you can find to prove or disprove the quoted statement. Consider vocabulary, grammar, idiom, and pronunciation. (3 and 5)

22. If you have traveled widely in the United States, especially by auto, classify dialect differences you have observed and see if you can explain why they have resisted "leveling." (3 and 5)

23. In William Faulkner's *The Reivers*, study the colloquial varieties of language used by the narrator, Boon, Miss Reba, Butch, Uncle Parsham, and Uncle Ned, to identify social levels within regional dialect. (3, 4, and 5)

24. Read all the available reviews of *Webster's Second International* and *Webster's Third New International* dictionaries and write a paper on the prevailing attitudes toward dictionaries and language revealed by the reviews. Refer specifically, for comparison or contrast, to principles of language represented in Parts 1 and 2 in this text. (1 and 2)

25. Study the language "coined" for fictional purposes in a work of science fiction, and write a paper on the language processes apparent in the neologisms. Aldous Huxley's *Brave New World* would be a suitable subject, embracing both British and American settings in the future. (2 and 4)

26. Certain religious groups, such as the Quakers or the Amish or the Mennonites, have preserved distinctive speech patterns, which in some groups retain foreign elements. From personal observation or from study of a work of fiction, such as Jessamyn West's *The Friendly Persuasion*, write an analysis of the vocabulary, grammar, and idiom of such a group. (3 and 4)

27. Mr. Micawber, in Dickens' *David Copperfield*, is probably the literary character most noted for use of literary rather than colloquial language. The dialogue in *David Copperfield* ranges from Micawber's pompous formality through the nonstandard speech of Mr. Peggotty and Ham. Analyze the distinctive characteristics of these varieties of style in dialogue: Micawber's formal speech, standard colloquial, and nonstandard colloquial. What conclusions do you arrive at concerning

the degree of informality in standard colloquial in nineteenth-century England in comparison with twentieth-century America? (4 and 5)

28. In Faulkner's "The Bear" a wide range of colloquial styles is represented. Study the dialogue of all the characters, classify it from most formal standard through illiterate substandard, and discuss the social and regional characteristics most notable in each variety. Note particularly individual social motivation or ambition as reflected in speech and comparable personal dress and behavior. (3, 4, and 5)

29. Select a practical number of topics, such as double negatives, from among those dealt with by both Bryant, *Current American Usage,* and Evans and Evans, *A Dictionary of Contemporary American Usage,* and compare the technique and content in the parallel entries. Where sources for quotations are given, look them up and examine the contexts. Arrive at a conclusion as to the soundness of the methods and sources used by Bryant and Evans and Evans in comparison with the treatment of the same points in a recent edition of a standard composition text. (4)

30. Select a category of television dramatic programs, such as domestic comedy or Westerns, and make a study of the levels of usage and varieties of style and their social implications. Use as a model for method and technique Theodore Williams' "Soap Opera Grammar," *American Speech* (May, 1957), 151–54. (4 and 5)

31. Make a study of the special vocabulary, slang, and idiom of a regional occupational group, such as Southern cotton-growers or Middle Western dairy-farmers, and prepare an analytical report of your findings. Arrive at a conclusion concerning the general principles illustrated by this speech group. Except for the lack of such a conclusion, a model may be found in Audrey Duckert's "The Lexical Cherry Orchard," *American Speech* (February, 1959), 65–67. (3, 4, and 5)

32. Using as a model Donald P. Costello's "The Language of *The Catcher in the Rye*" (*American Speech* [October, 1959]), write a study of a teen-ager, preferably a first-person narrator, in a current novel. (4 and 5)

33. Adapting the general procedure of Isaac in selection 29 to fit the language patterns you discover, write an analysis of the language of Blanche DuBois in *A Streetcar Named Desire* or Amanda Wingfield in *The Glass Menagerie,* both by Tennessee Williams, giving special attention to regional characteristics. (3, 4, and 5)

34. Write a paper discussing the facts about language presented in this text. How are they relevant to you as (1) a student, (2) a present or prospective teacher of English, (3) a present or future parent, and (4) a responsible member of educated society? (Omit 2 if you do not plan to teach.)

Contributors

HAROLD B. ALLEN, Professor of English at the University of Minnesota and Director of the *Linguistic Atlas of the Upper Middle West,* is the editor of *Readings in Applied English Linguistics, Linguistics and English Linguistics,* and *A Survey of the Teaching of English to Non-English Speakers in the United States.*

C. MERTON BABCOCK, Professor of American Thought and Language at Michigan State University, has edited *The Ordeal of American English, Focus: A Book of College Prose,* and *The American Frontier.* He has also studied various aspects of Mark Twain's rhetoric and use of language.

MARY C. BROMAGE, Associate Professor of Written Communication of the School of Business Administration at the University of Michigan, reports on some of the innovations in language brought about by technological developments.

CLAUDE BROWN, author of *Manchild in the Promised Land,* has observed at first hand the distinctive elements in the language of young blacks in America today.

FREDERIC G. CASSIDY, Professor of English at the University of Wisconsin, is director of the *Dictionary of American Regional English.* He is co-editor of *Dictionary of Jamaican English* (with R. B. Le Page) and of *The Development of Modern English* (with Stuart Robertson).

NOAM CHOMSKY, Professor of Linguistics at the Massachusetts Institute of Technology, is author of several works in linguistic theory, including *Syntactic Structures, Aspects of the Theory of Syntax, Cartesian Linguistics, Language and Mind,* and *The Sound Pattern of English* (with Morris Halle).

F. STUART CRAWFORD, editor of etymologies for the Merriam-Webster Dictionaries, has training and extensive teaching experience in classical philology.

BERGEN EVANS, Professor of English at Northwestern University, has written widely on problems of grammar and usage. His books include *A Dictionary of Contemporary Usage* (with Cornelia Evans), *Comfortable Words*, and *Dictionary of Quotations*.

W. NELSON FRANCIS, Professor of Linguistics at Brown University, is the author of *The Structure of American English, The English Language*, and *Computational Analysis of Present-Day English* (with Henry Kučera).

CHARLES C. FRIES, Emeritus Professor of English at the University of Michigan, is one of the American pioneers in the scientific study of language. His *American English Grammar* and *The Structure of English* are landmarks of American linguistic scholarship.

PHILIP B. GOVE, Editor-in-Chief of the Merriam-Webster Dictionaries and a careful observer of the American language, advocates a descriptive rather than a prescriptive approach to grammar and usage.

ROBERT A. HALL, JR., Professor of Linguistics at Cornell University, has specialized in Romance philology and in pidgin and creole languages. He has written *Linguistics and Your Language* (a revised edition of *Leave Your Language Alone!*), *An Analytical Grammar of the Hungarian Language, Spoken and Written French*, and *Italian for Modern Living*.

ARCHIBALD A. HILL, Professor of English at the University of Texas, has studied linguistic problems in Latin and English and is the author of *Introduction to Linguistic Structures* and the editor of *Linguistics Today*.

D. E. HOUGHTON is Professor of English at Sacramento State College.

DAN ISAAC, lecturer in English at Queens College, wrote his doctoral dissertation on Tennessee Williams.

MARTIN JOOS, Professor of Linguistics and Director of the Centre of Linguistic Studies at the University of Toronto, is the author of *The English Verb* and *The Five Clocks*. He has edited *Readings in Linguistics* and *Middle High German Courtly Reader* (with Frederick W. Whitesell).

EDWARD HANFORD KELLY, Associate Professor of English at State University College, Oneonta, New York, is interested in current developments in the usage of American words.

JOHN S. KENYON was Professor of English at Hiram College, and his research in linguistics resulted in *American Pronunciation* and in *A Pronouncing Dictionary of American English* (with Thomas Knott).

HANS KURATH, Emeritus Professor of English at the University of Michigan, is editor of the *Middle English Dictionary* and author of *A Word*

Geography of the Eastern United States.

WILLIAM LABOV, Associate Professor of Linguistics at Columbia University, is investigating the usage and structural patterns of speakers of nonstandard English. His publications include A *Study of Non-Standard English* and *The Social Stratification of English in New York City.*

J. J. LAMBERTS, Professor of English at Arizona State University, is interested in English usage and in the teaching of English in secondary schools.

RAVEN I. MCDAVID, JR., Professor of English at the University of Chicago, has been a fieldworker for the *Linguistic Atlas* and is coauthor of *The Pronunciation of the Eastern United States* (with Hans Kurath). He prepared a one-volume abridgement of H. L. Mencken's *The American Language* and *Supplements to the American Language.*

H. L. MENCKEN (1880–1956), a journalist and magazine editor by profession, was a self-trained philologist whose collections of material relating to all aspects of American English were published in *The American Language* (1st ed., 1919; 4th ed., 1936) and in *Supplements to the American Language* (1945, 1948).

WILLIAM G. MOULTON, Professor of Linguistics at Princeton University, is the author of *The Sounds of English and German* and A *Linguistic Guide to Language Learning.*

JOHN NIST, Professor of English at Auburn University, has written on Beowulf and modern Brazilian poetry, in addition to preparing A *Structural History of the English Language.*

WALTER J. ONG, S. J., Professor of English at St. Louis University, has written widely on rhetorical theory, the history of ideas, and modern poetry and criticism. His books include *The Barbarian Within, Ramus, Method and the Decay of Dialogue, The Presence of the Word, Knowledge and the Fortune of Man,* and *In the Human Grain.*

THOMAS PYLES, Professor of English at Northwestern University, has written *Words and Ways of American English, Origins and Developments of the English Language, The English Language,* and *English: An Introduction to Language* (with John Algeo).

PAUL ROBERTS, late Professor of English at San Jose State College, applied the methods of descriptive linguistics to problems of English composition, grammar, syntax, and usage in *Understanding Grammar, Patterns of English, Understanding English,* and *Modern Grammar.*

DONALD A. SEARS, Professor of English at California State College at Fullerton, has written *The Discipline of English* and *The Sentence in Context* (with Francis Connolly).

MARGARET SCHLAUCH, Professor of English at the University of Warsaw, is the author of *The Gift of Tongues* and *The English Language in Modern Times.*

HENRY A. SMITH is Publications Project Coordinator at the North American Rockwell Corporation.

Selected Bibliography

I. PIONEERING OR SEMINAL STUDIES IN LANGUAGE

Bloomfield, Leonard. *Language*. New York: Holt, Rinehart and Winston, 1933.

Chomsky, Noam. *Syntactic Structures*. The Hague: Mouton, 1957.

Fries, Charles C. *American English Grammar*. New York: Appleton-Century-Crofts, 1940.

——. *The Structure of English*. New York: Harcourt Brace Jovanovich, 1952.

Hockett, Charles F. *A Course in Modern Linguistics*. New York: Macmillan, 1958.

Jespersen, Otto. *Language, Its Nature, Development and Origin*. New York: Macmillan, 1949.

Leonard, Sterling A. *Current English Usage*. Chicago: Ireland Press, 1932.

Marckwardt, Albert H., and Fred G. Walcott. *Facts About Current English Usage*. New York: Appleton-Century, 1938.

Roberts, Paul. *English Syntax*. New York: Harcourt Brace Jovanovich, 1964.

Sapir, Edward. *Language*. New York: Harcourt Brace Jovanovich, 1921; Harvest Books, 1955.

Trager, George L., and Henry Lee Smith. *An Outline of English Structures*, Studies in Linguistics, Occasional Paper No. 3. Washington, D.C.: American Council of Learned Societies, 1956.

II. OTHER LINGUISTIC STUDIES

Allen, Harold B., ed. *Readings in Applied English Linguistics*. New York: Appleton-Century-Crofts, 1958.

Allwood, Martin S. *American and British: A Handbook of American-British Language Differences*. Mount Pleasant, Iowa: The New Prairie, Iowa Wesleyan College; Mullsjo, Sweden: Anglo-American Center, 1964.

Bolinger, Dwight. *Aspects of Language*. New York: Harcourt Brace Jovanovich, 1968.

Bronstein, Arthur J. *The Pronunciation of American English*. New York: Appleton-Century-Crofts, 1960.

Brook, G. L. *History of the English Language*. New York: Oxford University Press, 1958.

———. "America," in *The Language of Dickens*. London: Andre Deutsch, 1970, pp. 130–37.

Bryant, Margaret M. *Current American Usage*. New York: Funk and Wagnalls, 1962.

———. *Modern English and Its Heritage*, 2nd ed. New York: Macmillan, 1962.

Chomsky, Noam. *Aspects of the Theory of Syntax*. Cambridge, Mass.: MIT Press, 1965.

Chomsky, Noam, and Morris Halle. *The Sound Patterns of English*. New York: Harper & Row, 1968.

Craigie, William A., and James R. Hulbert, eds. *Dictionary of American English*, 4 vols. Chicago: University of Chicago Press, 1938–44.

Evans, Bergen. *Comfortable Words*. New York: Random House, 1962.

Evans, Bergen, and Cornelia Evans. *A Dictionary of Contemporary American Usage*. New York: Random House, 1957.

Follett, Wilson. *Modern American Usage: A Guide*. Edited and completed by Jacques Barzun et al. New York: Hill and Wang, 1966.

Francis, W. Nelson. *The English Language: An Introduction*. New York: Norton, 1965.

———. *The Structure of American English*. New York: Ronald Press, 1958.

Gleason, H. A., Jr. *An Introduction to Descriptive Linguistics*, 2nd ed. New York: Holt, Rinehart and Winston, 1961.

Hall, Robert A., Jr. *Linguistics and Your Language*. New York: Doubleday, 1960.

Hayakawa, S. I. *Language in Thought and Action*, 2nd ed. New York: Harcourt Brace Jovanovich, 1964.

Hill, Archibald A. *Introduction to Linguistics*. New York: Harcourt Brace Jovanovich, 1958.

Ives, Sumner. *A New Handbook for Writers*. New York: Knopf, 1960.

Jacobs, Roderick A., and Peter S. Rosenbaum. *English Transformational Grammar*. Waltham, Mass.: Ginn-Blaisdell, 1968.

Kenyon, John S. *American Pronunciation*, 10th ed. Ann Arbor, Mich.: George Wahr, 1961.

Kurath, Hans. *A Word Geography of the Eastern United States*. Ann Arbor: University of Michigan Press, 1949.

Labov, William. *The Social Stratification of English in New York City*. Washington, D.C.: Center for Applied Linguistics, 1966.

———. *A Study of Non-Standard English*. Washington, D.C.: Educational Resources Information Center, Center for Applied Linguistics, 1969.

Langacker, Ronald W. *Language and Its Structure: Some Fundamental Linguistic Concepts.* New York: Harcourt Brace Jovanovich, 1968.

Lloyd, Donald J., and Harry R. Warfel. *American English in Its Cultural Setting.* New York: Knopf, 1956.

Malone, Kemp. "Historical Sketch of the English Language," in *The Random House Dictionary of the English Language,* unabridged ed. New York: Random House, 1967, pp. xv–xxii.

Marckwardt, Albert H. *American English.* New York: Oxford University Press, 1958.

Mathews, Mitford M., ed. *A Dictionary of Americanisms on Historical Principles.* Chicago: University of Chicago Press, 1951.

Mencken, H. L. *The American Language,* rev. by Raven I. McDavid, Jr. New York: Knopf, 1963.

Muller, Herbert J. *The Uses of English.* New York: Holt, Rinehart and Winston, 1967.

Myers, L. M. *The Roots of Modern English.* Boston: Little, Brown, 1966.

Newsome, Verna L. *Structural Grammar in the Classroom.* Oshkosh: Wisconsin Council of Teachers of English, 1961.

Pike, Kenneth L. *The Intonation of American English.* Ann Arbor: University of Michigan Press, 1945.

Pyles, Thomas. *The Origins and Development of the English Language.* New York: Harcourt Brace Jovanovich, 1964.

———. *Words and Ways of American English.* New York: Random House, 1952.

Pyles, Thomas, and John Algeo. *English: An Introduction to Language.* New York: Harcourt Brace Jovanovich, 1970.

Roberts, Paul. *English Sentences.* New York: Harcourt Brace Jovanovich, 1962.

———. *Modern Grammar.* New York: Harcourt Brace Jovanovich, 1968.

———. *Patterns of English.* New York: Harcourt Brace Jovanovich, 1956.

———. *Understanding English.* New York: Harper & Row, 1958.

———. *Understanding Grammar.* New York: Harper & Row, 1954.

Robertson, Stuart, and Frederic G. Cassidy. *The Development of Modern English,* 2nd ed. Englewood Cliffs, N.J.: Prentice-Hall, 1954.

Rogovin, Syrell. *Modern English Sentence Structure.* New York: Random House, 1965.

Schlauch, Margaret. *The English Language in Modern Times.* Warsaw: Polish Scientific Publishers; London: Oxford University Press, 1964.

Sledd, James A. *A Short Introduction to English Grammar.* Chicago: Scott, Foresman, 1959.

Sledd, James A., and Wilma R. Ebbitt. *Dictionaries and That Dictionary.* Chicago: Scott, Foresman, 1962.

Stewart, George R. *Names on the Land*. Boston: Houghton Mifflin, 1958.

Trager, George L. "Language," in *The Encyclopaedia Britannica*, Vol. 13. Chicago: Encyclopaedia Britannica, 1960.

Warfel, Harry R. *Language: A Science of Human Behavior*. Cleveland: Howard Allen, 1962.

Wentworth, Harold, and Stuart Berg Flexner, comps. *Dictionary of American Slang*. New York: Thomas Y. Crowell, 1960.

Whitehall, Harold. "The English Language," in *Webster's New World Dictionary*. Cleveland: World, 1959, pp. xv–xxxiv.

————. *Structural Essentials*. New York: Harcourt Brace Jovanovich, 1956.

A 1
B 2
C 3
D 4
E 5
F 6
G 7
H 8
I 9
J 0